Michelle & Bert —
A token of great
appreciation for the
many kindnesses
shown us and especially
PATRIK.

Dennis Lund 6/5 '97

THE NEW DEAL'S BLACK CONGRESSMAN

THE
NEW DEAL'S
BLACK
CONGRESSMAN

A LIFE OF
ARTHUR WERGS MITCHELL

DENNIS S. NORDIN

UNIVERSITY OF MISSOURI PRESS
COLUMBIA AND LONDON

Library of Congress Cataloging-in-Publication Data

Nordin, Dennis S. (Dennis Sven), 1942–
    The New Deal's Black congressman : a life of Arthur Wergs Mitchell /
Dennis S. Nordin.
        p.   cm.
    Includes bibliographical references and index.
    ISBN 0-8262-1102-X (alk. paper)
    1. Mitchell, Arthur Wergs, 1883–1968.   2. Legislators—United
States—Biography.   3. Afro-American legislators—Biography.
4. United States. Congress. House—Biography.   5. United States—
Politics and government—1933–1945.   6. New Deal, 1933–1939.
7. United States—Race relations.   8. Afro-Americans—Illinois—
Chicago—Politics and government.   I. Title.
E748.M63N67   1997
977.3'11043'092—dc21
    [B]   97-4478
                                                                       CIP

∞™ This paper meets the requirements of the
American National Standard for Permanence of Paper
for Printed Library Materials, Z39.48, 1984.

Designer: Stephanie Foley
Typesetter: BOOKCOMP
Printer and binder: Thomson-Shore, Inc.
Typefaces: Palatino and Stone Serif

All photos courtesy of the Chicago Historical Society.
Publication of this book has had the generous assistance
of the Clifford Willard Gaylord Foundation.

CONTENTS

PREFACE

T his book deals with an African American of dubious character. For that reason, no objective biography of Arthur Wergs Mitchell will conform to usual patterns of modern African American scholarship. His primary interests throughout his life were too overwhelmingly self-centered; by birth a victim, he used the circumstances of race to personal advantage. To most of his contemporaries, he was neither admirable nor respectable. Many African Americans who knew him well despised him, and he viewed most African Americans with contempt.

There seemingly has been a reluctance among researchers and publishers to produce studies of African American leaders who could only be described as scoundrels. Instead, most studies have been concerned on the one hand with the victimization and exploitation of the minority by an unfair majority and on the other hand with tragic-heroic figures who were exemplary human specimens. Such historical literature provides the African American minority with superb role models and strengthens black pride, but does it offer a full account of the black experience in twentieth-century America? It perhaps could be argued that in recent decades historians have probed only selectively into the African American experience. From an understandable desire to avoid being branded with the stigma of racism or the label of Uncle Tom, they have neglected studying such tools of the white political structure as Arthur Mitchell. Moreover, the emphasis upon those few special individuals who rose from plantation and ghetto backgrounds to achieve prominence and acclaim tends to ignore the black masses, for whom revisionist tales of Horatio Alger have little relevance. For this author, after studying Mitchell's lifetime in great detail, there is less inclination today than previously to believe in the relevance of the American Dream for a majority of the black minority. The doubts exist partly because the ruling race has imposed no-win terms on black leaders. Mitchell's political career is a perfect illustration of the problem of white dependence.

If Arthur Mitchell represents in any significant way black leadership in the 1930s and later, it is understandable why African Americans have fared no better than they have: the power elite has wanted nothing more from them. Harsh as this conclusion may seem, it is justified by Mitchell's rapid rise from nowhere to a seat in the U.S. House of Representatives in 1935. Given a figurehead role by the Democratic party leadership of Chicago, he then willingly and eagerly did his political masters' bidding, handling whatever they had deemed vitally important to their interests. Mitchell's bosses regarded his most natural constituency, Bronzeville blacks living in the First District, only as votes to be counted. It is this sad and little-known aspect of the African American experience that represents this biography's value.

Two experiences—one personal and the other vicarious—presented to me the question of whether I should write a biography of Arthur Wergs Mitchell. Some years ago, a young African American law school graduate suggested that I abandon the project. She asked why anyone with decency would be interested in such a person, and argued that Mitchell would be better forgotten. In fact, it might even be racist to produce a biography of the fellow. On the other hand, a resident of south-central Los Angeles, in frank conversation with a Danish television reporter, gave me a good reason to complete the work. Speaking in the aftermath of the failure of a jury to convict Los Angeles police for the brutal beating of Rodney King, the African American interviewee stated flatly that Los Angeles's power structure, including its African American mayor, did not "care a thing about me." A similar assessment would have applied equally to Arthur W. Mitchell, the first African American Democrat in Congress. In essence, the Los Angeleno summarized the point of this book. Mitchell does not deserve a biography because of what he did for blacks; he deserves it because his career demonstrates how far an African American in the age of Franklin Roosevelt could go by making himself the tool of a power structure that also did not "care a thing" about the people he had been elected to represent.

This study reconstructs Mitchell's life from his birth in 1883 in rural eastern Alabama to his death in 1968 on an estate near Petersburg, Virginia. It was a checkered life. Although Mitchell was a great admirer of Booker T. Washington, he ran afoul of the famous educator while operating independent schools as an upstart competitor. The episode ended with a successful blackmail plot against Washington. Ultimately forced to leave Alabama by legal problems arising from disgraceful dealings with illiterate landowners, Mitchell relocated in Washington, where he dabbled in real estate and studied law. However, it was active membership in a black fraternity that gave him his first opportunity in politics. In 1928, because of contacts from the brotherhood, Mitchell went to Chicago to work as a paid Republican campaign organizer for Herbert Hoover. The experiences of working in a campaign and living in the Windy City added new dimensions to Mitchell's life, especially the determination that the District of Columbia was not a good place for individuals with his political ambition. Chicago, with its fifty wards, seemed a great choice for an African American with serious thoughts about pursuing elective office. Having just witnessed the election of Oscar DePriest, a black Republican, to Congress from Chicago's Bronzeville district, Mitchell knew African Americans had a chance to be elected to high office by this constituency. After having been to the Midwest, however, he realized a party switch would be the most expeditious way to realize his dream of going to Washington as an elected official. After joining the Democrats in Chicago, Mitchell devoted much time and energy to the party's Second Ward activities. Almost immediately, local Democratic party committeeman and ward heeler Joseph Tittinger discovered a remarkable quality in Mitchell that distinguished him from rival Earl Dickerson, Bronzeville's most outspoken African American Democrat and the white boss's greatest critic. Mitchell had demonstrated no tendencies for independence, and he obediently followed white leadership. As a consequence, Mitchell was fitting himself into the ward committeeman's face-saving plans. To relieve mounting pressures from Bronzeville residents who demanded support for African American candidates, Tittinger shrewdly saw in his unknown but docile follower a perfect nominee for DePriest's GOP seat in Congress. For Mitchell, the fortuitous combination of Tittinger's backing, the Great Depression, and white distaste for DePriest sealed victory in a racially split district with a white majority in November 1934.

Forewarned by both Chicago and Washington Democratic bosses not to be confrontational like DePriest, Mitchell accepted their advice. He announced a "safe" course of interesting himself only in constituent issues. Also to gain a desirable reputation, he praised the South and its Democratic officeholders and carried on heated public confrontations with the leaders of the NAACP and the National Negro Congress. By the end of a tumultuous first year, close followers of Mitchell were expressing either misgivings or praise for his conduct in office. The warmest endorsements came from Southern Democrats, and the harshest criticism flowed from impatient African Americans. Always insecure about his position, Mitchell solidified himself further by praising Franklin Delano Roosevelt and by voting with the Chicago congressional delegation. From a position on the Post Office Committee, he offered patronage assistance to his district's four ward committeemen. As a result of such loyalty, the Machine rewarded Mitchell with another nomination and then delivered enough votes in November 1936 to ensure his reelection. Although he continued attacking civil rights leaders, there were some better efforts to represent a national black constituency. For example, in 1937, he abandoned his personal antilynching bill in favor of an NAACP-supported measure. He also fought hard to reinstate an African American midshipman dismissed from the Naval Academy. Evidence of this new resolution to make a subtle move to greater independence showed itself clearly after he was oustered from first-class railroad accommodations during a trip through the South in 1937. Determined to obtain a redress, Mitchell brought a lawsuit against three railroad companies. Despite verbal warnings from leaders of the Chicago Machine not to continue the case, Mitchell did not surrender. His suit went to the Supreme Court, where the justices awarded his steadfastness with a favorable decision. It was to be Mitchell's last public victory because without discussion, the bosses informed him that William L. Dawson would be succeeding him on the ticket in 1942. Resigned to retirement, Mitchell faded quietly from politics and public life and took up a pastoral existence in Virginia that squared with his idea of gentlemanly splendor.

Despite eight years on Capitol Hill, and although he once was so well known that his name ranked below only athletes Jesse Owens and Joe Louis in a poll of African American college students, Arthur Wergs Mitchell has had nothing named for him in Chicago or anywhere else. In publications about African Americans during the Roosevelt era and in Windy City political histories of the same period, not much more than his defeat of Oscar DePriest is noted. Yet as a pivotal figure, Mitchell was important. By deliberately distancing himself from most responsibilities to a neglected constituency, African Americans, he had in many ways blazed a trail for several other self-serving black officeholders who also have depended upon fickle white electoral majorities for their positions.

For their help in the course of writing this book, many people deserve special praise. Wherever they might be, I want my greatest gratitude to reach Bronzeville friends Oliver Jackson, Sadie Gidron, Mattie Fox, Catherine Johnson, Charley Gilbert, Annie Perkins, and Hattie Sommers. Thirty-five years ago, when I was a naive teenager without firsthand knowledge of Chicago's Black Belt, these gracious ladies and gentlemen did better at introducing me to the harsh realities of race and powerlessness in the city of Chicago than any school or professor. While working with them in the Chicago suburb of Skokie, we talked; that is, I bombarded them with many questions, and my amazingly patient friends responded with enlightened drama about the daily trials and tribulations of living with second-class citizenship. Without having had the opportunity to experience such rare inspiration and candor, I must confess that insights into the effects of Organization politicians employing and exploiting figureheads such as Arthur Wergs Mitchell seem impossible to imagine. Thankful appreciation must also go to Archie J. Motley of the Chicago Historical Society. It was he who directed attention to Mitchell's manuscripts and advised a careful scrutiny to see if a book might come forth. I am also grateful to many others who graciously gave of their time in order that I might better understand my subject and the politics of

Chicago. Joseph Tittinger in Illinois, James Lee Johnson Junior in Washington, and all of the others interviewed were so kind and cooperative. Of the scores of individuals who opened themselves freely to my demands for information, Mrs. Clara Mann Mitchell deserves special praise; never shying from questions, she filled gaps with illuminating narrations. I must think as well of Mrs. Claude A. Barnett, who trusted me enough to provide first access to the valuable files of the Associated Negro Press; at the time of my research, she had them in storage at her Bronzeville home. For being as Professor Roy Vernon Scott has always been to former students—generous to a fault—and kind enough in my case to examine and criticize a roughly drafted biography, there is inability to express in words all the praise he deserves. Equal in generosity and worthy criticism was Emeritus Professor Augie Meier of Kent State University. Although several years had lapsed between our contacts, he never seemed doubtful about my determination to complete a study of Mitchell, and never neglected to provide good editorial advice. Archivists from Tuskegee Institute and Northwestern University are deserving of special mention, too; respectively, Daniel T. Williams and Patrick Quinn presented me with additional sources of information. Help from Chicago State University funded travel and photocopying costs. Last but by no means least among many contributors, everyone connected with the University of Missouri Press has helped. Anonymous readers and the editorial staff improved my focus and suggested necessary improvements. From outside the circles of Mitchell contemporaries, professional advisers, and countless kind people who assisted in one way or another, there is my family. Although not always fully appreciated by sons Peter and Patrik or wife Gun, my slipping away nightly to the confines of my quiet office was tolerated enough for me to organize and write this biography of Arthur Wergs Mitchell.

Dennis Sven Nordin

ABBREVIATIONS

ABE	Alabama Bureau of Education
Afro-American	*Baltimore Afro-American*
Annie	Annie Harris Mitchell
ANPR	Associated Negro Press Release
Argus	*St. Louis Argus*
BP	Claude A. Barnett (Associated Negro Press Files) Papers
BTW	Booker T. Washington
CAD	Corneal A. Davis
CCCR	Choctaw County Court Records
CD	Colored Division
CFD	Charles F. Davis
CHH	Carter H. Harrison
CHS	Chicago Historical Society
CR	*Congressional Record*
Defender	*Chicago Defender*
DNCC	Democratic National Campaign Committee
DsL	Davis Lee
EBD	Earl B. Dickerson
EGB	Edgar G. Brown
EJK	Edward J. Kelly
EJS	Emmett J. Scott
EKJ	Eugene Kinckle Jones
FBR	Freeman B. Ransom
FDR	Franklin Delano Roosevelt
FMDP	Frank M. Dixon Papers
FP	John Fitzpatrick Papers
HCCR	Hale County Court Records
ICC	Interstate Commerce Commission
IFL	Ira F. Lewis

JAF	James A. Farley
JEM	J.E. Mitchell
JET	James E. Tittinger
JFP	James L. Johnson Family Papers
JLJ1	James L. Johnson Sr.
JLJ2	James L. Johnson Jr.
Jmc	John McDuffie
John	John W. Mitchell
Journal and Guide	*Norfolk Journal and Guide*
JPD	John P. Davis
KM	Kelly Miller
LC	Library of Congress
M	Arthur Wergs Mitchell Sr.
McDP	John McDuffie Papers
MNR	Mitchell News Release
MotP	Robert R. Moton Papers
MP	Arthur Wergs Mitchell Papers
MWJ	Mordecai W. Johnson
NAACP	National Association for the Advancement of Colored People Papers
PBY	P. Bernard Young
PDJ	Percy D. Jones
RP	Franklin D. Roosevelt Papers
RW	Roy Wilkins
SCCR	Sumter County Court Records
SJ	Scipio Jones
SP	Anthony Sorrentino Papers
TIA	Tuskegee Institute Archives
TJD	Thomas J. Davis
TM	Thurgood Marshall
WAW	William A. Wallace
Wergs	Arthur Wergs Mitchell Jr.
WJE	William J. Edwards
WP	Booker T. Washington Papers
WW	Walter White

THE NEW DEAL'S BLACK CONGRESSMAN

Alabama Years

1883–1919

A s Arthur Wergs Mitchell surveyed the Capitol on January 2, 1935, before striding swiftly into the cavernous chamber of the House of Representatives, there was a moment to doubt what would soon occur. Here he stood, an African American one generation removed from slavery, and he was going to be sworn in as a United States congressman, the first of his race to sit on the Democratic side of the aisle. Yet despite some unlikely elements, Mitchell knew no drug had taken him beyond reality into a temporary fantasy world. His defeat of Oscar DePriest in the November 6 election was no figment of his imagination.[1]

Mitchell's road to Washington was most unusual, with many stops along the way. It began humbly and inconspicuously in the obscurity of a one-room cabin near Roanoke, Alabama, on December 22, 1883.[2] Former slaves Taylor Mitchell and Ammar Patterson Mitchell became first-time parents, and heralded his birth by naming him after President Chester A. Arthur. However, as a baby and small boy, the youngster seldom heard his given name; his parents preferred "Beauty" or "Beaut." For unknown reasons, the middle name of Wergs came later; Mitchell added it himself, with no explanation of its origin.

By the standards of the times for blacks in northeastern Alabama, the Mitchell household of eight was blessed. At first, Arthur, two brothers, and three sisters lived with their parents on rented land. The whole family farmed during springs and summers, and Taylor Mitchell logged timber between the last harvest and the spring planting. He grew cotton for cash

---

1. Unless otherwise noted, this and subsequent paragraphs on Mitchell's early life are based upon interviews with Mrs. Clara Mitchell.
2. U.S. Department of Commerce, Census Bureau, Records, 1900, 1910; Metropolitan Life Insurance Company, Policy, MP. There is some dispute about the year because official records list the birth year as 1880, and Mitchell always gave 1883.

and planted corn and sweet potatoes for home consumption. A perfectly tended watermelon patch was a source of special pride. To enjoy a melon from his father's vines required consent, an unsatisfactory arrangement for spirited Arthur. Having acquired a streak of independence and some stubborn self-reliance at a young age, he did not like seeking permission. Accordingly, Ammar Mitchell permitted her son's cultivation of a private garden. Soon young Arthur was boasting that "people now would have to ask me for a watermelon."

Like many black children, Beaut received only a rudimentary education. When he celebrated his sixth birthday, the nearest public school for blacks was ten miles away. Although illiterate himself, Taylor Mitchell knew if little Arthur and his siblings were ever to attend school, the family must move. However, the closest available cabin near a school was five miles away, on abandoned land that was blanketed with heavy brush. Desperate for educational opportunities for his children, the father accepted the challenge of reopening the land for planting. Arthur helped clear the land while attending four separate three-month terms. Unfortunately, the teacher was an incompetent, self-taught man who, according to Taylor Mitchell, knew less than his youngster. Disgusted with the situation, the father removed Arthur from the school and turned his education over to a white neighbor. Soon thereafter, all tutoring stopped for several years.

During the first fourteen years of Arthur's life, the Mitchell family got along reasonably well, given the time and place. From his logger's wages and sales of farm produce, Taylor Mitchell was able to clothe and feed six offspring. The family moved often, following the timber. Eventually, savings from cotton sales paid for a small farm. Meanwhile, Arthur was developing a reputation for diligence and detail. As a result, Ammar Mitchell could always recognize his fields from the others because his rows were straight. More serious than frivolous, Arthur seldom mixed with peers. Except for friendly relationships with two white boys, there was not much socializing.[3]

For a boy raised in the late nineteenth century, everything about Beaut's childhood appeared normal. Sitting by firesides and listening to James "Professor Jim" Smedley tell ghost stories was his favorite pastime, and like the fictional Huckleberry Finn, he had a pet dog and a hatred for cats. Arthur's lack of compassion for felines showed itself cruelly one day with his deposit of a kitten—strangled out of meanness—in a hog trough. Punishment for his sadistic deed followed, for Ammar Mitchell would

3. As will be noted in chapter 3, there was something lasting from Mitchell's boyhood relationships with these boys; they were among the people congratulating the congressman-elect in 1934.

not accept her son's explanation that the cat had drowned. During his parents' absence on another occasion, he delighted younger siblings by harnessing a hog for rides around the farmyard.

Arthur was close to his father and maternal grandmother. Trips to her home on a nearby plantation often netted fresh cheese, a treat he seemed to enjoy more than candy. Taylor Mitchell spent as much time as possible with his oldest son, who sought permission to accompany his father on visits to Roanoke because "daddy" was a "pushover," bending easily to his children's wishes for something special. On one such county-seat trip, Arthur coaxed a McIntosh coat and matching Wellington rain boots from his father. However, his good fortune changed quickly after he returned home with the new outfit. Not at all pleased by her husband's softness and extravagance, Ammar seized the clothing and refused to let her son wear it.

There was no doubt that Ammar Mitchell dominated her household. She was a proud descendant of field hands from the nearby Patterson Plantation. Her father was white according to family legend, and she herself was "a very light woman." Since she ruled so sternly, her sons Arthur and John determined that all pale-skinned women made poor wives because "they fussed too much." On the other hand, nothing so definite remains about Taylor. It seems from tidbits left in the oldest son's personal papers that Taylor Mitchell had been born and reared in the Cusseta community near Columbus, Georgia. How and under what circumstances he would later meet Ammar Patterson cannot be verified. In speeches, Arthur did mention enslavement, but there are no other facts or details about the man.

As a boy, Beaut had experiences that later would help him in shaping opinions and actions. Some awareness of racial pride was instilled early in the youngster. When his mother discovered him eating from a tin plate outside the home of white playmates, she forbade him to accept food there again under such humiliating circumstances. It was also as a boy that Mitchell began acquiring a lifelong dislike for gospel preachers. His ingrained hostility toward them apparently took root from the tendency of Baptist ministers to stop at Arthur's home for expected chicken dinners. The boy watched as they devoured the best pieces, leaving only neck bones, backs, and wings for everyone else.

Mitchell's ambitious nature showed itself during childhood, too. There were many turning points, but perhaps the most important came from a journey to town. Once when he and his father were visiting Roanoke together, they entered the county courthouse to observe an agenda of legal proceedings. The day's sessions proved so interesting to the youthful Arthur that he began proclaiming his intentions to study law. His new interest gave him renewed motivation to do well in school. He loved reading, but with no available library, books were difficult to obtain. As a means of purchasing them he chipped wood for charcoal, which he then sold at five cents per bushel. Resourcefully, Beaut developed some favorite tricks with primers; to master alternative solutions to problems from text examples, he would study ahead. Pride in such accomplishments undoubtedly contributed to a sense of superiority. Almost from the beginning, he placed importance on gaining an upper hand in every situation before him. Perhaps that accounted for the great pleasure he gained from buying penknives and other items from mail-order catalogs for eventual resales to other boys. Quarterly camp meetings were another source of income. At these, he cut hair and shaved at twenty-five cents a head.

Youth's pleasantries faded quickly in 1897. Typhoid fever carried to the Mitchell household by contaminated water brought disaster. The deaths of Taylor Mitchell and two younger sisters, plus a physician's fee, left the survivors destitute and at the doctor's mercy. Suddenly, the doctor took everything, including unharvested crops and the family's homestead. Desperately struggling to keep her family fed and together, the widowed mother with Arthur's aid would nightly "steal" from what had been "their own planted fields." Since it had been a white man who had confiscated land as payment for unpaid medical debts, the experience could have soured Arthur against the other race. Yet, it would not, because in the midst of hardship, some positive events were occurring, too. Two white friends gave him a sardine can and later treated him, two of his brothers, and his sister Tommy to ice cream. Years later, remembering the incidents with gratitude, Mitchell was still trying to repay for boyhood generosity with invitations to his Virginia retirement estate.

Young Arthur passed rapidly from childhood to adulthood, bypassing adolescence. Taylor Mitchell's death forced his rapid maturity into manhood, because his mother expected him to be patriarch over her depleted family. For many years, his assistance held the family together. Nevertheless, after he acquired a girlfriend, his mother advised marriage. Claiming to have more urgent business, Beaut spurned matrimony. From an uncle in Macon County, he had just heard of Booker T. Washington's Tuskegee Institute. Figuring there would always be ample time to marry, he concluded that not receiving an education would only be foolish. Almost eight years had elapsed since his last experiences with formal instruction, and now that Tuskegee was affording him an opportunity to renew a long-awaited education, he would avail himself of it.[4]

4. Mitchell interview, April 21, 1970; M to John J. Hagehorn, July 14, 1937; S. H. Tatum to M, November 10, 1934; M to S. H. Tatum, November 21, 1934; Z. Dallas

In 1901, Mitchell had an auspicious arrival at Tuskegee, which had been established some twenty years earlier for poor black youngsters' industrial and agricultural education. At seventeen, he departed Chambers County with all his possessions—"a dress-suit case, an extra pair of trousers, one suit of underwear and a few shirts"—intending to cover the sixty-five miles on foot. Upon reaching Macon County's celebrated school, Arthur had fifteen cents. Although he possessed so little money, he thought that would not keep him from entering Tuskegee's gates because he had heard of the school's mission to take in and educate penniless youths. However, the naive young man received a rude awakening from John H. Palmer, Tuskegee's stern registrar, who quickly informed him that there was a two-dollar entrance fee. The bad news disappointed Arthur, but it was not enough to send him home. On leaving campus, he was resolved to return with the money; then, nobody could deny him admission. Fortunately for him, his nearby uncle was kind. Wages from washing dishes in town and free board at his relative's house quickly enabled him to save the amount required for the admission fee. Accordingly, during the second week of September 1901, Arthur Mitchell reentered the gates, this time for middle-class placement in Tuskegee Normal and Industrial Institute.[5]

Soon after Arthur's entry, he was seeking special status. On October 13, 1901, or just one month after his late admission, he asked the school's council for permission to board at his uncle's and to attend night classes. Young Mitchell's letter to the school's governing body cited faculty members and a minister as character references, and it expressed his frustration at not being able to gain acceptable campus employment—such as in the tailor shop—and not having been granted time with the principal to discuss the reasons behind the requested changes. School authorities ruled favorably for admission to the night program, but they decided he could "not board outside."[6]

That Mitchell had asked for special consideration so soon after his admission to Tuskegee would indicate that he might be different and more difficult than many other students at the school. Mitchell had shown no fear of Booker T. Washington, and there had not been hesitancy on his

Hicks to M, November 26, 1934; James Smedley to M, November 18, 1934; M to James Smedley, November 26, 1934; William F. Smedley to M, November 22, 1934, MP.

5. Tuskegee Institute, *Annual Bulletin*, 1901–1902, 91. Mitchell in many autobiographical sketches claimed his arrival at Tuskegee had been preceded by one year at Talladega College, but circumstances and facts do not substantiate this. If anything, they contradict his assertion. See Buell G. Gallagher to M, December 4, 1934, and M to Gallagher, December 6, 1934, MP.

6. M to Councill [*sic*] of T.N.I.I., October 13, 1901; Council to M, October 13, 1901, WP.

part to ask for whatever he wanted. Moreover, he did not view himself as ordinary. In his bold letter to Tuskegee's board, there appeared a confident prediction of something exceptional: "I believe I can be a great man in the future." Washington would discover this for himself after the registrar assigned Mitchell to work in the principal's office.[7]

The appointment became a turning point. From this position, Mitchell learned much from Washington about running a private school, and he clearly mastered some basic lessons in operational management from being in close proximity to a mentor who by then was attracting many distinguished guests to Tuskegee. Being in the headmaster's office enabled Mitchell to observe much, including Washington's manipulations of whites for the achievement of goals. Years later as a public figure, Arthur Mitchell fondly credited the institute and Washington for his success.

The Tuskegee Idea and the man behind it would become indelibly etched on Mitchell's view of race relations. He would never forget what the principal had achieved through accommodation to another race's terms and standards. As we shall see, Mitchell would follow Washington's formula, and he would always argue with skeptics who doubted the wisdom of the so-called Wizard of Tuskegee's philosophy and methods. Fifty years after his educational experience and firsthand lessons from Booker T. Washington, he still defended—physically if necessary—the school's record and its founder's principles.[8]

Tuskegee offered discipline and regimentation as well as a fixed curriculum. A strong martial air prevailed at the institute, with its male students wearing required military-style uniforms. Everyone on campus moved in cadence to bells and commands, with demerits given for deviations from a daily program that began with morning prayer and ended with nighttime vespers. Rules and prohibitions at Tuskegee had multiplied to the point that many students were complaining that every pleasure had become a vice. Staff especially frowned upon liquor, tobacco, cards, and dice, and there was a special code of restrictions for women. Student Eula Mae King—later Mitchell's wife—offended simply for "going in the back to the big gate," a violation because there had not been an approved escort with her to the institute's outer limits; she received a full disciplinary citation. In academics, middle-class pupils such as Mitchell all studied literature, composition, grammar, English history, reading, mathematics, and science (under George Washington Carver). Between lessons and work, Arthur was achieving distinction with the Willing Workers Debating Club.[9]

7. M to Councill [sic], October 13, 1901; *Tuskegee Messenger* 10 (December 1934): 2, 8, WP.

8. Mitchell interview; *CR*, 75th Cong., 1st sess., 2110, 3149.

9. Tuskegee Institute, *Bulletin*, 1901–1902; Demerit Book, 1895–1899, WP; *Tuskegee Messenger* 10 (December 1934): 2, 8; Frank P. Chisholm to M, May 22, 1937, MP.

Mitchell, however, did not stay long at Tuskegee. Before completing his second year, he transferred to Snow Hill Institute, a grammar and secondary school staffed only with Tuskegee graduates and located in rural Wilcox County, Alabama, near Selma. It is not known why he chose to finish his studies and receive a teaching license from Snow Hill instead of Tuskegee. In later years when he described his education, he did not mention Snow Hill or the efforts of its principal, William J. Edwards; Mitchell would always call himself a Tuskegee man.[10]

With few blacks educated well enough to teach, there were desperate cries for young men and women with command of the three R's. Mitchell entered the profession in 1903 as a temporary teacher in Cusseta, Georgia, Eula Mae King's hometown. Just before the end of the school year, Tullibody Academy, the "colored" school of Greensboro, Alabama, named Mitchell principal. There in Hale County, the young bachelor was joined by sweetheart and recent Tuskegee graduate Eula Mae in teaching. However, there were several early indications to Booker Washington that this job assignment would not satisfy Mitchell. Days after getting the appointment, Mitchell was laying plans for a school modeled after Tuskegee.[11]

By the time his first letter reached Washington from Greensboro, Mitchell was engrossed with the project, galvanizing the support of the local citizenry. According to Mitchell, prominent whites were endorsing his plan, while the community's few educated blacks were offering resistance. Soon he was writing to Washington to grumble about a black physician who had "insulted the white board by saying you and none of your followers had not sense enough to do anything but teach the people to work." Besides negative feelings, Mitchell's letter contained pleas for advice, counsel, and a strong Tuskegee endorsement of the proposal. Mitchell—like many other former Tuskegee students—deemed Washington's backing indispensable to his plan's success because the Wizard's support commanded respect and bestowed legitimacy. Operators of fledgling schools besieged Washington with such requests, asking that he lend his name and reputation. They almost always offered the same deal to the great educator. Like Mitchell in Greensboro, several other founders of schools were offering Washington trusteeships as their bait to draw attention to their programs. Receiving no response from Tuskegee to his initial appeal, Mitchell persisted, repetitioning Washington several weeks later. An acknowledgment finally came with a disappointing message.

10. Glenn N. Sisk, "Negro Education in the Alabama Black Belt, 1875–1900," 134–35; ABE, *Negro Education,* No. 39 (Montgomery, 1911), 94–96; Arnold Cooper, *Between Struggle and Hope: Four Black Educators in the South, 1894–1915,* 3–16; Donald P. Stone, *Fallen Prince: Black Education and the Quest for Afro American Nationality.*

11. *Greensboro Watchman* (Ala.), May 3, 1906; M to BTW, May 27, 1903, WP.

Washington stated that he could neither take a place on Mitchell's school's board of trustees nor provide any more than a vague, conditional endorsement; withholding full support at this time was necessary because the school had not commenced its tasks.[12]

As the weeks rolled on and the summer of 1903 passed, Mitchell's plans for a new industrial school were progressing well without Washington's full blessing. Mitchell seemed to know the exact requirements for outfitting an institute. His experiences at Tuskegee had also apparently taught him some valuable financial lessons. Having observed how Yankee contacts and philanthropy had assured success at Tuskegee, he resolved to seek and interest wealthy men in his educational venture. As his first steps, he gave a most ambitious name to the proposed academy, West Alabama Normal and Industrial Institute, and then assigned it a motto, "Bend to the oar tho the tide be against us." With the academy's name and slogan conspicuously emblazoned on newly printed stationery, Mitchell became a fund-raiser. Booker T. Washington and Tuskegee again figured into his plans. Mitchell sought Washington's permission for a touring musician to play at Tuskegee. The request was met with hostility, however. Mitchell's great hope had been for helpful introductions by Washington to potential supporters. But Mitchell was simply asking too much of the Wizard; clearly, Washington would not intentionally undermine his life's work by assisting a young upstart like Mitchell. Besides, aid to Mitchell would siphon funds otherwise earmarked for Tuskegee.[13]

Periodically over the next five years, the *Greensboro Record* informed local citizens about West Alabama Normal and Industrial Institute. At every instance, Mitchell seemed to stress the need for practical studies and the interdependence of two races: "It is my opinion that for the present instead of putting so much stress upon the teaching of the higher sciences, we devote a good deal of our time to the trades . . . , and especially agriculture. . . . I make an earnest plea that all persons, both white and colored, join us in the building up of an agricultural school at this place. . . . This will effect [sic] the interest of the white man and the black man alike.

12. M to BTW, June 20 and 30, 1903; Register of Corporations and Societies, book 1, 88–89, HCCR; M to B. F. Beverly, November 21, 1934, MP. Dishonorable dealings with Greensboro blacks were contributing to Washington's suspicions. Mitchell's failure to honor a verbal agreement with predecessor Thomas Seay about paying for some books was not soon forgotten. See Seay to M, January 16, 1935, and M to Seay, January 18, 1935, MP; for details of Washington's relationships with other upstart educators, see Cooper, *Between Struggle and Hope.*
13. M to EJS, July 22, 1903, R. C. Bruce to EJS, November 16, 1903, M to BTW, June 20 and 30, October 12, 16, and 25, and November 10, 1903, BTW to M, October 14 and 22 and November 19, 1903, WP; M to WJE, June 30, 1903, BP; HCCR, Deeds, S, 55–57, 236–37, U, 392–93.

For indeed our interest is so interwoven that one cannot be helped without effecting [sic] the other." In the beginning when West Alabama's receipts were so inadequate that they could not sustain anyone, Mitchell continued as Tullibody Academy's principal.[14]

His experiences as a Hale County educator ended in 1908. After less than five years, West Alabama Normal and Industrial Institute closed. Mitchell then ventured to Birmingham and entered the real estate business. Experience gained in this field during previous summers had apparently prepared him adequately to abandon the Greensboro job. Besides, he had already met and entered a new business partnership with John A. Rogers, a white planter from Gainesville. Somehow, they had set in motion everything for the formation of the Afro-American Building Loan and Real Estate Company of Sumter County. The plans called for a subdivision of Rogers's Fair Oaks Plantation in the northern part of the county. According to their scheme, plots would sell to local blacks. Mitchell fit into the planter's project because a school would help attract residents. For a school, Rogers made "a donation" of eighty acres of prime timberland, and then assigned Mitchell to building and running the institution. Since this would be the only nearby Negro educational facility, Rogers was expecting all land located near the proposed school to boom in value. This was only phase one of Rogers's scheming. Once unsuspecting settlers were on the land and in debt, they would be trapped, unable to leave because of the binding effects of unfavorable credit terms. When Mitchell agreed to Rogers's "kind challenge" of teaching useful agricultural skills, he was probably foreseeing no linkages between education and peonage.[15]

During the early 1900s, teaching and establishing schools in west central Alabama were not the only things on Mitchell's mind. He first courted and then married Eula Mae King. Later in 1905, she had a son, Arthur Wergs Mitchell Jr. Nevertheless, as a father and husband, he was mostly indifferent; family obligations would never hold as much interest and importance for him as other parts of his life. In point of truth, he was always too self-centered to be an attentive family man; his goals and instincts were tangible and impersonal. He sought wealth and fame, not love and devotion. Hence, he distanced himself from both wife and child. Since Greensboro and Panola had less than two thousand inhabitants, his lack of affection could not pass without notice. Observant neighbors never recalled Eula Mae Mitchell going to town with her husband, and there was even gossip that he was locking her inside their house. Her death from

14. *Greensboro Record* (Ala.), January 12, 1905; *Greensboro Watchman*, May 3, 1906.
15. M to WJE, February 29, 1908, BP; unidentified newspaper clipping, MP; Goldston Interview; SCCR, Deed Records, book 26, 153–54; *Tuskegee Messenger* 10 (December 1934): 2.

pellagra in 1910 at age twenty-nine added to the speculation, precipitating the charge in the rural community that he had almost starved Eula Mae to death before having her committed to an insane asylum. Arthur Mitchell refused to dignify the rumors with a serious denial, preferring instead a stock reply that would do little to quiet gossipmongers but much to reveal his indifference to criticism: "You know how women are—they won't half eat anyway!"[16]

After only a brief stay in Birmingham, Mitchell moved to Panola's Fair Oaks Plantation. During his short stopover, he nevertheless experienced politics for the first time. In the wake of Theodore Roosevelt's public support of William H. Taft for president, he and a small group of Birmingham blacks, meeting at a local lodge, formed an "organization to promote the interests of colored Republicans" that became known thereafter as Jefferson County's "Taft Republican Club." Mitchell was on the executive committee. Nothing would come from the group's activities, however; within the local GOP, the African Americans lost power to a "lily white" faction. The shame of this episode so embittered Mitchell that he never participated again in Alabama political activities. For more than two decades, he neither campaigned for candidates nor attempted to register to vote. Accepting Republican patronage pay in 1910 as a census taker marked the closest he would come to engaging in politics before 1928.[17]

Nothing is known about the origins of the Rogers-Mitchell relationship. However, it is reasonable to assume that Mitchell's general conduct was a factor behind his role in the land liquidation scheme. During the fall of 1908 and not long after his arrival at Fair Oaks from Birmingham, Mitchell began giving black residents the sense that their new schoolmaster had come to help himself and not them. With suspicion, they watched Mitchell, a "dandy," in his role of overseer over timber-clearing operations and school construction. Despite their reservations, all work was proceeding swiftly. Fully transplanted to Panola and proclaimed ready for its first five-month term, West Alabama Normal and Industrial Institute reopened October 28, 1908, this time temporarily, in a small public schoolhouse built during Reconstruction. The shabby facility was used while work was progressing on a permanent structure. Within weeks after the start of school, the community recognized that bench work and traditional instruction in basic subjects were not the bases of Mitchell's educational

16. Mitchell, Goldston, Gilberts, Little, and Mason interviews; M to WJE, May 17 and August 12, 17, and 29, 1910, BP; unidentified clipping, MP.

17. Bureau of the Census, official credentials, MP; *Birmingham News*, March 19, 1908; *Choctaw Advocate* (Butler, Ala.), March 29, 1916; Mitchell, Goldston, Little, Gilbert, Mason, and Pinson interviews. Speech notes from 1912 in MP refer to Woodrow Wilson, but Mitchell's comments were vague and not at all antagonistic to the governor.

program. At its core was work. Surrounding the school were forests to fell and fields to plow, plant, dress, and harvest. Strenuous activities were as much a part of the principal's "education" as classroom lessons in the three R's and music. Some seventy years later, two elderly Sumter County residents recalled all this along with some general impressions of the operation's mastermind. When asked about him, octogenarian Fanoy Little snapped back that he remembered Arthur Mitchell as a "money man" who had "worked the devil out of students."[18]

Shrewdness as a farm manager and entrepreneur became matters of great pride for Mitchell. He often publicized noteworthy results in local newspapers, and the same reportage went to acquaintances at Tuskegee. The *Sumter Sun* recalled how black residents had once petitioned the county's school superintendent to withdraw its $125 in public funds from the principal because "they did not want their children to work 'but [to] learn out of books.' " Yet with his well-managed land now returning a bale or more of cotton per acre, the *Sun* article continued, even former critics were asking to "learn how to farm like Prof. Mitchell." There was also mention of Rogers and his full satisfaction with black tenants learning the value of intensive farming. To Emmett J. Scott, Booker Washington's chief assistant at Tuskegee, Mitchell told of pupil-worker achievements at Panola, and of the school's expansion plans. However, there was no complete disclosure of Fair Oaks. Obviously missing were details of the child labor that was being passed off as useful industrial education. Given in return for token lessons in general studies, toil was the children's offering to the headmaster.

Since Mitchell answered only to Rogers, the parents' negative reactions to questionable methods and achievements did not matter. Despite its exploitation of students, West Alabama Institute still was the only existing educational institution for blacks in northern Sumter County. Hence, work progressed until Mitchell had assembled a cluster of new buildings—each painted barnyard red—for "instructional" and agricultural purposes. By 1910, these included a three-floor, twenty-five-room wooden structure, a chapel, a workshop, and the principal's cottage. On the grounds were two mules, a horse, two cows, five hogs, chickens, turkeys, and assorted farm implements.[19]

West Alabama's "highly recommended" staff came from Tuskegee and Snow Hill bearing personal letters of endorsement from Booker T. Washington and William J. Edwards. However, full obedience, not credentials, was what was most important to Mitchell; he accepted no challenges to his

18. Mason and Little interviews.
19. Ibid.; *Livingston Sumter Sun* (Ala.), 1910; M to EJS, January 27, 1910, WP.

authority or to his management of the enterprise. In practice, Mitchell's enforcement of iron rule meant teachers forfeited all rights to disagree with his interpretations of Washington's educational philosophy. For such docile service, his staff received small compensations along with pleasant living quarters in the main classroom building.[20]

Financing West Alabama Institute was one of Mitchell's greatest concerns. From his experience in Greensboro, he had learned a great deal about the limits to Southern white largess, and he had witnessed Booker T. Washington's reluctance to part with Tuskegee support and funds. Mitchell also knew alternative monetary sources had to be found, or soon West Alabama Institute would close. It was receiving some state and county support, but in such paltry amounts that their impact on the school's budget was inconsequential. The public funds were not even paying teachers' salaries. Yields from sales of farm produce provided income, but again, it did not amount to much. Until such time as he could tap Yankee philanthropists for gifts, soliciting area residents for monetary support would have to suffice. Thus, Mitchell adopted a routine of teaching by day, followed by nightly appeals for funds at nearby African American churches. These efforts not only infused the school with needed cash but also honed Mitchell's skills as a public speaker.[21] A March 12, 1911, address at an African Methodist Episcopal church typified his speeches. An excellent presentation, it contained what would become familiar themes about the value of work and the patience of whites:

> Have your boys stop carrying pistols, teach them that it is better to use the Bible, song books, newspapers, magazines, plows, shovels, wagons and mules than shotguns, pistols, knives and things that are damaging us very materially in some sections of the country. Teach them that it is better to work for absolutely nothing than to spend time in idleness and foolish gossip, for work without compensation has in it ennobling power and virtue more than I can explain. Stop allowing your boys, girls and wives to go to town on Saturdays or any other times unless they have business there. As I have stated, the white man doesn't want to give us up for he is our friend, but he wants better results from the soil than ignorance and methods of fifty years ago are bringing him.[22]

As a means of promoting the school and himself as the person behind great agricultural feats at West Alabama Institute, Mitchell supplemented fund-raising at churches with assorted free activities on the

20. M to WJE, March 1 and 30, September 27, and October (n.d.), 1910, BP; Little interview.

21. Pamphlet, *The Principal's Story;* M to BTW, March 15, 1910, MP; *Tuskegee Southern Letter,* April 1910.

22. *Geiger Times* (Ala.), March 23, 1911.

school grounds. A Panola institute and fair held on February 16, 1910, was representative of the undertakings planned for black farmers. To herald the all-day event at the school, he covered northern Sumter County with professionally printed handbills. They noted the day's schedule and invited the participation of all interested African Americans in beneficial activities. According to the outline, morning hours were filled with brief seminars conducted by local residents on "How to Make Money on the Farm," "How to Break Land for Cotton and Corn," "The Cost of Producing a Bale of Cotton," "How to Grow Corn on Sandy Land," and "The Need of Improved Seed and the Use of Fertilizers." On a lighter side, the morning agenda also featured baseball and foot races. After a noon dinner, the day's events concluded with a literary program.[23]

While working with children in Alabama, Mitchell approached the two races very differently. Interactions with whites were obviously aimed at courting a favorable opinion of him. In the process of garnering respect for himself, he raised the doubts and suspicions of blacks. In practice, he gained their rebuke by mastering a uniquely twisted interpretation of Booker Washington's handling of race relations. The effects became especially evident after Mitchell had stressed to white listeners in his audiences the usefulness an educated black population would have on communities. He could be irksome because in his backhanded overtures to securing greater support for West Alabama, there were often derogatory references to illiterate African Americans. Resultant gains from strengthening Alabama's agricultural economy with practical lessons in farming, he lectured, would not be the only benefits accruing from assistance to his school; he also promised less tangible rewards: "Idleness is one of the greatest causes of so much crime being committed. It is our aim to teach the negro to love all honorable work however humble. . . . We are living in a great country, surrounded by . . . white friends, who have always trusted us. . . . We owe them a great debt of gratitude for having been so patient with us in our weakness. We are not slow to admit that the man is our sponsor and we are dependent on him to a large degree. We cannot hope to do anything here without the co-operation of the white people."[24]

While asking for financial help in early 1910, Mitchell launched a massive drive to place West Alabama Institute before as many blacks as possible. Once again, he enlisted Tuskegee's assistance, choosing the *Southern Letter* to disseminate news about his school's efforts to uplift the race with education. Letters from Mitchell, Eula Mae, and Rogers appeared in Booker T. Washington's monthly publication. All stressed allegedly fine

23. Handbills, *A Gala Day for the Negroes of West Alabama!* and *Big Industrial Fair for Negroes,* MP; M to WJE, September 19, 26, and 30, 1910, BP; *Geiger Times,* September 29 and October 20, 1910.

24. *Gainesville Times* (Ala.), February 17, 1910.

work among Sumter County youngsters, and each asked readers for contributions. After appealing locally and in a Tuskegee magazine, Mitchell was ready for a major collection effort among benevolent Yankees. At least once while at Greensboro, he had ventured to the Northeast after money. On this journey, a successful ten-day appeal, he had concentrated on religious congregations in Watertown, Connecticut.[25]

Consecutive Northeastern swings in 1910 and 1911 were noteworthy adventures for Mitchell. A winter tour brought him before audiences in Massachusetts, Connecticut, and New York. Generous with their monetary gifts, people at every stop were responding favorably to Mitchell's oratory about the challenges and handicaps facing students at West Alabama Institute. Typical were Mitchell's successful efforts at Palmer, Massachusetts. Large groups gathered to hear him, and his addresses were preludes to taking in much money. Before departing, he had spoken to three churches, a YMCA gathering, and a businessmen's club. Afterward, there was an eventful stopover at Watertown. While there, Mitchell recruited the Dean of Women from the Voorhees Industrial School of Denmark, South Carolina. Voorhees, begun in 1896 as a mission to train and educate young African Americans by Tuskegee graduate Elizabeth Evelyn Wright, had been employing Annie Cornelia Harris. Eventually destined by selfless love and steady devotion to become Mitchell's second wife after Eula Mae's death, Harris, a very mild-mannered woman, agreed to follow the persuasive fund-raiser to Alabama. Before an exchange of nuptial vows, she traveled home at the end of West Alabama's 1911 term. On her way home, Harris spoke and collected money for her fiancé's school. She hardly had time to settle in her hometown before Mitchell was present for her hand in marriage.[26]

Successful fund-raising in the North reflected Mitchell's abilities as a storyteller and orator. Much better at narration than his mentors Washington and Edwards, Mitchell usually prepared audiences well for solicitations, relying upon vivid detail and drawing from personal experiences like his office-boy work under the Wizard of Tuskegee. Suddenly shifting to a straight face and a sincere voice, he began exaggerating his own worth, noting how, for example, he had been favored most among the great educator's students. To legitimize these preposterous claims, Mitchell reached down into a breast pocket, producing what appeared to audiences to be impressive credentials and words of encouragement from Booker T. Washington, John A. Rogers, and William J. Edwards.

25. *Tuskegee Southern Letter,* February and April 1910; *Springfield Daily Republican* (Mass.), n.d.; M to WJE, n.d., MP.

26. Marriage announcements and unidentified clippings; Martin A. Manafee to M, February 21, 1935, MP; M to WJE, January 5, March 31, and May 9, 1911, BP.

Although the Wizard had not personally inspected West Alabama, his resistance to Mitchell eventually softened. With Mitchell's persistence, West Alabama finally gained Washington's superficial approval. Even if his letter to Mitchell was not a sweeping endorsement, Washington added considerable prestige to Mitchell's portfolio. Regardless, credentials alone did not render Mitchell's appearances special; this came from his outstanding oratorical talent. Each successive trip north exceeded the previous one at taking in dollars and producing additional invitations to speak. Clearly, Mitchell had become proficient at warming hearts and raising money. With the gifts of a talented actor, he conveyed earnestness and humility while dramatizing the trials and tribulations of educating indigent children. In addition to his speaking skills, Mitchell was a master promoter and organizer. As a case in point, he skillfully heralded an upcoming appearance at New York City's Salem AME Church. In advance of the event, he circulated flyers that announced program speakers and vocalists. Two New York ministers, a Brooklyn quartet, a soprano, and a journalist were on the platform with him for an evening of West Alabama fund-raising.[27]

Apparel collections represented another important part of Mitchell's work. Just his asking audiences for worn coats, shoes, trousers, shirts, and dresses seemed to give urgency to his efforts on behalf of underprivileged people. Unfortunately, because of Mitchell's greed, the gathered items all too often ended up profiting the solicitor more than the neediest people of Sumter County. Since his trips north netted barrels of used clothing from charitable Yankees, there followed garment sales that enriched Mitchell. For this kind of unscrupulous conduct, Mitchell's unsavory reputation in Panola grew worse; almost everybody in the isolated community had come to know him as a person who "wouldn't deal straight for five minutes."[28]

Indeed, among blacks who had made quick judgments of Mitchell, his standing in Sumter County had never been especially good. From the outset, neighbors saw through him and his schemes. From the beginning, Mitchell and West Alabama Institute were vested in altercations. On one occasion, an armed father came to the school to confront the already unpopular schoolmaster with an angry accusation. The parent claimed there had been a brazen attempt at fondling his daughter. Emphatically denying the charge, Mitchell managed to calm the irate man. Although nothing developed from the accusation, another incident involving a

27. *Springfield Union* (Mass.), n.d., 1911, unidentified clippings, and a flyer, *A Great Mass Meeting*, MP; M to WJE, January 5 and March 31, 1911, BP.
28. Little interview; *Springfield Union*, 1911; M to WJE, n.d., MP.

husband-wife teaching pair from West Alabama and a local white man would prove more serious. After the white man had tried to seduce the female instructor, her spouse challenged the would-be accoster, demanding to know his intentions. Unpleasantries were exchanged, and in an ensuing struggle, the white assailant fired a pistol at the husband, causing superficial wounds.

Shortly after the shooting, on Sunday, October 29, 1911, the main hall burned to the ground. Rumors circulated in Panola that the fire had been set deliberately. Whether it had been Mitchell trying to escape a troubled community, a spiteful white arsonist, or coincidence, no one knew. Given Mitchell's incineration of a barn on his Virginia estate some forty years later to collect on an insurance policy, there are grounds for suspicion.[29]

Only days after the fire, Mitchell announced plans to rebuild. A "Special Appeal"—which went out locally and nationally on November 1, 1911—reported an eight-thousand-dollar loss. According to Mitchell's estimate, rebuilding would cost ten thousand dollars. He hoped to raise money by inducing two thousand "friends" to give five dollars each. In pleas for generous donations, he asked potential patrons to remember how the institution had rendered so much service prior to the disaster. By Mitchell's account, the blaze had interrupted eight teachers' work among more than three hundred children. Instruction was both needed and appreciated so much, noted the principal, that he was pledging himself to the school's future if only the necessary funds could arrive quickly to replace what had been destroyed. Mitchell was depending upon both local and national supporters to contribute to the cause. In appeals, the *Geiger Times* proved especially helpful. Pronouncing Mitchell's work as "productive of too much good to lay smoldering in its ashes," it called on local citizens of both races to stand by him with assistance in his labors. For all who had already contributed, there was an editor's warm praise.[30]

The school was rebuilt, but not at Panola. This time, John H. Pinson, a white speculator-landowner from neighboring Geiger, led a small group of Sumter County entrepreneurs in showering benevolence and active support on Mitchell and West Alabama Institute. Beneath their generosity, however, was a hidden motive: what truly had brought the schoolmaster, Pinson, and others together was another grandiose scheme for subdividing idle plantation acreage into a new agricultural community for poor blacks. As sole owners of all principal businesses, including the *Geiger Times* and the local bank, white speculators imagined themselves title

29. Little interview; *Springfield Union*, 1911; M to WJE, n.d., MP, Mason and Mitchell interviews.
30. Circular, *A Special Appeal*, November 1, 1911, MP; *Geiger Times*, November 3, 1911, and May 30, 1912.

holders to a fiefdom of several thousand acres around the new town of Geiger. Mitchell was a central figure in the planning because, in large part, the operation's success would rest on the drawing power of a school that he had funds to develop. By publicizing a "famous" agricultural academy's educational work and its "professor," the developers hoped to bring potential black land purchasers to Geiger. For participation in the business venture, Mitchell's allotment was more than four hundred acres of land on which to provide "agricultural instruction."[31]

Booker T. Washington eventually learned that Mitchell was passing himself off as a Tuskegee product and was promoting a school of dubious merit as an authorized offshoot of Tuskegee Institute. For several years, the Wizard had suspected these activities. Thus, there had never been full cooperation with Mitchell's appeals for assistance. However, Washington waited until 1912 before sending an investigator on a truth-seeking mission to Sumter County. Washington concluded from the probe that Mitchell's efforts had not been giving children satisfactory education. The revelation infuriated him, because Mitchell had been identifying himself and West Alabama closely with Tuskegee. Mitchell not only had falsely claimed to be a Tuskegee product but also had shown the audacity to connect bogus activities directly to Washington's work. After tolerating all this for several years, Washington finally advised Northern contributors to spurn all appeals from West Alabama Institute. Mitchell was on the last leg of a fund-raising trip through the Northeast when reports of Washington's action reached him from a Boston informant, who urged immediate consultation about the matter in Massachusetts. So advised, Mitchell postponed everything else on his schedule.[32]

In subsequent correspondence with mentor and friend William J. Edwards, Mitchell pledged sooner or later to bring suffering on all parties responsible for defaming him. Credibility and income were at stake. Mitchell pulled out every weapon in his arsenal to gain Washington's public admission of an error in judgment. Moreover, white friends from Geiger were also adamant about the matter because they had more to lose than a black ally. Washington was so threatening to the land scheme that they were ready to support Mitchell if he chose retaliation against him. In a May 21, 1912, letter to Edwards, Mitchell predicted that "Mr. Washington will be the sufferer. . . . I do not wish Mr. Washington any harm while we have it within our power to strike him as he perhaps has

31. *Geiger Times*, August 13, 1914; Geiger's blueprint; Incorporation Records, book 2, 91–92; Deed Records, book 31, 14, SCCR; M to WJE, May 14, 1912, BP; interviews with persons whose identities have been withheld at their request; odd clippings and W. A. Rayfield to M, March 4, 1935, MP.

32. M to WJE, May 14, 1912, BP; Cooper, *Between Struggle and Hope*, 41–43.

not been struck before. . . . I shall not worry about it in the least, for . . . no one can positively hinder or keep us from finally succeeding."[33]

Fearful lest Mitchell might use his influence with whites to hurt Tuskegee, Washington acted. He handled opponents' charges through an intermediary, who was dispatched to west central Alabama for another investigation. To this examiner, Mitchell issued a tough ultimatum for Washington: retreat or suffer consequences. Later, Mitchell reported how his "white friends assured him [the emissary] that it must be done and have written Mr. Washington that he must make a public declaration that the first report was false." To Edwards, Mitchell expressed some regrets about having to deal so harshly with "Mr. Negro," but it was now a question of survival: "the only thing that has kept this matter out of the courts is the desire on my part not to injure any one further than I am forced to in order to take care of my self." What Mitchell did not mention to Edwards was the true reason for ignoring the courts. By a mix of cajolery and bribery, he had coaxed and induced a Tuskegee telegrapher to cooperate in a plot to spy on Washington. From Washington's office files, the coconspirator had gathered third copies of messages. With scores of these in hand, Mitchell had good reason to write confidently on June 7, 1912, that he and white friends "never felt better over the out look of our work." They had recognized a foe's vulnerability to their blackmail.[34]

The stolen messages contained secrets of Washington's life. According to Clara Mitchell, Mitchell's third wife, they revealed that Washington led something of a dual life. In public, the advocate of accommodation was following his own advice with a chaste, temperate existence, but in the messages there emerged a private person known to very few people, who ordered quantities of whiskey and arranged visits to white mistresses. Since no records now exist to substantiate such alleged improprieties, one must wonder whether Washington—a careful man known for discretion—would have risked his entire career and reputation by using a local telegraph office to reach liquor retailers and female companions. Still, the messages must have contained something that had given Mitchell an advantage and a basis for wringing concessions from Washington. As bitter as retreat surely must have been for Washington, he was at a protégé's mercy. The younger man had him, and there was no option but to comply with Mitchell's demands. Although Washington's papers at the Library of Congress do not mention retreat, other evidence supports grudging submission to Mitchell. To prominent Northern philanthropists, Washington was under threat to circulate a much-revised

33. M to WJE, May 21, 1912, BP.
34. Ibid., May 23 and June 7, 1912; Mitchell interview; EJS to M, July 22, 1914, WP.

evaluation of West Alabama. Furthermore, Mitchell exacted a strong character reference avowing that no one had ever matched his Tuskegee performance.[35]

After his reputation was restored, Mitchell never extorted additional concessions from Washington. However, he was fully prepared to do so if the need should arise. Hints that West Alabama Institute's principal was holding onto the cables unsettled Washington; the possibility of Mitchell resurrecting an advantage to press for further concessions haunted the Wizard. In 1914, his apprehension about Mitchell's potential to extract more favors at any time finally led him to push the telegraph company into a full investigation of the whole matter, to ascertain how copies of telegrams had found their way to Mitchell in the first place. Meanwhile, Emmett J. Scott pled for the cables' return. When the request came, Mitchell was in Cambridge, enrolled in Harvard University's noncredit summer proficiency program. Scott knew of Mitchell's whereabouts because Mitchell had written earlier in July, requesting printed information on "Tuskegee as a vocational school." Since the staff secretary had responded promptly and satisfactorily, Mitchell's answer about the stolen telegrams was courteous. However, he corrected Scott; an impression that there were still seventy-five to eighty outstanding telegrams was an exaggeration. Casually but most coyly, Mitchell dismissed the telegram affair as meaningless, and was careful to deny any earlier involvement: "I think you must be mistaken when you say you have secured some telegrams that were formerly in my possession. I am quite sure that the bundle refered to was either destroyed or is still my possession, and I am equally sure that I have seen no others. So you must be mistaken when you say you have secured any that I have seen."[36]

Meanwhile in Alabama, Washington continued to press for a complete probe. He informed District Superintendent W. C. Lloyd of the Postal Telegraph-Cable Company of Mitchell's alleged involvement in the scheme, but there was no mention of blackmail. Omitted in Washington's demand for an investigation was everything except Mitchell's mysterious possession of telegrams. After interviewing every employee at the Tuskegee office, Lloyd responded that his check of Macon County had uncovered nothing about missing files, but that he would continue his

35. Mitchell interview.
36. Ibid.; EJS to M, July 22, 1914; BTW to W. C. Lloyd, July 22 and August 6, 1914, WP; M to EJS, July 13 and 25, 1914, WP; M to WJE, November 13, 1914, BP. In addition to several summers spent at Harvard, M attended Columbia University under similar arrangements. At Columbia, he studied philosophy under T. V. Smith. A lasting relationship unfolded, with Smith viewing Mitchell "as a man of action as well as a mind of thought." Smith to Robert McCormick, January 19, 1941, MP.

investigation because nobody had questioned Mitchell about the cables. From all evidence at hand, however, Lloyd concluded preliminarily "that these telegrams were gotten out of the office in an unscrupulous way through this man Mitchell and we think that he deserves punishment." Finally, after a two-month delay, in a September 16, 1914, letter to the complainant, Lloyd released the accused's version of the affair. Mitchell had commented in his defense "that the report that I have in my possession copies of telegrams sent out by officers of the Tuskegee Institute is not true. As I remember it there did come to us through the mails several months ago a badly [sic] mutilated package of what appeared to be old copies of telegrams. But as it was absolutely worthless in so far as we could see, no effort was made to preserve it. . . . we have not the slightest idea who sent them or why they should have been sent to us." The controversy ended quietly with this explanation. Neither the telegraph company nor Washington wanted any further investigation. Thus for Mitchell, a flat denial of his involvement abruptly ended the curious affair. Yet he knew how he had successfully humbled Washington. In a confidential conversation with Clara Mitchell almost forty years later, after having lived with a secret skeleton in his closet for so long, he detailed the conspiracy and blackmail.[37]

Extortion had saved Mitchell, and the plans for reopening West Alabama Institute at Geiger stayed on schedule. Moreover, his troubles with Booker Washington had not affected raising funds. In fact, before encountering credibility problems with Tuskegee's founder, he had topped his previous collections in the North. He returned to Alabama "with a substantial sum and promises of such others, endowments, etc., that virtually settle[d] the question that two large brick and concrete buildings will soon grace the campus." With no one left to inform Northern well-wishers, there was no way that they could have known that their Dr. Jekyll was Mr. Hyde to blacks back in Alabama. Consequently, groundbreaking ceremonies for a third edition of West Alabama Normal and Industrial Institute were carried out as planned on July 19, 1912. Since it was an event to celebrate, Mitchell arranged a barbecue, a keynote speech by a visiting minister from Watertown, and reduced railroad fares on the Alabama, Tennessee and Northern Railroad for travel from York or Reform to Pinson's Crossing in Geiger. In the feature address, the Reverend William T. Holmes stressed Mitchell's value to the community as a teacher and praised the reciprocal generosity of Pinson for having endeavored to "do something for the colored people" after the blacks "had had so great

37. BTW-Lloyd exchange, July 22, 24, and 27, August 3, 6, 25, and 27, and September 16, 1914, and one undated letter, WP; Mitchell interview.

a part in making him prosperous." Contradictions in the assessment were clearly missed by Holmes.[38]

On land donated for education by the Pinson and Geiger Land Corporation, a large building rising north of Geiger became a modern, two-story structure that housed classrooms, an auditorium, and living quarters. Situated near the school were comfortable accommodations for the Mitchell family. Cleared fields awaiting eventual cultivation in cane, alfalfa, peanuts, corn, potatoes, and cotton were surrounding the neat compound. Soon some two hundred male and female student workers, ages seven to sixteen, would earn lessons in basic subjects. Supervising everything was "Professor" Mitchell, less known already in Geiger for his obvious talents as an organizer than for his dapperness and aloofness. Once more, warm friendships eluded him; soon after his settlement, he placed himself so far above his African American neighbors that equal relationships were impossible. Furthermore, his tendencies toward conspicuous consumption were not sitting well among villagers. His son Wergs had a Shetland pony, and he himself used an elegant black buggy pulled by a fine team for errands. In the past, blacks who had dared to flash such finery before poor whites had endangered themselves, but Mitchell seemingly enjoyed such defiance. In Panola, his pomposity and bombastic style had offended blacks without risks or serious consequences. Now, however, among whites, his tastes for well-bred horses, fine carriages, and tailored clothing were giving him a reputation as "an uppity nigger." This was an age of lynchings in the rural South, and nothing was more detrimental to a black man's prospects for a long life than an air of superiority. From a nearby plantation, the white overseer confessed to hating Mitchell because he had become "too big for his britches." When warned of the jealous man's comment that "Mitchell's meat was worth forty cents a pound," the teacher replied, "I suspect I am worth more than that!"[39]

Mitchell enjoyed much success at Geiger until word spread of his haughtiness. From several summers spent at Harvard and Columbia Universities, he gained so much culturally and educationally that the improvements manifested themselves in his publicity releases about West Alabama Institute. Prospective donors received professional-looking circulars. A fine sample of his newly acquired skills was a mailer that appeared late in 1912; it created strong impressions of West Alabama Institute's effect on racism. With a combination of textual claims and

38. *Geiger Times,* May 30 and July 11 and 25, 1912; *Montclair Times,* August 10, 1912; *Waterbury American,* March 25 and August 15, 1912; *Boston Transcript,* December 11, 1912; odd unidentified clippings; Rayfield to M, March 4, 1935, MP. W. A. Rayfield was Mitchell's Tuskegee classmate and the buildings' architect.

39. Gilbert, Little, and Pinson interviews; odd unidentified clippings in MP.

sobering statistical data for the Black Belt, the Mitchell-produced tract believably attributed many miraculous attitudinal changes in Geiger to West Alabama's influence. Readers were told that a lynching had occurred in 1908 on the site where the institute now stood, and that greater respect for Geiger's blacks after West Alabama's opening had made a repetition unlikely:

> The feeling of opposition that existed generally among the white settlers was of such nature as to render it unsafe for an educated Negro to spend even one night in this section. . . . opposition was born in the early days of freedom; at which time many Negroes sought education with the mistaken idea that it would liberat [sic] them from all forms of manual work and make of them powerful political factors. . . . Much of my time was devoted to the work of bringing about a better understanding between the white people and the educated Negro. Soon they were able to see thru the example that I tried to set that education along the right lines would not "ruin" the Negro. Even the white men that constituted a mob and lynched a Negro . . . are now making small contributions to . . . the school.[40]

If the example and work of West Alabama had favorably changed any white's attitudes, blacks were unimpressed. They had noticed no improvements in race relations. Oppressed and at the bottom of society's pecking order, they still feared white people. At most, Mitchell's efforts had succeeded at stabilizing political order and social interactions. He distorted the truth, telling fellow blacks about alleged white concerns with minority interests. His statements did not bring justice; instead, they encouraged passivity, subordination, and even more discrimination. On other fronts, there were accomplishments. By early 1913, Mitchell's work had become well enough known in philanthropy circles that West Alabama was attracting famous trustees. Mitchell had impressed Oswald Garrison Villard, editor of the *Nation*, so much that the journalist hosted fellow trustees at his New York office. A 1913 student harvest of six cotton bales and one thousand bushels of corn was impressive, too.[41]

Together, West Alabama Institute and Geiger experienced prosperity and growth until 1914, when a ban on foreign loans after the outbreak of World War I precipitated difficulties. Situated near the heart of Alabama's Black Belt, Geiger was bound to King Cotton. After cotton's abrupt collapse on export markets, its price fell sharply. In succession,

---

40. Handbill, *White Mob Lynched Negro on Suspicion; Afterwards Converted to Cause of Negro Education*, MP.

41. Mason, Little, and Goldston interviews; M to WJE, February 3 and October 8, 1913, BP.

John Pinson's land values and profits plummeted. Soon Mitchell's school's importance to land schemes vanished. Months prior to this, there had been gloom about West Alabama Institute's future prospects in Geiger. Mitchell, knowing the sham of operating a bogus academy could not last forever and aware of a school in need of an administrator in adjacent Choctaw County, prepared himself for a possible move there with regular appearances at rallies. As he was readying himself for an uncertain future, he made a fortuitous reacquaintance with land speculator–county solicitor John McDuffie, a contact from their years together in Greensboro. Renewing his relationship with the white leader was very important to Mitchell, because McDuffie would later foster Mitchell's move to Choctaw County.[42]

A combination of local resentment, low commodity prices, and opportunities elsewhere had been tempting Mitchell to leave Geiger, but his departure did not come until early in 1915. At dawn on January 13, fire raced through West Alabama's main building, totally destroying it. Nobody died, but only a piano and some clothing were salvaged. As supervisor of rescue efforts, Mitchell almost perished after being seemingly trapped on the second floor by flames racing up a lone stairway. He managed an escape by leaping from a window. The long fall jarred the teacher, but he sustained only assorted aches and bruises. While these discomforted him, he somehow arranged board with neighbors for all the dislodged pupils and staff. He also filed an insurance claim to collect two thousand dollars from a policy on the gutted building. Conflict over receipt of the sum ultimately sealed his fate in Geiger, prompting his quicker-than-expected move to Choctaw County. Controversy had raged over whether he or West Alabama Institute deserved the payoff. Since he had paid the premiums and had run the academy, Mitchell presumed it all belonged to him. His Geiger partners disagreed. By their reckoning, Mitchell had no entitlement; from its beginning, the school had always been a community asset. Hence, a payout must go either toward rebuilding West Alabama Institute in Geiger, or else it must revert to the Pinson and Geiger Land Corporation. Facing two unacceptable alternatives, Mitchell brazenly fled with the money to West Butler in Choctaw County.[43]

Awaiting him there in 1915 was a new opportunity to "educate" children, but unlike in Greensboro, Panola, and Geiger, he found a functioning school already in operation in Choctaw County. Compared to his past

42. M to WJE, November 13, 1914; *Choctaw Advocate,* July 8, 1914; handbill, *Educational Mass Meeting!* MP; Thomas J. Toolen to Frank Kloeb, February 2, 1933; folder, "The Plain Truth," 326; M to JMc, January 4, 1936, McDP.

43. *Geiger Times,* January 14, 1915; Gilbert interview; CCCR, Deeds, book 13, 635, book 18, 46, book 19, 58, 369–70.

experiences, assuming control of an existing area technical school was a simpler task. Instruction at Armstrong Agricultural Institute had begun in 1914. Among its proprietors, enthusiasm had prevailed for exploiting three hundred acres of virgin timberland; that the land surrounded a schoolyard was not coincidental. Mitchell's new position at Armstrong represented another of his well-laid contingency plans. A mixture of timber resources and supportive whites positioned the opportunistic Mitchell to exercise his twice-tested formula of exchanging token education for compulsory labor.[44]

Soon after Mitchell's arrival, Armstrong Agricultural Institute came under public scrutiny. As part of an overall survey of black education, the Alabama State Bureau of Education sent delegations to every county. An inspection team reached Armstrong in November 1915. After a complete study, it recommended county control of the private school and public administration of its finances. Its suggestions came without explanation, but the State Bureau of Education consistently opposed proprietor-operated schools; all too frequently, they were personal fiefdoms. Neither Mitchell nor the county responded.[45]

On the bright side, Armstrong, like Mitchell's previous schools, offered basic education to children who otherwise might not have received any formal instruction. Their learning experiences were not forgotten. Some sixty years after Mitchell had left Armstrong, his former pupils found for interviews recalled their studies more easily than the negative aspects of the institution. When asked to remember her experiences at Armstrong, Zola May told of receiving lessons in arithmetic, weaving straw mats and baskets, sewing, and cooking—as well as a recollection of a trip to the principal's office for a Mitchell-administered paddling. Participating in Saturday afternoon baseball games on a West Butler schoolyard diamond was the fixture in Golden W. Chaney's memory of Armstrong. When asked about Wergs and Annie Mitchell, the interviewees reminisced fondly about the boy. With nothing negative to recall about the school or its controversial but enterprising principal, Chaney and May appeared in full agreement with a father of four children educated at Armstrong, who offered his congratulations to Mitchell after his former neighbor's nomination for Congress in 1934. In the same letter, the parent expressed gratitude for the schooling Mitchell had provided many years earlier in Alabama.[46]

44. Harrison and Mitchell interviews; *Choctaw Advocate,* January–May 1915.

45. ABE, *Negro Education,* Bulletin 39: 101. Recommendations are found throughout the bulletin; see also Bulletin 38.

46. William R. Turner Sr. to M, August 29, 1934; Earl J. Hopkins to M, February 1936, MP; Chaney, May, and Collins-Levy interviews.

Although Mitchell did not change his demeanor in West Butler, there was one thing different about him in Choctaw County: he was out in the community more, appearing as a guest speaker at traditional black gatherings. Emancipation days were occasions for oratory in western Alabama, and Mitchell enjoyed these. On January 1, 1916, Arthur and Annie Mitchell were active participants in a local ceremony celebrating deliverance from slavery. During a short program, Annie read Lincoln's Gettysburg Address, and her husband gave forecasts for a new year before inspiring listeners with "Fifty-Three Years of Negro Freedom in America." Two months later, Mitchell joined black farmers in eulogizing Booker Washington, who had died in November 1915, with a final homage. Mitchell assumed responsibilities for staging a public memorial service that featured Scripture readings, prayers, hymns, silent vespers, and thoughts on dealing with the boll weevil.[47]

Of course, increased participation in community affairs also gave Mitchell new opportunities to woo white support. He managed this as always by telling blacks exactly what the other race wanted them to hear and believe. Since this was an era of mass migrations of blacks from the rural South to urban centers, there were opportunities to capitalize from the negative effects of the exodus on the region. By exploiting these, Mitchell endeared himself to whites by refuting claims of Northern labor agents and departees that there were better advantages for blacks elsewhere and by appealing to blacks to stay in the South. He purposely ridiculed "loafer[s]—the element that is so frequently seen hanging around barber shops and pool rooms. They are worthless. . . . There is no doubt about the race being done a serious injury by having that class of Negroes carried to the north and stationed among white people who are not only unfamiliar with the negro, but whose patience with him is very short." When Mitchell needed backhanded introductions to slip points by ruling whites, it was his common practice to resort to debasing soliloquies like this one. As his preface to indicating that failed race relations had accounted largely for the rural South's inability to hold onto its African American residents, he first besmirched migrants before urging "more vigorous action to put a stop to lynching and to see to it that negroes receive justice in the courts." Mitchell was a master of circumspection. First, he adroitly irritated the blacks in attendance to the delight of whites; after the ruse had minimized risks of repercussions, he gave advice to the ruling majority.[48]

47. *Choctaw Advocate*, June 16 and November 3, 1915, March 15, April 26, and May 17, 1916; handbill, *The Fifty-third Emancipation Celebration of the Negroes of Choctaw County and Great Educational Symposium*, MP.
48. *Birmingham Ledger*, September 7, 1916. Overall, condemning idleness and urging respect for law and order won Mitchell praise among Black Belt whites. Crime

Besides his apparent empathy for rulers' explanations and rational-izations, Mitchell relied upon patriotism. Sensing the popularity of the April 6, 1917, declaration of war by Congress, he closely associated himself with preparedness drives. Soon after the United States had gone to war, he temporarily closed Armstrong, dismissing students and imploring them to "return to the farm and engage in agriculture with a view of helping pro-duce food stuffs for the army." Then many weeks later, at the school's 1917 commencement, he gave a strong demonstration of symbolic commitment to the nation. Speaking from a stage fully decorated with American flags and red, white, and blue bunting, Mitchell used the occasion to address both blacks and whites. He appealed to blacks to contribute generously to the Red Cross, and he assured area whites of his race's intentions during the Great War: "Whatever else can be charged against the American Negro, it is to his credit that he has never been a traitor. . . . There are no Benedict Arnolds among the Negroes. The genial nature of the Negro makes him quick to forget injustice in the presence of trouble. . . . Inform us, equip us and give us orders . . . we are . . . ready . . . to help. . . . This is the only country the Negro knows; the American flag is the only flag he loves."[49] Although Mitchell did not volunteer for military service and was not drafted, he urged other young men to enlist. He was often at the depot, sending off trainloads of inductees. When, for example, seventy-three young blacks arrived from eastern Mississippi and western Alabama to leave for Iowa's Camp Dodge, he stood at attention on the platform, admonishing "them to cherish and love the flag of the United States" and urging "upon them the importance of obedience and of doing their duty."[50]

Mitchell remained in Choctaw County until late 1919. A portent of the reasons behind his eventual departure occurred in 1916, when someone stole Werg's sorrel pony. To enemies in the community, the animal symbol-ized what they disliked about their dapper neighbor. Because of Mitchell's ostentatiousness, lower-class whites and poor blacks had ironically found a common enemy in him. Mitchell finally overstretched his luck and their welcome; he purchased an expensive Packard touring automobile. The car caused a sensation as the first black-owned motor vehicle in Choctaw County and stimulated hostile reactions from both races. To blacks, the Packard was a tangible reminder of what an unprincipled man had netted by exploiting them. Poor whites also despised Mitchell's

concerned them because a disproportionate share of Alabama convicts came from cotton counties. Glenn S. Sisk, "Crime and Justice in the Alabama Black Belt, 1875–1917."

49. *Choctaw Advocate,* May 2 and 30, 1917, and June 12, 1918.

50. Odd clipping and *Army Registration Certificate,* September 12, 1918, MP.

success. According to what Clara M. Mitchell learned several decades later, the luxury car caused her husband so many problems that he began to fear serious trouble.[51]

The stage was set for a repetition of the Greensboro-Panola-Geiger routine of fleecing and fleeing. Fearful most for his wife and son, Mitchell packed them and steamer trunks full of family possessions into the Packard for an escape to Washington. After safely settling his family in the capital, he returned to West Butler in a risky venture, apparently to convert as many school assets into cash as possible. This time, however, Mitchell's attempt to liquidate school assets and run did not succeed; Armstrong's trustees intervened to save and protect the school's assets. In quick succession, they discharged Mitchell as principal, installed a successor, and retained an attorney to begin legal proceedings to obtain a judicial opinion of Mitchell's dealings. Precautions had followed their discovery of several mysterious land titles. According to these, Mitchell and not Armstrong held deeds to hundreds of acres around the school. Shaken by the revelation and the ensuing income losses, Armstrong barely survived. As for Mitchell, reports had him leaving West Butler with ten thousand dollars.[52]

The controversy surrounding Mitchell's dishonest management of Armstrong did not end with his escape from West Butler; instead, the dispute continued for more than a year after his departure. To recover lost property and obtain a desist order, Armstrong's trustees filed a lawsuit in Choctaw County Circuit Court; it charged Mitchell with continuing to raise money for personal benefit after all his ties with Armstrong had been severed. The litigation also sought to invalidate every Mitchell land deal on the grounds that "a prominent, well educated, shrewd, intelligent and influential member of the negro race" had taken advantage of the purported grantors, "mostly all ignorant, common every day, country darkies, living as farmers in the rural section of the state." The litigants also tried to recover all monetary subscriptions donated to the school but allegedly diverted into Mitchell's "own private ends." On May 9, 1921, after studying the case against Mitchell, Judge Ben D. Turner of Alabama's First Judicial Circuit announced the court's ruling in Mitchell's favor and dismissed all evidence as circumstantial. Therefore, official records do not show wrongdoing by Mitchell.[53]

51. Mitchell and Harrison interviews; *Choctaw Advocate*, September 27 and October 4, 11, 18, and 25, 1916.
52. Mitchell interview; *Choctaw Advocate*, September 24, November 12, and December 10, 1919.
53. CCCR, *The Armstrong Agricultural and Industrial Institute vs. Arthur W. Mitchell*, 1920–21.

In the final analysis, Mitchell enjoyed a charmed existence in Alabama, often taking advantage of opportunities to manipulate great men such as Booker T. Washington, white men such as John A. Rogers, and many hundreds of humble, anonymous people. Whenever he was seemingly cornered, he somehow escaped. His belligerence, flaunting style, and callous disregard for others won him few black friends. Furthermore, he disregarded an important unwritten rule while operating schools in Greensboro, Panola, Geiger, and West Butler. In rural communities like these, where people tended to know and trust one another and gave unquestioned acceptance to personal promises, there was little kinship for a newcomer who consistently broke commitments just because verbal noncontractual commitments were not legally binding. At least twice, Mitchell's actions landed him in court, but without evidence of wrongdoing, plaintiffs had no legal grounds for lawsuits.[54]

For Mitchell, the lure of Northern money combined with prevailing illiteracy among blacks had produced an interesting dilemma. Well-educated, well-intentioned philanthropists from the North provided opportunities both for good men and for charlatans to raise significant sums of money through promises to elevate the race's standing. Some, such as Tuskegee's Booker T. Washington and Lawrence C. Jones of Mississippi's Piney Woods Country Life School, used their talents and resources to improve the plights of rural blacks; others, such as Arthur W. Mitchell, gained personally from rich benefactors' gifts. Short of personal, on-site inspections, grantors had no way of distinguishing honorable men from hucksters. Only their instincts and references guided charitable women's and men's decisions about whom to trust. For affluent believers in Mitchell, no monuments to their generosity remain. Heavy growths of scrub, thorns, and trees blanket four former school sites, and passenger trains do not stop at Pinson's Crossing or West Butler. Yet as bad as Mitchell's schools apparently were, some pupils benefited from his educational institutions. For having experienced Mitchell, many students considered themselves fortunate, because they had progressed from his academies to careers in the professions.[55]

54. CCCR, *W. C. Horn v. Armstrong Agricultural Institute and A.W. Mitchell*, fall term, 1917.

55. Author's personal survey of four sites and Tuskegee; Booker T. Ridgeway to M, December 10, 1934; M to Richard Harris, November 23, 1934, MP; Barnett Memorandum on M, n.d., BP. The latter entry refutes several Mitchell claims about himself and substantiates the overall drift of this chapter.

Washington and Chicago

2

1919–1934

T he Washington that Mitchell entered in 1919 was a divided city emerging from a turbulent decade. The Treaty of Versailles, class conflicts, and the possible unionization of District of Columbia police had split the populace, and there had been tensions caused by omnipresent racism. Always a Southern city because of its location and population, Washington had become a barometer for black-white issues. The city's blacks had seen nightmares become stark reality as the Grand Old Party gradually lost interest in civil rights and as they endured Woodrow Wilson's presidency. Coinciding with losses of basic rights had been a sharp rise in the District's black population. Lacking defense plants and heavy industry, Washington had not gained as many blacks as Chicago or Detroit, but the 1920 census still showed a 16.4 percent rise. Settling 15,520 new arrivals into schools, houses, and jobs had not been easy, and returning servicemen had made these tasks even more difficult. Racial unrest had begun to mount because whites had blamed blacks for job and housing shortages. These circumstances had combined to produce an ugly atmosphere lethally charged with explosive hatred. Finally, on July 19, 1919, a series of isolated incidents and mass hysteria had generated ten days of rioting and interracial hostilities.[1]

1. William H. Jones, *The Housing of Negroes in Washington, D.C.: A Study in Human Ecology*, 30–32; Dewey H. Palmer, "Moving North: Negro Migration during World War I," 52–62; Constance M. Green, *The Secret City: A History of Race Relations in the Nation's Capital*, 184–200; Green, *Washington: Capital City, 1879–1950*, 207–29, 264–66, 270; Federal Writers' Project, WPA, *Washington: City and Capital*, 80–82, 89; *Washington Bee*, January-December 1919; August Meier and Elliott M. Rudwick, "The Rise of Segregation in the Federal Bureaucracy, 1900–1930," 178–84; Arthur S. Link, *Wilson: The New Freedom*, 245–54; Nancy J. Weiss, "The Negro and the New Freedom: Fighting Wilsonian Segregation," 61–79. Details of the receptions greeting Negro veterans are

Mitchell's first official interaction with this seething city came in September 1919. Earlier travel to the Northeast had taken him often through Washington, but he had never stopped. Now Mitchell was to testify before the House Committee on Interstate and Foreign Commerce, which was holding hearings on proposals to return all railroad carriers to private ownership. Why, and by whom, he had been invited to give testimony is unknown. With boldness, nevertheless, he pointed out how humiliating it was for self-respecting blacks to ride aboard separate coaches. For Southern blacks, he observed, only lynching surpassed the wrongfulness of the "Jim Crow car." What blacks wanted, he urged, was equality: "The Negro should have every railroad accommodation for the same money that is granted other races. He does not ask this as a matter of charity, but demands this as a right. The only way to have equal accommodations is to have the same accommodations for all. There can be no equality of accommodations with separation of passengers."[2]

Whether Mitchell's appearance before the House committee contributed in any way to his family's immediate departure for a new life in Washington is also unknown. On record, Mitchell never discussed why the District of Columbia had been his choice as the most suitable place for his purposes, plans, and family. He certainly was more familiar with New England and New York. Furthermore, his wife's family ties were in Connecticut. Although Mitchell left nothing behind to explain his move to the capital, a few conjectures make sense. One lies in his relationships with prominent Alabama whites such as John McDuffie, a planter, liberal Southern politician, and befriender of blacks. Could it simply have been that McDuffie and others with his outlook wanted a carefully placed observer in Washington? McDuffie's presence on Capitol Hill makes this conjecture feasible. Alabama's First District had elected McDuffie to Congress in 1918, and he had taken his seat on March 4, 1919. Since he had known Mitchell for more than fifteen years, had aided him in the past, and would help him again in the future, a relationship between the two men more than likely existed in 1919. Supporting the hypothesis are questions regarding how both Annie and Arthur Mitchell could have gained immediate government employment without insider assistance. Mitchell's receipt of a minor job at the Bureau of Internal Revenue at a time when many better-educated African Americans in the city were suffering from unemployment widens the mystery.

given in Arthur E. Barbeau and Florette Henri, *The Unknown Soldiers: Black American Troops in World War I*, 164–89.

2. DNCC, press release, November 8, 1934, MP; U.S. Congress, House Committee on Interstate and Foreign Commerce, 66th Cong., 1st sess., *Return of the Railroads to Private Ownership, Hearings*, 2026–29.

Circumstantial evidence adds to the likelihood that white intermediaries were behind Mitchell's foothold in Washington. The possibility that Mitchell was planted among radicals might explain his strange gravitation toward left-leaning blacks shortly after his arrival in the District of Columbia. Otherwise, there are few reasons for some out-of-character actions. There was something peculiar about Mitchell joining A. Philip Randolph, Chandler Owen, and other radicals to establish The Friends of Negro Freedom soon after his move north. Equally strange was Mitchell's odd behavior and introduction of Randolph at a Buena Vista, Maryland, rally of socialists on July 5, 1920. In the capacity of toastmaster, Mitchell, "in an earnest and eloquent appeal, made such a strong plea [for leftist causes] . . . that the dollar bills began immediately to come from the people." Oddly, two years earlier he had drummed up support for the American Red Cross and American Expeditionary Force. Mitchell's posture at Buena Vista was not at all in line with any of his previous or future stances.[3]

Speculation aside, Mitchell, unlike most migrants moving north from the Deep South, brought certain assets with him. He came to Washington with sophistication acquired from years of observing Booker Washington's methods at Tuskegee, profitably operating his own schools, touring the North, and studying with the likes of Columbia's T. V. Smith. One fact stood out about Mitchell: he knew how to handle himself. Long before he departed for Washington, D.C., he had mastered a cardinal principle of his life: "look after yourself because no one else will." When he began a new life in Washington, working capital was his major advantage. His savings estimated at ten thousand dollars and his prominent white and black contacts probably shielded him from many of the difficulties most black migrants from Alabama faced.[4]

Money alone, however, could not guarantee Mitchell a place in Washington's black community. Two other considerations—roots and physical appearance—also determined status in the District's pecking order. Perhaps his light complexion was the more important factor. Although he was never light enough to "pass," Mitchell's coloring and facial characteristics gave him more status than darker blacks with more pronounced Negroid features. Of course, he did not possess Washington roots. Those Washington blacks from established families of three or more generations' duration in the capital held societal status and access to the social whirl of the black aristocracy, points pressed on an envious newcomer. For "top 100" Negroes in literature, music, and society, there was the special honor of Mu-So-Lit Club eligibility. For a social striver such as Arthur Mitchell,

3. Handbill, *The New Independence,* July 5, 1920, MP; *Washington Bee,* July 17, 1920; Chandler Owen to John Fitzpatrick, April 7, 1922, FP.
4. Mitchell interview.

all this had meaning. Although summers at Harvard and Columbia might have sharpened his diction, society people always seemed to judge him as an outsider more interested in material possessions than in ideas or art. Since Mitchell would seek acceptance throughout his adult life, this caused him pain because acceptance always seemed to elude him. Out of bitterness, he belittled the feats of those above him in status and cowed those below him. No matter the lionization of self-made men in American folklore, few persons of Mitchell's humble birth have ever attained the fullest blessings or acceptance by society's inner circles.[5]

For Mitchell, the ten-year period from 1919 to 1928 proved pivotal. The twenties were profitable for him because of investments in the District rental market. Few blacks had developed properties when he began his career in real estate. Almost at once after forming the Mutual Housing Company in 1920, he prospered. Its incorporation obviously resulted from his insight into the District's acute housing problem. Public sales of stock enabled Mitchell and the Mutual Housing Company to accumulate enough money to purchase the Luray Apartment. A fine, sturdy four-floor structure located southeast of the Capitol building, it formally opened on November 23, 1920, with gala festivities. Speeches, dance music, and refreshments marked the grand opening. In giving the general public an opportunity to inspect the building, Mitchell and other Mutual Housing officers used the occasion to announce immediate goals and plans for a second stock offering, this to acquire more real estate. As blockbusting pioneers, these stockholders intended to "acquire apartment houses and blocks of residential property now occupied by whites and rent the same to colored people." Within a short period, additional public stock sales enabled the Mutual Housing Company to purchase two more multiple-dwelling complexes.[6]

Critics like Howard University professor William H. Jones foresaw negative effects such as increased crime and prostitution stemming from housing blacks in apartments like the ones rented out by Mutual Housing. But faultfinders neither affected nor deterred Mitchell, and their conclusions had no impact upon zoning laws in the District. As the founder of the Mutual Housing Company, he intended to hold on to a good investment for as long as it yielded satisfactory returns. Profits from leases and the inflationary growth of the properties' equity values increased his wealth. Through nonchartered lending agencies and banks, there was also considerable

    5. Ibid.; Green, *The Secret City*, 207–10; *Washington Bee*, March 1, 1919; M. C. Clifford to M, February 2, 1935, MP.
    6. Jones, *The Housing of Negroes*, 31–32, 70, 107; *Washington Bee*, November 27, 1920, and October 1, 1919; *Washington Tribune*, January 19, 1924; Mitchell interview; Mutual Housing Company, Financial Statements, MP.

borrowing against these properties to fund another enterprise, Mitchell's "loan sharking." According to Clara Mitchell, her husband never had qualms about cheating fellow stockholders. At least one victim, she said, took Mitchell to court, charging him with stock swindling. Then as in all previous (and subsequent) cases involving fraudulent practices, Mitchell freed himself of all accusations by convincing a naive judge. As the widow recalled her husband's description of the trial, he established his innocence in magistrate court with a legitimate-looking document produced from his coat pocket. After the bench granted Mitchell permission to read its contents, he began reading. He was so convincing that the unsuspecting judge dismissed the pending suit without ever inspecting the document. The widow remembered how her spouse had bragged that it had been a deed, but it had not borne on the case at hand.[7]

While managing three apartment houses and arranging street loans, Mitchell was on a continuous search for further income sources. In 1921, the *Washington Bee* announced his partnership with William H. C. Brown. The partners had formed Brown and Mitchell Employment Agency, a firm promising to "fill the position you wish. Reasonable prices." Failures at matching employees to employers, however, soon led to dissolution; Brown left to become president of the newly chartered Industrial Savings Bank, and Mitchell began studying law.[8] Preparation for the new career represented the fulfillment of the interest he had first expressed upon returning home with his father from the Chamber County courthouse; for many years, he had had neither the means nor the time to satisfy his childhood aspiration.

Like most black attorneys in practice before 1935, Mitchell never attended law school. His preparation combined home study and apprenticeships. By correspondence, Chicago's Blackstone School of Law offered him a comprehensive law course, which he supplemented with some intensive private study in the Washington law offices of several black attorneys, including Edgar Brown, Perry Howard, and Benjamin L. Gaskins. By 1927, he had absorbed enough law to gain admission to the bar of the District of Columbia, and later to the bar of Illinois.[9]

7. *Washington Bee,* October 1, 1919; Jones, *The Housing of Negroes,* 135, 140; Mitchell interview; George I. Borger to M, May 12 and June 20, 1932; W. C. A. Brown to M, June 11, 15, and 18, and July 18 and 22, 1932; M to Brown, June 13, 16, and 22, and July 20, 1932; M to James F. Shea, Inc., June 16 and 25, 1932; E. Roy Hill to M, June 23, 1932; Frank Stetson to M, July 1, 1933; M to Second National Bank, July 1, 1933; M to Jesse W. Lewis, July 11, 1933, MP.

8. *Washington Bee,* June 11, 1921.

9. Mitchell interview; Carter G. Woodson, *The Negro Professional Man and the Community, with Special Emphasis on the Physician and the Lawyer,* 187–89; G. W. Harms to author, January 20, 1975; District of Columbia Bar certificate, MP.

Mitchell soon discovered, however, what other black attorneys had found: a license did not guarantee success. Like others, he suffered from common misconceptions about a likely future practice. Without any direction and guidance, self-instruction in the law tended to create some false impressions in hopeful individuals. Mitchell, like many others in his situation, had thought a bare knowledge of some basic concepts would lead to a profitable career, but when he began his practice, black counselors typically were working exclusively with domestic grievances, petty criminal offenses, inheritances, and wills. Seldom were familiarity with profound legal matters or new interpretations of law needed. Mitchell's law practice followed the pattern. White bar associations denied him membership, and neighbors showed little confidence in his abilities. Behind his back, they were labeling him a "ham lawyer" or an "ambulance chaser" who was "working for 'Street and Walker,' pressing bricks." In other words, Mitchell was spending his time walking up and down streets, searching for clients. His caseload varied, but clients usually sought legal advice and assistance on such routine matters as theft, divorces, and insurance. Complex cases involving corporations, government, and individuals were not on his agenda; these remained solely in the hands of white lawyers. On the other hand, Mitchell was not after complex litigation. Testing a law or practice's constitutionality had been neither his intention nor his primary reason for becoming an attorney. Accepting many cases, with each one yielding a small fee, was his modus operandi.[10]

Only rarely, and then only after leaving Washington for Chicago, did Mitchell attempt to handle civil rights litigation. After 1928 and his work on Herbert Hoover's election campaign, he showed a fleeting interest. His first experience with a civil rights case apparently came in late 1931, or some three years after he moved to Illinois from the District of Columbia. The Negro Employees Improvement Association of Chicago retained his counsel to overturn a court-ordered injunction against its picketing a Southside chain of restaurants accused of unfair hiring. Mitchell argued for withdrawal of the restraint, but the superior court would not reverse the ban. After this defeat, Mitchell became involved in at least one other civil rights case before 1935. In an effort to secure a favorable settlement for a New York couple that had been "manhandled" in Aurora, Illinois, by a restaurateur and local police, he filed a twenty-five-thousand-dollar

10. Cephases, Mitchell, Cyrus, and Dickerson interviews; Woodson, *The Negro Professional Man*, 189–90, 194, 221–26, 228–29, 240–41; William H. Hale, "The Negro Lawyer and His Client," 59; August Meier and Elliott Rudwick, "Attorneys Black and White: A Case Study of Race Relations within the NAACP," 915–18; divorce transcript, *Clark v. Clark*, April 3, 1930; M to the Rev. Mr. Powell, February 6, 1932; M to James H. Poage, August 8, 1932, MP.

damage suit in 1933. According to Attorney Mitchell's brief, the alleged female victim's use of a cafe's rest room had set off a chain reaction of abuse. First, the proprietor had begun pointing to a backdoor, demanding that the woman exit there. Her refusal to do this had so infuriated the owner that he had her bodily removed from the restaurant. After these indignities, the New Yorkers filed a complaint with the Aurora Police Department. Thereupon, "instead of being helped . . . [they were] berated . . . and ordered . . . to leave town" because "This is a white man's business and white man's town. These people [the cafe owner] can do what they want to and nothing will be done about it. Now you two get out of this town and stay out. You are smart 'Niggers,' but if you don't get out of here quickly you'll be done away with and no one will ever know what happened to you." Although the case never went to trial, Mitchell could still claim one triumph. The lawsuit called attention to missing police records of the entire episode; the offending law officers' slovenliness led to reprimands and to a demotion of the captain on duty during the incident.[11]

Except for a brief period shortly after he moved to Illinois, Mitchell did not affiliate or work closely with the NAACP. Furthermore, he avoided other groups whose courses of action revolved around change through legal challenge, protest, or arrest; he did not foresee any promise for personal gain from such associations. Besides, he disagreed with activism. Having received early indoctrination in Booker T. Washington's gradualist philosophy, Mitchell retained a conservative's reservations about sudden reversals and radical departures.[12]

The biggest boost to Mitchell's political career from his Washington years came from his membership in Phi Beta Sigma, which was, according to Professor August Meier, "the least highly regarded social fraternity of black professional men." In 1925 after its annual December meeting of delegates, Mitchell's affiliation assumed altogether new importance; until he resigned nearly nine years later, he was the fraternity's national president. Consecutive service for so many years in the elected leadership position gave him many opportunities to establish strong fraternal relationships with a national membership that included prominent African Americans. Thus Mitchell was able to establish contacts that would eventually bring him into national politics.[13] Of his fraternal ties, those with Albion L.

11. *Chicago Whip*, October 10, 1931; *Defender*, October 14, 1933; Clarence J. Ruddy to M, February 12, 1935, MP.

12. Mitchell interview; for a longer discussion, see chapter 7.

13. *Defender*, January 7 and December 29, 1928, November 7, 1931, November 18 and December 30, 1933; M to Annie, December 26, 1927; John W. Johnson Jr. to M, February 3, 1933; Lewis to M, January 24, 1936; M to C. L. Roberts, July 29, 1935; *Crescent*,

Holsey and Robert Russa Moton proved the most significant. From key positions within the "Tuskegee Machine"—Moton was Booker Washington's successor and Holsey was *Tuskegee Messenger* editor, presidential administrative aide, and National Negro Business League secretary—the two men commanded power and prestige, realities that would not elude Mitchell's tapping. Holsey was an active Sigma, whereas Moton chose nonparticipation in brotherhood national conventions. Through Mitchell's efforts, Moton obtained regular reports and information about the annual proceedings. In the process, Mitchell and Moton developed close ties.[14]

Through influential Sigmas and other contacts, Mitchell started to move quickly and effortlessly from political obscurity to GOP notoriety. For men of his standing, gaining something from the Republicans was commonplace; there was a pattern of black attorneys committing themselves to the GOP's black political activities. For example, District of Columbia acquaintance Perry W. Howard had been politically active for many years before Mitchell became involved in 1928. What set Mitchell apart from his professional contemporaries was the level of his first political assignment. The GOP's Colored Division sent him to Chicago to seek black support for Herbert Hoover's presidential bid, a task not taken at all lightly by party bosses. There had been slippages in the party's conventional lock on African American voters, and since Hoover's campaign staff deemed retention of a large majority in Chicago pivotal to Hoover's chances of success in Illinois, Mitchell's work assumed importance. Altogether, the Republican party employed him for three months in Chicago, paying him almost one thousand dollars in salary and reimbursing all per diems and travel expenses for the period. Mitchell, a new face on the speakers' circuit and a relative stranger to the Midwest, canvassed the so-called Bronzeville district, the area of the South Side with the highest concentration of the Windy City's black minority. Here among African Americans, his assignment was to win precincts for Hoover by the largest possible margins to give the Republican nominee a leg up on a victory in Illinois. Although the exact details of Mitchell's arrangement with GOP bosses are sketchy, Moton must have been involved somehow with Mitchell's appointment.

Spring 1949, (and letters in) MP; Lawrence interview. There were occasions when Mitchell received more tangible rewards from his brothers. At one annual gathering, for example, the rewards for his "devotion and fidelity" were two hundred dollars and a silver loving cup.

14. Albion L. Holsey to M, January 12, 1927, May 16 and June 18, 1929, and December 8, 1930; M to Holsey, May 28, November 27, and December 13, 1929; M to Robert R. Moton, November 11, 1930, and February 4, 1933; Moton to M, August 29, 1927, and February 6, 1933; C. V. Troup to Moton, December 8, 1930, MotP. Chapter 6 details the Moton-Mitchell friendship during Mitchell's early years in Congress.

With regard to blacks and Republicans between World War I and 1932, few decisions were made without input from Moton. On "colored questions," his recommendations carried much weight.[15]

As a Hoover spokesman, Mitchell was confronted by the growing apathy and disillusionment among better-educated blacks for the Grand Old Party and its candidates. By late summer, when Mitchell began his work in Chicago, many African Americans who previously had been staunch partisans had already committed themselves to ignoring presidential politics. For them, W. E. B. DuBois's caustic conclusion written later for *Crisis* gave a correct reading of the 1928 contest: "It does not matter a tinker's damn which of these gentlemen succeed." Less cynical men were bolting Lincoln's party to support Democratic candidate Alfred E. Smith. Also, experienced veterans of elections such as Robert R. Church Jr., the Memphis black leader long associated with GOP national campaigns, had rejected jobs in the Colored Voters Division because of the party's broken promises to blacks during the 1920s.[16] Ready to exploit what appeared to be a superb opportunity for Smith, the Democratic party earmarked more than ninety-eight thousand dollars for marketing him to African Americans. The combination of the Democrats' largest budget ever for winning over traditional Republicans and a candidate who, despite DuBois's cynicism, was attractive to many blacks, added to abnormally high black apathy, disillusionment, and party abandonment, struck fear into many Republican strategists. Suddenly, tasks and responsibilities before Mitchell assumed greater importance in Hoover's campaign. To maintain the party's usually solid black majorities in 1928, GOP leaders recognized that holding onto black voters would require more than a few waves of the bloody shirt and the aged rhetoric about Lincoln's Emancipation Proclamation and Democratic outrages after Reconstruction.

With adjustments clearly needed in its approach to its most loyal supporters, the GOP responded by assigning the Republican message of peace and prosperity to several new spokesmen. Unlike so many before them,

15. Woodson, *The Negro Professional Man*, 229–30; Mitchell Expense Reports to the Republican National Committee, 1928, MP; Richard B. Sherman, *The Republican Party and Black America from McKinley to Hoover, 1896–1933*, 137, 146–47, 150, 158–62, 176, 226–29, 233–34, 250; author's survey, MotP; Lawrence interview; Ralph J. Bunche, *The Political Status of the Negro in the Age of FDR*, 193–98, 462–63; Donald J. Lisio, *Hoover, Blacks, and Lily-Whites: A Study of Southern Strategies*.

16. Sherman, *The Republican Party and Black America*, 232; Lisio, *Hoover, Blacks and Lily-Whites*, 106–16, 128–40; Roi Ottley, *The Lonely Warrior: The Life and Times of Robert S. Abbott*, 342–43; Charles H. Martin, "Negro Leaders, the Republican Party and the Election of 1932," 85; Joan H. Wilson, *Herbert Hoover—Forgotten Progressive*, 129; George F. Garcia, "Black Disaffection from the Republican Party during the Presidency of Herbert Hoover, 1928–1932," 462–77; *Defender*, November 3, 1928; *Crisis* 35 (November 1928): 381.

the fresh recruits were often vigorous, aggressive men of Mitchell's caliber. However, their assignments were not easy, for shadowing and stalking Hoover's spokesmen at every turn were equally persuasive Democrats such as Earl B. Dickerson, an ambitious attorney who became Mitchell's nemesis. Working from a Bronzeville office with a twenty-eight-thousand-dollar budget from the newly created Democratic Colored Division, Dickerson coordinated the Upper Middle West region for Smith's effort among Negro voters. He led a small team of subordinates who worked diligently to refute GOP claims. Despite this effort and Smith's rupture of old color lines within the Democratic party, the party's campaign to win over black voters showed few results. Only minor shifts in voting occurred, and these changes within the black electorate did not affect the election's outcome.[17]

For Mitchell, the three months spent on the Hoover campaign had more than fleeting importance. The campaign acquainted him with Chicago's internal political structure. The experience of campaigning and his insider exposure to election challenges were fascinating, but Windy City politics were more intriguing to Mitchell than was working for Hoover. He saw in the Chicago system's distribution of power something special; it opened up politics for minorities. The number of blacks with active political careers was particularly memorable. Their participation in public life was dependent upon a fifty-unit ward system. Unlike other cities with significantly fewer divisions, Chicago's very different representative framework almost guaranteed civic duties to every minority. There were black aldermen holding city council seats, and five African Americans were members of the Illinois General Assembly. Even more impressive to Mitchell, Oscar DePriest—Capitol Hill's only black member—was a Chicagoan.[18]

Also of interest to Mitchell was the patronage system that fueled Chicago politics. The system during much of the 1920s was largely GOP-driven, and Bronzeville officeholders were Republicans. Across the ghetto, this combination produced fierce competition for every opportunity and caused so much infighting that outsiders stood little chance of succeeding. Yet under William H. "Big Bill" Thompson, the mayor for twelve of the sixteen years between 1915 and 1931, the GOP Machine had

17. *Defender*, October 27 and November 10, 1928; Dickerson interview; John M. Allswang, *A House for All Peoples: Ethnic Politics in Chicago, 1890–1936*, 42; Edward T. Clayton, *The Negro Politician, His Success and Failure*, 55–56.

18. Mitchell interview; for background information about Chicago political opportunities, see Allswang, *A House for All Peoples* and Clayton, *The Negro Politician*. Although weak on Thompson's relationships to organized crime and black political organization, Douglas E. Bukowski's generally disjointed and contradictory 1989 dissertation "According to Image: William Hale Thompson and the Politics of Chicago, 1915–1931" is unfortunately the best account of Big Bill.

institutionalized its control over Bronzeville to such an extent that neighborhood Republican bosses were effectively mixing politics with policy and prostitution while collecting lucrative bootlegging kickbacks. Huge armies of patronage workers skillful at "gettin' out the vote" were the linchpins behind a successful operation. For jobs well done, Thompson's organization rewarded black lieutenants with plush "Loop offices" at City Hall and supervisory powers over vice operations in their districts. On the other hand, underlings—the system's foot soldiers—gained steady patronage employment on city work crews. Exchanges that empowered the black ward heelers and employed precinct captains for delivering election pluralities enhanced Thompson's reputation; to admirers, he was a "Second Lincoln."

Notwithstanding unique bestowments to African Americans, there was, insofar as Mitchell was concerned, a problem with the GOP Machine; he wondered if he, an outsider, could ever break into the setup. Concluding that he could not, he decided an all-for-nothing stake on a Windy City political career must take the matter into account. After wrestling with the dilemma, he wondered if taking a bigger gamble should not be contemplated. Rather than waiting for turnover to occur in the current organization, he wondered if betting his future on the Democrats might not be better. He surmised that risking all on the opposition might not be such a long shot after all. He recalled that work for Hoover had brought him into competition with Earl Dickerson. Since Dickerson had achieved a role for himself in the Democratic party, why, Mitchell apparently asked himself, could there not be opportunities for other blacks?[19]

Soon after the 1928 election, with much on his mind, Mitchell returned to Washington. In the capital, he wound down old commitments and prepared himself for life as a Democrat. His move to Chicago occurred sometime in the first half of 1929. He lodged with his wife's sister and brother-in-law. Although records are sparse for his first three years in Illinois, he apparently relied on income from three sources. After opening a law office at Forty-Seventh Street and South Parkway, Mitchell slowly developed a legal practice. His Washington rental properties still provided him with more income than did his law office. Yet inasmuch as his law clients were poor and all his property holdings were shared, dependence upon these for a livelihood provided Mitchell with no more than basic survival. Although not acknowledged by him, his independence derived from his wife Annie's contributions. Stable and supportive, she had made

19. Mitchell, Brummit, and Dickerson interviews; *Defender,* November 17, 1928; Borger to M, June 14, 1929, MP; Ottley, *Lonely Warrior,* 344–45; Clayton, *Negro Politician,* 43–46.

possible his freedom to move and dabble in different things since their move together from Alabama. She was a quiet, pleasant person who kept to herself and tolerated his moods as well as his interludes. Loving letters to her man revealed her devotion, and in order to keep a household solvent until something positive unfolded for him, she kept in the background in a serene, retiring way, performing clerical work in various Washington offices. As he dreamed of a political career, Annie Mitchell bettered her G-rating, going from the Post Office Department to a position in the General Accounting Office. After coming to Washington in 1919, Annie, except for a brief deviation in 1921 when she studied at New York's Wanamaker Beauty College in preparation for opening the ill-fated Mitchell's High Class Beauty Shop, held steady employment in federal offices. Income from her secretarial jobs allowed her "Precious" to keep dual residences, one in politically rich Chicago and another in secure Washington. Internal Revenue Service records show how much Mitchell depended upon Annie's earnings. According to a 1934 joint filing, her GAO salary of $1,260 represented more than 55 percent of the pair's income. Silent about her accomplishments, Mitchell did not even introduce her to anyone in Chicago; few of his new associates ever met her. But then again, parental and spousal duties never held a primary place in Mitchell's life; his obsession was to become a black copy of the genteel Southern white gentleman.[20]

While familiarizing himself with Chicago, practicing law, and learning the inner workings of Bronzeville politics, Mitchell looked ahead. Evenings spent at precinct offices and Second Ward party headquarters with fellow Democrats made him anxious to participate in the 1932 presidential election. He wanted an important role in the upcoming campaign. By 1932 Americans had stopped looking around the corner for prosperity, and Bronzevillians, like people elsewhere, despaired of looking for jobs that did not exist and of waiting in long soup lines that led into steaming church cellars. Moreover, in an area of Chicago that grew increasingly depressed, nightlife had all but vanished.[21] From Mitchell's personal assessments of 1932, the dismal state of the nation definitely held opportunity for him. Aware of campaign-job possibilities from his work for Hoover four years earlier, he began sending feelers to Democratic party leaders about possible roles for himself in the upcoming election. Notable due to his early conversion from the GOP, Mitchell looked to his good contacts to land something substantial in the National Committee's Colored Division.

20. Policy, Capitol Life Insurance Company, June 18, 1927; Mitchell Joint Income Tax Return, 1934, MP; *Washington Bee*, June 4, 1921; *Defender*, December 16, 1933; Cyrus, Spencer, Tittinger, Thornton, Dickerson, Mitchell, Gibson, and Cephases interviews.
21. Arvarh E. Strickland, *History of the Chicago Urban League*, 104–8; Spencer interview.

For assistance, his past experience had taught him to count on Alabama's John McDuffie. After departing the capital for a Windy City political adventure, Mitchell remained in periodic contact with the Monroeville native. During April 1932, for example, when McDuffie was looking for the "right kind of colored man," his friend understood. Mitchell introduced Emmett J. Scott, an administrative aide at Howard University after Booker Washington's death. In an accolade-filled letter to Congressman McDuffie, Mitchell described Scott as "without doubt among the most able, philanthropic, and outstanding men." More importantly, Scott had a "fair and just attitude toward matters and men," Mitchell double-talk to advise McDuffie that Scott was not a civil rightist. The dividend for suggesting such a suitable candidate occurred months later; this time, it was McDuffie—generally acknowledged by Capitol Hill insiders as one of Washington's most powerful men and a dominant figure in national party politics—presenting "colored friend" Mitchell to Democratic National Chairman James A. Farley. The timing proved to be perfect; the Democratic boss had just begun building a team to elect Franklin Delano Roosevelt.[22] McDuffie's recommendation netted Mitchell an important assignment in the 1932 campaign. Through the Alabaman's influence with Farley, Mitchell became a "trailer." Farley assigned him to follow Republican spokesman and Congressman Oscar DePriest into the West, to refute everything DePriest said. To enhance their presidential candidate's chances in pivotal states such as California, Democratic tacticians had concluded that employing truth squads would be the best approach for reaching frustrated African Americans who had grown tired of Herbert Hoover's alleged betrayals. Democrats were intent on marshaling discontent with Hoover into a galvanized black movement for Roosevelt.

In California, Mitchell's tasks were to monitor a small but potentially decisive African American electorate and to dog DePriest, the most recognized black political leader. Known often as "the lone black in Congress," DePriest enjoyed billing as a champion of civil rights and as a fearless Republican. Refusing to concede a thing to him, Democrats intended to issue tough challenges to him. Soon, it became clear that they were hounding him with a more gifted orator. Relentlessly, Mitchell reminded black audiences of recent GOP blunders such as "Lily-White" tactics in 1928, Hoover's ill-fated nomination of accused racist John J. Parker to the Supreme Court, sharp declines in black patronage, segregation and other indignities forced upon mothers of black World War I veterans during travels to their sons' French graves, and national economic maladies. No gifted public speaker, DePriest nonetheless had to deal with Mitchell's

22. M to JMc, April 5, 1932, MP; Mitchell interview.

shadowing him. Mitchell's presence on the campaign trail unnerved the two-term black lawmaker because with vigor and reason, Mitchell offered thunderous challenges. Yet as annoying as Mitchell's stalking was to DePriest, it had only a negligible impact upon California's black population. With rare exceptions on the West Coast and elsewhere, blacks voted much the same in 1932 as they had in 1928. Thoughts of Roosevelt's trips to Warm Springs, Georgia, his alleged authorship of Haiti's infamous constitution, and the Texas roots of his running mate John Garner were seemingly enough to convince blacks that FDR's "forgotten man" would not have dark skin and that a New Deal would exclude them. From a positive perspective, Mitchell's appearances in Oakland, San Diego, Los Angeles, and San Francisco were personal triumphs and a Democratic turning point. His activities—and others like them across the North and West—illustrated that the Democrats had not conceded the black vote to the GOP. And for Mitchell, trailer campaigning in the West had done much to establish him as an effective force in the party's Colored Division.[23]

Mitchell surfaced soon after the 1932 landslide as one of a handful of dominant black Democrats. Prominent among fellow black New Dealers in search of postelection favors, Mitchell's standing continued to rise. Even if the Colored Division workers had only contributed marginally to victory, there were general demands for tangible proofs of gratitude. Fearing a Southern backlash, Democratic committeemen were not making any promises. As a result of cowardly noncommittals during the immediate postelection period, there was so much strain on several black-white Democratic relationships that they approached open ruptures. Making matters worse, nobody close to Roosevelt had even been courageous enough to thank the faithful minority workers properly. Besides the snubs, the President-elect's inner circle avoided public discussions of the new administration's racial policies. On the other hand, members of the Colored Division were leaderless. For weeks, none of its members had ventured forward with viable counteractions to the Roosevelt administration's obvious Southern strategy.[24] As with many others in the Colored Division, Mitchell expected more from campaigning than per diem and travel reimbursements, but there all similarities ended. Since nobody else had assumed a mantle of leadership, he decided it might as well be his task. To provide unity, he urged formal reactivation of the Executive Committee of the Colored Division. After a reestablishment of this body, it could become

23. M to W. H. Loving, November 23, 1932; M to R. Bentley Strather, November 25, 1932; M to John W. Bussey, November 25, 1932; Frank C. Walker to M, March 31, 1933, MP; Martin, "Negro Leaders," 86–93; Sherman, *The Republican Party and Black America*, 254–56; Walter F. White, *A Man Called White, the Autobiography of Walter White*, 104.
24. M to C. Oliver; M to S. A. T. Watkins, November 25, 1932, MP.

a sounding board for minority grievances and a first step toward an overall administrative planning unit on race questions. To initiate all this, Mitchell advised a national meeting of outstanding black Democrats. His approach was persuasive because it followed a simple premise: if many black delegates assembled and established themselves as a constructive body, representation of African American interests could begin. From personal experience, Mitchell knew how divisiveness had placed severe limitations on blacks' effectiveness at championing their vital interests. Using this premise as an argument for action, Mitchell broached the idea of a postelection assembly of black Democrats with party minority chieftains Robert L. Vann and William J. Thompkins. Since both men agreed on the advantages of holding a conference, they pledged their cooperation and their intention to steer as many leading black Democrats as possible to Mitchell. Receiving positive feedback aided and encouraged Mitchell. The local arrangements were quickly made for convening African Americans in Chicago. Once finished with these details, Mitchell asked John McDuffie to attend and to invite U.S. Senator Pat Harrison of Mississippi and Vice President-elect Garner to come as well.[25]

Although Mitchell was the moving spirit behind the conference, there was also minor assistance from other Bronzeville Democrats. Yet it was Mitchell who invited fellow black Democrats and white party leaders to Chicago on January 20–21, 1933. According to everyone's invitation, the stated purpose was "obtaining some definite knowledge as to the attitude of the president-elect on matters affecting the interest of the Race." Before the opening session, disappointing news reached Mitchell from the Southern trio of Harrison, McDuffie, and Garner; citing "other commitments," they sent regrets for being unable to attend. Too late either to invite other white leaders or to cancel the conclave altogether, Mitchell proceeded without them. The conference began with a dinner that he had billed as a "nonpartisan banquet," but in point of fact, it honored National Democratic party leaders. Mitchell was the toastmaster. As such, he read Garner's telegram of greeting and introduced out-of-town guests. Outstanding blacks from across the country were in attendance at what should have been called the Mitchell Conference of Negro Democrats. In effect, it was the first-ever national caucus of black Democrats. Inasmuch as delegates desired definite statements from the incoming Roosevelt administration about its intentions and stands on such diverse racial questions as anticipated roles of blacks in managing Mississippi River

25. M to Oliver and Watkins, November 25, 1932; M to Robert L. Vann, December 31, 1932; Vann to M, December 22, 1932; M to William J. Thompkins, January 9, 1933; JMc to M, January 14, 1933, MP; *Defender*, January 14, 1933.

flood-control and flood-relief efforts and in terminating peonage practices, there would be disappointment; Garner's short telegram was the only official response. During the delegates' first hours together, their resolutions revealed anger and frustration. They demanded strong actions, and there was also consensus about the desirability of pinning down Roosevelt on racial questions. Tenacity and a will to fight did not last, however. The men in Chicago avoided alienating actions because they were politicians first and civil rightists second. Hence in their summary comments, mildness replaced the initial angry tone. From their perspective, pushing too aggressively on racial issues would preclude them from future political considerations. Since they were seekers of personal power, they had no desire to jeopardize their positions with wild actions that might upset influential interests in their party. In the bigger scheme, jumping to premature judgments would have no ultimate value; weak as a component within the Democratic party, African Americans still were too impotent to demand anything.

Without convention minutes or news reports available to reveal the inner workings of the Chicago gathering, it is impossible to know with certainty who steered the assembly onto its final moderate course. If Mitchell's severed ties with Vann and Thompkins mean anything, full responsibility rested with him. Mitchell not only always distrusted Vann and Thompkins after the convention but also shamelessly labeled them troublemakers or worse. Making the case even stronger, the Chicagoan later charged Vann and Thompkins with disloyalty to the Democratic party. Obviously, inside the hall it had been two against one, with Mitchell for softness and adversaries Vann and Thompkins united behind a hard line. Whatever the circumstances, the black Democrats' two days together were important for Arthur Mitchell; after all, he had proposed, planned, and chaired the conference.[26]

After the assembly's failure at steering Roosevelt on a new course in race relations, Mitchell still wanted a payback for what he considered campaign debts to him. Again trying to exploit John McDuffie's good reputation and contacts for intervention at the highest levels of executive government, Mitchell believed his influential ally could land him an important post in the new regime. McDuffie cooperated, pleading several times to James Farley for aid. In one letter, McDuffie even went so far as to suggest the wisdom and advisability of running Mitchell against DePriest in 1934. Despite his powerful friend's sincere efforts, Mitchell

26. JMc to M, January 14, 1933; Committee of Non-partisan Chicago Citizens in honor of Democratic Visitors, Banquet Program, January 21, 1933; Vann to M, February 22, 1933, MP; *Defender*, January 14 and 28, 1933.

did not obtain a job. After McDuffie's intervention failed, he tried personal persuasion. Using strong character references as a means to impress, he contacted Clark Foreman of the Department of the Interior for suitable employment. However, Foreman gave him an unwelcome suggestion that he took as an insult. Foreman directed Mitchell to officials in Robbins, Illinois, who might offer Public Works Administration employment. Of course, Mitchell had imagined his California campaigning bringing him a more impressive appointment than a laborer's job in an all-black town; he had hoped for supervision of a Washington bureau, preferably with some control over economic or legal matters involving African Americans.[27]

Ambitious for himself more than accountable to the race, Mitchell used every trick at his disposal to achieve his goals. "Uncle Tomming" remained in his repertoire, and he was a masterful flatterer of whites. With minor adjustments, he adapted the lessons learned years ago in Alabama from "dealing with the man" to white politicians. Just as his skillfulness with appropriate words and phrases had worked many years earlier with plantation owners, Mitchell expected a modified strategy of recognizing and praising important office seekers and incumbents for achievements, election victories, and milestones would work wonders for him in Chicago. Whenever individual Democrats had done anything of importance for themselves, the city, or the party, Mitchell was likely to offer them his help. Quite transparent, these trivial messages nonetheless were carefully calculated ploys aimed at ingratiating him with top party figures. His letters, however, compromised African American respectability. To Mitchell's discredit, he often used congratulatory occasions to denigrate fellow blacks. To promote himself in correspondence to white politicians, he often attempted to distinguish blacks who deserved no consideration from others who warranted privileges. Notwithstanding his general feebleness at identifying and isolating the two groups, these were still disturbing suggestions from Mitchell that he might be personally useful if a need should arise to manage and control troublesome African Americans.

In 1933, Mitchell approached Judge Harry M. Fisher, Mayor Edward Kelly, State's Attorney Frank Loesch, and at least twelve other prominent Chicagoans in this way. Upon Ed Kelly's selection by the Chicago City Council to fill Anton Cermak's unexpired term, Mitchell advised the new mayor that "the best thinking Negroes of Chicago . . . have the highest regard for you and unshaken confidence in your honesty and integrity."

27. M to JMc, March 11, May 3, and November 9, 1933; M to John Foscoe, June 10, 1933; M to Clark H. Foreman, October 14, 1933; Foreman to M, October 23, 1933; JMc to JAF, June 29 and September 13, 1933, MP.

Due to efforts such as this, Mitchell was emerging as a black politician and backslapper with an unscrupulous willingness to sacrifice anything or anybody for a chance to achieve his personal goals. By seldom missing any tricks or means for advancement, he was weaving himself skillfully and quickly into the Chicago Machine's good graces. To the political bosses, he above all demonstrated dependability and circumspection. His instincts for bridled power and readiness for compromise moved him closer and closer to those in power. Few Bronzeville contemporaries noticed this, and to those who did, Mitchell offered no explanations or apologies. Somehow, he had known that displaying disregard for an action's impact on others would have positive and significant effects on the outcome of his calculations to move forward in the organization. Cleavages were the basis of Chicago's fieflike system, and for giving loyalty and obedience to the Machine, bright men of Mitchell's caliber received rewards and also roles in daily operations. Windy City bosses were experts at finding and promoting "safe" people from many diverse racial and ethnic backgrounds. Powerful city and county Democrats were on the lookout for street-smart, crafty individuals with ambition who could hold in personal disappointments and who would ungrudgingly pay homage to party leaders. Mitchell was one of their finds. Fifteen years after his farewell to Alabama, Mitchell had nothing more fixed in his plans than a burning ambition to succeed. His changes in employment, residence, and political allegiance had all been geared to achieve this one overriding goal.[28]

28. M to EJK, April 15, 1933; M to EBD, February 14, 1933; EBD to M, February 15, 1933; M to Harry M. Fisher, March 11, 1933 (same to many Illinois notables); M to Frank J. Loesch, January 30, 1933; Loesch to M, January 31, 1933; invitation, Judge Harry M. Fisher Testimonial Dinner (Mitchell headed the dinner committee), May 31, 1933, MP; Dickerson interview.

Halcyon Days for Chicago's Perfect Black Politician

1934–1935

C hicago's record of electing blacks impressed Arthur Mitchell. After almost a month in Illinois for Hoover, he would not forget Mayor Thompson's application of what has succinctly been called "recognition politics." Early in his turbulent Windy City political career, "Big Bill, the Builder" made a crafty adjustment to accommodate the wave of blacks arriving in Chicago. Thompson was several years ahead of other politicians in employing African Americans to gird up his political organization. Blacks in Chicago were rewarded with patronage opportunities and elective positions in return for their support. Thompson does not deserve too much credit, however. Chicago's fifty-ward system accounted for the city opening itself to greater ethnic and black political participation. Clever mayoral policies and peculiar municipal districts notwithstanding, Mitchell noticed how Chicago's predominantly black-populated precincts responded. City Hall observers dubbed the area "Uncle Tom's Cabin," and called Thompson "The New Lincoln." To Mitchell, the inclusion of blacks in the Machine was "democracy." Although he never elaborated much about what he had observed in Chicago in 1928, Mitchell clearly appreciated the opportunity Chicago offered for an African American eager to gain entry into politics. Hence Mitchell, with seemingly no greater desire than to win a political office, was willing to move from Washington to Chicago in 1929.[1]

Mitchell soon found that Chicago, upon closer examination, had fewer distinguishable characteristics than he had first imagined. Like so many other black contemporaries, Mitchell discovered flaws. Except for more

---

1. Edgar Litt, *Beyond Pluralism: Ethnic Politics in America,* 62; Mitchell interview; Elmer E. Cornwell, "Bosses, Machines, and Ethnic Groups," 28; for black migration to Chicago, see James R. Grossman, *Land of Hope: Chicago, Black Southerners, and the Great Migration.*

black-held offices with all their accompanying power and privileges, life in Chicago's ebonyville was not better than it was in other Northern ghettos. Bronzeville's stark poverty and its awful blight of pitiably overcrowded, unilinear neighborhoods were clear to see. Between 1920 and 1930, Chicago's black population soared, growing 134 percent and reaching 233,903 residents by the end of Mitchell's first year there. African Americans were severely restricted in their choices of housing. In terms of total acreage, black areas pushed outward every year, but this expansion did not keep pace with pressures from new residents on existing housing stock. The failure encouraged "partitioning." After being bisected and quartered, housing units were beset with overcrowding's side effects. Such problems as inadequate recreational facilities, infant mortality, communicable diseases, and classroom shortages increased manyfold.[2]

Still, midway through 1929, Mitchell was sampling "massive psychic gratification." He entered a city where Thompson's ward heelers rewarded political favors with patronage and public offices. Returns were in proportion to correct voting. To offset Al Smith's anticipated strength among Chicago's Roman Catholics, Thompson's Machine had pushed hard in the 1928 elections for a massive black turnout. Compared to previous elections, there was more "visual slating" this round. For the first time in Bronzeville's history, there was a complete slate of black GOP office seekers. Subsequently, African Americans won election to posts at all levels of government. Mitchell might not have understood urban politics very well, but he understood the implications of the 1928 vote. If African Americans represented Bronzeville in Chicago, Springfield, and Washington, why, he asked, would there be any barriers to his plans?

However, Mitchell did not make naive assumptions about white largesse in the Midwest. From the start, he paid proper homage to the system's operatives because he recognized that municipal power passed downward from the mayor's office. As with blacks in city, county, state, and national elective offices, there was not much concern on his part with particulars. He was not interested in whether Chicago was fair and

2. Otis D. Duncan and Beverly Duncan, *The Negro Population of Chicago: A Study of Residential Succession*, 6, 21–23; Carole Marks, *Farewell—We're Good and Gone: The Great Black Migration*; Grossman, *Land of Hope*; Allan H. Spear, *Black Chicago: The Making of a Negro Ghetto, 1890–1920*; Edith Abbott, *The Tenements of Chicago, 1908–1935*, 117–26; Mary E. Ogden, *The Chicago Negro Community, a Statistical Description*; Charles S. Newcomb, ed., *Census Data of the City of Chicago, 1934*; Esther M. Phillips, *Negro Health in the State of Illinois*; "Social Data for Chicago Communities," *Community Fact Book, 1938*; St. Clair Drake, "The Negro Church Associations in Chicago: A Research Memorandum," 202–3; the best description of Chicago's evolving ghetto is Thomas L. Philpott's *The Slum and the Ghetto: Neighborhood Deterioration and Middle-Class Reform, Chicago, 1880–1930*.

representative to Bronzeville; reforming a city had not been a motive for his coming. As he had in Alabama and in Washington, Mitchell was looking above all for opportunities to better himself. From survival lessons learned in the South, he had a good understanding of how to find success in Chicago. Hence, he knew when bosses expected his silence. When, for example, he observed a wide-open numbers racket operating in Bronzeville, he knew his survival would depend upon him seeing nothing. Since shares from "the wheel's take" were never equally divided among its players, he preferred an opportunity to spin the big wheel over a chance at winning. He reckoned it to be logical; spinners did not lose.[3]

Thus, Mitchell had good reasons for settling in Chicago. Most of all, he had political goals. Specifically, he set himself in pursuit of Oscar DePriest. Aware that DePriest and black Chicagoans in public office were Republicans, Mitchell pondered if continuing his membership in the GOP would not present too many obstacles. With Congress a coveted objective, his target was DePriest's First District, which included Bronzeville in the Second Ward as well as major portions of the First, Fourth, and Eleventh Wards, and which possessed a multiracial population that was approximately 60 percent white. After assessing his options, one always emerged as least favorable. As an upstart waiting out a man of similar age, he could face a long postponement if he waited for something to happen to DePriest. A political career was more than enough bait to lure Mitchell coldly to the only option that would favor him. To dislodge a black Republican, Mitchell chose to desert the Republican party. The possibility of the GOP losing favor and the low percentage of black Democrats may explain Mitchell's bolt from his party. Republican leaders possessed such smug overconfidence about black political loyalties that they had already driven reform-minded African Americans such as Chicagoan Earl B. Dickerson half-heartedly into the opposition. Mitchell sensed immediate opportunities from their switches. Regular attendance at local Democratic precinct meetings taught him about insiders and outsiders of Chicago politics. After a few sessions, he made contact with an influential political boss, Joseph E. Tittinger, the beleaguered white committeeman from the predominantly black Second Ward. Race was placing "Joe" in an awkward position. Continuously pressed by the relentless intentions of Dickerson and others to have a black appointed to the party post, Tittinger needed

3. Clayton, *Negro Politician*, 40–47; an unpublished thirty-seven-page report on the numbers racket in Chicago, SP; Tittinger, Mitchell, and Dickerson interviews; Harold F. Gosnell, "The Negro Vote in Northern Cities," 267; *Defender*, January 26, 1929; Ottley, *Lonely Warrior*, 344–45; St. Clair Drake and Horace R. Cayton, *Black Metropolis: A Study of Negro Life in a Northern City*, vol. 2, 470–94; Litt, *Beyond Pluralism*, 45, 156–57; Cornwell, "Bosses," 30.

black allies to stave off a successful rebellion. Learning of Tittinger's predicament, Mitchell gambled a second time, betting the white ward heeler could provide more help than black malcontents. Hence, Tittinger and Mitchell formed an alliance that would prove invaluable to both men: the white boss gained an articulate black supporter, and the ambitious newcomer obtained a useful sponsor. For all to note, Tittinger's relationship with Mitchell served the committeeman as his conclusive proof that he was not a racist.[4]

To win office, Mitchell needed more going for him than a frustrated ward heeler; such an achievement required patience and luck. Between 1929 and 1934, many factors contributed to an improved political outlook for Mitchell. Locally and nationally, Hoover and his party lost much of its support with the onset of the Great Depression. The Republicans' losses appeared first during the 1930 off-year elections. In 1931, Thompson absorbed the full impact: Chicagoans toppled the once-mighty mayor and his Machine from power, electing Democrat Anton Cermak in his place. All across America in campaigns before the 1932 elections, GOP incumbents faced equally bleak futures. A revolutionary swing toward the Democrats continued after Franklin D. Roosevelt's humiliation of President Hoover. Suddenly, with a Democrat already in City Hall and another awaiting the Oval Office, Mitchell's change of party affiliation seemed a stroke of genius. There was only one problem, however; Cermak was not cooperating. Unlike his GOP predecessor, Cermak was not elevating many Bronzevillians to political positions.

Within an instant on February 15, 1933, the situation changed. On that date, an assassin's bullet meant for FDR mortally wounded Cermak. For the city's black populace, two years of frustration, harassment, and neglect ended. Longing for empathy and improvement, African Americans were encouraged from the first words uttered on race relations by Cermak's successor, Edward J. Kelly. Kelly immediately declared just intentions. Shrewdly recognizing from the Thompson regime how potentially valuable and useful African Americans could be, Mayor Kelly and Chairman

4. Mitchell, Tittinger, and Dickerson interviews; in a remarkably well-researched account of black political personalities from Bronzeville, Charles R. Branham examined both major and minor figures in his 1981 University of Chicago dissertation, "The Transformation of Black Political Leadership in Chicago, 1864–1942." There is unfortunately too much effort put into boosting such efforts at the expense of earlier scholarship because many of Branham's themes require further development and attachment to City Hall. Reading his characterizations of prominent figures such as Louis Anderson, Oscar DePriest, William Dawson, and Earl Dickerson without understanding the backdrops of their situations leaves the impression that these politicians were powerless because of their pettiness rather than the hopelessness of Bronzeville in the overall scheme of machine politics. Branham also dismisses the true genius of Mitchell, that is, his ability to time moves and play odds perfectly.

Patrick J. Nash of the Democratic Central Committee of Cook County began including Bronzeville in their machine-building plans. For participating, its inhabitants eventually received Chicago patronage and hundreds of newly created WPA jobs, and for being fairer than Cermak, Kelly earned respect and even admiration from the city's largely Republican-oriented black minority. Within less than two years, accolades and support from the leading black newspaper the *Defender* and black Republican politicians followed. Words from the mayor were speaking louder than his actions, however; almost no blacks emerged as his anointed candidates for office. In contrast to Thompson's careful slating of minority members for offices, Kelly kept most ward and patronage supervision under Tittinger and forty-eight other white committeemen (Edward Sneed was the only exception). A consequence was that Tittinger faced persistent anger and resentment from African Americans. As determined as blacks were to challenge Tittinger, their complaints went nowhere because of steadfast refusals by patronage generals Kelly and Nash to dismiss a reliable lieutenant.[5]

Although Tittinger needed Mitchell, there were questions about how Mitchell might assist. Two facts dominated all other considerations in the two men's odd relationship. By Tittinger's own admission, he had been on the lookout for a man like Mitchell. To quiet persistent critics who bemoaned the neglect of African American constituents, Tittinger wanted a black figurehead to run for prominent office. In Mitchell, he confessed in 1971, a perfect person had been discovered, because Mitchell would be forever indebted to the ward heeler's Second Ward Democratic organization and to others in the Machine who would have a hand in electing him. In late January 1934, or roughly ten weeks before the April primary, Tittinger courted and encouraged Mitchell. As early as January 30, at a Roosevelt birthday celebration in the heart of the Second Ward and before a large crowd of Democratic regulars, he hailed Mitchell as his probable choice for Congress in the upcoming primary. The endorsement heartened the largely black audience, but the crowd was gladdened even more by the announcement that local favorite Bryant A. Hammond would be the Organization's candidate for the Illinois Senate.[6]

5. Branham, "The Transformation of Black Political Leadership"; Christopher R. Reed, "Black Chicago Political Realignment during the Depression and New Deal," 242–56; John M. Allswang, "The Chicago Negro Voter and the Democratic Consensus, A Case Study, 1918–1936," 171–75; Martin Meyerson and Edward C. Banfield, *Politics, Planning, and the Public Interest; the Case of Public Housing in Chicago*, 61; Clayton, *Negro Politician*, 55; Arnold R. Hirsch, "Chicago: The Cook County Democratic Organization and the Dilemma of Race, 1931–1987," 63–70; Roger Biles, *Big City Boss in Depression and War: Mayor Edward J. Kelly of Chicago*, offers an interesting view of Kelly; *Defender*, March 23, 1935.

6. *Defender*, February 3, 1934; Tittinger interview.

A loner by nature, Mitchell did not seem to possess the charm and personality required of Chicago politicians. Friendships came with difficulty, and according to interviewed witnesses, Mitchell made few acquaintances and apparently no sincere friendships during his first five years' residence in Bronzeville. Most odd and peculiar as well for a man with political ambitions, few area residents knew of his existence. In addition, those aware of Mitchell's entry into the tightly knit world of the community's professional elite generally agreed that he was hostile and combative. In most instances, these were two more negative traits for an aspiring politician. After Mitchell's arrival in the spring of 1929, his tendency to rub people the wrong way was also noticed. As one person summed it, "The more men Mitchell met, the more enemies he made." Mitchell's harshest contempt was for persons below him in status, such as black panhandlers begging for handouts.[7]

For whatever satisfaction it might have brought Annie Mitchell alone in the District of Columbia, her husband's only known Bronzeville mistresses were law and politics. Life in the Windy City was a serious ordeal. Workaholic routines apparently had greater seductive power than any woman. Mornings found Mitchell in his office at 417 East Forty-Seventh Street for a full schedule of activities. There, he ritually read newspapers, wrote letters, talked to cronies, and practiced law. An hour for lunch at nearby cafés—usually with associates who generously overlooked his shortcomings—seemed his only consistent social indulgence. His pleasure came from attending precinct and ward meetings and other political work. All this was possible because nothing else occupied his evenings and weekends. Above all, establishing strong ties to Tittinger was the goal of this schedule, because it might lead to a congressional seat.[8]

On another front, Mitchell made himself somewhat better known among black and white Democrats. Organizing honorary dinners was his favorite way of introducing himself. During the spring of 1933, for example, he chaired a committee of the black Chicago Democratic Lawyers Club to fete Judge Harry M. Fisher of the Cook County Circuit Court. A testimonial dinner was the climax; it attracted a partisan gathering that included black attorneys and their friends. For sixty cents, participants dined with Fisher and listened to endless praises. Like Mitchell's ingratiating letters to political figures, the dinners showcased a man anxious to display indebtedness to whites. In the final analysis, however, these efforts worked to Mitchell's long-range benefit.[9]

---

7. Cyrus, Gibson, Thornton, Spencer, and Tittinger interviews; the first indication of Mitchell having taken up residence in Chicago was a letter addressed to him at 417 East Forty-Seventh Street, Borger to M, June 14, 1929, MP.

8. Cyrus, Gibson, Thornton, Spencer, Tittinger, and Mitchell interviews.

9. Testimonial Dinner Invitation, MP.

Bolstered by Tittinger's two announcements, Mitchell and Second Ward precinct workers braved arctic cold weather in early 1934, gathering enough names on petitions to meet the filing deadline for participation in the April primary election. Additional support, however, was lacking from other First District political organizations. In particular, Mitchell received no encouragement from Michael "Hinky Dink" Kenna, Joseph P. Geary, or Hugh Connelly, the white ward committeemen of the First, Fourth, and Eleventh Wards, respectively. These three men, who presided over white-majority wards, stuck with a different candidate, Harry Baker, an old friend who had gained only 43 percent of the 1932 vote against DePriest. In the upcoming primary, all signs pointed to white committeemen favoring a dull personality like Baker over the risk of imposing an unknown black candidate on constituents. Obligingly, Kelly and Nash relented. Nevertheless, Tittinger continued engaging precinct workers to help Mitchell challenge Baker. Tittinger also obviously feared Edgar Brown, a black insurgent who was challenging both for his committeemanship and the nomination to contest DePriest. Stridently and militantly, Brown criticized Tittinger, labeling him a "foreign incumbent" guilty of denying Bronzeville its fair share of patronage. Tittinger clearly used his support of Mitchell as his buffer against these attacks.[10]

For blacks in the First District, the 1934 Democratic primary was an interesting contest. Never in Chicago political history had two African Americans vied for the same opportunity to run as Democrats against an incumbent black. In urging voters to give him a chance, Mitchell used three themes. First, he told them frequently that no other Democratic candidate could possibly defeat DePriest in the general election. Second, he claimed his intent to place Chicagoans first and not last as DePriest had allegedly been doing. Third, every Mitchell speech expressed full devotion to the New Deal. He promised, if elected to Congress, to give Roosevelt unwavering support. Meanwhile, the contest settled into a Baker-Mitchell race: lacking money and organization, Brown's campaign died for all practical purposes long before primary day. In the First, Fourth, and Eleventh Wards, Baker won white support without effort. On the other hand, Mitchell worked hard to make himself known among Second Ward voters and to win over voters in the three white wards. In the midst of this most unusual "salt-and-pepper" campaign, something unexpected happened. Mitchell received an accidental boost from Mayor Kelly. Whether by design or blunder, Kelly assisted Mitchell's cause by appearing at the regular Tuesday night ward meeting in Bronzeville and saluting his presence in the race. Kelly not only acknowledged Mitchell

10. Tittinger and Dickerson interviews; Primary Petition, MP; *Defender*, February 24 and March 17, 1934.

but also offered him words of encouragement. Mitchell alertly added a favorable twist to remarks by the mayor, sanguinely interpreting a kindness as his endorsement. It was a most hopeful assessment, because after just one year in office, Kelly certainly had not intended to do more than court Bronzeville. But by coming to the Second Ward under such circumstances during a primary campaign, he had only himself to blame if Mitchell extracted political advantage from casual remarks. Yet in the final analysis, it was race and not Kelly's ill-timed, misinterpreted appearance that determined the election's outcome. In what became a Pyrrhic victory for Machine forces, white Democrats chose Baker, and blacks cast ballots for Mitchell. By amassing large pluralities in the white wards, Baker survived an African American bloc effort in the Second Ward, gaining 7,236 votes to Mitchell's 6,812.[11]

With his loss behind him, Mitchell traveled home to Washington for a visit. After the spring primaries, everything seemed to be going De-Priest's way. DePriest had survived a stiff challenge from a disgruntled Republican rival, and for a second time, his Democratic foe would be bland Harry Baker. Then the situation changed dramatically. Baker died of heart failure, thus opening the way for a new contestant. In the bizarre turn of events, Mitchell, the obscure newcomer, emerged with the Democratic nomination. According to Tittinger's account years later, Mitchell gained the opportunity because two factors favored him: he was safe, and he was unknown. Mitchell was a dream candidate, Tittinger explained. Tittinger had feared losing control of the Second Ward to a popular, charismatic African American because of his failure to reward blacks with places on tickets. After a few exchanges with Mitchell, Tittinger knew he had found a godsend. Strong in appearance and robust in speech, Mitchell possessed excellent physical characteristics for a candidate. After Baker's death, un-concealed contempt for other blacks along with obvious selfishness suited Mitchell ideally for a key role in Tittinger's plans. Without expressed concern for anyone and without a loyal following to give him a power base and independence, Mitchell possessed qualities a boss in Tittinger's predicament could only dream of finding. From all perspectives, Mitchell fit the bill perfectly. There was no risk of him becoming like DePriest and bucking ward overlords and white leaders, and unlike better-known Second Ward blacks such as Dickerson, he had no means for political independence.[12]

11. M to Kelly, March 22, 1934; News Release, The Illinois Liberty League Second Ward Club, MP; *Defender,* March 17, 1934; *Chicago World,* February 10 and March 6, 1934 ; *Chicago Tribune,* August 4, 1934.

12. Tittinger and Dickerson interviews; M to JET, January 12, 1934, MP.

By Tittinger's account, he had no trouble selling Mitchell to colleagues from the other First District wards. After Tittinger had secured their consent, he turned to members of the Cook County Organization for their approval. Here atop local politics, only loyalty and electability really mattered. Expertly schooled in the ways of the Machine, Tittinger knew just what to say on Mitchell's behalf. Thus, he presented Mitchell to the leadership with one simple sentence: his man would defeat DePriest without adverse consequences for the Organization. Proudly crediting himself for reaching this political conclusion, Tittinger claimed that he alone had uncovered the ideal candidate and had ascertained his eagerness to run for Congress. Whatever doubts he might have had about pushing black candidates, there was no skittishness about offering Mitchell.[13]

These recollections contradict Mitchell's version of events. To account for his Democratic nomination in 1934, Mitchell stressed his connections as the only feasible explanation. According to Mitchell, immediately after news of Baker's death had reached him in the District of Columbia, he planned a quick return to Chicago. A place on the ticket then resulted directly from a close relationship between Congressman McDuffie and James A. Farley of the Democratic National Committee. On Mitchell's behalf, McDuffie persuaded Farley to write to key Democrats in Chicago. Then with a copy of Farley's letter in hand at the emergency slating session, Mitchell allegedly sold himself. Awed and dumbfounded by his performance, the leadership speechlessly succumbed, for there now existed a most compelling reason to thrust an opportunity of running on the bold political nobody in their midst. According to Mitchell, the party kingpins reasoned his likelihood of success in a contest against DePriest would be as good as anyone else's.

Given Mitchell's interpretation of the nomination, Tittinger shrugged before dismissing it as illogical nonsense. Had Farley or for that matter anyone else of importance written such a letter ordering Cook County Democratic party leaders to nominate Mitchell, then Nash, Kelly, or some other leader would have simply placed his name on the ballot. Certainly regarding this particular nominee, Tittinger remembered, nobody at City Hall, the County Building, or Springfield had commanded anything. Still clinging to Mitchell as a personal discovery, Tittinger reasserted that he had gone to the Cook County meeting with resolve to "get Mitchell over, and I did." Manuscript evidence supports the existence of a McDuffie letter. It introduced and praised Mitchell, but there is no correspondence in Mitchell's files or elsewhere to suggest outside intervention by Farley. In fact, nothing points to any interference and pressure. There were McDuffie

13. Tittinger interview.

letters written much earlier to Kelly and Nash, but they were character references and not political endorsements. In a letter to Farley, on the other hand, McDuffie characterized Mitchell as a "decided improvement over the Republican Member, DePriest, and I hope the National Committee will find it feasible to lend its support to Mitchell." Back in January before officially seeking the Democratic nomination, Mitchell had left a Mc-Duffie letter with Tittinger. General in content, it was a recommendation of Mitchell, and it contained a Southerner's complaints with DePriest. Here again, though, none of the Alabaman's statements imply anyone in Chicago was expected to do anything special for Mitchell.[14]

After the die had been cast for Mitchell at an emergency session of Cook County committeemen, Tittinger, Kenna, Geary, and Connelly joined in a districtwide, united Democratic effort to drive DePriest from office. During the Republican's three congressional terms, he had acquired national fame as a fighter for African American causes. Always ready to confront Southern Democrats—whether over his wife's right to attend White House receptions or an assistant's entitlement to dine in the Capitol restaurant—DePriest enjoyed verbal sparring with Southern politicians and traveling defiantly to their region. No special friend of books or intellectuals, DePriest was erratic and irrational at times. Different from his new Democratic opponent who carefully planned moves ahead with a chess master's skillfulness, DePriest jumped pell-mell into diverse issues. Oratorical eloquence came only spontaneously. For all those times when he knew in advance of talks, only nervous mutterings babbled forth from his mouth. Conversely, Mitchell preferred texts for speeches.[15]

Although DePriest was a waverer, fleeing one issue for another without seeing anything through to a conclusion, he demonstrated loyalty and steadfastness to his party. He had special commitments as the lone black on Capitol Hill, but these rarely conflicted with his role as the highest ranking African American member of the Republican party. With the

14. *Ibid.;* JMc to JAF, September 13, 1933, February 7, 1934; M to JMc, December 29, 1942; JMc to M, February 7 and December 31, 1942, McDP; M to JET, January 12, 1934; JMc to Pat Nash, March 6, 1934; JMc to EJK, March 6, 1934; Nash to JMc, March 16, 1934, MP.

15. For this and following paragraphs on DePriest, the author's conclusions are based on Harold F. Gosnell, *Negro Politicians: The Rise of Negro Politics in Chicago,* 164–94; *Chicago Broad Ax,* 1914–1915; *Chicago Tribune,* April 1915; *Defender,* 1914–1935; *CR,* 71st–73d Cong., with special analyses of DePriest voting patterns and his speeches; DePriest-related correspondence with the NAACP such as the subject to William Pickens, January 30, 1931; to WW, November 25, 1931, March 30 and April 4, 1933, and February 17, 1934, NAACP; letters in MotP, 1929–1933; coverage of DePriest's battle for Capitol eating privileges is in Elliott M. Rudwick, "Oscar DePriest and the Jim Crow Restaurant in the U.S. House of Representatives," 77–82; White, *A Man Called White,* 139–40; Martin, "Negro Leaders," 86.

United States engulfed in its worst domestic crisis since the Civil War and Herbert Hoover firmly committed to a wait-and-see policy, young blacks—unlike many of their elders—were questioning old ties to the GOP. DePriest did not fluctuate, however; throughout its darkest hours, the party could depend on him to defend Hoover's record and positions. On roll calls, his votes indicated undiluted support for party positions. On all types of issues during his Capitol Hill tenure, the record shows him with a majority of his party. Roughly translated, his votes signified support for Hoover's agenda and dogmatic opposition to the New Deal during FDR's first two years in office. In some respects, Thompson's defeat by Anton Cermak in 1931 was a defining moment for DePriest. With Democrats running Chicago politics, DePriest was no longer accountable to a white leader, but a basic fact about him was unchanged: he remained an idealogue wedded to libertarianism. Throughout a profitable life, he remained a conservative Republican, believing in protection of property owners and rights of businesses. Big government and public welfare went against his views and instincts. To him, the New Deal had little to promise the populace, while it threatened much in the longer term because it could neither inspire confidence nor restore sound money. His formula for stopping the Great Depression reflected the ideas of Hoover and other fiscal conservatives: invest business with opportunities to pull the nation from its economic malaise. Like many other men of considerable means, DePriest wanted a restoration of the dollar's full value and a reestablishment of investment incentives. The essentials of Republicanism were so deeply etched in DePriest's soul that he could not contemplate any changes. Herein was a major difference between the two men vying for the First District congressional seat. DePriest, the political philosopher, believed in constancy, while Mitchell was an opportunist. Both candidates were conservative, but Mitchell did not allow ideals to obstruct his quests for personal goals. Probably neither politician gave first consideration to the wishes of constituents nor offered long-term solutions. In different ways, both were extremely selfish. DePriest cared so much about a philosophy intended to protect personal interests that he neglected basic constituent needs. While an increasing number of Bronzevillians suffered from hunger and cold, he stood fast, persistently opposing plans that gave the federal government a role in relief distributions.

DePriest's problems went beyond Republican decline and Mitchell's challenge; once-unified wards were disintegrating all around him. To some extent, unity was a product of patronage. Soon after the GOP's displacement at City Hall in 1931, the party was weakened to such a degree that Republicans were experiencing seemingly irreconcilable intraparty battles over control of Second and Third Ward party committees. This kind of situation had occurred in the past, but Thompson had always appeased adversaries. Unresolved problems left from a 1930 falling-out between DePriest and the mayor over a Senate nomination had resurfaced in 1932. Not willing to forgive a transgression of authority, Thompson resented DePriest's open defiance so much that there was an attempt at unseating him in the 1932 primary. Black voters did not allow this, though. DePriest amassed a huge vote margin over Alderman Louis Anderson, Thompson's revenge candidate. Nonetheless, the contest with Anderson was no boost to DePriest's bid to set up a political machine among black Republicans. Out of leftover bitterness and many snarls, intraparty warfare reemerged in the Second and Third Wards. Although DePriest retained his powers in the Third, there was no chance to savor victory; developments in the nearby Second Ward were not at all beneficial. William L. Dawson, DePriest's unofficial choice for committeeman, lost. The defeat meant that antagonistic William King was in control of a pivotal ward. More than ever, therefore, DePriest was vulnerable. His traditional sources of strength and power had either vanished altogether or had atrophied. In 1934, Mitchell was on hand to exploit his weaknesses.[16]

Once Mitchell had been given the Democratic nomination, the Kelly-Nash Machine asserted itself with armies of interracial precinct workers. With patronage jobs on the line pending the outcomes of the 1934 elections, Democratic captains converged on voters of the First, Second, Fourth, and Eleventh Wards, soliciting as large a turnout as possible for party nominees on election day. Since they sought straight-ticket voting, the identities of individual candidates did not matter. According to Tittinger, Mitchell's name on the ballot did not have significant bearing. In point of fact, Tittinger observed, only a few of his precinct workers liked Mitchell, whereas a majority found him personally offensive. What they disdained most about Mitchell, noted Tittinger, were his demeaning condescension and general unsociability. But their feelings were inconsequential; patronage jobs resulted from electing the party's friends, and not the workers' choices. Thus for the greater cause of winning, the Democratic legions willingly subdued their personal emotions. For executing this duty, persuasion often worked best with the electorate. If it failed, there were always other means; Tittinger sheepishly related how some people in Bronzeville had developed better understandings of money than others. *Chicago World* owner-editor Jacob Tipper, explained Tittinger, had accepted such "help."

16. *Defender,* April 12 and November 1 and 8, 1930, August 1, 8, 15, 22, and 29, September 5 and 26, and October 10, 1931, April 9 and 16, July 9 and 23, September 10 and 17, October 29, and November 12, 1932, February 25 and December 16 and 23, 1933, January 13 and 27, February 3 and 24, March 17, and April 7, 14, and 21, 1934; *Chicago Tribune,* April 12, 1934; Moton to DePriest, November 10, 1932, MotP; Allswang, "Chicago Negro Voter," 167–68; Clayton, *Negro Politician,* 53.

Partisan viewpoints in a struggling black weekly were open for bid. In reality, Tittinger speculated, cash to Tipper had probably bought little more than party "donations" to storefront preachers. Then again, it probably was better to have these people with you than against you.[17]

In terms of publicity, the nominees' personal appeals overshadowed the importance of the patronage workers' tireless and methodical campaigning in the backwaters of precincts. However, in 1934, the candidates in the First District were attracting more than usual attention. For an off-year House race, DePriest versus Mitchell drew a large, racially mixed audience from the entire nation. Of course, the attention was due to the nature of the struggle. Whites from Dixie were generally interested in the election because they were hoping for DePriest's defeat. Top Republicans in turn watched the race carefully for the election's implications and ramifications on the GOP. For similar reasons, key Democrats observed closely, too. Gaining or losing a minority as large as the black electorate would have lasting strategic importance for both parties. African Americans were curious onlookers as well; they followed the Mitchell-DePriest contest to learn which candidate would make the most promises to mind special racial interests. As a result, electing a representative for the First District became a major spectacle for Americans of both races.[18]

Mitchell and DePriest were both confident of victory. The GOP incumbent and his supporters were quick to ridicule Mitchell's candidacy. As early as mid-March, when Mitchell's hope of running had still been a distant dream, Morris Lewis, DePriest's secretary, predicted his boss would have little to fear from the unheard-of Mitchell. Later, with Mitchell in place on the ballot, DePriest spokesmen cited some statistical evidence for their contention that the district looked like a safe bet for their man. During the 1934 primary, 19,088 voters had requested Republican ballots, while only 16,150 had voted Democratic. The difference of 2,938 votes had been an accurate measure, they said, of the GOP's and DePriest's strengths in the First District. The opposition was equally optimistic. One theme appeared throughout Mitchell's speeches and correspondence: he would fulfill a great mission with a victory. Since changing parties and coming to Chicago, Mitchell had kept to his goal of wanting to contest

17. Tittinger interview.

18. *Pittsburgh Courier*, August 18, 1934; *Chicago Herald and Examiner*, September 6, 1934; if letters to M from people across the nation indicated interest, the race was generating strong feelings for both candidates. In MP, see to M from: Ella R. Hutson, August 15, 1934; L. D. Reddick, August 15, 1934; Turner, August 29, 1934; George A. Parker, August 30, 1934; Henry J. Richardson Jr., September 25, 1934; Alain Locke, October 5, 1934; Daniel L. H. West, October 12, 1934; W. C. Patton, October 14, 1934; Robert White Lanier, November 1, 1934.

the GOP officeholder. Now that he had come this far, replacing DePriest in Congress would follow. A month before the election, he claimed to have "beaten and out-generaled [his rival] at every stage of the game." Furthermore, Democratic committeemen expected at least a 10,000-vote Mitchell plurality.[19]

There were good reasons for these assumptions. Despite attempts to restore harmony, First District Republicans were still divided. King and DePriest—bitter rivals since DePriest's covert support of William Dawson for ward committeeman—had reunited to endorse each other's candidacies, but rancor continued among their backers. At a gigantic GOP rally, whispers followed King's entry into the hall. The commotion totally unnerved Dawson, who was speaking. Noticing what had been causing the murmuring, he rushed excitedly through his remarks before dashing from the podium. There had not been as much as token acknowledgment for King's presence. Nothing was more indicative of DePriest's problems than the formation and growth of the Mitchell Republican Boosters. As an obvious sign of disgruntlement with the three-term congressman, the dissidents' organization was a direct outgrowth of Mitchell's proposal to Caswell W. Crews, DePriest's most outspoken Republican critic. In August, shortly after Mitchell had met with Crews to "talk turkey," Crews assembled other disenchanted men and women for an open forum with Mitchell. Easily swayed, the group not only announced for the Democrat but also issued a call for others of like mind to follow suit. Louis Anderson, DePriest's opponent in the Republican primary, was one who heeded the advice, becoming in the process Bronzeville's most powerful dissenter to hop on Mitchell's bandwagon.[20] Meanwhile, Mitchell and Democratic bosses were succeeding much better at forging party unity. Mavericks, independents, and dissidents such as Earl B. Dickerson had united under the party's banner, and even critics and former rivals such as Edgar Brown had shelved their differences with Mitchell and Tittinger long enough to assist with campaigning against Oscar DePriest. In some instances, support for FDR and a common belief in the New Deal accounted for Democratic togetherness. More often, however, DePriest had been responsible himself for fostering strong opposition to his reelection. During thirty-plus years in public life, he had made many enemies. Passionate animosity toward him existed, and it accounted for many reluctant swings

19. *Afro-American*, March 17, 1934; *Chicago Evening American*, August 28 and September 25, 1934; M to: EBD, August 8, 1934; Lawrence C. Jones, August 28, 1934; Locke, October 6, 1934, MP.

20. M to Caswell W. Crews, August 14, 1934; Crews to M, August 27, 1934; M to Louis B. Anderson, October 8, 1934; Campaign Bulletin, "What Lie Will They Tell Next?" MP; *Defender*, August 18 and 25 and September 15, 1934.

to Mitchell. According to several people close to the campaign and to Bronzeville politics, Mitchell had done little himself to aid his cause. Openly acknowledged as the lesser of two evils by many residents tired of DePriest, and as the unlikeliest of persons to reap a bonanza from a popular president, he was, indeed, the beneficiary of divergent support.[21]

Regardless, Mitchell was superb at keeping DePriest off balance. Except for a few casual acquaintances in the legal profession, not many people knew the challenger. Moreover, nobody had ever gotten very close to him. Yet he escaped close scrutiny during the election. There were no investigations by newspaper reporters or Republicans into his background to collaborate the credentials and claims he had provided. As a result, truths behind his lies and deceit remained secret throughout the election. According to an autobiographical sketch distributed to Bronzevillians, Mitchell had received degrees from Tuskegee, Harvard, and Columbia; Snow Hill Institute and Blackstone were not mentioned. In addition, for obvious reasons, there were no divulgences of the controversies surrounding Mitchell's career as an Alabama educator. All through the contest, he successfully deceived prospective voters. Despite puzzling circumstances and contradictions about his past, First District residents accepted him as a person of achievements and distinction in education and law. Amazing as well, no hurt or deceived person from Mitchell's past emerged to volunteer tidbits to the pro-Republican black press or to DePriest. Only Snow Hill's William J. Edwards tried to set events straight about Mitchell's education, but there was no intended vindictiveness. The headmaster had tucked away a correction of Mitchell's school record in a Birmingham newspaper's letters-to-the-editor section.[22]

Of course, there were factors contributing to Mitchell's charmed life that accounted for why he was able to hide his past without being suspected or detected. Most of all, his distinguished appearance and clear diction gave feasibility to everything about him. He combined pomposity, self-confidence, and flowing, error-free speech to great personal advantage. To contemporaries, there were no tipoffs that the person before them was a fake. His refined parlance was not the patois of a Southern black migrant with only minimal schooling. In addition, Mitchell's campaign, which emphasized impersonal appearances at rallies and large gatherings, perfectly matched his strengths. The campaign became an enjoyable encounter with the citizenry of the First District because Mitchell was able to impress people while keeping them an arm's length or farther away. Always a

21. Dickerson, Tittinger, Gibson, Cyrus, Spencer, and Thornton interviews; EBD to M, August 3, 1934; Edgar Brown to M, August 30, 1934, MP.

22. *Birmingham Advertiser* clipping, n.d., BP.

person in front of crowds rather than at close range, Mitchell exhibited neither personal inhibition nor circumspection. Not having the benefit of close contacts, the electorate, in its superficial comparisons of Mitchell and DePriest, understandably favored Mitchell. Although enigmatic and not adept at making or keeping friends, Mitchell fared better in front of audiences than his inept foe.[23]

None of this passed without notice. Mitchell, a master at detecting and exploiting human shortcomings, adroitly built a whole campaign around DePriest's weaknesses. In contrast, the incumbent—aware of his own deficiencies and cognizant of Mitchell's strengths from their 1932 presidential campaign encounters—avoided Arthur Mitchell as much as possible on the campaign circuit. DePriest definitely did not want head-on meetings with his rival in front of critical audiences. As a result, with one man wanting confrontation and the other not, Mitchell charted an offensive course, while DePriest became a hapless victim. Mitchell sensed DePriest's timidity and reluctance to debate. Having discovered DePriest's discomfort with public exchanges, he set everything in motion to exploit his advantage. The best campaign strategy, he decided, would be to trap DePriest with public challenges to square off at any time or place. Then only one of two things could occur: his foe would accept the bait, or he would reject it. Either response, Mitchell craftily calculated, would be a victory for him because both options exposed DePriest's vulnerability before the voters.

Given no place to hide, DePriest dealt Mitchell every trump card. No matter if there were face-to-face debates or attempts at dodging challenges, DePriest was bound to lose. Convinced that exposing his rival as tongue-tied or fainthearted would aid his own bid for Congress, Mitchell went at DePriest, persistently annoying him with open and private calls for public face-offs. Each time, the incumbent refused. Unable to admit why he had been avoiding discourse on the issues, DePriest desperately searched for campaign momentum. To compensate, he concocted strange rationale for opposing debates. In good conscience, fretted the overwhelmed incumbent, there could be no participation with someone guilty of hiding secret Southern backing. To debate openly, he countered halfheartedly, Mitchell must accept one condition: he must reveal all correspondence from Congressman "Duffie" of Alabama. Obviously tired of being hounded by Mitchell, DePriest was now hoping to place his aggravating adversary on the defensive. But to the Republican's consternation and surprise, Mitchell immediately complied and then renewed a call for debates. Perhaps worse than a new challenge, there was nothing

23. See chapter one and Dickerson, Tittinger, Gibson, Cyrus, Spencer, and Thornton interviews.

revealing in McDuffie's letters. Mitchell not only had foiled DePriest's attempt at shifting the campaign's drift but had also removed DePriest's weak excuse for not wanting exchanges. Nevertheless, it did not change DePriest's resolve; he adamantly opposed joint forums with Mitchell right up to the election. Of course, avoiding challenges opened up DePriest to attacks. With a miserable congressional record, Mitchell chided, DePriest had everything to fear from debate.[24]

At every turn, Mitchell assailed DePriest. Portrayed as Hoover's man and a New Deal enemy, the Republican remained on the defensive throughout the campaign. Candidly asked in flyers to explain votes against relief measures and for bailouts of wealthy men such as Charles Dawes, DePriest responded unconvincingly. His attempts at counter-punching failed to generate enthusiasm. One example of DePriest missing the mark completely involved Secretary of the Interior Harold L. Ickes. For incorrectly implying that the New Dealer had been holding up Public Works Administration funds earmarked for Chicago because of a personal dislike of machine politics under Mayor Kelly, DePriest only solidified the opposition's claims that he was uninformed. As desperately as DePriest wanted to kindle a fire with this issue, it yielded only more embarrassment after Ickes's immediate release of money. Elsewhere, DePriest encountered additional difficulties. Even among traditional allies, the GOP candidate found new sources of opposition. The black churches, which traditionally had supported the Republicans, were in flux. Following the example of past elections, DePriest's campaign planned to rely heavily on letter-writing blitzes to supportive ministers. In 1934, however, these appeals were not always garnering desirable results. Once-trusted churchmen had already begun to have second thoughts about Grand Old Party candidates. A few pastors had become Democrats after Roosevelt's election, and of Bronzeville's many church alliances, only one, the African Methodist Ministerial Association of Chicago, stayed with Oscar DePriest. Worse than defecting, Baptists were closing their sanctuaries to him and opening them to Mitchell and his election team. DePriest also hurt himself: his insensitivity at an inopportune moment further damaged his relationship with pastors. Angered by the betrayals of some prominent Baptists, DePriest remarked that "Negro ministers of Chicago are a bunch of hungry beggars, and that you could buy them and their entire congregation with a Thanksgiving turkey." Advised of his foe's faux pas, Mitchell immediately turned it to his advantage.[25]

24. M to DePriest, October 4, 15, and 26, and November 3, 1934; DePriest to M, October 14, 1934; undated position paper entitled "DePriest Afraid to Meet Mitchell in Debate," MP; *Chicago World*, October 20, 1934.

25. Campaign pamphlet, "Let DePriest Answer!" n.d.; untitled and undated draft of a MNR; position paper, "DePriest against Public Work and Relief Program," n.d.,

Mitchell's disclosure of his uncomplimentary assessment of churchmen became another nasty problem for DePriest to overcome. Unable to turn the campaign into something positive, DePriest continued to suffer from his clever upstart's impregnability. Almost always under siege, he was too occupied with dodging debates, soothing hurt ministers, or defending a weak legislative record to mount anything resembling a counteroffensive. Whenever calm seemed about to appear, Mitchell reappeared with new charges. DePriest retaliated ineffectively because he had not found a really explosive issue. That so little was known about his opponent made Mitchell impervious to attacks. When DePriest was not defending himself, he went on boringly with prattle about the Republicans' wonderful treatment of blacks and Democratic homage to the Ku Klux Klan. No DePriest speech was ever complete without his repetition of Frederick Douglass's famous metaphor about the "Republican Party being the ship and all the rest the sea." As for Mitchell, DePriest tried frantically to tie him to a grand Southern conspiracy, but the challenger smartly took the issue away by pointing to constructive Southerners. With regard to FDR, DePriest babbled in abstractions about coming perils from the New Deal. There was no sting in the incumbent's bid, and worse, his rallies lacked excitement and new faces. Reflecting their candidate's dullness, GOP-sponsored events featured old-timers such as Roscoe Conkling Simmons rehashing worn tales of Lincoln, Emancipation, and Reconstruction. Short on funds and effective field-workers, DePriest sunk to addressing "dear friend" letters to constituents. But because of his misuse of congressional franking privileges, even these got him into trouble. Given a sample of what DePriest forces had sent, Mitchell went to postal authorities for an opinion and to reporters for publicity. Fearing negative attention and even prosecution for mailing political messages at the expense of taxpayers, DePriest sheepishly ordered campaign staffers to stamp all future election-related mailings.[26]

In contrast to the GOP's uninteresting campaign, Mitchell's bid was colorful. It featured new faces and clever, attention-grabbing literature, and everything about it appeared brisk and imaginative. To show exactly what FDR had done for blacks, Democrats arranged for Sylvester Harris and his mule to come to Chicago from rural Mississippi. National fame

MP; M to DePriest, November 3, 1934; Albert B. George to the Rev. D. Z. Jackson, October 10, 1934; Jackson to George, October 16, 1934; M to Dr. L. K. Williams, August 28, 1934, MP; *Chicago Sunday Bee*, August 26, 1934; *Chicago Tribune*, August 22, 1934; *Defender*, August 25, 1934.

26. DePriest to "My dear friend," n.d.; M to Patton, October 16, 1934; M to JAF, August 27, 1934; Mitchell handbill, "Mitchell Declares DePriest will not Tell the Truth," n.d., MP; *Chicago Daily News*, September 25, 1934; Spencer interview.

had come earlier to the black farmer. For help with a debt-ridden farm, the Mississippian had talked on the telephone with "Mr. Roosevelt." Harris's conversation had brought presidential intervention that forestalled bankers bent on seizure. In Bronzeville as Mitchell's honored guest, Harris made several cameo appearances in his bib overalls and with his mule. As curious First District residents listened attentively, he told them of his mortgage problems, his telephone call to the White House, and FDR's personal help. Unlike the humble Harris, whose notoriety had come from naïveté, several black Democrats in the campaign were professional men and women who shared Mitchell's rationale for leaving the Republican party. Like Mitchell, they had come as white-collar newcomers to Chicago, and they also had "tired of butting head[s] against a brick wall and not getting anywhere." Unseating Oscar DePriest had become many gifted people's outlet, and there was spirit in their response; they gave the Democratic drive an element missing in the humdrum effort of the GOP. In terms of outside talent drawn to Bronzeville, Mitchell enjoyed a decisive advantage. After all, his bid was tied to Roosevelt's and Kelly's popular administrations. Immediately after the emergency slating, the mayor was on hand in August, assisting Mitchell at a giant kickoff rally held at the fashionable Regal Theatre. Afterward, for dissemination among First District residents, the Machine provided a voluminous flood of eye-catching, colorfully drawn campaign leaflets.[27] Fresh and provocative with flattering endorsements by most noteworthy Democrats, these materials were spread by brigades of paid Democratic precinct workers to voters. Aimed mostly at black residents who were unsure of switching their allegiance to the Democrats, these slick pamphlets touted the party's accomplishments among the minority. Filled with pictures and biographical sketches of black officeholders and public-sector employees, these slick booklets appealed to both racial pride and partisanship.

Of the many handbills tailored and circulated to benefit Mitchell, the works of political cartoonist Proctor Chisholm were the cleverest and most artful. Short and to the point, Chisholm's penetrating comic strips were extraordinary at picturing DePriest and the Grand Old Party in embarrassing situations. Chisholm's jestful captioned drawings successfully captured all the key criticisms of the Republican incumbent, and they injected degrees of levity into an otherwise serious campaign. Of the talented artist's cartoons, none showed more creative genius and vitality than his rendering of "DePriest and The Negro Gold Star Mothers,"

27. Tittinger, Spencer, Cyrus, Thornton, Gibson, and Dickerson interviews; pamphlet, "President Roosevelt Saved His Little Farm"; Locke endorsement, n.d.; Owen to M, October 17, 1934; three position papers, n.d., MP; *Pittsburgh Courier,* September 29, 1929; *Chicago World,* October 27, 1934; *Crisis,* December 1934.

tandem sketches that poked sarcasm at DePriest on hand in silence to watch as sad-faced black pilgrims bound for their soldier-sons' European graves faced the indignity of traveling on a cattle ship. These drawings recalled DePriest's passive unwillingness to challenge President Hoover's and Secretary of War Patrick J. Hurley's shabby treatment of the mothers of African Americans who had died in World War I. The penetrating sketches were representative of the creativity and brilliance of Chisholm's contributions.[28]

Although bombarding prospective voters with imaginative campaign literature and bringing special people such as Sylvester Harris to Chicago required financing, the party's response was often inconsistent with its stated goals. To hear many Democrats, the party was united behind Mitchell. But they were not always willing to contribute. Setting a poor example, Pat Nash's Cook County organization was most stingy with its funds. Three weeks before the election, it had contributed only $250 toward Mitchell's financially pressed campaign. The limited funding affected Mitchell's bid for Congress. Always short of cash, his war chest needed constant replenishing. By election day, after he had exhausted all his liquid assets, only his stock in Mutual Housing remained. According to records and to Mitchell's testimony, his severe underfunding had reduced his personal worth by almost $2,000, and it had forced alterations or cancellations of several plans. During the campaign's closing week, his miseries over the dismal state of monetary affairs forced him to begin a major appeal for funds. From all indications, the last-hour solicitations absorbed as much of Mitchell's time as did a canvass for votes.[29]

As disheartening as poor finances had become, Mitchell gathered encouragement from other factors. Unlike many of his predecessors, Roosevelt's popularity was not waning at midterm, and his New Deal programs were retaining popularity with voters. Reasons for optimism were coming as well from several black newspapers, although as a whole the Chicago press was polarized and often vituperative. Unlike the *World*'s

28. Proctor Chisholm cartoons: "Hasn't He Been at the trough long enough?" "Mitchell challenges DePriest to debate," "He knows how to make Promises when he wants votes. He knows how to double-cross after getting votes," "MITCHELL! Stopped him," and "DePriest and The Negro Gold Star Mothers"; pamphlets, "The Truth About Oscar DePriest and Arthur W. Mitchell" and "A New Deal for the Negro!"; M to Chisholm, January 24, 1935, MP.

29. JMc to JAF, September 2, 1934; JMc to M, September 21, 1934; M to JAF, October 3, 1934; M to Emil Hurja, October 13 and 31, 1934; M to Nash, October 16 and 31, 1934; Hurja to M, October 22, 1934; M to Jacob M. Arvey et al., October 30–31, 1934, MP. M's general ledger shows receipts of $50 from Howard's Alain Locke, $100 each from two Chicago politicians, and $100 from DePriest foe, Louis B. Anderson. M contributed $546 of the $1,325 collected. Printing and publicity costs were the largest outlays.

Jacob Tipper, who declared early for Mitchell, the *Defender* gave its endorsement to DePriest on November 3. This stand was no surprise, because staff writer Douglas Bainbridge had been preparing readers for eventual opposition to Mitchell with a series of pro-DePriest articles. In these, Bainbridge had depicted Mitchell as a "carpetbagger" under the control and sponsorship of Southern forces who had been responsible for peonage, Scottsboro, and lynching. The endorsement contained some of this old-fashioned GOP rhetoric, but its main appeal was more to common sense than to partisanship. Clearly "not a political bird of passage," DePriest, noted the editor, deserved another term because of his record of service to "his state, his country, and his Race. He has served them well and faithfully. . . . He helped to make the opportunities for Race men and women what they are today."[30]

Given a choice for congressional representative, First District voters decided a New Dealer was preferable to a conservative. Mitchell outpolled DePriest, winning 27,963 votes to the incumbent's 24,829. With almost seventy years of voting traditions in apparent flux, few experts could have forecast the final result. There was also the DePriest factor to contemplate—how popular was he? Having never contested another black in a general election, he finally had received a fair test of his personal popularity. Without an African American opponent in earlier contests, there had been no way of knowing whether blacks had supported him or simply voted against his white opponents. Notwithstanding the many unusual circumstances surrounding a race with two black candidates, DePriest had done well by winning 47 percent of the votes. Throughout a hard, bitterly fought campaign, he had been the object of public scrutiny and harsh criticism; Mitchell, on the other hand, had been an aggressive shadowboxer capably landing blows at will but totally impervious to counterattack. Mitchell had known where and when to strike him, while he had not ascertained his opponent's weaknesses. He had also suffered from the Republican party's disarray and from poor judgment. Meanwhile, Mitchell had benefited from many advantages, not least of which were the Kelly Machine's manpower and FDR's New Deal.

Pondering his victory, Mitchell immediately deceived himself into thinking it had been a measure of his personal appeal. He assumed in particular that a majority of voters had sought "intelligent, courageous, honest and capable representation in the Halls of Congress, which I contend the First District has not had during the past six years. I think

30. Editorial survey, *Journal and Guide, Pittsburgh Courier, Afro-American, Cleveland Gazette, Argus,* and *Amsterdam News* (New York); *Defender,* October 20 and 27 and November 3, 1934; *Chicago World,* August 11, 1934.

the people are tired of bombast, ballyhoo and noise, where we should have constructive thought, honest action and real statesmanship." While perhaps true of his white supporters, Mitchell's assessment definitely did not hit the mark among blacks who had voted for him. DePriest might have been feuding for years with a minority of blacks, but fighting was only one of many causes accounting for his defeat. During three earlier elections to Congress, DePriest had overcome dissidents, but a change over which he would have no control had already begun by November 1934. Enough African Americans had bolted Lincoln's GOP for Roosevelt's Democratic party to precipitate problems. More than other factors, the impact of party switching had been most damaging to DePriest. His defeat occurred because many Bronzevillians had concluded that he had stayed "too old fashioned and out of date for the streamline age of [the] New Deal."[31]

By no means a major shift, the changing allegiances of 1934 were only a prelude to a much greater movement of Chicago blacks to the Democratic party later in the decade. In 1934, DePriest could take one pleasure from the voting statistics: they revealed him as Bronzeville's clear favorite. He had still won a majority of the black vote. He had done almost as well among longtime constituents in 1934 as he had in three previous elections. Among blacks, Mitchell had obtained just enough votes from the emerging Roosevelt Revolution to win. Using 1932 and 1934 election statistics from the mostly black Second Ward, one sees an unfolding shift. A precinct-by-precinct comparative analysis of the two years reveals only a slight movement to the Democratic column, but the percentage change was insignificant. Yet coupled to Mitchell's overwhelming plurality among whites, it was enough to defeat DePriest.[32]

On Wednesday morning, November 7, 1934, as news of Mitchell's decisive victory spread across the nation, excitement and expectation were evident throughout the First District. The mood was somewhat subdued, however, at the East Forty-Seventh Street address where Mitchell had his office. Since mid-morning, a friendly, orderly crowd had been assembling there. An optimistic but patient assembly of curious neighbors, inquisitive reporters, and hopeful supporters was jubilantly filling an entrance foyer and anteroom and was crowding the outside sidewalk. All had joined in common resolve to see and hear their new leader. When the noon hour struck, Mitchell emerged from solace and solitude to face the several hundred well-wishers on hand to greet him. Already clad in his overcoat,

31. Undated MNR; Marshall L. Shepard to Jackson, November 2, 1934; Elvy E. Callaway to M, February 14, 1939, MP.
32. *Chicago Tribune*, November 8, 1934.

he had hoped to join Annie and Wergs Mitchell for a quiet lunch at their apartment, ten blocks north on South Parkway, but the throng at his doorstep did not permit it. Occasionally as a gesture of a desire to leave, Mitchell put on his hat. Since nobody was taking the hint, the victor resigned himself to staying. For thirty-odd minutes, he accommodated the crowd with a winning politician's entertainment of reading telegrams, shaking hands, and being gracious about the attention. Undoubtedly more for the special benefit of reporters putting pencils to pads and less for curious citizens, Mitchell delivered a rambling monologue about the election, his life, and his plans. The win, as he interpreted it, was both "a vote for Roosevelt and recovery" and a "turning point in the campaign of bitterness waged by some northern Negro leaders against southern white people." Then, as he often did on such occasions with an audience to impress, he retold how a sixty-six-mile walk to Tuskegee had brought Booker T. Washington's guidance and influence into his life. Regarding his goals as a member of Congress, Mitchell asserted that nothing was any more important than a proposed "American citizens first" bill. Without elaboration, he simply noted that Americans and not aliens should receive first preference for jobs. There were also pledges to work "incessantly" for antilynching legislation and for legal action against job discrimination.

The spontaneous session revealed sides of Mitchell rarely seen in public. He pointed affectionately to Annie's picture and produced another of Wergs, whom he proudly noted was a University of Michigan graduate finishing an advanced degree nearby at the University of Chicago. For a man known to keep such family matters private, these were rare public glimpses. His patience was remarkable as well a day after his greatest triumph. Mitchell could be brusque and unkind after there had been interferences with his plans. Now during these moments together with mostly strangers, he was generous, showing even compassionate empathy. By appearances, the victory and its consequences had had a cathartic effect on him. For once, there appeared no traces of inferiority and anxiety; instead, he was enjoying the role of political spoiler. Unshackled and released on center stage, the often dour man's smile and humble words now radiated warmth, pleasure, and even gratitude. As he put it before leaving for his later-than-planned lunch, "Oh, yes, thank you. It was a fine victory and I owe it to all of you."[33]

Not far away another story unfolded. DePriest, with only a loyal secretary at his side, counted and recounted election returns. Edgar Riley of the *Home News* described a broken and weary man in defeat, looking "indeed, the shaggy lion of Illinois politics; a wounded lion though,

33. *Chicago Daily News*, November 8, 1934.

striking out at enemies that were too numerous for his clutches." As Congress's only black lawmaker, DePriest had devoted himself to African American burdens. After having assumed the duty with fervor, he felt betrayal and abandonment. Election results revealed for him just how many Bronzevillians had opted for an opponent proud of Southern white friends with hateful pro-segregation records. Engulfed in bitterness, the congressman still generously wished Mitchell well.[34]

Since Mitchell's rise had been sudden, most Americans were not acquainted with him or his views. Therefore, reporters searching for answers besieged him for information. Without explanation, Mitchell granted only one day-after interview. The honor strangely went to the *Gary American*'s Frank M. Davis. In the afternoon when Davis entered the Forty-Seventh Street office, he found Mitchell seated behind a messy desk cluttered with legal papers, congratulatory mail, and telegrams. Davis described Mitchell as "light brown, pleasant faced and voiced with hair almost totally gray. Smaller in stature and without the striking appearance of DePriest, Mitchell nevertheless has a quiet distinction and his words carry strong conviction when he speaks." Mitchell's reluctance to talk about himself surprised the newspaperman. After considerable coaxing and prompting, there were confessions to liking Howard-Lincoln football games, baseball, fishing, and drives alone on open roads in responsive but comfortable cars. Probing further, Davis ascertained Mitchell's plans for operating a congressional office. Claiming to "detest formality," the victor promised to be unaffected by Capitol Hill. "It will not be necessary to go through a lot of red tape to see me. I plan to be as easy to reach and talk with as I have ever been." After trying to focus on personal matters without great success, Davis turned to politics, asking Mitchell for his impressions of the election. Suddenly, the conversation became animated. Mitchell said his opponent's defeat had confirmed the New Deal's and Roosevelt's great popularity. His campaign for Congress was "one of the cleanest ever waged in Chicago" because its focus had set the record straight about an incumbent and his party. A strategy of informing the electorate had functioned according to plan. The First District had expressed itself for change, and truth and facts had triumphed over lies. At least, these were Mitchell's interpretations for Davis. The victor volunteered something else about the results as well. By making the election a mandate on Southern whites, Mitchell said, the win had given them vindication; none of the Republicans' desperate attempts at character assassination by association had succeeded. Besmirching and trying to link a black Democrat to Southern extremists had failed with the electorate

34. *Chicago Home News*, November 10, 1934; DePriest to M, November 7, 1934, MP.

because the voters had recognized all the outrageous charges for what they were: thin covers for DePriest's inadequacies. Mitchell explained that only die-hard GOP partisans had been foolish enough to accept shallow accusations about a Dixie plot aimed at removing an affront to segregation. About the charge that he was too friendly with certain lawmakers from below the Mason-Dixon Line, Mitchell had no apologies to make for these or any other relationships because "a man ought to have as many friends as he can make and retain." Besides, he was intending to "plan for the best interests of both races without sacrificing one particle of principle or character."[35]

The NAACP was particularly interested in Mitchell. After having enjoyed a good working relationship with DePriest, NAACP officers were disturbed by the election's outcome because it cost them a personal friend in Congress. Thereafter, several of them joined national efforts that honored DePriest. Meanwhile, when the disappointing news of the election reached the executive board, there were no leadership files on or firsthand knowledge of Mitchell; only tidbits assembled from newspapers and hearsay picked up here and there were available in New York. Short on information, the organization turned to Chicago resident and news expert Claude Barnett. The founder and head of the Associated Negro Press used the opportunity to portray Mitchell as a man unworthy of NAACP trust and support. Better knowledge of him, observed Barnett, inclined people to "discount him" more. Help to the candidate during his bid for office came only because of supporters' "grudges" with DePriest or desires for personal rewards. According to Barnett, Mitchell seemed at first blush "a reasonably friendly and intelligent personality," but on closer contact, he revealed himself to be "a four-flusher and an Uncle Tom." Barnett noted how a check into Mitchell's educational records had identified exaggerations. In point of fact and contrary to all claims, he had "from all the records available . . . little more, if any, formal training than DePriest." As for the black Democrat's Southern white friends, Barnett quoted Frederick Sullens of the *Jackson Daily News*. Obviously elated that Oscar DePriest would no longer "strut his stuff in the halls of Congress," Sullens, an unabashed racist editor, was happy as well because the incumbent's replacement was a " 'white man's nigger.' " Barnett ended his unflattering evaluation of Mitchell with DePriest's advice to blacks about why they should not befriend white Southerners: "It is impossible to satisfy the southern white man and serve the welfare of the American Negro." Negative opinions from Barnett did not affect the NAACP's first official statement about the DePriest-Mitchell contest. In a short article

35. *Gary American*, November 16, 1934.

entitled "New Congressman," *Crisis,* the monthly house organ of the NAACP, repeated Mitchell's own educational claims and summarized campaign high points such as Sylvester Harris's appearance. Without commentary or criticism, the essay stated Mitchell's New Deal devotion, his support for a soldiers' bonus bill, and his intention not "to stress the race issue in congress." Exchanges between Walter White and Roy Wilkins in December explain in part the willingness to give Mitchell an impartial first hearing. Previewing Wilkins's article for January's *Crisis,* White reminded that "newspaper reporters, intentionally or unintentionally, misquote persons they are interviewing." Hence, he thought it "a little harsh to accept at full value the statements put into Mr. Mitchell's mouth." White suggested replacement of "modifying phrases such as 'he declared' by 'he was quoted as follows.'" Restraint and a wait-and-see policy were in the NAACP's best interest. Annoying and alienating a new representative over some alleged remarks without first ascertaining their validity or context would obviously serve no useful end. Indeed, if Mitchell were a tool, as his many critics were charging, the fact would reveal itself soon enough. White reasoned premature judgments could drive a permanent wedge between his organization and Congress's lone black, and that would be a disheartening development certain to strengthen the will of segregationists to foil civil rights progress and antilynching legislation.[36]

For the most part, African Americans reacted to reportage of the upset victory without Barnett's rancor or the NAACP's caution. Many greetings came from humble working people, but many more arrived from black professionals. Some like Chicago Urban League Executive Secretary A. L. Foster had written more to instruct than to congratulate. Foster exhorted Mitchell to maintain DePriest's most cooperative record with the local chapter. More to the point of how to succeed, President R. R. Wright of Wilberforce College also advised pursuit of the loser's agenda "with the same dignity and fearlessness."[37] Understandably, correspondents often combined congratulatory words with speaking invitations. Had Mitchell dared to accept every offer, much of his first year in office would have

36. KM to WW, December 7, 1934; WW to KM, December 12, 1934; Claude A. Barnett to Frances Williams, November 15, 1934; Memorandum, WW to RW, December 11, 1934; RW to WW, December 12, 1934, NAACP; Pickens to M, November 8, 1934, MP.

37. A. L. Foster to M, November 14, 1934. For a cross section of responses, check the following letters to M from: Rhonda A. Hanley, James A. Yard, John A. Royall, C. B. Broussard, George N. White, November 7, 1934; Mary Williams, DeWitt T. Alcorn, November 8, 1934; Thomas W. Turner, Willard Morrow, November 9, 1934; Charles M. Jenkins, November 10, 1934; Wendell Erwin, Jesse M. Jamieson, November 12, 1934; Oliver, November 13, 1934; Jose G. Inerarity, December 11, 1934; R. R. Wright to M, November 14, 1934, MP.

been occupied with touring college campuses and speaking before various groups.[38]

Mitchell was not prepared for the inundation of invitations. Before seeing that there would be no way to accommodate everybody, Mitchell tended to irritate, frustrate, or anger many of those asking him to appear. Obviously at a loss to know how to deal tactfully with the problem of refusing people, he overextended himself and invariably disappointed his hosts by canceling appearances or by last-moment wavering. In his mix-up with Pure Food Co-Operative Grocery Stores of New York, both offenses occurred. Mitchell's first response predicated acceptance on the New Yorkers' agreeing to round-trip airfare and a free admission policy. After they had granted his wishes and set in motion a December 20, 1934, engagement, Mitchell wrote his hosts a vaguely worded note about the date's inconvenience. Embarrassed and peeved by his response, they had trouble grasping the full implications. Was he not able to come because of scheduling problems, or had something else caused a last-hour cancelation? Their uncertainty about his motives ruffled Mitchell. Upset that his strange explanations had not sufficed, he snapped back a response that stated his general displeasure with everything associated with the New Yorkers' invitation.[39] After a few such mishaps, Mitchell learned some important lessons; the New York mix-up led to policies on speaking appearances. Most importantly, he learned to say no firmly, promptly, and diplomatically. For releases from promises, his favorite excuse became pressing constituent and legislative duties. For spurns, he often used sponsoring bodies' racial makeups. For rejecting offers on this basis, he had no hard-and-fast applications, however. One group could be too black, and the next one not black enough. He refused some requests for appearances because organizations did not have strong enough interests in African Americans, and he spurned invitations from others because they were obsessed with race. Mitchell also set new conditions for accepting engagements. He generally did not want event sponsors charging for admission, and if the specified events were many miles from Washington, he required round-trip airfares. In pressing for the first, he liked to emphasize "that a Congressman should be heard by the citizens of the country, and that they should not be required to pay as they do in theatres and other forms of amusement and entertainment."[40]

38. See MP between November 7 and December 15, 1934.
39. George W. Hicks to M, November 19 and December 3 and 8, 1934; M to Hicks, November 26 and December 6 and 10, 1934, MP.
40. M to: William N. DeBerry, November 24, 1934; Eugene F. Cheeks, November 26 and December 6, 1934; J. W. Jones, November 27, 1934; Alan L. Dingle, December 11, 1934; J. M. Ragland, December 14, 1934, MP.

Most letters directed to Mitchell during the joyous interval between the election and the Seventy-Fourth Congress's opening in early January were supportive, but there were exceptions; not every writer complimented DePriest's conqueror or invited him to speak. William H. Davis of the *Amsterdam News* was the faultfinding correspondent who best communicated misgivings. After reading an overview of the politician's thoughts, Davis had no need to wait for explanations. Just seeing Mitchell's opinion that there was "no prejudice against my people in the present Administration" was enough to sour his assessment of Chicago's new congressman. From Apostle Saint Paul, Davis found appropriate rebuttal to an overly generous conclusion about the Roosevelt government, asking the rhetorical question, too, " 'Oh death, where is thy sting, oh grave, where is thy misery.' " Few longtime Mitchell enemies with scores to settle struck with Davis's vigor and vituperation. Some, such as District of Columbia attorney Charles S. Cuney, did not strike at all. Years before in 1919, Cuney had introduced Mitchell to municipal Washington and had assisted him with law studies several years later. Although a dispute over money subsequently damaged their relationship, the one-time friend offered after the election to "let bygones be bygones" and to "assist . . . in any and all the ways it is humanely possible . . . to assist." As Cuney perceived reactions, resolving to forget seemed generous in contrast to other Washington blacks who "have their axes all sharpened up to do all they can to make things unpleasant for you." Honing their weapons must have occupied the "axe-wielders" because none ever bothered Mitchell with threatening letters. On a more pleasant note, many friends who had not communicated with him for years resurfaced during the honeymoon period with congratulations. From Mitchell's hometown in Alabama, Roanoke postmaster S. H. Tatum was one who remembered him. Tatum's message pleased him almost as much as the victory over DePriest had. Clara Mitchell later recalled her husband speaking fondly of his boyhood companion and of how the two had lost track of each other, only to be reunited after the 1934 election. Tatum and his "little family cheered last Tuesday [on election] night when we listened over the radio, that you had beaten DePriest by four to one. Then we went to bed feeling fine that one of my boyhood friends of another color had been so signally honored." Not surprisingly, there were also offers of help. If quarters in New York City were ever needed, nephew Roosevelt Mitchell Stubbs would have a room ready for "Uncle Arthur." Alain Locke and Edgar G. Brown, longtime Mitchell associates from the District of Columbia, tendered driving skills. Thinking a restful ride would be helpful to the Mitchells, Locke and Brown suggested a drive "about the hills and valleys of Virginia, where trod the mighty Washington and immortal Jefferson, for like them you are the representative of the new order in the life of the Race and a noble champion of President Roosevelt's New Deal."[41]

On the other side, DePriest's many black enemies and detractors were gleeful. Disgusted with the defeated incumbent, they could not restrain their joy. Hailing his foe became their outlet for ventilating happiness for DePriest's misfortune. The Reverend William S. Braddan of Chicago's Berean Baptist Church typified this category of defilers. Feeling DePriest had slighted and insulted him early in the congressional race, Braddan had been unable to forgive his tormentor; rather, he had chosen Mitchell. Jubilant on election night that "modern David" had triumphed over "the Goliath of Egotism, the promoter of Race Antagonism, and do Nothing," the minister decided, nevertheless, to delay communicating with Mitchell because he wanted to give the congressman-elect's "multitude of new friends . . . an opportunity to shower . . . admiration, born over night." Mitchell did not become David to every grudge-holder, but some postelection expressions of support were attributable to DePriest's strong tendencies for abusiveness and ruthlessness. As a generalization, Claude Barnett's immediate characterization was correct. Much of Mitchell's support was lukewarm; letters to him implied as much. Ballots cast for him often were proxy votes against an incumbent whom many political insiders had considered arrogant and oppressive. Even outside Bronzeville, there were some disgusted individuals who found requital in backing Mitchell.[42]

Many correspondents missed the election's special significance. Inasmuch as the winner had broken a color barrier in the Democratic party, there was little recognition of Mitchell's victory as a black Democrat. The racial minority gave little notice or attention to the achievement of this milestone. Of many hundreds of African Americans complimenting him, only Howard University history professor Carter G. Woodson and two others recognized this historic "first." Woodson aptly called it a "new chapter." In terms of the election's overall meaning for racial politics, Southern whites attached greater initial significance to Mitchell's victory than did most blacks. On front pages and in editorials, even obscure papers such as the *Durham Morning Herald* and the *Anniston Star* chronicled the special "negro news." The triumph over the much-hated Oscar DePriest focused their attention. Here in the region where human bondage had

41. William H. Davis to M, November 9, 1934; Charles S. Cuney to M, November 17, 1934; MNR, with undated *Chicago World* quote; Roosevelt M. Stubbs to M, November 22, 1934; EGB to M, November 8, 1934, MP; Mitchell interview.

42. William S. Braddan to M, November 9, 1934; Broussard to DePriest, November 7, 1934; C. S. Hammond to M, November 11, 1934, MP; Barnett to Williams, November 15, 1934, NAACP.

its roots and where race influenced development, there appeared something of a consensus among the majority that the newly elected black Democrat was somehow "one of them." Like Southern whites, Northern white Democrats also tended to recognize the special context of Mitchell's victory. They heralded a party triumph, while sensing "a most important political development, THE NEGROES HAVE LEARNED TO VOTE DEMOCRATIC." As party chairman, James A. Farley was worried its immediate ramifications might create something of a paradoxical dilemma for Democrats. Undoubtedly like others in the party's upper echelon, he privately had misgivings about Mitchell. Later, when reporters pressed him for his initial reactions, there were no revealing public comments. Aware of the Democrats' fragile coalition and afraid of adverse reactions to a black's presence in party and congressional circles, Farley refused to assess or predict anything. He simply did not want to engage in public speculation about a Southern response to Mitchell. Indeed, the win was a strange affair for the Democratic chairman. As party spokesman and its highest-ranking official, Farley wanted to attract votes, but as a realist and skeptic, he wondered how to handle segregation, the South, and Mitchell without jeopardizing Roosevelt. Lacking answers for the moment, he deflected all matters relating to the Chicago win to Emil Hurja, an underling. Ostensibly to test for reactions and weaken opposition, Hurja presented Mitchell in the best possible light, linking him to John McDuffie and distinguishing him from trouble-making Oscar DePriest. Hurja kept options open for Farley and the party. If Mitchell's election caused embarrassment, the chairman could disavow his assistant's statements as an individual's opinions and not the official pronouncements of the administration or the Democratic party. Privately, Farley gave stern advice to Mitchell. Without being specific, he counseled against "making any commitments, or in any way tying up with any special group." Entering office devoid of entanglements and promises would ensure "greater freedom" and "greater possibility for success." Farley was not explicit about any of this, but the instructions were clear enough for Mitchell to understand. If he wanted to have a long political career and rewards, he must set Democratic party interests first and shun all disruptive programs and dissident individuals.[43]

43. To M from: Carter G. Woodson, November 20, 1934; Ransom, November 20, 1934; Theophilius M. Mann, November 7, 1934; C. C. Spaulding, November 15, 1934; W. L. Walker, November 14, 1934; G. R. Saxon, November 9, 1934; JMc, November 7, 1934; S. W. Bowen, November 9, 1934, JAF, November 15, 1934; undated MNR; undated *Norfolk News and Observer*, MP; *Durham Morning Herald*, November 13, 1934; *Anniston Star* (Ala.), November 18, 1934; *Montgomery Advertiser*, November 9, 1934; *Raleigh News and Observer*, November 9, 1934; *Jackson Daily*

Being directed and instructed by the likes of Chairman Farley, Mayor Kelly, and Representative McDuffie did not upset Mitchell, but being besieged by clamorers after his attention and favors annoyed him very much. From many wrong perceptions of his postelection tribulations, Mitchell exaggerated African American expectations of him. He incorrectly sensed that every black man and woman was asking for something from him. There were prison inmates petitioning his help with paroles, and a Fisk University student looking for a public relations job. Even Mitchell's personal haberdasher from Bronzeville was looking for something. According to the clothier's request, he "would much more desire to be a messenger of Congressman Mitchell, in Washington, than selling suits and overcoats" in Chicago. Worse yet were the scores of blacks who had concluded that procurements of assistance with sundry problems should come easier from Mitchell than from their own white legislators. Some naive people actually assumed the new lawmaker to be so generous and rich that he would loan or give them money. Even more alarming for somebody needing to demonstrate restraint for bosses were demands on him to act responsively on behalf of African Americans. If pursued as directed, most of this unsolicited advice would have placed Mitchell at risk. Unknown to the race, he was under clear orders to be much more circumspect and far less obstinate about turbulent racial matters than Oscar DePriest had been.[44]

Almost every request made of Mitchell after his election transcended realistic expectations, especially when laid against the realities of what an inexperienced congressman could change in a legislative body dominated by seniority and of the obstacles created by Roosevelt's dependence upon Southern Democrats. Like others new to Capitol Hill, Mitchell did not possess enough clout to effect major changes. For coping with a floodstream of diverse requests pouring into him from everywhere, he adopted a standard, no-help response. He explained politely why a House member

News, November 9, 1934, with unidentified clipping and commentary, BP; *Defender,* November 10 and 17 and December 8, 1934; *Chicago Herald and Examiner,* December 10, 1934.

44. JAF to M, November 15, 1934; EJK to M, December 20, 1934; M to JMc, January 4, 1936; in 1934, M had received advice and request mail from: Harry C. Brown, C. H. Calloway, J. H. Clinton, and George W. Prince, November 7; K. David Cammack, November 8; Hazel D. Johnson and Bert Cumby, November 9; Edwin L. Clarke, November 10; Catherine S. Scott, November 15; Royall and Dingle, November 16; Loving, November 17; Fred Minnis, November 22; Robert Perkins, November 26; Robert C. Von Stinson Jr., December 7; Henry R. Tolliver, December 12; Adlene Davis, December 16; Isaac Webb, December 28. M responded to: Smedley, December 3; George E. Washington and Perkins, December 7; Toliver and Mrs. A. B. Knox, December 19; Ridgeway, December 14; Webb, December 31, MP.

from Chicago could not serve both a district constituency and every black American. Logical as his answer might have been, it lost Mitchell much favor because he also suggested blacks with problems should try their own elected officials first before turning to him for help. Given the complicity of many legislators in the issues at hand, his advice appeared callous if not ludicrous, especially when the petitioners were from the Deep South and their complaints concerned discrimination.[45] With regard to interracial activities, another factor about Mitchell should not be missed; he deliberately wanted to placate Southern whites. Nobody knew any better than he why DePriest had become such a focal point of Southern rage and hatred. Now, on the eve of a congressional career, when he was under the closest scrutiny and the most pressure to please, Mitchell did not intend to provoke a key element of the ruling coalition.

One of the most humorous results of Mitchell's meteoric rise to national prominence involved Talladega College. Biographical sketches released during and after the 1934 election listed it as one of several schools Mitchell attended. Naturally enough as president of the Alabama school, Buell G. Gallagher had special pride. When he congratulated the winner, there was the impression that the school "had a share in your career." In the excitement of wanting to honor "one of Talladega's sons," the registrar checked for Mitchell's academic records and found no evidence of his attendance at the college. Apparently unsuspecting at this point and sensing nothing odd, Gallagher became "considerably embarrassed over this fact." In a second communication, the educator noted how much school officials would appreciate knowing details of Mitchell's studies and graduation. Here, in what could have been a damaging discovery, the politician bluffed successfully. Without a moment's hesitation, he coolly responded with a correction about his time at Talladega. A gap in the records and confusion existed, he confided, because presumptions about him being an alumnus were wrong. During the 1899–1900 school year, he claimed, he had attended but not completed a study program in the college's normal department. Hence, nobody had kept enrollment records. The explanation satisfied Gallagher, and there were no further probes.[46]

Amid the hoopla of the halcyon days when Mitchell was not personally involved with acknowledgments, requests, reporters, or law, he was busily touring, speaking, and vacationing. Since he was away from

45. Typical responses to Southern blacks went from M to: Smedley, December 3, 1934; Washington and Perkins, December 7, 1934; Tolliver and Mrs. A. B. Knox, December 19, 1934; Ridgeway, December 14, 1934; Webb, December 31, 1934, MP.
46. Gallagher to M, November 8 and December 4, 1934; M to Gallagher, December 6, 1934, MP.

Illinois most of the time, a "wonderful turkey dinner" held in his honor November 20 at a Bronzeville hotel and hosted by the Chicago Democratic Lawyers Club became the memorable highlight of his few days spent in the First District. The dinner attracted a biracial crowd of more than two hundred judges, politicians, and lawyers to the Vincennes Hotel for an evening with Mitchell. After many introductions and short toasts, the podium belonged to the black New Dealer. As with Mitchell's speeches at this time, the pre-Thanksgiving address made one point "plain" for all to realize; becoming "a Negro Congressman" was not his goal.[47]

Black professional colleagues who feted Mitchell in Chicago had been forced to wedge the dinner into their guest's hectic travel schedule. His first trip as a newly elected official followed only by days his triumph over DePriest. For unknown reasons, before he could leave on a Dixie pilgrimage November 10, Mayor Kelly insisted on assigning a plain-clothed policeman to Mitchell. The Louisville home of a Sigma brother was the first official stop. To celebrate the occasion, the host invited several prominent blacks to an informal pre-noon buffet luncheon meeting with Mitchell. Those who came heard a rambling, disjointed eight-point discourse on goals and several unflattering references to DePriest's "bombast, ballyhoo and noise." The morning's highlight came after the Kentuckians had obliged "their" new congressman to join in a spontaneous motorcade through Louisville. In the midst of assembling automobiles for a parade, two patrol cars appeared. The police chief sat in one, and the head of detectives was in the other. Anticipating legal problems, nobody in the procession dared to move. Indeed, the participants were pleasantly shocked at learning just why the officers had rushed to the scene; they had come to lead the caravan! What followed, therefore, was an eventful tour of downtown and black residential neighborhoods that featured Louisville's highest-ranked law officers in two clearly marked police vehicles—sirens blaring and lights flashing—to note Mitchell's visit. Afterward, the policemen escorted the visiting Chicagoans to the city limits and the road to Birmingham.[48]

The rest of the trip south went without notice, and Mitchell arrived for a family reunion with his mother, now old and feeble, his brother John, and his sister Tommy. For several years, the oldest son's relationship with his mother had been improving. She looked forward to her offspring's weekly letters and depended upon his cash enclosures. On a meaningful visit to her bedside, a crisp ten-dollar note that the bedridden matriarch

47. MNR, n.d.; banquet invitation, the Chicago Democratic Lawyers Club, n.d., MP; *Defender*, November 17 and 24, 1934. Black attorneys, including Mitchell, founded the CDLC for social and political reasons.
48. *Louisville Leader*, November 17, 1934.

managed to squeeze into her son's palm best symbolized closer bonds. Always fondly treasured, the bill became Mitchell's lucky charm in his wallet for the remainder of his life. For several days after the Birmingham visit, he visited familiar places in Alabama. At Tuskegee, there was informal dining with old friends. It was during a peaceful lunch—one unpunctuated by political discussion—that the special visitor spotted George Washington Carver. Thereupon, the former student had the honor of introducing his bodyguard to "the greatest scientist in the world." The triumphant return to Macon County ended with poses for the school photographer at Booker T. Washington's statue and a memorable send-off by several hundred cheering female pupils. Mitchell then stopped at Montgomery and Greensboro, renewing old acquaintances and reminiscing nostalgically.[49]

After Alabama, Mitchell and his escort traveled west to Hot Springs. A few days of soaking and relaxing in warm water at the Pithian Bath House revived him enough for the long drive north to Chicago. After spending only a few days there at his law office, Mitchell was on his way again, this time to his Washington home to handle long-neglected personal and business affairs. Absorbed with the campaign, he had not bothered with routine matters such as paying telephone bills and managing the Mutual Housing Company. There was also the matter of Sigma responsibilities and pressures; he perceived that he must do something to free himself from these. After consulting with fellow officers in the District, he resigned, ending his many years as president. His departure did not pass without rancor and personal bitterness, however; the Sigmas hurt Mitchell's feelings because they had not showered "little Napoleon" with enough praise and appreciation for his long service.[50]

Before taking office in January, Mitchell caused some startling developments in party alignments. His high-profile status—as evidenced in Louisville, Birmingham, and Tuskegee—inadvertently became a contributing factor for the subsequent shift of African Americans from the GOP to Roosevelt. At this, the pinnacle in Mitchell's life, neither actions nor words mattered; it was his presence that counted most. Fame as DePriest's conqueror packed auditoriums and banquet halls; almost everyone wanted a glimpse of the black Democrat, and those who caught

49. Mitchell interview; *Journal and Guide*, September 25, 1937; *Birmingham News*, November 12 and 21, 1934; *Birmingham Age-Herald*, November 13, 1934; *Tuskegee Messenger* 10 (December 1934): 1, 8; M to Beverly, November 21, 1934, MP.

50. M to Griffith Consumers Company, November 10, 1934; M to Credit Service Corporation, November 20, 1934; M to Lewis, November 21, 1934; Lewis to M, January 24, 1936; M to Fellow Greeks, November 23, 1934; M to Roberts, July 29, 1935; *Crescent* (special edition, 1949), MP.

one often pointed or stared. In an era of disenfranchisement, lynching, and discrimination, the white police chief in segregated Kentucky was just as struck with Mitchell fever as the young Tuskegee women. Astute Democrats realized early how the phenomenon could be harnessed to political advantage. Sensing opportunities to lure votes, they clamored for every chance to be associated with the new black hero. Mitchell's decision to shun independent political forums in favor of speaking appearances for Democrats gave party pragmatists a godsend. His coattails gathered white Democrats with good political instincts. In their quest after "recognition politics" on a grander scale than Chicago's, visionaries with common sense about their party's future imagined endless possibilities developing from the curious spectacle of an African American Democrat on his way to Congress. Never in the party's long history had a black elected official caused anything comparable to this stir. In fact, before Mitchell's November victory, there had never been a black catalyst in the National Democratic party.[51]

Alert to the political possibilities, Boss Thomas J. "Tom" Pendergast of Kansas City, Missouri, was among the first politicians to conclude that there might be benefits from associating with Mitchell. Upon learning of Mitchell's planned visit and address to a local gathering of black Democrats, Pendergast apparently pondered over ways to garner maximum public relations from the event. Sensing obviously positive implications for his organization, Pendergast decreed that "his boys" must be conspicuously represented at the Chicagoan's December 4, 1934, appearance. Seated, therefore, at the head table with Mitchell and Pendergast that night were local luminaries such as Senator-elect Harry Truman, Congressman Joseph B. Shannon, Representative-elect Jasper Bell, Mayor Bryce B. Smith, City Counselor John Gershon, and several other municipal and county officials. Shannon thought the occasion sufficiently important that he pulled himself "out of a sick bed to . . . attend the banquet and speak."[52]

Between the election and the opening of Congress, Mitchell was also involved in private study and consultation. Away from public pressures, he prepared for his congressional term by formulating policies on a number of issues. There was also time to express his gratefulness

---

51. Although speculative, these conclusions are from evidence found in sources noted hereafter; they definitely suggest an awareness of a political asset.

52. Quincy J. Gilmore to M, November 8 and 17, 1934; M to Joseph B. Shannon, December 6, 1934; M to FBR, December 3 and 20, 1934; Banquet Program, December 4, 1934, MP; *Kansas City Star*, December 4, 1934; *Kansas City Times*, December 5, 1934; *Kansas City American*, December 6, 1934; *Kansas City Call*, December 7, 1934; *Indianapolis Recorder*, December 15 and 23, 1934.

to Mayor Kelly and all the other influential Chicagoans who had entrusted in him the responsibility of representing City Hall on Capitol
Hill. The *Defender's* A. N. Fields understood better than most other contemporary black reporters just what stood behind the Machine-Mitchell
relationship, but even he did not perceive the bond's complete implications on Mitchell's future. After the election, Fields correctly credited
Mitchell's win to Ed Kelly. Comprehending that Kelly had been more
supportive of Tittinger's candidate than anyone else of importance in
the city, Fields praised the mayor for "creating possibilities and level-
ing down prejudices." For these realizations, Kelly deserved "a unique
place among the advanced thinkers of the nation." There was, nevertheless, one fault with Fields's analysis; he was seemingly unaware of
Mitchell's commitments to the Kelly-Nash Machine in return. To impress
unity upon Mitchell and other representatives of the Illinois Democratic
party, County Chairman Pat Nash arranged a dinner in their honor at
a Loop hotel on December 13, 1934. It was then that he ordered everyone to Springfield for a caucus. One central theme emerged from
these sessions; bloc voting was expected from the twenty-person Democratic delegation from Illinois to the House of Representatives. As a
first obligation, the group must support Chicagoan Adolph J. Sabath's
bid for Floor Leader. Overtly, in an obvious ploy to please party titans,
Mitchell gave zealous support to Sabath. Upon receipt of Nash's directive, the servile congressman-elect initiated personal letter-writing to
members of Congress, informing them of Sabath's credentials. A portent
of what to expect from the Kelly-Mitchell partnership occurred on December 20, 1934, when the mayor pushed a second early request on his
new lackey. He commanded Mitchell to give firm support to Chicago
homeowners' need for more government-funded emergency loans. In
calling for increases, Kelly noted how an immediate influx of $60 mil-
lion in credits would save an estimated fifteen thousand houses from
foreclosure proceedings. Mitchell now faced what sponsors had always
planned for him in the House, a grasp of obeisance's obligations. In what
would become typical of his responses to superiors, he publicly echoed
Kelly's conviction about sharply increasing federal appropriations to the
Home Owners Loan Corporation. Although one issue by no means tested
Mitchell's overall intentions to render obedient service, it nevertheless
gave some inkling of what to expect from him. Incidentally, when a bill
reached the floor for additional funding to protect mortgages, Mitchell
supported it.[53]

53. *Defender*, November 10, 1934; M to John J. O'Connor, December 15, 1934; Nash
to M, December 8, 1934; M to Nash, December 10, 1934; M to John D. Dingell,

During the honeymoon period before January's commencement of congressional duties, the black Democrat also signaled the administration in Washington what it could expect from him on Capitol Hill. There is no better example of him hard at work pleasing whites than his treachery toward Armond W. Scott. At the outset of a nine-month dispute over who should fill a vacancy on the District of Columbia Municipal Court, Scott had received Mitchell's early endorsement as James A. Cobb's replacement. Mitchell's support came in late May when he had nobody to please. On behalf of Scott, a friend of many years and a Washington attorney who had once helped with legal studies, Mitchell, unbridled by obligations, wrote James A. Farley and the Department of Justice. But after his election victory, with reason to worry about interpretations of his recommendation, Mitchell exhibited fear and uncertainty. With rumors circulating about the administration's opposition to his candidate, Mitchell wondered if a pro-Scott position taken several months before the November victory might not have been premature and politically unwise. To get a better reading on Scott, Mitchell sounded out Attorney General Homer S. Cummings "in the strictest confidence," for there was "not [a] wish to embarrass the administration or to be embarrassed in this matter." Admitting to doubts and lack of direction about the court appointment, Mitchell offered on December 8, 1934, to withdraw his endorsement if his candidate were "found objectionable to . . . Justice." Meanwhile, Scott was obviously unaware of a turnabout. Assuming continued support, he asked his "friend" on December 18 to contact Congressman Vernon Lowrey of Mississippi about influencing some Southern Democrats. Although Mitchell soon learned that Roosevelt had not decided on anyone and had not ruled out Scott's candidacy, the letter to Cummings was revealing. Here were signs of the pliancy and passivity that would eventually endear the black politician to the administration. After enduring so many problems from a meddling predecessor, perhaps the Democratic leadership could relax, knowing Mitchell, unlike DePriest, would establish himself as a person willing to abandon anything and anybody for Roosevelt's favor and an important political coalition. December correspondence not only showed the unlikelihood of Mitchell breaking with the administration over an issue as personal as a close friendship but also demonstrated the extremes to which he would go. The nomination eventually went to Scott over the angry protests of many prominent black Washingtonians, including the Colored Bar Association; its membership had supported Howard law professor William Hastie. Since the administration had no objections to

---

December 14, 1934; A. J. Sabath to M, December 19, 1934; EJK to M, December 20, 1934; M to EJK, December 29, 1934, MP; unidentified clipping, BP.

Scott, Mitchell dared to endorse him publicly. Although his efforts did not affect Roosevelt's choice, Scott's foes blamed the congressman for an unwanted selectee.[54]

Having already passed some preliminary loyalty tests for Kelly and Roosevelt and having visited many places as a congressman-elect, Mitchell had only minor tasks to complete before the January 3, 1935, opening of Congress. One was to gather information about lynching for possible use in floor or committee debates on the subject. For assistance, Mitchell enlisted Director Monroe N. Work of Tuskegee's Records and Research Department. Work complied, forwarding a full report to Mitchell prepared from files kept on the topic. To prepare himself better on African American affairs, Mitchell appointed a personal advisory board on race. Work, AME Bishop Reverdy C. Ransom, Professor Alain Locke, and Little Rock attorney Scipio Jones accepted placements. Although no exact duties were ever specified, Mitchell indicated the appointees would be "helping work out a program to meet the needs" of African Americans.[55]

With much accomplished, Mitchell approached the holidays with unusual cheerfulness. Everything during 1934 had seemed to go his way, and in less than two weeks, he would be taking the congressional oath as the first black Democrat to join the House. As congressman-elect of the First District, he had heard few criticisms of his performance. Other than clashing a few times in the Second Ward with fellow black Democrat Bryant Hammond over gratitude for the Machine's friendly overtures to Bronzeville, Mitchell had not encountered major problems in Chicago. Even the pro-DePriest *Defender* showed uncharacteristic restraint in wishing the new officeholder well, and all across the nation, press responses to him had been correspondingly positive. In general, African American editors had held back harsh comments, and some had even praised Mitchell. While waiting to see what might in fact develop from his most annoying actions and odd statements, potentially hostile groups such as the NAACP had not wanted to appear impatient or intolerant toward him. They had kindly attributed his alleged weaknesses to misunderstandings, idiosyncrasies, and variant judgments. Mitchell had already established

---

54. M to Homer S. Cummings, December 8, 1934; Scott to M, December 18, 1934, MP; *Washington Evening Star*, December 15, 1934. (For the 1935 battle over Scott's appointment, see: M to FDR, January 16 and March 20; FDR to Cummings, March 22; Cummings to FDR, April 19; M to Cummings, May 2, RP; M to FDR, January 12 and April 17; M to William H. Dieterich, March 18; Scott to M, May 9; Cummings to M, May 3; M to Cummings, March 20 and May 9, MP; *Washington Tribune*, May 18; *Washington Post*, April 25; *Washington Daily News*, April 23; *Washington Evening Star*, April 26.)

55. Monroe N. Work to M, November 14, 1934; M to Ransom, November 22, 1934, MP.

a political record of loyalty and usefulness to bosses in Chicago and Washington. After assessing his overall situation at the dawn of a new career, he had sufficient cause to extend "season's greetings to all of the people of the First Congressional District."[56]

Mitchell spent the remaining hours of 1934 acclimating himself to Capitol Hill and completing unfinished business. December 30 was especially busy. He settled in his congressional office, met members from both political parties, and performed final tasks. In spite of constant interruptions from future House colleagues stopping to introduce themselves, he still managed somehow to accomplish two important jobs: naming an office assistant and designating "the official organ." Mitchell selected Claude Holman, a young black attorney better known in Chicago courtrooms for exceptional stenographic skills than for law, to perform administrative and secretarial duties. To acquaint the appointee with the Capitol, Mitchell escorted Holman on a tour. By their account, they encountered "absolutely no discrimination"; instead, everybody was "cordial in their treatment." In choosing an official publishing organ, Mitchell could not forget how unenthusiastic and unsympathetic Robert S. Abbott of the *Defender* and Claude Barnett had been toward him. Holding grudges as a result of their persistently negative attitudes, Mitchell bypassed them for the job of distributing press releases; the honor went to Editor-Publisher Jacob Tipper of the smaller *Chicago World*. Independent and best known among Bronzeville politicians for his self-interest and unscrupulous dealing, Tipper had rendered "splendid service" during the election.[57]

In the *Defender's* first issue of 1935, Mitchell conceivably saw enough to feel good about the decision of ignoring the popular newspaper for the *World*. Reflecting upon 1934, *Defender* editors chose twelve events as the most important news involving African Americans. Although Mitchell's victory ranked first, Oscar DePriest received the editors' award as "The most outstanding personality of 1934."[58] Mitchell had reason to complain about the decision. Two contrasting scenes the morning after the election indicated the people's choice for the award. Jubilant supporters had surrounded the Democratic winner, and everyone but faithful Morris Lewis had abandoned DePriest. Still, the eight weeks after Mitchell's victory proved rather deceptive. On the one hand, black and white crowds

56. Metz T. P. Lochard to M, November 7, 1934; Barnett to M, November 8, 1934; PBY to M, November 10, 1934; M to Mauvolyene Carpenter, November 23, 1934, MP; *Chicago World*, November 10 and December 22, 1934; *Washington New Negro Opinion*, November 17, 1934.

57. MNR, December 30, 1934; M to Jacob Tipper, December 30, 1934, MP; *Defender*, February 17, 1935; *Chicago World*, November 10, 1934.

58. *Defender*, January 5, 1935.

amassed wherever he went, and everyone seemed to cheer his every utterance. Civil rights organizations such as the NAACP were silent and patient, and the few warnings from individual dissidents such as Claude Barnett and William H. Davis passed without regard. During this period, there could only be one Hero of the Moment, one Negro of the Year, Congressman-elect Arthur Wergs Mitchell. Yet, he had allowed himself to be deceived. Every appearance had been nothing more than a cameo pose for friendly crowds. By ignoring all but the most partisan pro-Roosevelt black organizations, he had managed to avoid exposure to potential hostilities. At every stop during two months of almost nonstop appearances, he had seen only the friendliest African Americans—gradualists and fellow Democrats just like himself—who had already made peace with a party that had anointed irreconcilable segregationists with congressional committee chairs, cabinet and executive appointments, and the vice presidency. In sum, by having deliberately shunned more militant leaders with more radical approaches to racial problems and injustice, Mitchell had not given his formulations a full hearing. Ultimately, as the most carefully watched black public servant, Mitchell would have to face black critics or else alter his approach to issues of race. But any changes would mean confrontation with the Chicago Machine and the Democratic party leadership. Either way, the halcyon period of 1934 was destined for a short life; African American reactions given during the eight-week interval had not previewed the perils Mitchell would face in Congress.

Chicago Machine
Representative in Congress

4

1935–1943

The Capitol was the setting on January 3, 1935, for a history-making event. When House Speaker Joseph W. Byrns faced Arthur W. Mitchell to administer the oath of office, he was installing the first black Democratic congressman. Of course, this swearing-in ceremony was special because of race and party affiliation, but there were incongruities in it as well. For parts of four decades as a representative from Tennessee, Byrns had often been a willing partner in the shaping and passing of legislation that either created or continued some form of segregation and discrimination. Moreover, he had fought civil rights measures and antilynching bills. Yet, there in front of him stood an African American, and the Southerner was lending himself to an act of integrating Capitol Hill Democrats and, in the process, sealing a black's bid for membership in the legislative body. As unlikely as Byrns's role might have seemed, few people noticed the absurdity of his participation or, for that matter, considered the matchup's improbable character. After all, their eyes and thoughts were on not Byrns but Mitchell. On this, Mitchell's great day, his mere entrance into the House was sufficient to draw attention from the floor, gallery, and nation.

From all indications, Mitchell was bringing new perspectives to Congress. From his previous statements, actions, and associations, his approach to elective office promised to be unique for a black man. His record carried no traces of a Reconstruction agenda, and it looked as if all that had characterized his black Republican predecessors would be absent from his actions in Congress. For unlike Oscar DePriest and other loathers of Southern Democrats, Mitchell did not want to impose a new order on Dixie. At the start of his legislative career, he seemed to have respect and even admiration for men with Byrns's background; he even had been calling some of these people his friends. On matters related to Roosevelt and the New Deal, Mitchell promised to take a new direction. Throughout the Seventy-Third Congress, with frightful conditions and a depression affecting several million African Americans, dogmatic DePriest had kept to a politically conservative philosophy, consistently opposing Roosevelt's liberal legislative program. Poised in 1935 to replace DePriest in the Seventy-Fourth Congress was a pragmatic African American Democrat with a solid commitment to FDR.

In regard to civil rights, Mitchell had showed more ambivalence and inconsistency than DePriest. Occasionally, as the representative-elect from the First District, Mitchell had acted as if a role of black delegate at large would be desirable, but he did not share DePriest's conviction that this role was a foremost responsibility. Rather, Mitchell had frequently touted attention to First District constituents—regardless of color—as his first duty. There would be legislative fights to punish lynchers and eliminate unfair hiring practices, but Mitchell had not promised more to blacks. Furthermore, he had never pledged himself to anything like DePriest's clamor and boisterousness. As for the House restaurant, there would not be any repetitions of the disturbances created by DePriest and Morris Lewis. By every account, if Mitchell's intentions were compared to DePriest's acts, his tenure promised to be more peaceful and certainly more bearable for Southern rulers.

Once Mitchell was officially in the House, another wave of congratulatory letters and telegrams arrived, and once more there were requests that he make clear his objectives and expectations. In response, he stressed again that he was "not going into Congress as a Negro with a chip on my shoulder" but rather "as the Representative of all the people of my district." Mitchell also reiterated that he had no intention of acting like DePriest, who "devoted himself to stirring up race prejudice" when he "arrayed race against race." Mitchell gave a frank reply when asked to comment if he foresaw negative reactions to his positions. He observed that anyone in a challenging position should "expect some opposition, but overcoming barriers makes victory all the sweeter. I may offend some people, but on the other hand some people may offend me."[1]

For Mitchell, the first weeks in Congress were extremely busy. There was the supervision of answering 1,250-plus letters and responding to 110 telegrams. He was also accessible to the press, granting fifty-odd interviews. In addition, he entertained approximately 500 guests on Capitol Hill and handled the arrival of 360 speaking invitations. Also during this period, he introduced H.R. 4457—an antilynching bill—and attended every House roll call. Yet wedged in the middle of everything was still time for diversion. On Monday, January 21, 1935, he got a resolution of

1. MNR, January 12, 1935; *Journal and Guide*, n.d., MP.

support from the Washington Ministers Conference before leaving later in the week for New York, where on the following Sunday, he garnered "fine words of commendation" for an address to fifteen hundred people at Bethel AME Church. A climax occurred on January 31, when he and Annie attended a Roosevelt-hosted White House reception.[2]

As hectic as his first month in office was, Mitchell cherished one event more than all the others. Almost one year later, he recalled John McDuffie's help during the first weeks of adjusting to legislative life. In particular, Mitchell was mindful of their meeting soon after his arrival in Washington from Chicago. He remembered how McDuffie had pulled him aside for expert advice on congressional ways and customs. Recalling their encounter as well as its overall positive effects on his House debut, Mitchell thanked McDuffie again for "those words of counsel which you gave me immediately after my coming to Washington." As he put it, "Everything has worked out as you prophecyed [sic]"—a House member of another race could make friends in "all sections of the country"—while "doing something in the way of bringing about a better understanding between the two groups [of different color]."[3]

In addition to using these first weeks to reestablish himself with Mc-Duffie and to make new contacts, Mitchell improved his relationships with Chicago by pursuing a useful committee assignment. Throughout his campaign and prior to the opening of the Seventy-Fourth Congress, he had been belaboring one theme. First and foremost, his district's welfare, not the interests of African Americans, would be his major concern. Thus as a substitute for developing and fostering a national black constituency, Mitchell implemented a policy that benefited the Chicago Organization in its daily operations. Appeals for assistance from residents of other districts were consistently met with stock replies from Mitchell's office. In almost all cases, he directed these solicitors politely but firmly to their own elected officials.[4]

In support of this approach, Mitchell rejected all recommendations from African Americans that he should only think about their best interests when considering committee assignments. There developed a general consensus among civil rightists that Mitchell could accomplish much

2. MNR, n.d.; M to Pauline B. Rinaker, January 18, 1935; M to Robert G. McGuire, February 5, 1935; White House invitation to the Mitchells, MP. Being part of this reception meant much to Mitchell; he wanted to make a favorable impression. Hence, he borrowed "one of the best cars" for the trip to 1600 Pennsylvania Avenue.
3. M to JMc, January 4, 1936, MP.
4. M to: Charles M. Holly, January 18, 1935; Thomas L. Dabney, January 21, 1935; James Pughsley (handwritten note by Claude Holman on letter of same of January 23, 1935); Earl L. Sykes, March 11, 1935; Alfred Crowther, March 13, 1935; A. Morris Williams, April 30, 1935, MP; *Chicago Tribune,* April 29, 1935.

more for the race on the House District of Columbia Committee than anywhere else. However, this assignment did not interest him. Instead, he opted for placement on the Committee on Post Offices and Post Roads. Adamant about this, Mitchell indicated that he wanted "to be free to attend to the demands of my Chicago constituents" because he had no interest in being "swamped with Negro friends here [in the capital] asking for jobs." Because of his demands and the intervening efforts of friends such as Adolph Sabath, who had worked to get him on this committee, he obtained the appointment.[5]

Once on the Post Office Committee, Mitchell quickly showed the rationale behind his choice. Close ties between his committee placement and his role for Chicago ward bosses rapidly became apparent. Almost immediately, "worthy" First District citizens began finding postal employment. Patterns established in early 1935 remained operative during Mitchell's entire congressional tenure. It was a simple carrot-and-stick operation, with patronage at the core. It involved the Chicago Post Office in a circular path that began and ended with city postmaster Ernest J. Kruetgen. As openings developed for custodians, special messengers, substitutes, extras, and other sundry jobs uncovered by Civil Service Commission procedures, the partisan head of the nation's busiest postal operation promptly notified Mitchell. Meanwhile back in Chicago wards, committeemen were at work, screening residents to identify the Machine's best servants. After their names reached Washington, Mitchell passed the applicant recommendations along to Kruetgen for eventual processing. Usually in the exercise, Machine bosses were unconcerned with their nominees' abilities to do postal work; their recommendations were based on the applicants' good service to the regular Democratic party. Every other consideration had no importance. Thus, it was common for the postmaster to report back about a particular applicant's unfitness. For example, one appointee for a Christmas rush turned out to be illiterate. As a result, he could not work as a mail sorter. From 1935 to 1943, Mitchell used his post office clout to do more than place Democrats in low-level patronage jobs. Often, he worked closely with Kruetgen and ward heelers to assist "more deserving constituents." Still, as Mitchell would have to

5. Unidentified-undated clip and MNR; Sabath to M, January 9, 1935; M to James M. Mead, January 19, 1935, MP; *Chicago Evening American*, January 7, 1935; *CR*, 74th Cong., 1st sess., 373; interestingly, in *Race and Ethnicity in Chicago Politics: A Reexamination of Pluralist Theory*, Dianne M. Pinderhughes concluded much the same about William Dawson's relationship to the Machine. Dawson, Mitchell's successor in Congress, also concentrated on bringing selective benefits to constituents, avoiding in the process sensitive public policy, committee assignments, and all substantive discussions involving discrimination. Dawson also understood "decisions are made downtown" and not in the wards. See especially pages 64 and 238.

note for a precinct captain who had sought consideration for a fireman's job in the new post office outside the Loop, "No one can approach the Civil Service Commission with a view of asking them to pass anyone. . . . if you pass the examination, it is possible that assistance can be rendered." For every "qualified" applicant, intervening with Kruetgen was always possible.[6]

Generally, Republicans and First District residents who had not channeled job interests into city hall's patronage "pipeline" did not have a chance at Kruetgen's post office. Backing for a postal position came only as a consequence of the committeemen's letters of recommendation to Congressman Mitchell; clearly spelled out, all the opportunities for work, moves, transfers, upgrades, promotions, and anything else within reason at the post office were for hire to the Machine. Without the benefits of a powerful friend stationed in a ward office or at city hall to aid a lowly constituent, there was no point to independent actions with Mitchell. He was placed in office to help the Organization, not every clamorer from outside the Chicago System. From a Machine perspective, residents of the First District without any clout might as well have lived elsewhere; ward bosses did not count them as constituents.[7]

On postal labor issues, Mitchell was sympathetic to the actions of the National Alliance of Postal Employees, but he shunned every Chicago-based drive to eliminate unfair promotions at Kruetgen's post office. Furthermore, outsiders were unsuccessful at enticing him to demand employment opportunities for African Americans as supervisors. Since providing ten people jobs at one thousand dollars each offered the Organization more advantages than chasing one position at ten thousand dollars, Mitchell showed no interest in participating in fairness-in-hiring drives sponsored jointly by the Chicago Council of Negro Organizations and the Chicago and Northern District Association of Colored Women. On a regular basis, officers of both bodies had called on him to join; he resisted their pleas. In 1940, after five frustrating years of attempting to enlist Mitchell, black activist Irene M. Gaines finally gained assurances

6. Ernest J. Kruetgen to M, January 20 and March 13, 1936, and March 22 and 28, 1938; M to Kruetgen, March 15, 1938, and February 19, 1940; Geary to M, March 17, 1938; M to Geary, March 30, 1938; JET to M, April 6, 1938; M to Michael Kenna, February 19, 1940; M to Curtis J. Poree, March 30, 1938; M to C. R. Davis, April 28, 1939; M to John Small, February 13, 1936; Aaron H. Payne to M, February 11, 1936; M to Payne, February 13, 1936; JET to M, April 24, 1939; M to Kruetgen, April 27, 1939; M to Daniel Williams, April 27, 1939, MP; Tittinger interview.

7. James L. Casey to M, March 15, 1935; M to Kruetgen, August 7, 1936; JET to M, August 7, 1936; Hugh Connelly to M, March 4, 1938; M to Connelly, March 14, 1938; M to Laura M. Beaty, February 4, 1937, MP (only a sample of several letters to First District residents who had petitioned for jobs without sponsorships).

from him. If through "proper investigation" she or any group could substantiate charges of discrimination at the post office, he promised he would personally oversee that all arrangements be set for Kruetgen to hear verifiable complaints against the Chicago Post Office. Mitchell, of course, knew that his promise would never materialize into anything because without any access to post office hiring records, Gaines could not build such a case. Neither Mitchell, ward organizations, nor the Chicago Post Office kept placement records for long periods. Thus, the full extent of patronage funneled through Mitchell cannot be determined. However, from indirect sources it is fair to state that he contributed invaluably to the Machine's patronage pipeline. From the only remaining tally of Mitchell nominations, one covering just the first seven months of 1937 and Tittinger's predominantly black Second Ward, fifty-four clerks and mail carriers were directly tied to Mitchell. If these positions were representative and a fair measure of overall effectiveness, his impact on patronage was indeed significant.[8]

Mitchell's role in post office patronage represented just one example of his value to Chicago bosses. In him, they had a reliable man. During his eight years on Capitol Hill, he consistently gave them dependable, trustworthy service. Throughout his tenure in Congress, there were special favors to Ed Kelly that exemplified his willingness to show gratitude. On February 15, 1935, with municipal elections approaching, Mitchell offered whatever help the mayor might need. Then almost eight years later, just before Mitchell's retirement, there was a parting gesture of indebtedness to Mayor Kelly "for the hundreds of favors you have shown me"; the outgoing congressman appointed Robert Halligan—a son of one of the municipal leader's good friends—to the U.S. Naval Academy in Annapolis. Between these two acts, Mitchell did just about all an underling could possibly do for superiors in the Organization. When Kelly or Nash demanded something of him, he complied cheerfully. On two separate occasions in 1937, the trustworthy lackey illustrated perfectly what kinds of services he could render bosses from the House of Representatives. During May, Kelly expressed a strong desire to have unrestricted versions of two appropriations bills enacted into statutes. As a consequence, he directed the Chicago congressional delegation to vote down all earmarking amendments to a $1.5 billion relief bill. About two months later, Congressman Thomas J. O'Brien, the city's own House whip, ordered Mitchell to read a telegram addressed to the Chicago caucus. The cable

8. Reprint, *CR*, 75th Cong., 1st sess., August 25, 1937; Sarah McCune to M, February 27, 1936; Foster to M, September 24, 1936; M to Irene M. Gaines, February 5, 1940, MP; Thornton and Tittinger interviews; *Argus*, July 30, 1937.

had been "requesting" solid support for Roosevelt's domestic program. In both cases, Mitchell confirmed his cooperative intentions. He fought first against hamstringing alterations, and thereafter, he rededicated himself to Roosevelt. As he put it to Chairman Nash, "I had already very strongly and loudly announced that I expected to support the President's program 100%. I recall that this is the instruction that you and Mayor Kelly have given from time to time. I am glad to do this because it is the request of the head of our organization."[9]

The Illinois Democratic party split in 1936. Afterward, there were many chances for Mitchell to demonstrate public loyalty to Kelly. Overwhelmed by two strong men, the party could not support the overreaching ambitions of both Governor Henry Horner and Chicago's mayor. Since both executives were after authority in Illinois, and ultimately the other's homage, a long-drawn contest for supremacy was inevitable. Oddly, after his victory over DePriest, Mitchell had joked about the prospects of serving a Protestant in the White House, a Jew in Springfield, and an Irish Catholic in City Hall, but now he would have to choose someone to support in the power struggle. Some six months before the end of his first term, he like all others belonging to the city's delegation to Congress bet on the mayor to reign supreme. Consequently, it was Kelly, with Nash's assistance, who continued setting policies and priorities. If there had been any doubts about Mitchell, they disappeared before a jammed Second Ward hall on March 10, 1936. Kelly had come to explain why Horner must be removed from the Democratic ticket, and Mitchell had returned from Washington especially to take sides in the fratricidal fight. He had the honor of introducing the mayor to the thousands gathered that night. No reconciliation took place after the primary. The ongoing race offered more chances for expressions from Mitchell against Horner. One occurred in 1938 when a *Defender* reporter asked Mitchell for an evaluation of a Horner backer and Kelly challenger, Assistant State's Attorney Thomas J. Courtney. With candor and spontaneity, Mitchell described the governor's man as "too small" for the mayorship, finding "no comparison" between the two mayoral candidates; Kelly was a "broad statesman with deep humanitarian interest void of prejudice, courageous and honest," while Courtney was "conceited, filled with bigotry and prejudice."[10]

9. M to EJK, February 15, 1935, and December 16, 1942; EJK to M, May 28, 1937; M to Nash, July 21, 1937, MP.

10. M to Henry Horner, November 22, 1934; M to JEM, April 4, 1936; Bruce A. Campbell to M, August 12, 1935; MNR, December 17, 1938, March 6, 1939; John H. Sengstacke to M, January 21, 1939; M to EJK, November 14, 1938, MP; *CR*, 76th Cong., 1st sess., 2153, 3059; *Chicago Evening American*, March 11, 1936; *Defender*, December 17, 1938.

After Kelly easily won the Democratic primary, Mitchell did some public relations for him on Capitol Hill. Upon returning to Washington the morning after the election, Mitchell proceeded directly from the railroad depot to the Capitol and his seat in the House. Mitchell could not wait to speak about Kelly and the previous day's Chicago primary. In an address that followed, he interpreted Kelly's triumph as a victory for the White House, advising, "If there are sections of our country that are growing lukewarm toward the President and his great program through the misrepresentation of partisan Republicans and a partisan press, they should take fresh courage from the hearty approval Chicago gave the President and the New Deal in . . . Tuesday's election." Looking to 1940 and Democratic prospects if FDR should follow the two-term presidential tradition by stepping down, Mitchell pushed Kelly as "Presidential timber."[11]

As willing as Mitchell was to help the mayor, he rarely asked for return favors. On April 1, 1937, in the midst of violent labor unrest at two South Side garment factories, there developed an unusual exception. From what had begun in February as simple demands by underpaid black workers to obtain better wages and union recognition, the struggle progressed to daily battles, pitting largely female picketers on one side against strikebreakers with bodyguards on the other. On behalf of six hundred strikers, local labor organizer Mary Redmond pleaded twice to her congressman, appealing for assistance in the conflict. Either Redmond had known of Mitchell's susceptibility to flattery or she had incorrectly believed his campaign literature from the 1936 reelection campaign, because Redmond left him with exaggerated impressions of his power, influence, and importance. According to her stated perceptions, Mitchell had developed so much clout in Washington that he could easily order capital contacts to prevail upon the president for intervention against sweatshop conditions. Meanwhile, Mayor Kelly's reputation for fairness was being diminished because his policemen were escorting "scabs" into plants. Sensing a need to assist Kelly with some face-saving gestures, Mitchell arranged a summit meeting at City Hall. It brought together Kelly, Cook County officials, and several Bronzeville pastors. Although the boss apologized at the session for the police department's overzealousness, nothing changed afterward. Apparently, Kelly intended to do nothing more than capitalize on a superb public relations opportunity. Other than posing with black clergymen for the newspaper photographers' pictures, Kelly only assured the ministers of plans to investigate charges of brutality. Despite the mayor's promises, labor unrest and violence continued until the women's strike collapsed. For Mitchell's part, his final words on the subject came in a May letter to Redmond. He reminded her of the conference arranged at the mayor's

11. *CR*, 76th Cong., 1st sess., 2153, 3059; MNR, March 6, 1939, and one n.d., MP.

office, and he reaffirmed empathy for the strike's general goals. Although he agreed with her that a weekly wage of six dollars was too low, he differed with Redmond over who was ultimately responsible for the violence erupting at the plants. Contrary to her claims, he blamed strikers for the disorder. According to reports before him, he said, picketers had stripped police of nightsticks and grabbed their badges. As a result of allegations of spontaneous, provocative actions against authority figures, Mitchell found union members' actions so unacceptable that he lectured Redmond sternly about respect for law and order.[12]

By personal admission the perfect "organization man," Mitchell was loath to complain about his placement in the Chicago setup. In his judgment, "going straight down the line with regular organization" would be best in the long run because it had already proven itself as "the only way . . . to succeed." He thus had few qualms about recommending to trusted political aspirants that they try compliance as well. To one budding politician, there went this advice: "It seems . . . any one aspiring to office and expecting support of an organization should identify himself as closely with the organization as it is possible for one to do." Communications to him from ward offices were daily reminders of his obligations to the Organization. In this, an era of high unemployment, most demands on him were job-related. Except for bounties from his membership on the Post Office Committee, he did not always have many positions to dispense. Yet, every contribution satisfied ward heelers. Occasionally, when there were unusual circumstances, such as a surprise request for workers in 1935, Mitchell had a few bonanzas to spread among constituents. To repair and service its fleet of automobiles, the Chicago offices of the National Recovery Administration needed ten mechanics to be available for a week or so every month. More jobs came from the Census Bureau at the end of 1939; it had several hundred vacancies to fill. Early rumor had Mitchell giving supervision over these jobs to a white, but the position went eventually to James A. McLendon, Annie Mitchell's brother-in-law.[13]

For the Machine, WPA and CCC jobs were more important than all others, and Mitchell had a major role in providing these. As soon as Congress approved funds for Chicago projects, he was eagerly checking into pertinent details for the Machine. Thereafter, he passed the information along

12. Petition, Nelly Ann–L. Sopkin Strikers Committee to M, 1937; M to EJK, April 1, 1937; EJK to M, April 2, 1937; M to Mary Redmond, May 14, 1937, MP; *Defender* and *Chicago Tribune,* February to May 1937.

13. M to C. C. Wimbish, November 17, 1937; Connelly to M, March 4 and April 4, 1938, and April 21, 1939; JET to M, March 7, 1938; Kenna to M, February 1, 1940; M to Kenna, February 5, 1940; Holman to M, letter and telegram, February 22, 1935; M to Kenna, February 20, 1940, MP; Tittinger interview; *Defender,* December 2, 1939; *Chicago Sunday Bee,* April 7, 1940.

quickly to ward heelers. Weeks before any state employment office or relief agency could publicize openings, politicos were already tipping off candidates about them. In effect, then, Mitchell—like other congressional members under Nash and Kelly—served as an invaluable conduit between their sources in the federal bureaucracy and a network back home. The procedure required close monitoring in Washington and constant communicating between officeholders and committeemen. At some New Deal offices, insiders entered the circular path, feeding back superior information from more direct, closer involvements with agency developments than congressmen could provide by themselves. These leaks then fed information to Machine operatives. For example, with candidate names supplied to Mitchell from four wards, H. K. Seltzer, WPA Director of the Third District, directly arranged employment for carefully selected constituents. Until 1938, everything had gone smoothly for Seltzer, the WPA, and the Machine. Then, sharp appropriation cuts and a followup drop in projects brought havoc. Although Mitchell did not recognize it, the decline was a premonition of a much greater problem about to confront Windy City bosses and Mitchell. On their front pages, Windy City newspapers reported a breaking scandal. It concerned possible Hatch Act violations, and there were allegations of WPA participation in Chicago patronage practices. The reports engulfed Mitchell, and they were so damaging that his political career was jeopardized. Troublesome as dwindling WPA resources had been for bosses, legal complications and embarrassments exposed by Chicago's Better Government Association on November 17, 1939, dwarfed everything heretofore encountered. It was on that date that the anti-Machine reform organization released a bombshell: Mitchell's frank letter detailing exactly how WPA work could be obtained in the First District. The letter was Mitchell's candid reply to a constituent. According to the letter, jobs went only to seekers with Machine sponsors. Such candidness about political prerequisites and connections was proof, the BGA claimed, that "politics is being played with human misery systematically and ruthlessly by the Kelly-Nash machine." Hence, it "shows that the taxes you pay, which are supposed to bring relief to the needy, are being used to build and maintain an impregnable political organization, apparently with the assistance of the WPA in Washington." Even more sinister, it was affecting the integrity of democratic values. "It shows why the relief areas in Chicago have such a high percentage of Democratic votes. It explains why fraudulent voting is so easy and so prevalent in relief areas."[14]

14. M to Connelly, March 16, 1938, and April 28, 1939; Connelly to M, March 22, 1938; JET to M, February 12, 1936, and March 22, 1938; Geary to M, March 14, 1938; M

During the next two months in Washington and Chicago, attention was focused on the BGA's alleged "proof of political blackjacking." The WPA denied an accessory role in the affair. In defending the agency in an attempt to assuage capital press corpsmen, WPA spokesman Corrington Gill was adamant about its independence from politics. According to Gill's brief statement, there had been no WPA complicity because every "department has repeatedly and insistently advised workers of their rights and . . . freedom from political interference." Gill conceded that there had been aborted attempts at violating venerable principles, but strong adherence to operating standards at the WPA had foiled would-be usurpers. As for impressions that patronage was an integral part of its Chicago practices, a WPA records check had "failed to disclose any communications . . . containing recommendations for any relief applicants." Had such links existed at the WPA, offenders would have immediately lost their jobs. Regarding possible fallout for Mitchell's alleged participation, Gill advised reprimands were impossible due to Hatch Act exemptions of congressmen. The briefing ended with Gill's advice to all prospective WPA workers: "No applicant need see a politician. It does him no good. He should visit his local relief office, not a committeeman."[15]

Unofficial responses were livelier than the WPA's cover-up. News accounts in Colonel Frank Knox's *Chicago Daily News* concealed a special interest. Owned and controlled by the 1936 GOP vice-presidential candidate, it had first rights to the explosive news story. Being a Republican newspaper, the *Daily News* tried to extract as much as possible from the mess, and it did not treat the letter as an isolated act or an aberration. In "Get A Letter!" readers learned how Mitchell had corroborated all charges against himself, the Machine, and the WPA. His final words in the last paragraph confirmed his personal role in the Machine's exploitations of federal relief. As he described normal procedure, "It is the unbroken rule of the Democratic organization . . . that each person seeking help . . . must first get a letter from his ward committeeman requesting the congressman to take care of the matter." The Seventy-Sixth Congress was in session when the BGA exposé broke. To stave off further embarrassment for the WPA and to prevent additional patronage scandals, lawmakers amended an appropriations bill, declaring certain political intercessions felonies. Furthermore, members talked over the merits of holding investigations

to Joseph A. Hale, June 2, 1936; M to Milton C. Smith, March 18, 1935; for 1935–1939, see also Mitchell's complete correspondence log with the four ward committeemen 1935–1942 as well as with H. K. Seltzer of the WPA 1935–1939, MP. *Chicago Daily News,* November 17, 1939.

15. *Chicago Daily News,* November 21, 1939; Tittinger interview.

into irregularities. In the meantime, capital rumormongers wrongly reported that Mitchell had been served a subpoena.[16]

During the first weeks of the exposé, Mitchell remained coy, saying and doing nothing. There was no point anyway because his purloined words had been so clear that explanations for seemingly indictable evidence would have looked foolish. As for official explanations or comments, they were promised following personal delving into the incident. Finally after almost six weeks, Mitchell showed his readiness to discuss the charges and allegations with Publisher P. B. Young of the *Norfolk Journal and Guide*. In a bizarre twist to the BGA's revelations, Mitchell accused Republican partisans and the intended recipient of "taking the W.P.A. into politics." Among other things in his rather peculiar, shameless explanation of his self-explanatory words of instruction to a naive job seeker, Mitchell argued duty had forced him to confirm the applicant's worthiness before giving him "help from the tax payers of the country." However, because of GOP resolve to regain the First District, a cabal of grudge holders led by Emmett J. Scott had distorted and smeared with "gutter snipes" an honest probe of a complete stranger's qualifications and background. With two final gasps, the patronage saga passed. One occurred during Capitol floor debates on antilynching legislation when a speaker strayed to read "the letter" to the Chicagoan caught in the middle. Critical of Mitchell's nonsupport of the bill under discussion, the attacker proceeded, accusing his Democratic colleague of playing "politics with the necessities and privileges of his constituents." Mitchell's final words came in a January 22, 1940, refutation. Claiming there had not been "a scintilla of truth" in GOP reports of a scandal, he asserted the letter had not related "even in the remotest way" to "W.P.A. job juggling." All blame for the uproar should fall upon Joseph Parvis, the white applicant denied help "until he identified himself through some one in Chicago, favorably known to" a municipal authority.[17]

Being a beneficiary of favors, Mitchell offered no objections to the Machine's racism. It is no wonder that when information reached him from a former partner about alleged discriminatory hiring practices at WPA Project 3519 in Chicago, he had no response. According to Attorney

16. *Chicago Daily News*, November 17, 1939–January 1940; ANPNR, "WPA Politics Gets Congressman Mitchell in Bad," December 20, 1939, BP.

17. ANPNR, "WPA Politics Gets Congressman Mitchell in Bad," December 20, 1939, BP; M to PBY, January 4, 1940; M to Anthony Overton, January 22, 1940, MP; *Journal and Guide*, January 6, 1940; *CR*, 76th Cong., 3d sess., 181–82. According to Bonnie Fox Schwartz (*The Civil Works Administration, 1933–1934: The Business of Emergency Employment in the New Deal*, 89, 93), the CWA was also beset by graft problems in Chicago.

William E. Lilly's report to Mitchell about racism, there had been a systematic replacement of talented black seamstresses by inexperienced white women. Early in 1937, approximately two-thirds of the thousand or so garment makers at the Bronzeville WPA facility were African Americans. During seven disruptive months of discharges and demotions, a sweeping black-to-white changeover "at the rate of four and five to one" had transformed personnel at the plants. Presented the problem, Mitchell showed no interest in "fuller details of the situation." Hence the sour Lilly-Mitchell relationship deteriorated further, but this did not upset Mitchell. Earlier in the year, Lilly had been audacious enough to imply that his former associate had not always acted independently. In rebuttal, Mitchell handled the inferences of Uncle Tom behavior this way: "My record is straight and will be. I am not acting under advice of anyone." A 1935 inquiry into the Civilian Conservation Corps to ascertain whether employment existed for African American reserve officers as project administrators and instructors was as close as the careful lawmaker ever came to urging reform on a federal agency operating in Chicago. At the time of the check, Illinois had been employing no black CCC supervisors. Therefore, a plea to hire black supervisors in the state's segregated CCC facilities was overdue. Mitchell's action was a sequel to a petition by Lieutenant Edward C. Johnson of Bronzeville's 449th Infantry Reserve. Speaking for Secretary of the Interior Harold Ickes, Howard W. Oxley insisted that all inquiries about the complaint should be directed to Sandford Sellers Jr. of the Sixth Army Corps stationed in Chicago. Rather than monitor Sellers's office to guarantee progress, Mitchell lost enthusiasm. Hence, the situation did not improve.[18]

However, he remained assertive with the Civil Service Commission. On a regular basis, forthcoming examination dates flowed from Capitol Hill to ward heelers. Furthermore, Mitchell made several inquiries into pending cases of constituents. When pressed on behalf of specific citizens, he investigated their test scores and eligibility. In some cases, he had to remind overanxious committeemen that congressmen did not always have clout. To "Hinky Dink" Kenna of Chicago's vice-ridden First Ward, his excuses signaled weakness. More used to "pull" than any other political wheelhorse, Kenna had trouble believing Mitchell's February 19, 1940, answer that "no political influence is permitted" at Civil Service. Apparently, Kenna, who ran political affairs from his saloon, thought a "good Chicagoan" had followed instructions sufficiently to receive a job.

18. Memorandum, William E. Lilly to M, August 2, 1937; M to Lilly, April 13, 1937; M to John W. Studebaker, June 10, 1935; Howard W. Oxley to M, June 12, 1935; Edward C. Johnson to M, June 25, 1935, MP.

After all, he had taken a required test; nobody had ever bothered to say anything about passing it![19]

Many of the causes brought before Mitchell would have caused serious repercussions for him had he dared to intervene. Both municipal public housing in all its ramifications and the Federal Theatre in its special manifestations illustrated his dilemma, and they demonstrated his abilities to pick with savvy which issues to ignore. In his relationship with the Machine, there was overall brilliance on Mitchell's part for knowing which actions would be ill-advised and which would lead to reprisals and disciplinary actions. Good perceptions proved helpful, indeed. Without many reminders to serve as warnings, he still made few wrong moves. Plain and simple, he recognized pitfalls and knew how to avoid the worst temptations. Good judgment steered him onto a safe course. In both housing and the Federal Theatre, African Americans confronted unfairness. But in placing grievances about the blatant operational injustices before Mitchell, they demonstrated total naïveté about his ability to assist. Clearly in calling on him to address wrongs, black petitioners had no idea of the Machine operatives' rule about subordinating racial matters to politics. Reversing bosses' priorities and still maintaining a credible position with the Organization was an impossible task. Change through petition was not exactly "Democracy" in action in Chicago. As a constituent with complaints about racism in Bronzeville operations of the Federal Theatre discovered, such matters did not interest her congressman. Working with Bronzeville students to restore ROTC programs to a high school curriculum represented the limits of Mitchell's intervention.[20]

Successful as the bosses and Mitchell were at skirting matters involving discrimination and racism in the city, they could not ignore altogether Chicago public housing. The questions raised by federally funded residence projects were complex. Difficulties and differences were conspicuously visible for everyone to see, and the city's decisions often overlapped and affected several population segments simultaneously. In Chicago, where ethnic minorities clustered in and clung to separate enclaves, preserving neighborhoods was almost sacrosanct. Furthermore, in its "recognition politics," the Machine depended upon defined residential areas for each of the municipality's major subgroups. The first real signs of trouble with Windy City public housing policy came in 1935 with a

19. M to Walter L. Dickson, March 12, 1935; William C. Hull to M, April 24, 1935; M to David H. Orro, May 20, 1936; M to Kenna, March 23, 1938, and February 19, 1940; M to Connelly, March 16, 1938; Connelly to M, March 4, 1938; M to Geary, March 29, 1938, and February 2 and 19, 1940, MP; for more on Kenna, see Lloyd Wendt and Herman Kogan's *Bosses in Lusty Chicago: The Story of Bathhouse John and Hinky Dink.*
20. Tittinger interview; Pearl G. Pachaco to M, December 5, 1936, MP.

flood of complaints about slow progress on WPA-sponsored housing in the Second Ward. On thirty-seven acres of densely developed land, the Department of the Interior had taken over rows of mostly crumbling structures that had housed several hundred impoverished black families. After dispossessions and demolitions had relieved them of their tattered residences, these poor people were resettled in deplorably overcrowded "temporary" facilities, with little more than promises that better living accommodations would be provided as soon as the government could complete Federal Housing Project Number 1402, euphoniously named South Park Gardens. In contrast to the barren field where new residences for blacks had been scheduled but not begun, three other completed public housing developments awaited white occupants. Overtly glaring discrepancies in priorities and fairness generated unfavorable news that caused doubts and displeasure to multiply in Bronzeville. Making matters worse, one newspaper even reported the PWA was abandoning altogether its plans to build the South Park project. The unhappy state of affairs was especially trying for many Democratic precinct captains who had to confront angry neighbors. At a loss to know what to expect and how to explain the racism to inquiring residents, one foot soldier unburdened his personal pessimism and Bronzeville's general heartbreak on Mitchell. In the process, the captain detailed his frustrations and difficulties with overcoming GOP propaganda about the public-housing fiasco. Due to stalling at the site of South Park, Republicans were regaining the confidence of voters. Oscar DePriest and William King were having good success at arousing Bronzeville; Second Ward inactivity and corresponding progress elsewhere gave them easy marks. In the face of all this, the distressed captain wondered what he should be doing to overcome an opposition that had evidence to substantiate charges of prejudicial intentions. Wanting to undermine the Republican onslaught and to regain his own party's credibility, he appealed to Mitchell, pleading, "do all you can in this matter." Resolved to intervene, the congressman responded favorably, listening with ears normally deaf to all Bronzevillian distress cries. No matter if bosses in Chicago had not been responsive, he was determined to carry his constituents' frustrations and grief to Roosevelt. With carefree abandon, he pleaded with the president, "please read this letter and give serious attention to the questions raised by" a faithful Democrat. For residents expecting evidence of immediate progress in public housing for blacks, the drive for results stalled with Mitchell's September 23, 1935, appeal on behalf of Bronzeville.[21]

21. Monographic studies about Chicago's ethnic ramifications, specifications, and manifestations abound, to cover this subject diversely from sociological, historical,

With Congress's passage of the Housing Act of 1937, the federal government relinquished much of its authority over public housing. Subsequently, city administrations found themselves empowered to make more
of the decisions. Localizing control did not benefit Bronzeville, however.
It only caused new hardships for blacks; the power transitions mandated
in the 1937 law only exasperated an already bad situation. Political to the
core like everything else in Chicago, the city's housing authority applied
discretionary home-rule powers to every responsibility related to housing.
This meant abuses and unfairness in everything from picking building
sites to renting out units. A free hand, with corresponding negative effects,
did not pass unnoticed for very long. Walter T. Bailey, "the only registered,
licensed Colored architect in Chicago," was the first constituent to complain about it to Mitchell. Under the PWA's Housing Division in 1935, the
Department of the Interior had hired Bailey and four white architects to
draft plans for South Park Gardens. Subsequent contracts ensured their
conditional employment until the project's completion. There was one
stipulation; work must commence by July 1938. Apparently, this meant
nothing to the Chicago Housing Authority. After its assumption of major
responsibilities, Bailey experienced change. Through inside sources, he
and three fellow architects learned that the CHA had shelved their plans
and had discharged them. The illegal firings promptly brought Bailey into
contact with Mitchell because it was the architect's mistaken expectation
that Mitchell might show interest in arranging an appointment at the
CHA. However, Bailey's January 28, 1938, appeal for assistance went
nowhere.[22]

Eventually, thirty months after Mitchell's appeal to Roosevelt, precinct
captains showed renewed impatience with the continuing inertia at South
Park. Their frustration reignited Mitchell. Again, it was the frustration
of enduring so much anger from Second Warders that brought him to
respond. Rambunctious enough once more to push for building federally
funded, low-rent residences in Bronzeville, Mitchell this time carried the
struggle directly to Nathan Strauss of the Federal Housing Authority. As

cultural, and political perspectives; author's surveys of the *Chicago Tribune, Chicago
Daily News, Defender,* 1934–1936. Fairness to Mitchell dictates a mention of him heeding
Robert Moton's advice, that is, there was an effort at opening up the city housing
office's bidding process to minority contractors. After an initial request had brought
nothing, no further pursuits were attempted. M to B. M. Pettit, June 7, 1935; M to FDR,
September 23, 1935; Mannie Manuel to M, October 4, 1935, MP.

22. Good discussions of politics and public housing are provided in Timothy L.
McDonnell, "The New Deal Makes a Public Housing Law: A Case Study of the Wagner
Housing Bill of 1937" and William Wheaton, "The Evolution of Federal Housing
Programs"; Walter T. Bailey to M, January 28, 1938, MP.

he had with Roosevelt, he reviewed the human suffering inflicted upon Chicago black families, first by displacements and then by interminable postponement. In reply, FHA administrator Strauss explained that federal officials could do nothing about delays because members of the Illinois General Assembly were causing the bottlenecks. Due to intraparty feuding and partisanship, downstate interests were allied, blocking enactment of necessary enabling legislation. Without passage, all municipalities lacked prerequisite home-rule powers to establish the independent housing offices required by the Wagner-Steagall Law of 1937. Strauss's answer pacified Mitchell. For another eighteen months, he did not pester about Bronzeville's stymied housing project. Without congressional pressure to speed up the Second Ward development, nobody with any authority seemed in a hurry to proceed. Finally midway through 1939, Mitchell reinterested himself in housing. Earlier on behalf of black architects and engineers with firsthand knowledge of the CHA's consistent prejudice against the employment of black professionals, the leadership of the Chicago-based National Technical Association petitioned Mitchell to lodge protests for its membership with Mayor Kelly. In a June 6, 1939, plea for concerted action, NTA Executive Secretary James W. Lucas informed Mitchell of a recent CHA call for applications from engineers and architects. Although they were for employment at South Park, the CHA refused to take applications from professionally qualified African Americans. After originally promising the race a major role in all decisions, the CHA broke its pledge. Lucas's appeal could not have reached Mitchell at a more opportune moment; shortly before, he had appeared in court for a lawsuit against three corporations accused of practicing discrimination. That experience aroused unusual militancy. Mitchell's personal frustration from having battled three defendants' lawyers over civil rights and equality worked in Lucas's favor. Ready seemingly to extend a personal struggle for equal rights further, Mitchell responded untypically on a delicate matter. Acting on the NTA officer's instruction and complaint, he went directly to Kelly. A surprising reaction followed; the mayor embraced the petition to hire black architects and engineers. Whenever possible, suggested Kelly in his initial reaction to Mitchell, eligible African Americans should get promotions to jobs with authority and responsibility. Afterward, however, the mayor wavered. Before blundering with an overcommitment, Kelly wanted to "see if satisfactory arrangements can be negotiated for taking care of competent engineers and architects of the Negro race on this particular project." For CHA reactions, he sent a feeler to Joseph W. McCarthy. Disinclined to offer these kinds of job opportunities, the CHA head resisted Kelly's overture. Receiving no follow-up support, the city boss abandoned plans to elevate blacks at a project ironically renamed Ida B. Wells after the pioneer Bronzeville civil rights champion.[23]

Soon after work finally commenced on the Wells homes in late August 1939, another conflict engulfed the project. Early in September, with many building sites already excavated for foundations, all work halted; the unions were resisting labor-saving methods. Planned use of ready-mixed concrete by a subcontractor caused the brotherhood of cement workers and laborers to stop construction. Unions blocking entrances with picket lines infuriated Mitchell. Terming their blockade "criminal," he threatened legal actions against everybody connected with stoppages at Wells. Furthermore, the irate legislator wanted both Congress and attorneys from the Justice Department to intervene with "a sweeping . . . investigation of the whole building system in Chicago." Chicago Building Trades Council head and CHA member Patrick J. Sullivan, he said, "should go to jail" because he was guilty of conflict-of-interest crimes. Mitchell also had a solution for ending senseless labor problems; strikers' jobs should pass to unemployed Second Warders. Following his usual pattern, Mitchell's unbridled early harsh reactions never generated corresponding actions. Upon completion in 1940, Wells immediately increased the clout and control of the Second Ward Organization. Desirable as a source of patronage, the housing development strengthened the Machine's leverage in surrounding black precincts. Meanwhile, pundits and cynics noticed something peculiar about its effect upon Bronzeville. According to their complaints, its residents were receiving crap games, relief, and public housing, and whites were getting jobs and city contracts. Even if Mitchell did not have much sway over transpirings at Wells, many constituents had the common misconception that he had the means to assist them with jobs and apartments. Despite his dismal record before the Wells project was completed and his helplessness afterward, Mitchell became a beneficiary. After his appeal for a presidential presence at the project's dedication, Roosevelt designated Secretary of Agriculture Henry A. Wallace to attend "as a testimonial to Congressman Mitchell's work."[24]

Unlike public housing, South Side vice lords posed no problems for Mitchell and the committeemen. Mitchell did no more than blink a blind eye at First District operators of illegal activities. Probably as much as anyone in the Organization's middle ranks, he depended on and cooperated

23. *CR*, 75th Cong., 3d sess., 2201; James W. Lucas to M, June 6, 1939; M to EJK, June 8, 1939; EJK to M, June 20, 1939; EJK to Joseph W. McCarthy, June 20, 1939; Thornton to M, June 20, 1939, MP; Thornton interview.

24. *Defender*, September 2, 1939; unidentified clipping entitled "Aldermen Sift Tieup of Housing"; Augustus L. Williams to M, April 16, 1940, MP; Spencer interview; memo to Edwin M. Watson, August 8, 1940; Watson to Henry A. Wallace, August 16, 1940, RP.

with mob members. Of the many underworld figures operating in and around Bronzeville, Julius Benvenuti was Mitchell's favorite. Described as "a millionaire who looked like a bum," the congenial Sicilian emigrant was, by all appearances, moving as freely throughout Tittinger's Second Ward as any signore in southern Italy. Notwithstanding race or background, members of the Organization were glad just to have Benvenuti's acquaintance. That the numbers operator enjoyed such approval from Party insiders did not surprise people familiar with Tittinger's setup; the gangster almost single-handedly bankrolled the entire ward operation. Like many others at party headquarters, Mitchell counted the extroverted Benvenuti among his closest friends, and he always replied favorably to Benvenuti's infrequent requests, even when it meant turning a blind eye toward Italy's dubious invasion of Ethiopia. Most sensitive about his roots, the Sicilian-American gangster requested that Mitchell refrain from condemnations of Italy's Ethiopian adventures. Besides being a precinct captain in the Second Ward and a generous contributor to Democratic campaigns, Benvenuti gave little personal favors such as ringside tickets to outstanding championship boxing matches. In 1937, Mitchell and Tittinger were his guests at Joe Louis's title bout against James Braddock. Forever friendly, the mobster liked nothing better than chatting with whoever was around Second Ward headquarters. Benvenuti was easily pleased and did not expect many favors; concessions to run numbers and opportunities to meet and associate with leading politicians satisfied him.[25]

While the numbers chieftain was content with a supportive godfather role in Second Ward activities, there were ambitious and assertive hoodlums who wanted more from First District bosses. One was John "Greasy Thumb" Guzik, a mobster who had advanced in less than twenty years from waiting tables in Michael Kenna's South Loop ward to leading Chicago's racketeers. Except for four years' incarceration for federal tax problems, Greasy Thumb had experienced no legal problems. He, like so many other dues-paying Chicago "businessmen," did not suffer interference from municipal police. Guzik was immune to every prosecution, save one; federal revenue authorities did not tolerate his tax evasions. Although he had served one prison term for underreporting his income, Treasury Department officials were not satisfied with his punishment, and they continued to investigate him. At the beginning of 1939, they asked Greasy Thumb to cover delinquent taxes and interest for 1924–1928. His IRS bill was almost $629,000; frantic, he sought a compromise

25. M to Julius Benvenuti, January 4 and April 20, 1935, and May 29, 1937; Holman to M, October 25, 1935, and December 4, 1936, MP; Spencer, Gibson, Tittinger, and Thornton interviews.

settlement with the government, but nobody at the Treasury was budging. Frustrated that his attempts had come to nothing, Guzik unburdened his predicament on Michael Kenna. Supplied a detailed account of the gangster's dilemma, Hinky Dink appealed to Mitchell, asking without explanation or elaboration that the congressman receive "one of my most trusted friends." Kenna noted only that Guzik would be on "a mission of which he will explain to you." Kenna asked Mitchell as "a good favor, take care of him, . . . a very Good friend of yours in Past." Days later in Washington, Mitchell gave the "mission" a receptive response. Then on Greasy Thumb's behalf, he met with IRS officials to gather as much information as possible. Generally satisfied that the IRS men had been "cordial and fairly agreeable" and not especially "hard boiled," Mitchell reported on his findings. He assured Guzik "that with the proper handling your case can be settled without any great degree of trouble." For the purposes of reviewing the IRS case and developing a proper legal course, he suggested a second meeting in Chicago. Decoded, Mitchell's suggestion meant that if the case were to proceed any further, he and Guzik would have to agree about a fee and other basics. Their next session together concerned money and a demand that Guzik replace his legal adviser in the District of Columbia with Washington attorney George E. C. Hayes. The hiring of Mitchell's friend as the case's legal functionary was an obvious move to capitalize on Guzik's misfortunes without risking a public career over something so imprudent as being the lawyer of record for a gangster guilty of tax evasion. Everything was acceptable to Guzik, who deferred the responsibilities to Hayes. Meanwhile, Mitchell spent much of the next two years advising his partner and conferring with Washington and Chicago IRS officials. In 1941, after exchanges and discussions with a "special functionary," the IRS gave Greasy Thumb a more favorable judgment; it reduced his debt to one hundred thousand dollars. For assisting, Mitchell earned fifty thousand dollars from Guzik.[26]

Mitchell rarely interfered in party affairs. After 1934 and through his four congressional terms, his constituents often solicited support for nominations, but appeals for political consideration rarely involved him. It was his unequivocal policy to offer nothing that bosses could misconstrue as

26. *Chicago Evening American* and *Sun-Times*, February 22, 1956; *Chicago Daily News*, February 23, 1956; Treasury Department to Jack Guzik, April 7, 1939; Carter H. Harrison to Jack Guzik, June 7, 1939; Kenna to M, May 10, 1939; M to Guzik, May 16, 1939; M to Guzik, June 29, 1939; Richard L. Tedrow to Guzik, June 13, 1939; Tedrow to Guzik, June 13, 1939; M to CHH, June 29 and August 4, 1939; George E. C. Hayes, Brief of John (Jack) Guzik for Failure to Pay Income Tax, 1924–1928 Inclusive, Before the Commissioner of Internal Revenue in Washington through the Collector at Chicago, July 3, 1939; Guy T. Helvering to Hayes, February 25, 1941; Hayes to Helvering, March 17, 1941, MP; Dickerson and Thornton interviews.

meddling. On January 5, 1935, in an unmistakable response to former Mitchell-for-Congress campaign coordinator Alfred T. Lucas, Mitchell indicated the extent of his unwillingness to insert himself into local politics. Mitchell would not help Lucas secure an important job in the upcoming municipal elections. Nothing could be done, shot back the cowed legislator, because his aid might be interpreted as "dictating to those gentlemen [Kelly and campaign manager Jacob Arvey] what they should do in the situation." Although he would have liked to have been helpful, there was no alternative but to excuse himself. As Mitchell explained it to Lucas, he must "proceed with the greatest possible caution in meddling with local affairs in Chicago" because of specific "instructions given to the Congressmen relative to local matters." When it came to Chicago political decisions, Mitchell maintained a rigid hands-off approach. His stance placed him in an awkward position, and his silence also gave him some discomfort at times. After notifying allies of his inability to assist, he often appealed for their understanding and empathy. As he clarified the tough situation for one anxious solicitor, "You can understand the embarrassing position it would place me in to endorse any person for such a place who might not have the endorsement of my organization. . . . This being true, it will not be possible for me to endorse any one until I am informed what the wishes of the Second Ward Democratic Organization are." Explaining himself further to another associate, he underscored his dilemma. "I knew that whether I agreed with some of the changes which have taken place or not, it was good sense and loyalty to keep mum about those things until such time as everything became adjusted."[27]

Nothing in practice illustrated Mitchell's obedience any better than his relationship with Earl Dickerson. From the beginning, the two men disliked each other, but Machine considerations demanded that they submerge their hostility. As long as independent-minded Dickerson retained official backing, his most unadmiring colleague in Congress did nothing to sabotage him. The two men's devotion and loyalty to the Democratic party were most visible during the wild derby for Second Ward alderman in 1939. The infighting affected both Democrats and Republicans. Because of an intraparty split, the GOP had two hopefuls, William King and William Dawson. On the other side, the Democrats were just as disrupted, with Dickerson and Corneal A. Davis fighting proxy battles for Ed Kelly and Tom Courtney, respectively. Bewildered by the development of fixed alignments, Mitchell misjudged Davis's popularity with the Machine so

27. M to Herman E. Moore, May 15, 1936; Wimbish to M, November 12, 1937; Alfred T. Lucas to M, January 5, 1935; M to Lucas, January 9, 1935; Harry H. Pace to M, May 25, 1937; M to Pace, May 27, 1937; M to WAW, January 29, 1940, MP.

completely that he secretly loaned him fifty dollars. Throughout an intriguing campaign that pitted a Machine-backed reformer against a former insider with dissidents' support, Mitchell was fed detailed accounts by his wife's brother-in-law, James A. McLendon. As a consequence, Mitchell was aware of Tittinger's and Kelly's initial opposition to Dickerson's candidacy, as well as the pair's bungling efforts at blocking Dickerson at a Second Ward slating session. Furthermore, Mitchell learned of Dickerson's success at upstaging others with precinct-captain endorsements and of the Machine's full capitulation to the candidate-inspired rank-and-file rebellion. The swing to Dickerson occurred just after Davis's threatened defection to Governor Horner and Tom Courtney if party bosses were to deny him a spot on the Democratic ticket. At this point, Kelly and Tittinger judged Davis's demands more damaging to Organization interests than the rumblings from precinct captains. After the settlement on Dickerson, Davis balked. Although Mitchell had always enjoyed better relations with Davis than with the slated candidate, there was no option but to place Davis on notice: "line up with the Wimbish [Horner] faction in the Second Ward" and "here is where we break." Mitchell's words reflected "absolute loyalty" to Kelly. If he "had named you," Davis learned from Mitchell, "I would have gone up or down with you, hook, line, and sinker." Meanwhile, Dickerson and Mitchell had saccharine exchanges. At least for the moment, the Organization's candidate for alderman felt good about his congressman. Indirectly, in one of Bronzeville's great political ironies of the Depression decade, Mitchell shared a role in his enemy's elevation. Months before the Second Ward's slating session and the Organization's endorsement of Dickerson, Tittinger had committed the Democrats to fielding a full ticket in the Second Ward. Largely as a result of Mitchell's persuasiveness, previous inclinations to ignore the aldermanic race altogether faded. Here, in one of the few instances when Mitchell's reluctance to participate in local affairs had given way to adamant doubts about the wisdom of conceding a council seat to the GOP, he accounted for a turnabout. Dickerson praised Mitchell's outburst of "independence and manhood" and appreciated "the fact that there are such men as you still holding political office." Years later, when asked to comment about such flattery, a blushing Dickerson shrugged in obvious disgust with himself: "If I ever said anything nice about that bastard, it must have been for a good reason!" Following King's and Dickerson's primary victories, Democrats and Republicans reacted differently. The Democrats united behind Dickerson, but GOP partisans did not coalesce. Refusing to support Republican nominee King, GOP Second Ward committeeman Bill Dawson championed Dickerson, a move that so stunned Mitchell that he wondered what to make of pledges from somebody as "treacherous" as this ward heeler. Except for a minor flare-up during the campaign, Mitchell and

Dickerson enjoyed pleasant exchanges. A lone blemish in their otherwise peaceful relationship came after disclosures of Edgar Brown's assistance to the Democratic nominee. Piqued that Dickerson had wanted to "fool with such a Negro," Mitchell requested explanations.[28]

In return for his obedience and loyalty, the Machine rewarded Mitchell every two years with its support in his bids for reelection. Although "putting Mitchell over" became a routine matter for First District committeemen, Tittinger always worried before congressional campaigns. With Republicans and independent-minded Democrats trying to capitalize on Mitchell's unpopularity, the Second Ward boss doubted the Organization's ability to deliver enough votes to carry Mitchell to victory. Due to his haughtiness, Mitchell's prestige sank so low in Bronzeville that jokes were circulating about him in 1936. According to one tale, first DePriest and then Mitchell petitioned Saint Peter for entry into heaven. However, before opening the gate to them, the keeper asked Angel Gabriel about the two men's credentials. Allegedly, Saint Peter allowed DePriest to proceed after he had disclosed all his good works for blacks, but when it was Mitchell's turn for judgment, neither Gabriel nor Peter could recollect the Democrat ever doing anything for anyone. In answer to their doubts, the now troubled petitioner replied that he had once given a "blind woman a nickle [sic] and a cripple man a dime. Thereupon, Peter asked, 'What should be done with Mitchell?' Gabriel said, 'Just give him back his 15 cts. and tell him to go to hell.' "[29] In one form or another, the story's lesson and the issue of Southern friends emerged and reemerged as dominant themes in anti-Mitchell campaign literature and speeches. As unpopular with blacks as he was during three campaigns, Mitchell escaped questions being raised about his role in the Chicago spoils system. In contrast to his rivals, he rarely resorted to mudslinging. An abiding confidence in the Machine's abilities to control the nomination process caused him more or less to ignore primary opponents. Similarly, his general election as a sitting lawmaker required little attention. Unlike black Republicans, the Democrat drew support from and appealed to white and black voters. To overcome Second Ward GOP strength, he depended upon large Democratic margins in the other, largely white wards. To succeed in largely ethnic areas and in the Loop, he placated constituents with election literature

28. CAD to M, January 4, 1939; M to CAD, January 6, 1939; MNR, December 17, 1938; James H. McLendon to M, January 16 and 18 and March 25, 1939; M to CAD, January 20, 1939; JET to M, January 21, 1939; EBD to M, January 22 and April 7, 1939; M to McLendon, March 27, 1939; M to EBD, January 22, March 27, and April 5, 1939; EBD to M, April 7, 1939, MP; Dickerson interview; *Defender*, March 25, 1939.

29. Spencer, 1936 Political Meeting Notes; Holman to M, December 4, 1935, MP; *Argus*, October 18, 1935.

that exploited a theme of partnership between him and popular politicians such as Kelly and Roosevelt, and he downplayed racial issues as much as possible. With prominent Democrats' endorsements and upbeat political cartoons depicting a statesmanlike, light-skinned black flanked by the president and the mayor, Mitchell subtly created positive impressions of a team player with strong interests in everybody.[30]

In his first bid to continue on Capitol Hill, there was little concern for the GOP. After the surprise defeat of 1934, successive Republican candidates represented an unraveling party in Bronzeville. From a hard-fought primary, DePriest resurfaced in 1936 in the role of challenger. DePriest not only represented a splintered party but also provided little evidence that he had learned much in the previous two years about First District political realities. By portraying Mitchell as "The Ego-maniac" who "does Not NEED the colored vote," DePriest hoped to defeat "one of the most unpopular men in public life in the community." However, he once again forgot the value of the Machine in soliciting white votes. Therefore, Mitchell's victory margin increased to more than seven thousand votes. Mightier than "the intrepid forces of FDR and the New Deal," carrot-and-stick measures used by ward heelers on behalf of Mitchell were simply too much to overcome. While Democratic bosses celebrated a second congressional landslide in Chicago, on the East Coast in New York, a suffering Walter White of the NAACP was wondering "whether Mr. Mitchell ran with, ahead of, or behind the ticket." For the record, Roosevelt had outpolled Mitchell all across the First District.[31]

After Mitchell's reelection, one matter remained for the victor to settle. Having battled the *Chicago Defender* from the outset, he appeared in superior court, seeking five hundred thousand dollars in damages from Robert S. Abbott's newspaper. In a clear case of irresponsible editing, someone had cleared for publication a letter allegedly written by a racist

30. From 1936: W. B. Bankhead, February 3; John M. Houston, January 30; and Dingell to M, January 31; *CR* reprint, February 12; M's Campaign Literature: "Take a Look at the Record," "Weigh the Records of the Two Candidates for Congress," "Let DePriest Answer!" "What Lie will Tell Next?" MP.

31. From 1936: Spencer to M, April 2, 3, and 4; *Chicago Second Ward Square-Dealer*, February 5 and 26; M to Westbrooks, February 22; M to PBY, April 4; Casey to M, April 24; Wyatt to M, May 11; Payne to M, February 11; M to Durden, May 9; Durden to M, June 4; M to Augustus Bierd, June 1; M to DePriest, November 1; DePriest Campaign Literature: "The Ego-maniac" and "Republican Leaders Endorse DePriest for Congress"; S. H. Seelo to Friends, October 30; *Chicago Second Ward News*, May 9 and 23; M Campaign Literature, "Take a Look at the Record," MP; *Chicago Tribune*, February 23; *Defender*, March 21 and 28, April 22, October 31, and November 7; ANPNR, "DePriest and Mitchell Win Nominations for Congress," April 22 and "Mitchell Wins Although Chicago Southside Remains Slightly Republican," November 11, BP; WW to Irwin C. Mollison, October 17 and November 5, NAACP; Cyrus, Gibson, Spencer, Tittinger, Thornton, and Dickerson interviews.

from Mississippi and intended for a stranger in Chicago. If believed, the dumb scenario followed this sequence. A Dixie correspondent had supposedly been so concerned about the First District seat that he wrote to a Chicagoan with an appreciation of Southern views. However, the writer mistook the addressee's identity. Hence, the warped analysis did not reach a sympathetic white but instead fell into a black's possession. Thinking the racist's arguments for Mitchell's retention might alert Bronzeville, the recipient surrendered the letter to the *Defender*. Mockingly composed, with words chopped, stretched, or otherwise mutilated to affect an ignorant Southerner's accent, it certainly could not have been printed as anything but a bad joke on Mitchell. In what had been clumsily passed off as a Mississippian's advice to a white Chicagoan, the composition's author had supposedly tried to appeal to its recipient for Mitchell's victory. Unlike DePriest, Mitchell "has not forgot what he lerned in the South that a nigger must stay in his place. We are interestd in him down here. Mitchel is the first nigger who we white people helpted that didnt get beside hisself." Suspicious and unbelievable as the letter and the peculiar circumstances surrounding its arrival had been, apparently no one at the *Defender* hesitated to foist the sham off on readers. The paper not only published the scurrilous, moronic composition in its election edition but also printed thousands of copies for last-hour GOP distribution. The court dismissed the case because the newspaper had only been guilty of poor judgment. Hence, it could not be sued for participating in a dumb prank. As transparently ill-conceived as the whole affair had been, it certainly did not warrant a lawsuit. Of the silly caper's main characters, Wallace Johnson figured most prominently. As recipient and deliverer of the slur, he attracted immediate suspicion because of his open animosity toward Tittinger. His dismissal from duties as a Second Ward precinct captain no doubt had motivated Johnson's revenge against the committeeman and Mitchell. As absolutely idiotic as his half-baked nonsense was, a magnanimous victim should have laughed at Johnson's clumsiness instead of seeking retribution.[32]

Mitchell's opponents changed in 1938, but other things remained very similar. As in his previous elections, the Machine's backing was again so decisive that he had no need to be concerned about the intraparty rivals lined up against him in the April primary. While they reintroduced the usual charges about Ku Klux Klan friends, carpetbagger status, and servile dependency upon an insensitive white committeeman who had

32. *Defender*, October 31, 1936; *Defender* handbill, "It Speaks for Itself, Read It!" October 31, 1936; Complaint, Superior Court of Cook County, Illinois, *Arthur W. Mitchell v. The Robert S. Abbott Publishing Co., Inc., a Corporation and Robert S. Abbott;* M to Abbott, January 27, 1937, MP.

only dispensed demeaning jobs to blacks, Mitchell limited himself to one week of campaigning. On the Republican side, after a "nip and tuck affair," William L. Dawson polled just more than 31 percent of the GOP vote to win a four-man race. With a new foe, Mitchell expected "a bitter fight in the fall." Compared to DePriest, Dawson appeared a much tougher and more pragmatic opponent with seemingly brighter prospects in the white precincts. Every bit the fighter, Dawson appeared more "level-headed" than DePriest. Disinclined to philosophize, he wasted no time attempting to convert loyal Roosevelt supporters with attacks on New Deal programs. Yet, Dawson's effort showed just how little campaigning had changed in the First District. As in the past, Mitchell remained "the tool of southern reactionary congressmen." Dawson summoned a GOP tradition based on Reconstruction rhetoric to claim deeper "rabble rouser" roots for civil rights and freedom than his rival. But although the Machine and its practices should have been made an issue, the GOP did not suggest that it was a corrupting influence on the representative process. Among black Republican observers of Bronzeville, Claude Barnett was the only one who consistently acknowledged the Democratic Organization as an invincible obstacle to recovering a congressional seat. Writing on June 18, 1938, about Mitchell's unpopularity, Barnett did not foresee it as much of a negative factor because "the democratic party controls city, county and state, and is not insensible to the advantages accruing from this position in Washington." For GOP congressional committee chairman Joseph W. Martin, Barnett gave a pessimistic assessment of Dawson's situation. There were no imagined positive influences affecting voters because "the power which relief and other democratic advantages weilds [sic]" would give the GOP candidate "a tremendous handicap to overcome."[33]

Of course as a beneficiary of the Machine, Mitchell did not have to concern himself with the ramifications of machine politics on Republicans. His task was to adjust to the new and apparently greater challenges of Dawson, and he did well. Without Oscar DePriest's negative record to attack, he concentrated more than previously on his own personal accomplishments and less on his adversary's weaknesses. Three other features distinguished his third campaign. In his campaign literature, there were no referrals to or mentions of Dawson. This subtlety was a major departure for Mitchell. The cartoons on leaflets that had so unmercifully ridiculed and assailed DePriest were gone. By climbing above the fray, Mitchell

---

33. From 1938: *Chicago Sunday Bee*, n.d.; *Chicago Truth*, March 12; Wimbish to M, January 28; M to JET, March 14; Horner-Courtney-Durden-Wimbish Handbill; State of Illinois, *1938 Official Vote*; M to John, May 17; *Chicago Midwest Daily Record*, June 18; Dawson Campaign Literature, "Drive out Mitchell, the Menace," MP; *Defender*, April 16 and October 29; Barnett to John Hamilton, May 12; Barnett to Joseph W. Martin, June 18, 1938, BP.

clearly strove to project statesmanship and a positive image. At mass meetings, though, surrogates "lambasted" GOP leaders and Dawson. As a means of intimidating voters, patronage workers also used a new tactic. For the first time on a large scale, complaints circulated that Democrats were threatening to "cut off" relief checks from all registered Republicans. Finally, in what "was perhaps the most bitterly fought election ever staged between Race candidates . . . sound wagons rolled the streets night and day bearing signs of the various candidates." With so much working for Mitchell and the Democratic party, they were able to overcome Dawson's tough challenge. Afterward, with another victory registered, Mitchell just sighed, realizing his closest race had been won with 53 percent of the vote and with a plurality of 3,811.[34]

In less than one year, the greatest irony of Mitchell's political career occurred. During the 1939 Second Ward aldermanic race, Tittinger increasingly emerged as the main issue. Tittinger's defenders were oblivious to whether or not he "drew the color line" or was otherwise unfair to blacks. They simply dismissed all the complaints as the work of "disgruntles" endeavoring "to embarrass him and make trouble for the Party." Like Tittinger's other defenders, Mitchell felt replacing him "would be a fatal mistake."[35] Eventually, intraparty discord caused by reformers' outspokenness and Tittinger's indefensible position presented Bill Dawson with a golden opportunity. On a self-serving "I-told-you-so" mission to Democratic kingpins Kelly and Nash, Dawson—the able chieftain of GOP interests in the Second Ward—reminded his hosts of Tittinger's insistence on a full slate in 1939 and the resultant insurgency among black precinct captains. Had Tittinger not persisted, the good instincts of the county chairman to sit out an ill-advised 1939 aldermanic race would have prevailed. The crafty Dawson then laid out a convincing package deal that would help the Democratic kingpins to overcome tough challenges from the reform-minded Dickerson, resentment directed at Tittinger, and unruly party rebels. In return for the party's ward committeemanship, Dawson offered himself and his loyal GOP organization. As an all-in-one solution, his proposal punished Tittinger for not anticipating intraparty problems from running a full slate of candidates and for being inept at

34. From 1938: Mitchell Campaign Literature, "Congressman Mitchell Has Made an Outstanding Record," "Congressman Mitchell Opens Fight on Jim Crow"; Precinct Vote Count, MP; *Defender*, November 12.

35. M to Nash, June 27, 1939; M to John L. Fry, February 5, 1935; M to MCS, March 11, 1935; M to Clarence H. Robinson Sr., March 20, 1935; M to Durden, February 6, 1936; M to John Scott, February 22, 1936; M to Wimbish, February 1, 1938; JET to M, August 6, 1935, and May 20, 1937; M to JET, January 15, May 19, and October 29, 1937, and May 10, 1939; Holman to M, January 2 and 4, 1936; M to Holman, December 4, 1935, MP; *Defender*, March 16, 1935; Tittinger, Dickerson, Thornton, Cyrus, Gibson, and Spencer interviews.

silencing critics like Dickerson. Also, the package empowered an African American, thus creating the appearance of Machine dedication and responsiveness to Bronzeville. Arguably more important to Kelly and Nash, Dawson promised delivery of many new votes to the Organization. The tempting proposition came amidst a Dickerson-supported petition drive against Tittinger. Hence for party bosses, the offer was irresistible. In obedient unison at the regularly scheduled Monday meeting of the Cook County Central Committee on October 30, 1939, party delegates unceremoniously dumped Tittinger in favor of "treacherous" Dawson. Perhaps on account of well-known animosities between Dawson and Mitchell, their unfriendly relationship came under floor discussion. At the closed-door session, there were politicians who favored a strategic replacement of Mitchell with Dickerson in order to remove a major source of conflict within the party and to corral reform elements. Figuring Dickerson's elevation would rid them of an embarrassment, they argued the move might also obligate Dickerson to Dawson. After a brief discussion, there was little enthusiasm left for taking the gamble. As important and symbolic as Tittinger's anticipated removal would be for everyone connected to the Second Ward, nobody from the Central Committee bothered to solicit Mitchell's reactions. Such disregard of his opinions proved how little worth the bosses attached to his thoughts. Their slighting had significant consequences for Mitchell. The only news to reach him in Washington about the transpiring developments in the Second Ward came belatedly from gossipy secondhand sources. His informants urged him to arrange immediate travel to Chicago to get a personal grasp on the situation. But a pending personal lawsuit against several railroads delayed his departure from the capital. For a confirmation of what he had heard, he asked Nash to verify hearsay about Kelly's "disrupting the Organization and placing my former opponent Dawson in charge of patronage. I cannot understand this movement, if true." Although Mitchell probably deserved information, the party's county office confirmed nothing to him about the dismissal and shakeup. Bronzeville was in a total uproar over Dawson's ascendancy, and Congressman Mitchell found himself in complete isolation, not knowing who or what to believe. Being under strictest instructions not to delve into local politics, he was forced by the circumstances to move somewhat deftly between curiosity and coyness. Having been outmaneuvered by an adversary, Mitchell seemed a total outsider who desperately needed a reliable surrogate to protect his vital interests in the new setup.[36]

---

36. Tittinger interview; *Chicago Daily News*, November 14 and 17, 1939; CAD to M, September 18, 1940, MP; Fred J. Smith to M, October 28, 1939; M to Nash, October 30,

Indeed, Mitchell would learn that his worst fears were realities. As an informant verified, Dawson had taken over the Second Ward, and worse, Dickerson's initiatives had felled Tittinger. Dickerson had pushed for blacks' signatures on ouster petitions. According to a version of events that reached Mitchell in Washington, "trickery was born in the distorted mind of Dickerson in order that he might possibly be put on the ticket by Mr. Dawson for Congress." Threatening to Mitchell, the duo of Dawson and Dickerson was probably "working hand-in-hand." The changes had unsettling effects on many Second Ward veterans, according to Democratic insider-turned-outsider James Durden in a communication to Mitchell on January 2, 1940. As a result of the turmoil, Durden entreated Mitchell "to see face to face the set up." Other equally gloomy reports also reached Mitchell; each one stressed that the situation was filled with uncertainty and confusion. Judging by details in Mitchell's possession, Dawson's position was "precarious." As one critic put it, "Things are in such a turmoil here in the Second Ward that it is difficult to make a fairly accurate observation." Had Mitchell heard from both sides, he would have learned that under Dawson's leadership Second Ward politics were changing quickly. Dawson moved the ward headquarters east along Thirty-Fifth from Michigan Avenue to Calumet, and then he assigned his longtime ally, Augustus L. Williams, to the Organization's legal affairs. Shuffling personnel, the new boss appointed several well-known Democratic outsiders such as C. C. Wimbish to a reorganized party apparatus. In many cases, their places resulted from Dawson's ruthless purges of former insiders. Naturally, with new men in power, wheelhorses of the old regime found themselves stripped of authority and influence. For Mitchell during those first days of 1940, there was still no indication about how the restructuring would affect him. This was obviously a difficult period for the congressman. By mid-January, many of Dawson's harshest opponents had already organized a challenge, and Mitchell was tempted to join them. Under leadership from Myron M. Frazin and Perry C. Thompson, a dump-Dawson organization was established to participate in the 1940 spring primaries. Frazin and Thompson solicited Mitchell's support and assistance. For the Second Ward 1940 Regular Democratic Organization, they wanted a candidate with years of experience to head the ticket against "downtown" bosses and Dawson's Second Ward Regular Democratic Organization. From informal surveys in Bronzeville, Frazin surmised there were "several groups unable to stomach our 'appointed' committee man" and concluded that "confusion runs riot" in the Dawson camp;

1939; Frederick D. Larkins to M, November 1 and 6, 1939; Durden to M, December 23, 1939; M to Durden, December 27, 1939, MP; Tittinger interview.

"he cannot win even with the support given him." All this left Mitchell pondering whether he would have a future in Chicago; there was much to consider. For six years, his original sponsor and supporter Tittinger had done much to help him, but now Tittinger was allied with a rebellious faction as a candidate for the state house of representatives. Many friends and supporters clamored against former enemies who now posed as the Democratic party's sudden guardians. Facing pressure from both sides and with much at stake, Mitchell did not rush a decision. Coolheaded and detached, he listened but refused to commit to persuaders from one side or the other; he would shape his own future. Even though the postponement of a decision showed "very good foresight," he could not delay forever. However, he could wait for an opportune moment to announce his intentions. Finally, after almost fifteen weeks, Mitchell ended his procrastination. On February 10, 1940, he was in Chicago; his dinner companion was Bill Dawson. Something of a relationship must have developed because within forty-eight hours, they reunited at the ward office. There, the two men buried their past differences long enough to unite behind Mitchell's campaign for a fourth term in Congress.[37]

The logic of siding with Dawson outweighed personal factors. Negotiating with him made more sense than committing political suicide. When given a choice, Mitchell decided cold realities must outweigh personal debts to old friends such as Joe Tittinger. More than once, he had witnessed mavericks from the Machine fare poorly in campaigns because they had neither jobs, housing, nor relief to dispense. Therefore, he obviously figured another group of malcontents would have no chance as well. Having been a beneficiary of the Machine's support three times, Mitchell appreciated more than most people just what the Machine could accomplish in Bronzeville. Besides giving thought to practical factors, he was a sincere believer in Kelly's and Nash's abilities. Five years before the latest squabbling over patronage and leadership, he had received specific orders from them to ignore local affairs. After they had told him not to be intrusive or inquisitive, he obeyed instructions in order to net their rewards. For the Machine's part, it kept its promises, too. In exchange for his good service and silence, it twice gave him large reelection pluralities that returned him to Capitol Hill. Now for his tergiversation about Dawson, Nash and Kelly would grant him a fourth term in Congress. Pragmatic and loyal

37. Durden to M, January 2, 1940; McLendon to M, January 4, 1940, and n.d.; Larkins to M, January 8, 1940; Myron M. Frazin to M, January 17, 1940; Campaign Pamphlet, "The Life Work and Political Background of Perry C. Thompson"; Frazin and Thompson to Second Ward Precinct Captains, January 24, 1940; handbill, "Refuse to Sign Dawson's Suicidal Petitions," n.d.; *Second Ward Political News*, January 24, 1940, MP; Tittinger interview; *Pittsburgh Courier*, February 17, 1940.

like always to superior forces, Mitchell did not demur about abandoning former allies for a declaration for Dawson. Besides, the Second Ward's new boss also considered Dickerson "hardheaded." The 1940 primary was in progress when Mitchell had his meeting with Dawson. Dawson was under pressure from Alderman Dickerson to dump the party's most unpopular and least effective standard-bearer. Hearing of a plot against him, Mitchell altered his official opinion of Dickerson. From being "the ablest man running for alderman," the city council member became "the most conceited man in the United States." So in swift, remorseless trans-formation, Mitchell shifted assessments and allegiances. After a double-talk reevaluation of personalities, Mitchell endowed former enemies with goodness and castigated former allies from the Second Ward Organiza-tion such as Joe Tittinger for being turncoats hungry for power. A first private sign of his realignment came on February 16, 1940, four days after his long session with Dawson. "My dear Committeeman," began his patronage-related correspondence to Dawson. To Democratic chairman Farley, Mitchell was positive and kind on an even grander scale toward Tittinger's ambitious replacement. Dawson, Mitchell wrote to Farley, mo-tivated precinct captains and was "a very able man working heart and soul for . . . the Party." Miraculously, with Dawson in command, precinct and ward meetings were filled with a "Democratic spirit never seen . . . so high as it is at this very moment." Besides, the change to Dawson "thoroughly disrupted the Republican Organization" because he had "brought with him hundreds of the most outstanding political workers in the ward who formerly were Republicans but are now Democrats." In choosing sides, Mitchell had demonstrated again his uncanny talent for picking winners. In Bronzeville, the groundswell of angry support the anti-Dawson faction envisioned from an aroused electorate never materialized.[38]

The primary and general elections of 1940 were Mitchell's first political battles without Tittinger. Dawson now headed Second Ward political af-fairs for the Democrats. Since resistance movements against his leadership had never been tested, there was speculation going into the 1940 pri-mary about party cleavages affecting incumbents like Mitchell. Although two challengers were contesting the Machine for his renomination, only Redcap president Willard S. Townsend, running under an "anti-bossism" banner, appeared formidable enough to test Bill Dawson's abilities to deliver votes to Mitchell. Because Townsend was unknown outside union circles and had no political record, even Mitchell's harshest critics were

38. M to J. Gray Lucas, January 26, 1940; M to EBD, April 15, 1942; M to William Dawson, February 16, 1940; see also A. L. Williams to M, April 1, 1940; M to Williams, April 16, 1940; M to JAF, March 13, 1940, MP; Tittinger interview; *Kansas City Call*, February 24, 1940; *Chicago Tribune*, March–April 1940.

unenthusiastic about his chances to succeed. Before the primary campaign, friends and supporters of Dickerson had been pleading with him to announce, but in a defining moment like this, the alderman had refused to heed reckless advice from the unauthorized Dickerson for Congress Committee; this would have defied Dawson's decision to stick with Mitchell. Hence with nobody of importance in the field to contest him, Mitchell coasted easily into November and an election showdown with Dawson's old Republican enemy; William E. King had outpolled eight contenders for the GOP nomination. In a desperate search for something substantial upon which to base a successful effort against Mitchell, King requested Walter White's help with "any material . . . that may be effective in this campaign," but the NAACP leader could do nothing. Besides, additional information could not be King's panacea. Dawson and a "fine group of captains" represented a powerful, unstoppable force. With them "taking care of . . . [all his] interests," Mitchell felt "absolutely safe in the hands of our Organization." With Bill Dawson in control, nothing had deteriorated in the Second Ward, and FDR's popularity had grown in Bronzeville. As a consequence, Mitchell approached the November 5, 1940, election with few worries. Election results then substantiated his faith in the new committeeman and the Machine's abilities to deliver votes. For the first time, Franklin Roosevelt carried a majority of black precincts, and Mitchell accumulated enough votes outside Bronzeville to pick up a fourth term.[39]

Eight years on Capitol Hill presented Mitchell with many opportunities to break commitments to his first constituency, the Kelly-Nash Machine, but rather than do this, he reaffirmed frequently and diversely his strong intentions to remain an "Organization man." During Democratic party squabbles and the ouster of Tittinger and Dawson's elevation, through his silence over endorsements and nominations, and in his compliance with Machine patronage procedures, there was constancy in Mitchell's loyalty and obedience. Here in essence were the alpha and omega of his entire legislative career. House roll calls indicated his unwavering devotion and faithfulness. On these, he followed Kelly's and Nash's instructions, voting almost always with other Chicago Democratic House members against Republicans. No other congressional bloc commanded as much of his allegiance as the one representing Windy City interests

39. *Chicago Tribune,* March 10, April 10 and 11, and September 15, 1940; *Chicago Daily Times,* January 23, 1940; *Chicago Sunday Bee,* February 11, 1940; McLendon to M, January 16, 1940; WAW to M, January 31, 1940, M to CAD, September 19, 1940; Mitchell Handbill, "Congressman Mitchell in the Capitol," November 5, 1940, MP; *Defender,* February 10, 1940; Dickerson interview; King to WW, April 19, 1940, NAACP; *Voice,* November 2, 1940; *Defender,* November 9, 1940; *Chicago Tribune,* September 15, 1940; *Pittsburgh Courier,* September 7, 1940.

on Capitol Hill. In every type of issue from farm bills to welfare proposals, Mitchell broke rank substantially less often with fellow Chicagoans than with all other subgroups in the House. An analysis of Mitchell's voting on roll calls confirms him as a supporter of Chicago and a foe of the GOP.[40] Besides voting correctly most of the time on Capitol Hill, he behaved favorably in other ways, too. Most importantly, he obeyed rules covering constituent requests. When requests arrived without a ward committeeman's support or sponsorship, he had clear instructions to ignore them. After each election, Machine bosses carefully lectured loyal charges to do nothing for residents who were bypassing official channels for employment and assistance; Mitchell adhered to this policy. Hence, his activities became an integral part of a powerful political organization's daily operation. In the final analysis, Mitchell performed most satisfactorily, fulfilling obligations to the Machine, following its rules, voting correctly on roll calls, bestowing patronage and assistance to only the "right" people, and distancing himself from "local affairs." Mitchell was not especially popular with Bronzevillians, but nevertheless, in terms of voting percentages, each successive reelection showed him gaining more of their votes. Yet, the pattern of his first victory of 1934 repeated itself three more times; white votes delivered every Mitchell triumph. In race-conscious Chicago, his victories proved how willing Kelly and Nash were to dispense their ultimate rewards to "safe" individuals who kept promises and achieved according to party and Machine expectations. For an ambitious but relatively unknown black who came to Chicago in 1929 from Washington, it all translated into four congressional terms, modest wealth, and fleeting fame.

40. Based upon the author's exhaustive analytical survey of House voting patterns from roll calls, *CR*, 1935–1943.

"Professor" Arthur W. Mitchell, principal of West Alabama Institute, c. 1912.

*First wife Eula Mae Mitchell
and son (Arthur)
Wergs Mitchell, c. 1908.*

*Annie Harris
Mitchell,
Mitchell's
second wife.*

*Mitchell after his move to
Washington in late 1919.*

*Eighteenth Phi Beta Sigma convention, December 30, 1933, Chicago. President
Arthur Mitchell is seated in the middle of the first row.*

Mitchell challenges DePriest to debate.

Amateur cartoonist Proctor Chisholm's genius and imagination helped Mitchell to effectively attack opponent Oscar DePriest in the 1934 campaign. In "Mitchell challenges DePriest to debate," voters are reminded that DePriest has refused to take part in public debates, and Mitchell is pictured as the champion of the New Deal. In "DePriest and the Negro Gold Star Mothers," DePriest is criticized for not protesting the Hoover administration's mistreatment of African American mothers traveling to France to visit the graves of sons killed in World War I.

DePriest and
The Negro Gold Star Mothers

Meeting of Chicago's Second Ward Democratic Organization. Seated to the right of the sign is Congressman Arthur Mitchell. Earl B. Dickerson is to Mitchell's left.

Mitchell seated at his Capitol Hill desk.

*At the statue of Booker T. Washington on the campus of Tuskegee
Institute. From left: Congressman Mitchell, registrar John H. Palmer,
president Frederick D. Patterson, trustee Richard Harris.*

Designed to downplay Mitchell's race as an issue in the 1940 First District
congressional election, this postcard-size handout showed a darkened picture of Franklin
Roosevelt and a light-colored portrait of Arthur Mitchell. With a handwritten caption
reading "For Arthur W. Mitchell from his old friend Franklin D. Roosevelt," Roosevelt
gave Mitchell a personal boost in his first campaign under the Second Ward leadership
of Republican-turned-Democrat William L. Dawson.

1940 agreement for a common legislative cause on antilynching measures. From left: Representative Raymond McKeough of Illinois, Mitchell, and Joseph Gavagan of New York.

After receipt of a congressional appointment to the Naval Academy at Annapolis in 1936, James L. Johnson Jr. receives some pointers from sponsor Arthur Mitchell.

Congressman Mitchell escorting West Point appointee James D. Fowler around the Capitol in 1939.

*Attorneys Arthur Mitchell and Richard
Westbrooks ready to battle against railroad
discrimination before the United States Supreme
Court in 1941.*

*Congressman Mitchell delivering the 1941 commencement
address at Howard University.*

Secretary Christine Ray and Mitchell in 1942, packing for his departure from Congress.

The Mitchell mansion at Rose-Anna Gardens outside Petersburg, Virginia, nearing completion in 1942.

Retiree and Southern country gentleman Arthur Mitchell poses at Rose-Anna Gardens.

Arthur W. and Clara Mann Mitchell posing after their marriage at Rose-Anna Gardens, March 20, 1948.

Wreath-laying ceremony at Booker T. Washington's grave during Mitchell's 1951 stop at Tuskegee Institute while touring the South for the Southern Regional Council. From left: Clara Mann Mitchell, Arthur W. Mitchell, USDA field agent T. M. Campbell, field coordinator J. Henry Smith, school vice president I. A. Derbigny, business agent Luther H. Foster, assistant to president Robert R. Moton Jr., director of public relations Charles E. Tout.

New Deal Democrat

5

T he Chicago Machine and the Roosevelt administration clearly
benefited each other. Numerous cultural activities, relief and aid
programs, housing, beautification and conservation projects, in-
frastructure improvements, and above all endless opportunities to express
"recognition politics" were the Kelly-Nash Organization's rewards from
the White House. The Chicago Machine's paybacks to the president were
equally significant, especially in the form of consistent support from loyal
Democratic members of the Chicago Caucus for FDR's legislative agenda
and massive Democratic pluralities in Chicago to ensure that pivotal
Illinois would vote for the Democrats every four years in the electoral
college. In effect, the Machine and the administration sustained each
other's survival. Hence, there were reasons enough for keeping all the
secondary participants in the process under strictest instructions to cooperate fully and deliver as directed. At comprehending roles and accepting
directions, Mitchell proved himself exceptionally gifted. Already in full
grasp of these stakes upon entering Congress in 1935, he was completely
resigned to compromising racial matters to other political interests for as
long as necessary. He also knew and accepted another fact of survival:
embarrassing challenges over civil rights such as Oscar DePriest's protest
at the House of Representatives' restaurant could not be repeated if he
wished for a long congressional tenure. Thus, when Mitchell commented
that his legislative efforts would primarily benefit the First District and
FDR, he was engaging in skillful double-talk; it was his way of masking
servitude and his true motivations for not actively championing the minority's causes. An astute politician, Mitchell allowed himself to accept the
rules of the game as they related to race. He had served his apprenticeship
in Alabama. For him, discerning a taboo subject from a safe topic was easy.
Since his future House career depended upon pleasing an odd coalition of
Northern urban and Southern rural Democrats who had been giving vital

support to the Roosevelt administration, it was important to remember what life in Alabama had taught him. In the past, Mitchell had adjusted well to other people's priorities and parameters, and from all indications, he would be doing so again in Congress.[1]

When Mitchell entered Congress, Roosevelt was approaching the middle of his first term. Already, reassessments of the once-feared man had begun. Mixed reviews were coming from a black minority that had supported him in 1932. Compassionate interest in common people and New Deal programs for relief of human suffering comforted this group. There were also signs that none of the dire predictions about a Democratic presidency were going to become reality. Many African Americans, for example, had feared FDR's running mate, John Nance Garner. After nothing horrible had happened, the *Pittsburgh Courier* reminded black doomsayers of all their predictions about Garner's evil influence and their warnings. According to them, the Texan, "if made President of the Senate, would destroy the last vestige of constitutional protection now enjoyed by Negroes [and] . . . that the South would be in the saddle, . . . and that Negroes would be lynched by the wholesale and trampled under foot like so many worms." Nonfulfillment of these prophesies gladdened Roosevelt's black supporters, but they were still a bit reserved in their judgments because the president had done so little to "translate the principles of Jefferson into action." Nonetheless, these critics had been seeking more presidential "courage" in dealing with people who needed "a better attitude" toward the minority.[2]

Other African Americans were less generous in their appraisals. Speaking for "the thinking Negro," scholarly Horace R. Cayton viewed "the Hoover and Roosevelt administrations . . . as similar as 'The Gold Dust Twins,' neither meaning him any good or glory. However, if it is to be Hobson's choice in the next presidential marathon, Roosevelt versus Hoover, the former should not only get the Negro vote . . . , of two evils choose the dumbest, but may the gods be sufficiently propitious on those occasions, to save us from both." Cayton had harsh conclusions because "Roosevelt has been and is as silent about the ever mounting number of Negro lynchings as an Indian statue at the door of a cigar emporium and gives no evidence of changing." As the perceptive journalist put it, presidential silence occurred logically enough, because why would

1. Early proof of Mitchell's resolve to obey the rules before him came on March 11, 1935. After a mixed delegation from Father Divine's Los Angeles temple had been denied service in the House restaurant, Mitchell announced his neutrality, stating that he thought "the issue involved too small to devote much time to or to make a noise about, it," *Louisville Leader,* March 16, 1935.

2. *Pittsburgh Courier,* March 9, 1935.

Roosevelt have an "intention of committing political suicide"? According to the critic, the Roosevelt administration considered maintaining peace with the "solid South . . . more greatly desired than justice for the masses, hence, 'mum is the word.' "[3]

Hostile as Cayton was toward the president, his views did not coincide with the opinions expressed by an increasing number of African Americans. Their "Mister President Roosevelt" was a friend. Even without overt gestures to the race, his popularity was rising. During Mitchell's first year on Capitol Hill, a tenant farmer's positive expressions perhaps reflected these new feelings better than discontented intellectuals' attacks. He not only appreciated President and Mrs. Roosevelt but also foresaw the day when many other "colored folks . . . [would be] on the side of the Democrats." For those in search after concrete assurances from the chief executive, there was the much-cited July 5, 1935, Roosevelt pledge to President C. C. Spaulding of the North Carolina Mutual Life Insurance Company. In an encouraging first sign, FDR indicated his personal desire for better relations and greater justice for the minority. As he assured a black leader, "the Administration intends that every recovery and regular agency of the Federal Government be administered with absolute equity and fairness."[4]

All of this had significance for Mitchell. Emerging in the aftermath of an election triumph as Roosevelt's best-known African American defender, he sought credibility as the one race leader who could work effectively with Democrats. With few opportunities to observe firsthand, blacks who viewed Roosevelt from distant vantage points did not have Mitchell's privilege of evaluating him from personal experiences. Several face-to-face meetings positioned him uniquely to assess the president's attitudes about minority issues and leaders. During his eight-year tenure on Capitol Hill, Mitchell had open communication lines to the Oval Office. Almost without exception, when he requested an audience with FDR, private sessions would follow. According to every report, both men enjoyed their brief encounters together, finding them useful and cordial. For Mitchell's part, there was a respectful deference to the statesman. As a result, he did not take advantage of his chances to press for changes and improvements. Instead, he usually minimized complaints with the administration. At every meeting between the president and the lawmaker, Roosevelt controlled and dominated the agenda in predictable fashion. At the appointed hour, a secretary escorted Mitchell in to Roosevelt. The congenial leader

3. Horace R. Cayton to M, October 22, 1935, MP.
4. M. D. Dilworth to JAF, October 20 and to FDR and M, October 22, 1936; Spaulding to FDR, June 20, 1935; FDR to Spaulding, July 5, 1935, RP; *New York Age,* March 2, 1935; *Journal and Guide,* July 27, 1935.

smiled and stretched out his hand before asking Mitchell to be seated. Then, as first priorities, Roosevelt commenced by inquiring about his guest's wife and his activities in Congress before soliciting Mitchell's indulgence to tell a funny story. After chatting about trivialities and amusing Mitchell for several minutes, FDR looked at his watch. Acting astonished, he then excused himself for talking so much without inquiring Mitchell's concerns. Then with little time left for discussion, Mitchell haltingly presented a major issue for presidential attention. Smiling and laughing at this point, the domineering host consoled his guest, telling him not to worry because everything would come under control. Following docile expressions of humble gratitude for Roosevelt's time, Mitchell departed, gladdened and satisfied that he had discussed something of importance with the president. In addition to private conferences, Arthur and Annie Mitchell, without fanfare or attention, attended many White House social functions for House members and spouses. The awkwardness associated with Mr. and Mrs. DePriest's appearances at similar receptions disappeared almost completely. There was also considerable correspondence between Mitchell and Roosevelt. At one stage, their contacts were so close that a black domestic worker at the White House confidentially warned the NAACP leadership that "Mr. Mitchell is a bad influence . . . so far as the affairs of Negroes are concerned."[5]

From the moment of Mitchell's arrival on Capitol Hill until his departure in 1943, he tried to help FDR fill positions. Since White House staffers seldom sought the congressman's many evaluations and recommendations, not much thought was given to his input. At no time was Mitchell's lack of influence on the selection process more apparent than after Roosevelt's June 25, 1941, Executive Order 8802 establishing the Committee on Fair Employment Practices (FEPC). With several appointments forthcoming, Mitchell desperately wanted a role in the selections. Therefore, he tried calling in debts from influential Democrats who had once benefited from his actions, and he engaged in personal lobbying. With a written request for a private audience with FDR about the matter, Mitchell went to White House favorite and former Supreme Court justice James F. Byrnes and Speaker of the House Sam Rayburn, begging their help. Likely in repayment for past favors, they were favorable to

5. MNR, March 25, 1935; M to Hurja, July 26, 1935; M to Marvin H. McIntyre, August 20, 1935; M to JAF, August 26, 1936; M to C. B. Powell, September 1, 1936; FDR to M, March 7, 1935, and November 18, 1942; M to FDR, March 4 and August 8, 1935; M to Cummings, August 8, 1935; M to Mary M. Bethune, December 18, 1937, MP; confidential WW memo, October 7, 1935, NAACP; Mary Bethune's "My Secret Talks with FDR" described how the president distracted visitors with stories and flattery. By so dominating sessions, he left no time for serious discussions.

arranging for Mitchell to be involved in the committee. Rayburn wired and Byrnes telephoned the White House. These efforts succeeded in freeing Roosevelt's appointment diary for a Mitchell visit, but nothing else came from their activities. Timid salesmanship and Mark Ethridge's selection as FEPC chairman destroyed whatever chances Mitchell might have had to influence developments. Exasperating matters further, White House insider and Eleanor Roosevelt favorite Mary Bethune was successful at nominating Machine and Mitchell enemy Earl Dickerson to the FEPC. Upset as Mitchell was with the choice, Mayor Kelly telephoned Ethridge, complaining that Dickerson's place on the committee would give the troublemaker unfair advantage over an incumbent black lawmaker. To equalize matters, Kelly demanded either a forced resignation or the agency's enlargement to accommodate Mitchell. Since the mayor could not prove allegations of Dickerson intending to politicize FEPC activities, Ethridge did not change the committee's composition.[6]

On those rare occasions when there were requests for Mitchell to submit candidates for executive department assignments, he usually turned to one of several well-established networks for names. Of these, the Chicago Machine was the greatest source of personnel. When he reached outside the Organization's patronage setup, his favorite choices were colleagues from the Colored Division of the Democratic National Committee, Sigma brothers, and members of Washington's black professional elite. From the latter group, Mitchell selected either friends connected to Howard University or attorneys. For example, he secured a Federal Writers' Project grant for Professor Carter Woodson.[7]

Although Mitchell's contributions to White House policy-making and staffing were irregular and infrequent, he voiced few complaints. The notable exception occurred on August 24, 1937, when Mitchell uncharacteristically confronted Democratic leaders over Justice Department appointments. Confessing his agitation to James Farley over treatment received from Democrats and the administration, the generally docile Mitchell claimed to have been "much discouraged and disgusted [so as]

6. M to FDR, May 15, 1939, and February 6, 1942; M to Henry Morgenthau, May 27, 1941, MP; M to FDR, July 3, 1941; Mark Ethridge to James Early, December 29, 1941, RP; Dickerson interview; citing newspaper sources in *A New Deal for Blacks*, Sitkoff contradicted Dickerson and correspondence found in the Roosevelt Libary in Hyde Park. According to his twist of events, the Machine had opted for Dickerson's placement in Washington as a ploy to get "him out of its hair"; see also Kirby, *Black Americans in the Roosevelt Era*, 116.

7. M to Joseph L. McLemore, September 18, 1935; T. V. Smith to McCormick, January 19, 1941; Woodson to M, November 20, 1934; 1934 Campaign Financial Report; KM to M, May 20, 1938; FBR to M, September 13, 18, and 25, 1935; M to FBR, September 16 and 19, 1935, MP.

to note that there is apparently no appreciation for what little I have done." Once the complaints had begun flowing, Mitchell unleashed all his disappointment, noting "Honors and appreciation continue to go to those of my Race who have supported the Party on one hand, and fought it and filchered the Party on the other hand." In this, perhaps the congressman's most revealing letter, he did not mince words about his inner feelings. As he reminded Farley, "I have been very modest in pushing myself forward; I have not been to you nor to any other high official and attempted in any way to dictate appointments among my people." According to Mitchell, there were justifications for grievances. In his judgment, he had "played the major part in bringing the Negro support to this administration." Nevertheless, the administration had consistently given greater consideration to less-deserving African Americans. More than anything else, Mitchell did not look favorably on the fact that his suggestions were often being bypassed in favor of Robert L. Vann's. To Mitchell's stunned amazement, the Pittsburgh journalist's harsh editorial campaign against FDR's proposals for reorganizing the Supreme Court did not seem to affect him; regarding appointments, the publisher of the *Courier* retained an active role. Perplexed and hurt by the favoritism shown Vann, Mitchell could not refrain any longer from decrying his perceived unfair treatment. Since Vann's antagonisms had contrasted so sharply to his own unwavering support for the presidential program, he understandably could not fathom why Rooseveltian loyalty had been costing him influence. Hence, as his sarcastic remedy, Mitchell offered opposition to the president. Upset as the Chicago Democrat had clearly become over his powerlessness, he was discrete, keeping all bitterness between himself and Farley. After venting his rage, Mitchell retired briefly from Washington, taking a vacation to regain composure and a better perspective. Sobered, he returned to the Capitol resigned to his role as Roosevelt's staunchest black defender. Forced by bosses Kelly and Nash to go hat in hand to party and administration officers, Mitchell lacked sufficient leverage to demand more. Trapped as he was in an elective position that enforced his almost complete obedience, he found himself without enough independence to serve responsively and act freely. His 1937 complaints to Farley substantiate his awkwardness and dismay with having a weak role, and demonstrate that his shackled existence had been bothering him because of the limitations he faced whenever African Americans attempted to enlist his involvement with the Roosevelt administration or after their complaints had reached him through the executive department. For example, when Farley quizzed him about criticisms from black Democratic leader and Indiana industrialist Freeman B. Ransom, Mitchell's predicament forced him to advise that the administration could totally disregard Ransom's unwarranted evaluations of the government's mishandling of black applications. They had come, Mitchell responded cautiously, from "a high class man inclined to be pessimistic," who "dwells over long on things that are a little out of line, often forgetting the many things which are in line and which merit special commendation."[8]

For blacks appealing directly to him for intervention with members of the administration, Mitchell had two standard replies. To correspondents unknown to him, he often offered beratings for their ignorance of his commitments to a Chicago constituency or for their partisanship. Harsh and intolerant as he frequently tended to be with critics, the race of correspondents did not figure much in his treatments. Without hesitation, Mitchell fired equally vilifying charges at white or black correspondents who annoyed him. In his responses, he labeled one white a "nitwit interloper" and another an "economic royalist." For Democratic Colored Division insiders with complaints about a lack of good opportunities for blacks in the administration, he advised either more organization-building among the race or more deferring to important white Democrats. Without sufficient kowtowing, minority members could be perceived as "not altogether in sympathy with the New Deal" and "rather free with adverse criticism."[9]

Regardless of how others in Washington might have rated Mitchell as a race spokesman, House Democrats liked him. Through four terms as a partisan lawmaker, he gave party members ample opportunities to appreciate his consistent roll-call voting with Democratic majorities. Moreover, his commitments to the New Deal and Roosevelt impressed them as earnest and steadfast. Inasmuch as all these factors were significant, they played only an incidental role in Mitchell's overall popularity. His approach to interracial relationships was what likely separated him from other blacks and endeared him most to many Democrats. When they were in his presence, there was no need for them to feel condemnation or recrimination. He was reassuring toward fellow Democrats on Capitol Hill. House members from the South were quickest to sense and appreciate Mitchell's unalienating quality. After DePriest, they found Mitchell a pleasant relief. For years, they had listened to both white and black Republicans blame them for the poor plight of the South's African Americans, but

8. M to JAF, August 24, 1937, and June 6, 1940, MP.
9. Samples of Mitchell's correspondence with critics include Roswell A. Benedict to M, July 15, 1936; M to Herman Weinberger, January 26, 1940; M to W. W. K. Sparrow, April 1, 1937; see also M to Jasper C. Horne, April 24, 1935; FBR to M, September 18, 1935, April 24 and 29, 1936, and June 12, 1940; FBR to Sherman A. Minton, April 15, 1936; M to FBR, April 27, 1936, MP.

in contrast, Mitchell was restrained in his dealings with Southerners. He enjoyed telling mixed audiences and reporters how blacks had benefited under their truest friends, Southern whites. In the presence of Southern whites he brought delight, especially after noting how much more at home blacks were in Dixie among understanding whites than they were above the Mason-Dixon Line among strangers. In several well-publicized statements resounding Booker Washington's counsel to blacks, Mitchell shifted blame from the sources to the victims, claiming each individual had responsibility for his own self-improvement. Whites present at one large mixed gathering in Virginia derived so much satisfaction and comfort from hearing such "brutal frankness" from Mitchell that they recommended his speech be published in the *Congressional Record*. Among other things, Mitchell had "made it plain that what becomes of the Negro and his future is largely a matter for the Negro himself to settle." As he put it, blacks would see personal improvement if they "did not spend as much time cursing the white man as . . . in showing the Negro his duty and responsibility."[10]

Halfway through his first term in Congress, Mitchell's solace and gentleness to the formulators, perpetuators, and defenders of racial inequality and segregation had removed most of their concerns about him. All of a sudden, the white South gave him its endorsements. In a short note, similar to others sent to Mitchell by grateful Southern congressmen, Sam Hobbs of Alabama captured the region's positive sentiments, complimenting the Chicago lawmaker for rendering such "outstanding service" to African Americans. "While other Parties are more sympathetic with the social equality aspirations of one element of our negro population, the Democratic Party is, as you have repeatedly and ably pointed out, the Party which has conferred the only real benefits upon the negro since his emancipation." In expressing relief for the black legislator's conduct, white Southerners were not alone; Northern Democrats were glad, too. Wearied by rightists' battles and guilt by association for being in the same political party as their Dixie brethren, they accepted FDR's viewpoints about recovery and black people. In regard to compromises over segregation in New Deal agencies, they chose enacting a plan for economic improvement over becoming bogged down with side issues such as the program's discriminatory features. As its cosupporter and as a fellow partisan politician who assisted Democratic candidates, Mitchell proved himself an asset to the party. He attracted crowds and gave Democrats inside tracks to minority voters. Furthermore, it was nice having him assail

10. Reprint, *CR*, 77th Cong., 1st sess., March 7, 1941, MP.

Republicans for keeping blacks "in political slavery for seventy years." Thus Mitchell's presence on Capitol Hill took pressure off Democrats and exonerated them for their policies toward blacks.[11]

Also during his first year on Capitol Hill, Mitchell forged a reputation for reliability. In 1935, while crisscrossing the eastern half of the United States and speaking before Northern and Southern audiences, most commonly at strictly Democratic functions, he delivered one basic message: "Only a pessimist can say, there is no chance for us in this country. Under the New Deal you have the opportunity of a life time if you measure up to it." Given in many different forms, the theme was adapted for use at a North Carolina courthouse gathering, a New Rochelle banquet, and several dozen other functions. Before concluding with a pitch for the New Deal and praise for Roosevelt, Mitchell coupled the common point of his messages to condemnations of the GOP. "The Republicans," he said, "have used the Negro as a football, kicking him from place to place in the last 25 years. If you follow that party, the cause of the Negro is well nigh hopeless."[12]

Unmitigated partisanship became Mitchell's forte. As a regular feature of his congressional tenure, he assaulted the GOP's record on civil rights. In many respects, his August 13, 1935, speech, "The New Deal," ushered in a new era in the national debate over which political party now placed the minority's best interests at its foundation. Mitchell counterattacked Lincoln's political successors, accusing them of gross misconduct and exploitation. Originating from a congressional pulpit as a pioneer African American effort against Republicans, his address contributed much to reversing the GOP's claims on blacks. Heretofore, as part of Lincoln's legacy, Republicans had monopolized almost everything associated with civil rights on Capitol Hill. GOP House members had pointed to the South in particular with accusatory fingers for its blatant unfairness and segregation. Now with Mitchell refuting their arguments, the Republican party was under assault for racist attitudes and prejudicial policies. With slight variations and minor adjustments to reflect upon particular events, Mitchell's subsequent congressional speeches were repetitions of the August address. Even his last major congressional speech, "The New Deal

11. Sam Hobbs to M, January 24, 1936 (see also letters from Sam Rayburn, Tom Blanton, John H. Kerr, Maury Maverick, John A. Martin et al. to M, January 24, 1936; James P. Buchanan to M, February 24, 1936); M to Benjamin H. Fisher, May 4, 1936, MP; *Louisville Courier-Journal*, June 1, 1936; *CR*, 74th Cong., 2d sess., 1903–4.

12. From 1935: M to Petry Fisher, February 15; Randel Toliver to M, March 2; M to Toliver, March 5; M to Turner, July 9, MP; *Birmingham Age-Herald*, March 30; *Nashville Tennessean*, February 17 and March 5; *Athens Limestone Democrat* (Ala.), July 25; *Athens Alabama Courier*, August 15; *New York Times*, August 11; unidentified clipping, February 17, BP.

and the Negro," did not contain anything not found in his first partisan attack delivered to Congress. His farewell talk of October 14, 1942, like his speeches before it, rehashed African American accomplishments under the Democrats. The one thing differentiating it was a scathing rebuff to black Washingtonian Edgar G. Brown's charges of racism leveled at FDR. Labeling the discharged federal employee "a superconfidence man," Mitchell asserted that he belonged "to that group of racketeering so-called race leaders that always go around with their hands out seeking money, prestige, recognition, and power for themselves only, at the same time caring absolutely nothing for the group [minority]. Brown will sacrifice any interest of my group [race] or any other group if it means a few paltry dollars in his own hand." Certainly as subjective and antagonistic as any other House member's discourses, Mitchell's oratorical outbursts served their purposes. First, they garnered headlines. Often during Democratic election campaigns, party workers distributed reprints of the officeholder's sensational congressional oratory among blacks. Good for party propaganda and publicity, his speeches offered a rationale for abandoning Abe Lincoln in favor of FDR. Perhaps more importantly, the black Democrat filched the race issue from the Grand Old Party. From a congressional soapbox from 1935 to 1943, he charged Republican officials with pursuing detrimental policies toward African Americans, and it was he who led Democrats against an opposition unaccustomed to attack, harassing it continuously with tags of racism and minority bias. Hence, it was a combination of his oratory and New Deal programs that finally choked to death Republican predominance on civil rights discussions in Congress. Here as well, he linked black prosperity to the enactment of a liberal economic program. Heretofore, black congressmen had been teetering between their party's left and right wings, ignoring in the process connections between civil and material issues.[13]

Although there were some broad hints about a philosophy of government in Mitchell's campaign speeches, he did not really know at the outset of his House career where he would stand on most issues. Thus, survival preoccupied him in the beginning. As a result, he followed fellow Chicago Democrats' leadership; gradually, however, after confronting many different bills before Congress, his ideas evolved into patterns. His suggested regulation of holding companies incorporated in the Rayburn-Wheeler Public Utility Act of 1935 was clearly the first sign of his evolution.

13. Reprint, *CR*, 74th Cong., 1st sess., August 13, 1935; reprint, 74th Cong., 2d sess., June 1, 1936, MP; *CR*, 77th Cong., 2d sess., 8128–29; *CR*, 74th Cong., 2d sess., 5886–88, 8551–53, 9285–86; 76th Cong., 1st sess., appendix, 4041–42; *Washington Post*, May 5, 1936; *Washington Tribune*, June 8, 1936; *Washington Evening Star* and *Afro-American*, April 25, 1936; *Baltimore Sun* and *New York Times*, April 23, 1936.

His initial impulse was to agree in general with FDR that electric power companies were "parasites." When Mitchell was taking a hard stand, there were indications of his belief that these enterprises had done "more to destroy and handicap the free workings of legitimate business than any single single [sic] institution in the whole land. . . . I, up to this point, have seen no reason why I should not support the bill."[14] Yet, after his vote with a House majority on July 2, 1935, to control or eliminate all utility holding companies operating or marketing securities in foreign and interstate commerce and to regulate both interstate transmissions and sales of electric energy as commerce, he mellowed. At first, he opposed all amending to weaken the initial legislative proposal's heart in section 11. Then with it stuck in a House-Senate conference, he voted against a motion instructing representatives to strike at public utilities. More evidence of an evolving attitudinal change occurred during the next roll call. Then, he voted against restricting the rights of power-company lobbyists to represent investor interests.[15] Mitchell had an explanation for adopting a moderate philosophy. As he explained it and his reversals to a correspondent:

> I write . . . to say that the legislation in which you were so deeply interested was passed by the House but only after the "death sentence" was eliminated from the bill. This "death sentence" was the occasion of the strong opposition which developed among security holders and stock holders of utility interests. I think we all agree that these hugh [sic] financial concerns should be controlled in the interest of investors and there should be some Government supervision, but the better thinking people of the Country do not believe that they should be destroyed at the expense and to the detriment of the investors. The bill as passed by the House is not calculated to injure the interest of the holders of securities and stock in these companies.[16]

Interestingly placed in the middle, Mitchell found himself squeezed between the power companies, who wanted no legislation, and Roosevelt, who sought their "death sentence." Torn, the black Democrat ignored the final two roll calls on Rayburn-Wheeler.[17]

The Guffey-Snyder Coal Bill became another early test. Designed as the legislative replacement for Court-invalidated NRA codes governing

---

14. Samples of M's mail on utilities are: Sarah Blackman to M, March 4, 1936; Joseph A. Klein to M, April 1, 1935. For an initial reaction, see: M to Fred D. Porter, June 28, 1935, MP.

15. *CR*, 74th Cong., 1st sess., 11048, 11050, 12766, 12769.

16. M to Frances V. S. Clinch, July 3, 1935, MP.

17. *Ibid.*; Arthur M. Schlesinger Jr., *The Age of Roosevelt: The Politics of Upheaval*, 302–24.

bituminous coal manufacturing, marketing, and mining, it proposed the establishment of a national coal board with regulatory powers over wages and hours, collective bargaining, minimum prices, and trade practices. Since it was an attempt at stabilizing production and distribution, conservatives were aligned against it while the administration, the United Mine Workers, and progressives sought its adoption. For Mitchell, support for Guffey would come easier than it had for the unamended Public Utility Act; the coal bill was mostly regulatory legislation, and it contained no confiscatory features. Therefore, it fit nicely into Mitchell's evolving middle-of-the-road ideas about government and society. Seen as the people's servant, government should only serve enterprise and labor as arbiter and regulator. If anything upset the lawmaker about the campaign for the Bituminous Coal Act, it was blustering from John L. Lewis. A threat to initiate a national strike if Congress failed to enact appropriate legislation hurt the labor czar's cause with Mitchell. Similar to his reactions to the Chicago garment workers' actions, there was sympathy with wage-and-hour demands but not with strong-arm tactics. Given Mitchell's respect for law and order, he had problems endorsing anything that defied or eroded society's foundations. Since he strove for balance, it is easy to understand why he could not stomach "labor racketeer" Lewis. As such, Lewis had the lawmaker's stamp of disapproval, being classified along with all those "who seek to use and who do use labor for the benefit of themselves."[18]

On the subject of government-provided social welfare, Mitchell demonstrated consistency. Throughout his tenure in the House, he accepted overall the notion of public responsibility and roles for the state in its citizens' lives. Inasmuch as he backed relief appropriations, his support would increasingly reflect concerns. As he approached the end of his legislative career, he voiced increasing fears about blacks becoming so dependent upon government for handouts that they might lose all incentives to improve. As he put it, "The people of the Nation must realize that the Government is getting near the end of the rope in the matter of creating jobs and taxing the people to keep these jobs going; when many of the people who are the beneficiaries of these jobs are not interested beyond that particular job, and will not seek to secure work outside the Government." These concerns notwithstanding, Mitchell remained pro-administration in his early roll-call record and even subsequent congressional votes, out of loyalty to Roosevelt and his overriding opinion about

18. Schlesinger, *Age of Roosevelt*, 334–36; *CR*, 74th Cong., 1st sess., 13823, 14136, 14654; *CR*, 77th Cong., 1st sess., appendix, 5320–21; WW, T. Arnold Hill, Asa Philip Randolph to M, August 14, 1935, MP; *Chicago Tribune*, November 20, 1941.

Congress's obligation to foster improvements. Mitchell revealed as much to a conservationist, observing that the "Congress has very deep interest in trying to conserve human beings. . . . the resolution adopted by your [Audobon] society should be taken up after we have done something to relieve suffering among the people. I am sure that we must consider men and women before we consider ducks and geese." In addition, engaging government in pensions was a legitimate public-sector activity. Between April and June 1935, while facing the issue of retirement benefits, Mitchell sided with Democrats, keeping the Social Security Administration bill on course. Reflecting on this four years later, during heated congressional debates over equalizing payments with a central system, he commented, "It is the duty of the Congress of the United States to provide a pension for old people." However, unlike many other representatives from rich states who wanted revenue returns to match collections, Mitchell lacked sympathy for any plan that would distribute pensions unevenly. "We do have poor counties and poor States, we do have rich people and poor people, and if this Congress owes the old people of this Nation a duty to pension them, we ought to do it without regard to State lines." With similar regard to the issue of giving cash bonuses to World War I veterans, Mitchell was an outspoken advocate. More so than with any other issue before him, he defied the White House over helping the doughboys and sailors. Despite presidential opposition to rewards to veterans, Mitchell persisted about granting them. Beginning with his campaign against Oscar DePriest and running through 1935, no cause commanded greater support from him than bonus checks. In fact, its passage was so important to Mitchell that he made no efforts to conceal his differences with Roosevelt over an endorsement. In order to enact this legislation, as Mitchell was easily conceding to veterans of the War, voting to override presidential vetoes would be the only action that he could not contemplate. One year later, nevertheless, on January 24, 1936, he reversed himself, joining a bipartisan House majority to overcome a stubborn administration on the Vinson Bill for Adjusted-Service Certificates. For his steadfast independence, Mitchell received a citation from black veterans. It represented more than commitment to war heroes; it also symbolized his only clean break with FDR.[19]

19. Herbert Caro to M, April 17, 1939; M to Caro, May 2, 1939; M to Mrs. William J. Anderson, January 18, 1935; World War Adjusted Service Campaign, Citation, March 15, 1936; M to Lionel T. Thorsness, January 12, 1935; Thorsness to M, January 23, 1935; M to Michael B. Gilligan, January 15, 1935; M to Walter Krirtoff, January 24, 1935, M to George J. Tidd, February 19, 1937, MP; *CR*, 74th Cong., 1st sess., 5658, 5692–93, 6289–90, 11788–89; 76th Cong., 1st sess., 6909, 9733; *CR*, 74th Cong., 2d sess., 268, 312, 837, 986; *Journal and Guide*, January 18, 1936.

Every major legislative proposal and foreign-policy initiative aimed at strengthening America gained Mitchell's automatic support. This meant, for example, opposition to Louis Ludlow's attempts at circumventing congressional powers to declare war. In 1939, Mitchell placed himself squarely behind Roosevelt's cash-and-carry and neutrality proposals, and two weeks before the attack on Pearl Harbor, he campaigned for American ships taking more weapons to the armies allied against the Axis Powers. He argued for arming them because "materials furnished involve a far less sacrifice than furnishing an expeditionary force composed of our sons." Mitchell's outspoken advocacy of conscription and preparedness was not necessarily popular. For example, these stands further alienated him from Bronzeville's radicals. After voting for the Burke-Wadsworth Conscription Bill of 1940, he returned to Chicago and met many organized protesters who disapproved of his affirmations of the president's programs. With picket lines, the South Side Council of the American Youth Congress tried to block Mitchell's path. According to the demonstrators' official statement, "Congressman Mitchell has shown no independence of thought in voting for measures in congress that effect [sic] the Negro. He is a regular Charlie McCarthy, [a puppet who] . . . seems to care little . . . what the Negro voters in his district think. . . . He seems to be of the opinion that he owns the district, the voters be damned." Mitchell read his constituency differently. Disbelieving that First District residents were not "100% in favor of the Preparedness Program," Mitchell wanted some proof of their disloyalty. As he explained his pro-draft stand, "I believe in the full and complete defense of my country and I shall vote my convictions . . . , notwithstanding the foolish threats and intimations coming from the 'know all' who speak loudly but never act."[20]

Opposition to Martin Dies's House "committee investigating un-Americanism" was about the only fault self-proclaimed patriots could ever find in Mitchell's record. Disproportionately and oddly, Illinois Democrats were more libertarian on this issue than any other state caucus in the House. Of twenty-one members who voted for its dissolution in 1939, five—counting Mitchell—represented Illinois districts. Labeling the quintet "the five little Red Congressmen from Illinois," the opinionated *Chicago Tribune* suggested voters "remember these" at election time. Indeed, for all that, Mitchell emerged a winner from the controversy, at least in the estimates of progressives who long disliked Dies's classifications of un-Americanism. For them, his concerns were too narrow; he should

20. *Arkansas Democrat* and *Hot Springs Sentinel-Record,* October 10, 1939; M to Alice Lockwood, January 10, 1938; M to Harry Kosovske, September 25, 1939; M to George W. Johnson, September 5, 1940, MP; *CR,* 77th Cong., 1st sess., 8857; *Defender,* August 24 and September 14, 1940.

pursue right-wing and racist organizations vigorously, while ignoring everybody interested in humanitarian and liberal causes. Undoubtedly when Mitchell voted a stop to Red-baiting activities, he had none of this in mind. He simply disliked Martin Dies's "ballyhoo rampages for the purpose[s] of getting his name in the newspapers and deceiving those who do not know the actual facts in the case." If his stance was, in fact, a personal campaign against Dies and not a vote against witch-hunting, it illustrates Mitchell's selectivity in dealing with Southern Democrats. Although critics claimed he was a "tool" of the white South, the truth is that his negative or positive judgments resulted from individual merit. A good case in point occurred at the start of the Seventy-Fifth Congress when his party was split along sectional lines over the selection of Speaker Joe Byrns's successor. If Mitchell owed debts to Dixie, there would have been strong assistance to Sam Rayburn of Texas. Instead, he campaigned for New York's John O'Connor. As Mitchell advised a colleague, "We feel that our interest will be better taken care of under the leadership of Mr. O'Connor. . . . I can assure you that a vote for him will be greatly appreciated by the fourteen millions of Negroes in the United States." Although Mitchell offered no elaborations for these conclusions, on his part, there was a general trust of aristocrats and disdain for populists like Rayburn.[21]

At no time would his bifurcation become more apparent than during battles over the Supreme Court. First, Mitchell disappointed African American leaders because he trusted "the President 100%" to reform the judicial system fairly. His support of FDR on court packing was unpopular, but it paled in comparison to the repercussions he faced from his enthusiasm for Senator Hugo Black as the presidential nominee to the nation's highest tribunal. Writing as one Alabaman to another, Mitchell claimed some familiarity with Black's "work in that State" among African Americans. As the Negro politician put it, "Your attitude toward my people for the most part has been one of genuine friendliness." Even after the NAACP's sensational disclosure of Black's past membership in the Ku Klux Klan, Mitchell still referred to the selectee as "one of the fairest and squarest men in Washington." According to the Machine Democrat's unique reasoning, something rather courageous and positive followed KKK affiliation. "When Hugo L. Black renounced the Ku Klux Klan, that act was alone the secret order's death knell." NAACP leaders did not concur with Mitchell's opinion. They insisted the negative revelations

21. M to Marvin B. Pool, January 12, 1939; M to Joseph A. Dixon, December 31, 1936, MP; *Chicago Midwest Daily Record*, February 9, 1939; *Chicago Tribune*, February 1–28, 1939, February 5–9, and April 28, 1940; *Defender*, February 11, 1939; *Pittsburgh Courier*, March 16, 1940.

should lead Roosevelt to withdraw Black's nomination. As for Mitchell, they recommended he stop embarrassing African Americans with foolish talk. Almost four years later in 1941, the same scenario played itself out again. This time the controversy was over the nomination of James F. Byrnes. Although no hint of KKK membership turned up in Byrnes's Dixie-rooted background, civil rights forces were still mobilized against him. Having gained a record of filibustering and "uncompromising opposition to any and every form of justice and equal treatment" as a lawmaker from South Carolina sufficed. Hence for Mitchell, who supported Byrnes's nomination and scoffed at critics, this episode brought a sense of déjà vu because for a second time Roosevelt presented an outstanding Southern candidate for the Supreme Court and African Americans maligned the nominee, Roosevelt, and his own defiant backing of the bid. By refusing again to cave in to pressure to withdraw support for a Dixie nominee, Mitchell allowed a friendly thirty-year relationship with Byrnes to stand as proof enough of the Charlestonian's "fair and just" demeanor toward blacks.[22]

Besides his support for bench nominees and his pro-administration voting record, Mitchell tried to be useful in other ways to FDR. On three different occasions, he strove to be the president's goodwill envoy to the West Indies. The primarily black population of the Caribbean feted the unofficial ambassador, giving access to important officials and showing him places not ordinarily on tourist itineraries. Each of Mitchell's visits to the islands had some importance, but he particularly expected his ten-week excursion of 1935 to achieve significant breakthroughs in American-West Indian relations. Although he surveyed nine British and two French colonies, the Virgin Islands were his primary interest, occupying 40 percent of his time on land. In retrospect, Mitchell's distribution of presidential portraits and biographical sketches of famous African Americans to island schools was the only positive accomplishment during his journey. Otherwise, every phase of his introduction to diplomacy failed to achieve

22. Tipper to M, February 15, 1937; M to Edith Bleili, February 11, 1937; M to Roscoe Dunjee, March 8, 1937; M to Dickerson, March 15, 1937; M to Wimbish, March 15, 1937; M to Joseph B. Keenan, March 15, 1937; Lilly to M, March 16, 1937, M to Hugo L. Black, August 13, 1937, unidentified clipping, n.d.; M to FDR, May 17, 1941; James F. Byrnes to M, May 20, 1941, MP; *Omaha Call*, March 20, 1937; *Oklahoma City Black Dispatch*, n.d.; H. A. Robinson to WW, August 13, 1937; J. L. LeFlore to RW, August 13, 1937; Charles A. J. McPherson to WW, August 14, 1937; Louis T. Wright to Henry F. Ashurst, August 16, 1937; WW to Black, August 16, 1937; WW to FDR, September 16, 1937, NAACP; *Oklahoma City Oklahoma Eagle*, October 16, 1937; *Columbus Advocate*, August 28 and October 9, 1937; *Defender*, September 18 and October 16, 1937, and June 28, 1941; White, *A Man Called White*, 266–67; WW to FDR, June 12, 1941; Watson to WW, June 16, 1941, RP; *CR*, 77th Cong., 1st sess., appendix, 2855.

his expectations. Long intrigued by the tropical region, Mitchell wanted to establish himself as a reliable source of West Indian information and to influence the appointment of a judicial nominee to the Virgin Islands. Simultaneously, key leaders of the New York–based Federation of American Virgin Islands Societies had hoped to coax him into lobbying for greater autonomy. When the House Committee on Insular Affairs held hearings on an administration-backed bill, members asked Mitchell to share overall impressions and to testify. Reading from a prepared text on April 3, 1936, he credited the United States with improving residents' lives and with upgrading overall conditions in the Virgin Islands. "My observations and study bring me to the conclusion that the trend of affairs in these islands is steadily upward . . . and that through . . . the Federal Government . . . [they] will be brought to . . . self-supporting and self-governing." He therefore was "heartily in favor of" the Roosevelt administration's Organic Act. However, when pressed hard to note if every feature had his approval, he sheepishly confessed that "I cannot recall it." Due to lack of preparation and ignorance of the bill under scrutiny, Mitchell failed to establish himself as an expert worthy of the committeemen's time. He lost also by supporting the administration's position on autonomy. In counterpoint to Federation wishes, his stand let down its officers who had been "feeling that somehow you are destined to play a very important part in the reconstruction of the Virgin Islands."[23]

Mitchell's other goal for his trip also turned out badly. A few weeks prior to departure, he advocated the nomination of one of two black Democratic lawyers from Chicago for an appointment to a vacant Virgin Islands' judgeship. Candidates C. Francis Stradford and Richard E. Westbrooks received equally strong endorsements from Mitchell for the post. Prior to his return to Washington from the West Indies, the candidates were under the mistaken impression that their congressman commanded substantial clout with Roosevelt. It was soon thereafter that they discovered just how little influence Mitchell really wielded. If Mitchell had ever possessed an opportunity to do something for either Stradford or Westbrooks, he lost it

23. M memo on Caribbean trip, n.d.; M to Holsey, December 13, 1929; M to Dantes Bellegarde, March 19, 1932; Bellegarde to M, March 21, 1932; Eustace Gay to M, December 20, 1935; M to FDR, n.d.; *New York Age* and unidentified Barbadian newspaper, n.d.; A. C. Burnét to M, March 11, April 14, and August 10, 1936; M to Burnét, March 13, 1936; Alonzo G. Moron to M, November 27, 1936; Lawrence W. Cramer to M, March 13 and 23, 1936; Federation of American Virgin Islands Societies, Resolution of December 12 and Circular of December 14, 1935, MP; *Defender,* January 7 and December 29, 1928; Committee on Insular Affairs, U.S. House of Representatives, 74th Cong., 2d sess., *Hearing on H. R. 11751—A Bill to Provide a Civil Government for the Virgin Islands of the United States,* April 3, 1936, 9, 17, 36–40.

completely because of some uncomplimentary remarks uttered inadvertently while in the presence of Virgin Islanders. Nobody had recorded his
exact words, but enough tidbits survived to damage whatever chances he
might have had to affect a decision. Island Governor Lawrence Cramer
filed a damaging report on his visit for his superiors in the capital. From
it, administration officials learned the full details of Mitchell's contempt,
arrogance, and uncooperativeness. Worst of all, he had loudly blurted out
within earshot of several St. Johns residents that they were "a lazy and
dirty set of people." According to Cramer, the congressman's indiscretion
rendered him an unrespectable influence on Virgin Islands affairs. Tread-
ing now with extra caution and greater sensitivity in order to choose an
African American with acceptable credentials, Roosevelt was disinclined
to take Mitchell's advice. The position eventually went to William H.
Hastie, a Harvard Law School graduate whose candidacy Mitchell had
been trying to block from the outset. From their days together in the
District of Columbia, Mitchell and Hastie did not like each other. There
was a revealing sidelight behind FDR's choice of an NAACP activist. In a
memorandum "Not to be seen by anyone except N.A.A.C.P. Executives,"
Walter White explained how useful Mr. and Mrs. Irwin H. McDuffie had
been to him. From overheard conversations in the White House, the valet
and maid had been leaking out damaging information about Mitchell. It
came because Mrs. McDuffie "believes that Mr. Mitchell is a bad influence
on the President so far as the affairs of Negroes are concerned."[24]

Later Caribbean "missions" indicated Mitchell had learned basic
lessons in diplomacy, discretion, and courtesy. From his cruise liner's
docking to departure during a 1937 stopover in Havana, Arthur and
Annie Mitchell enjoyed superb Latin hospitality. Cuba's president and
other high officials served as the Americans' hosts, escorting them around
the republic's capital. Even the normally anti-Yankee Cuban reporters
trailing after the entourage exhibited friendliness. A story in *Diario de
la Marina* typified how the American visitors had not evinced hostility

24. *Philadelphia Tribune*, September 5, 1935; Edward T. Lee to M, August 14, 1935;
unidentified letter to FDR, August 26, 1935; Stanley Reed to FDR, September 14, 1935;
FDR to M, August 28 and November 4, 1935; M to FDR, September 4, 1935; M to
Burnét, December 10, 1935; Burnét to M, December 1, 1935, and March 11, 1936; John
Henry to M, November 14, 1935; Harold L. Ickes to M, November 8, 1935; M memo
on Caribbean trip; Lionel Roberts to M, January 25, 1936, MP; "Congressman Mitchell
Makes Sensational Virgin Island Speech but Reporters Forget it," November 13, 1935,
BP; WW to Charles H. Houston, October 7, 1935; WW to William H. Hastie, October 7,
1935; WW memo, October 7, 1935, NAACP; Cummings to FDR, August 26, 1935; FDR
to M, September 17, 1935; FDR to Reed, August 31 and September 3 and 7, 1935; FDR
to Ickes, September 19, 1935, RP; Gilbert Ware, *William Hastie: Grace under Pressure*, 85;
Fishel, "The Negro in the New Deal Era."

among newspapermen covering the event. The story's author considered Mitchell "one of the most outstanding leaders of the Negro citizenry in the United States, one of the politicians with the best futures and most influence in the Democratic Party, and a personal friend of . . . Roosevelt." If the attention had underlining meaning, it was not spelled out for the congressman until his return to America. Awaiting him then from the republic's undersecretary of justice, Miguel Angel Cespedes, was an explanation about what Mitchell should have "liked most" about Cuba. "To you the pleasantest experience of your stay has been that nobody has given any sign that he has noticed you belong to the colored race. In your country, the fact that you are a Negro causes you constant vexation." Mitchell's final West Indian trip as a visiting official produced a noteworthy result. In 1941, during America's buildup of naval and air bases on British-held Caribbean islands, African Americans were concerned about a rumor that Great Britain was not granting them employment visas in British territories. Without sponsorship, Mitchell went on a fact-finding mission to the Caribbean. A tour of the islands did not resolve much, however. Just because he had not found African American workers anywhere in the islands was not a justification for him to accuse or suspect England of being guilty of employment discrimination. As a prelude to completing his assessment of the situation, Mitchell sought answers to questions from the British ambassador in Washington. Neville Butler responded to the inquiry for England's absent envoy to America. According to the senior staff member's reassuring note to the concerned American, there was "no foundation for the suggestion that the British authorities wish any discrimination as regards colour made in the selection of those persons who may be sent from the United States."[25]

As his three Caribbean experiences illustrated, Mitchell's status as Congress's only black member gave him notoriety and access, but station did not offer him input or power. Both on Capitol Hill and in the White House, his counsel was seldom solicited. However, he often proved himself an asset to the Democratic party. In terms of personal accomplishment, aid to fellow members was his greatest value; he was their showpiece. As such, he received many honors and rewards from the party. An invitation to the annual Jackson Day Dinner, on January 8, 1937, was one payback. Just happy to be included, Mitchell could add the privilege to his list of

25. *Havana El Mundo, Havana El Pais, Havana El Crisol, Havana Diario de la Marina,* December 28–30, 1937 (Spanish-to-English translations by author); M to Havana's Mayor, November 2, 1937; Miguel Angel Cespedes to M, December 30, 1937; M to Carl Murphy, January 10, 1938; Neville Butler to M, March 27, 1941; *Port-of-Spain Gazette,* January 2, 1941; *Port-of-Spain Trinidad Guardian,* January 29, 1941; *Afro-American,* December 27, 1937.

"firsts." While seated among 2,079 diners for an evening of backslapping partisanship and speeches, he attracted little notice; Roosevelt's presence capped off the event.[26]

On other occasions, such anonymity did not occur. When Mitchell spoke at the Democratic National Convention in Philadelphia on June 25, 1936, he attracted considerable attention. His address followed a black minister's invocation. Senator Ellison D. "Cotton Ed" Smith of South Carolina immediately attached negative connotations to a procession of African Americans. Appreciably disgusted that his political party had allowed a black's opening prayer, the headstrong racist ceremoniously vacated the auditorium before the blessing. Then just as the South Carolinian was resettling in his seat with the Palmetto delegation, Mitchell arose to address the assembly. Another black at the podium proved more than Cotton Ed could tolerate from his party in one day; it drove Smith to leave the arena for the session's duration. Whether staged deliberately for effect or not, Smith's farcical series of stunts in essence gave fellow Democrats an excellent shot at convincing black voters that there was nothing to opponent charges about Ku Klux Klansmen running FDR's administration. Of particular note about the episode, fellow Southerners summarily condemned Cotton Ed. From North Carolina where a professor ventilated total "humiliation and disgust" at Smith's "silly demagogic and ungentlemanly conduct" to the Heart of Dixie where both the *Birmingham News* and *Montgomery Advertiser* editorialized against his alleged opportunism and arousals of passions, there was resultant embarrassment because Cotton Ed's actions were judged "representative of the South's attitude, when in fact it was not." In cynical contrast, the *Selma Times Journal* had no objections to including blacks in party deliberations, but the editor did not approve of what he interpreted as conspiring to showcase their presence for the South's disapproval. Seeing what effect an African American preacher had on Smith, "master minds of the convention got busy and rushed Congressman Mitchell . . . onto the platform in an effort to pour oil on the troubled waters." Of course, the boycotter's ploy for attention afforded opportunities to other party members to disassociate themselves completely from a colleague's foolishness. Thus, their negative reactions to Cotton Ed gave the episode significance; under Chairman Farley's leadership, the Democratic Colored Divisions exploited Smith's antics to maximum effect. Naturally, Mitchell was asked for reactions, and his response elicited praise from everybody but extreme white supremacists. By attaching clever commentaries to the boycott, Mitchell managed to silence many of his harshest critics. In a

26. Unidentified clipping, MP; *New York Times*, January 9, 1937.

statement for the press about the incident, he began mercifully before lambasting Cotton Ed with "God forgive him, for he knows not what he does. If the Senator intends withdrawing every time a Negro participates in the activities of the Democratic party, he should go into training for the walkathon, as he will have much walking to do. I feel the Senator is ignorant and steeped in prejudice. He belongs, probably, to the Ku Klux Klan, at least in mentality. I have no confidence in his statesmanship, and the sooner we get rid of his type the better. He is a disgrace to his state and to our party." After Mitchell's response, even longtime critic A. N. Fields complimented him. Calling his announcement "the most manly statement yet made by Mr. Mitchell," the *Defender* reporter praised the officeholder because "for this he is entitled to high commendation."[27]

Two important issues related to civil rights and the Democratic party were deflected and forgotten in the confusion over the sensationalism of Smith's boycott. First of all, few noticed National Bar Association demands for a resolution related to ending discrimination had not reached the convention floor. Besides doing nothing about the black lawyers' concerns, delegates had ignored *Defender* challenges to the racial composition of the Illinois delegation. At the convention, except for Mitchell, a national alternative delegate chosen at large, the state lacked African American representation. The content of Mitchell's speech had been lost as well in the uproar. Delivered in Philadelphia, his speech had been another patented attack against modern Republicanism. Among other things, he had charged "The so-called generous attitude of the Republican Party toward the Negro ended 30 years ago. The Grand Old Party long since deviated from its ancient doctrine of human rights in quest of material prosperity." In contrast to the Republicans' weak record, countered Mitchell, the Democrats represented common people. Come election day, he predicted confidently, a large black majority would remember, giving the Grand Old Party its final notice. "History shows that we have always stood by our friends. . . . The name of . . . Roosevelt is indelibly stamped upon the mind and heart of every Negro in this country. We look upon him as our greatest friend and benefactor. . . . 'Mr. President, we are with you all the way.' "[28]

Mitchell's political address was a prelude to a more important role in the Democratic party's bid to become the choice of African Americans in the November elections. On July 29, 1936, as a natural outgrowth of

27. *Defender*, June 27 and July 4, 1936; *Selma Times Journal*, June 28, 1936; Schlesinger, *Age of Roosevelt*, 598; C. H. Hamlin to Ellison D. Smith, June 26, 1936, MP; *Montgomery Advertiser* and *Birmingham News*, July 11, 1936.

28. Lawrence to M, June 16, 1936, MP; Lawrence interview; *Defender*, June 27, 1936; CR, 74th Cong., 2d sess., 10782–83.

his steady service and partisanship, Mitchell and Boston attorney Julian Rainey became chairs of the Western and Eastern sectors respectively of the Democratic party's "Colored Division." Although *Newsweek* incorrectly identified each man as "a Harvard-educated mulatto," there was a correct realization that selecting Rainey and Mitchell reflected another attempt at weaning black voters from Lincoln and Frederick Douglass. Once considered an absolutely hopeless task "like Jews backing Hitler," efforts were now going well under the current administration because of FDR's appointment of "50-odd Negroes to important executive positions" and a fairer "share of Federal jobs, relief, agricultural benefits, CCC jobs, and housing projects." Accordingly, benefits and accomplishments along with corresponding political breakthroughs for blacks in boss-ridden cities such as Chicago, New York, and Kansas City improved the party's prospects and worried GOP presidential candidate Alfred M. Landon. *Newsweek* was not alone in its predictions for 1936. Democrats were hopeful, too. For "colored division" leaders Rainey and Mitchell, high expectations meant tremendous responsibilities and stress. They were on the reelection team for different reasons. In Rainey's case, it was experience that landed him an important role, whereas Mitchell's selection resulted from recognition. The party leadership considered both men capable of giving unity and purpose to varying state "colored divisions," and there were expectations that the work of the "colored" leaders would interlock in a general reelection effort. Since Rainey and Mitchell had specific tasks and budgets, the Democratic National Committee demanded regular reports. Although responsibilities were tough and anticipations sanguine, party superiors never vested full confidence in Rainey and Mitchell. For instance, the two men lacked power to assemble state Negro organizations, and they had no input in the selections of state chairmen; these tasks belonged to James Farley. Individually for each state, on advice and recommendations of national committeemen and local party bosses, the chairman named every state director of Negro operations.[29]

The first indications that Mitchell would have trouble managing the Western Division came from Nebraska. Soon after Mitchell's selection, journalist David Lee presented the appointee with an unusual challenge. Quiet for weeks after "serious difficulties" at the *Afro-American*, Lee, a discharged employee, finally resurfaced in Omaha as the general manager of the little-known Western Newspaper Syndicate. In a strange, somewhat incoherent letter to Mitchell, Lee "emphasize[d] the fact that I am not for

29. *News-Week,* September 12, 1936; *Defender,* August 8, 1936; *Baltimore Sun,* July 30, 1936; M to Moton, August 3, 1936; M to F. W. Littlejohn, August 17, 1936; James C. Quigley to M, August 3, 1936, MP.

sale," but sought "recognition" and "opportunity." Threatening Mitchell supposedly in his "own language," Lee promised "to raise 'hell' " if his demands were not met. Although at first Lee never spelled out to Mitchell the exact terms of his blackmail, there were hints of possible research in Alabama to expose the officeholder's shadowy past. Sensing his threats had not daunted Mitchell, Lee became more explicit, claiming his intended victim would soon see his early life in Alabama presented in words and pictures. In explaining his motives to Mitchell, Lee underscored his regrets with the congressman's conduct. "A Negro of your type and attitude is not fit to be in Congress as a representative of our people or any other people, and I will go plum to hell to bring about your defeat after the way you spoke about me. I lost a day, drove to Washington and spent the day, at my expense and wrote a long story on you in an effort to present you to the public in a different light from the one in which you had previously been painted. . . . You can mark me down with the rest of the colored newspapermen who are out to bring about your political demise." Fearless of Lee and blackmail, Mitchell gambled correctly against appeasement; Lee's retaliations did not materialize.[30]

During the 1936 campaign, nothing caused Mitchell more severe problems than Farley's control over appointments. As late as August 31, Farley had not selected black directors in five states under Mitchell's command. Worse yet were the leadership crises occurring after selections. In Nebraska, the incompetence and immaturity of those in charge undermined efforts to win over black voters. The young man at the head of the drive was an inexperienced organizer. All his attempts at commanding rank-and-file workers produced so much rancor and dissension among veterans that they finally established a rump organization to galvanize support for Democratic candidates. Conditions were even more volcanic in other states. Indiana went into complete disarray for weeks after its directorship had gone to Indianapolis businessman Freeman B. Ransom. State Chairman Omar S. Jackson's recommendation had come without counsel from the Indiana Negro Democratic Central Association. Despite having no input in Ransom's selection, Mitchell nevertheless received INDCA's blame because the state's African American Democrats in general wrongly believed his authority extended to Ransom's appointment. Indiana's black Democratic leaders did not look favorably on Ransom. Characterized as a "dud," the cosmetics manufacturer was disliked because of alleged undermining of INDCA. Consequently, this was no easy matter for Mitchell to sort out and settle. In response, Mitchell, acting on Farley's orders but with no help or suggestions from headquarters, was to resolve a

30. David Lee to M, August 11 and 30, 1936, MP.

difficult crisis. Under these circumstances, he had an impossible mission. First, he appealed to Jackson for assistance. Then, he ordered Ransom to ascertain Jackson's advice for settling the matter. In presenting a frank assessment of how disunity could wreak havoc on Democrats in Indiana, Mitchell minced no words. He promised only a personal investigation into the situation. However, there were no hints that Ransom should resign. To Mitchell's urgent appeals for a peaceful resolution, Ransom offered assurance "that all differences and difficulties of every sort have been ironed out." Unfortunately, Mitchell chose not to believe Ransom. Had he accepted Ransom's positive report of a settlement, he would not have made an unnecessary trip to Indianapolis.[31]

Across the western division, there were several other personnel problems that demanded investigation and resolution. The case of Ohio illustrated a typical problem. Months before Farley's appointment of Mitchell as western director, Roosevelt-Davey clubs had been forming among blacks to boost FDR and Governor Davey in their bids for reelection. Thomas J. Davis had been organizing these clubs when new directives came. Davis was well known to Mitchell, being "the fellow who [had] made such an ass of himself when you [the Congressman] talked" last in Cleveland. By most estimates at cross-purposes to Davis's efforts, Chairman Francis W. Poulson of the State Central Committee appointed Linell L. Rodgers to manage Ohio's "colored" activities for the national ticket. The selection was an invitation to problems because with two rivals in place for support and favors, conflict was inevitable. Within no time, Davis complained to Farley about "a gross mistake," a competitor who did "not enjoy the good-will of the Ohio State Democratic League, which is the one and only Negro organization in Ohio." Making matters worse, Davis had no intention of assisting Rodgers, for that would be asking "me to pull chestnuts out of the fire." With Ohio in tumult, Mitchell had no choice but to leave for Columbus. There, before seeking to consult with three blacks on the governor's reelection committee, Mitchell conferred first with Poulson. The African American trio convinced Mitchell that Rodgers was "a misfit" for the job at hand. Thereupon, without any further consultation, Mitchell acted decisively, replacing unpopular Rodgers with

31. M to JAF, August 31, 1936; Harry Leland to JAF, August 19, 1936; M to Frank Murphy, February 29, 1936; J. J. Hoover to M, March 26, 1936; Mrs. D. E. Hood to M, March 27, 1936; Marshall A. Talley to M, March 27, 1936; M to FBR, August 6 and 31, and September 3, 1936; Richardson to Louis Ludlow, July 30, 1936; FBR to M, August 7 and September 2, 1936; Littlejohn to M, August 10, 1936; Central Association petition to JAF, August 14, 1936; Hoover to JAF, August 14, 1936; Hoover and Hood to Minton, August 15, 1936; Jackson to JAF, August 25, 1936; W. Forbes Morgan to M, April 27, 1936; M to Jackson, August 31, 1936; M to Hoover, September 2, 1936; nameless clipping, September 12, 1936, MP; *Indianapolis Recorder*, September 12, 1936.

friend and confidant Percy D. Jones as chair of a three-man committee for the president. Since Davis received one of the slots on the board, the arrangement pacified everyone except Rodgers. At mending fences in Ohio, Mitchell displayed excellent judgment and was magnanimous enough to disregard his personal dislike of Davis. Mitchell had used prudence and initiative to fabricate a viable political body out of confusion and intrigue.[32]

His difficulties were not always so easy to settle. The problem unfolding in Kansas, for example, was totally different. Here, the issue was race. For state colored director, the chairman of the Kansas Democrats angered and insulted blacks by naming Joseph S. McDonald, a white state senator. In particular, the appointment offended Colored State Chairman Dorsey Green and Colored Speakers Bureau Chair Earl Reynolds. Mitchell agreed with the critics; the state chairman had lacked judgment and sensitivity. In a protest to Farley, Mitchell called the naming of McDonald a "serious mistake" because it was ammunition for the GOP to use in its struggle to hold and recapture African American votes. To study and correct the "delicate situation," Mitchell promised personal investigation. But in the final analysis, there was not much he could do officially about McDonald without some cooperation from Kansas's white Democrats. Aware of probable problems from trying persuasion, he compensated by privately negotiating with Davis Lee of Topeka to forge an improvised solution. Unrecognized, the Topekan became ex-officio head of the black campaign with Mitchell's consent to storm Kansas on behalf of Roosevelt.[33]

As the leader of Western Colored Democrats, Mitchell also confronted intrastate rivalries. For example in Missouri, St. Louisans resented the state directorship going to a Kansas Citian. Since the recipient was District of Columbia Recorder of Deeds William J. Thompkins, Mitchell could hardly feign impartiality. Absolutely not his favorite candidate to lead blacks anywhere, Thompkins had long been considered "sinister" and trouble-some. Making matters worse, after a disruptive meeting with Mitchell, Thompkins griped to Farley about Mitchell's leadership deficiencies. After word shot back to Mitchell of Thompkins's backbiting remarks, bad blood between them boiled openly. In retaliation for the bad report to the national chairman, Mitchell tried limiting Thompkins's activities to

32. PDJ to M, July 25, 1935; Davis to JAF, August 15, 1936; M to Linell L. Rodgers, August 6, 1936; M to JAF, September 12, 1936; M to Frazier Reams, September 22, 1936; PDJ to JAF, September 24, 1936, MP.
33. DsL to M, September 29 and October 21 and 25, 1936; DsL to FDR, September 15, 1936; M to Earl T. Reynolds, September 18, 1936; Reynolds to M, September 24, 1936; Reynolds to Lynn H. Brodrick, September 10, 1936; M to JAF, September 13, 1936; Joseph H. McDonald to JAF, September 29, 1936, MP.

Missouri. The attempted grounding, however, brought another appeal by Thompkins to Farley. By now totally disgusted with the petty spatting, Farley issued a cease-and-desist order to Mitchell. Under no conditions was there to be more contact with his nemesis.[34]

Although minor problems with state directorates continued into autumn, most of the serious difficulties with appointees happened during Mitchell's first six weeks as western director. Except for a brief pause taken to attend his mother's funeral in Birmingham and a last-hour rush to campaign in Chicago, Mitchell endured two months of managing a major political organization. Surely, nobody behind the Colored Division's inception had imagined he would become involved in disputes between different warring factions. His first priorities were to propose an operating plan and to submit an activities budget. In the preparation of these, Mitchell relied heavily upon Rainey. With a budget of $106,000, Mitchell estimated 1.5 million African American voters could be reached in 179 western counties; the largest outlays would be for salaries, travel, literature, and communications. As director, Mitchell asked for $1,650, with another $60 per week set aside for his wife's stenography during the campaign stretch month.[35]

Keeping the division functioning was Mitchell's role after the appointment of state directors. To plan and standardize procedures, he invited subordinates to Chicago during late August. As a preparation, "each State Director . . . [was asked to] map out his own program." Disappointing results nevertheless came from the Chicago staff gathering. Attendance was poor because not many state organizations had delegated their directors to travel. Except for Bill Thompkins, whose absence had been in reaction to Mitchell, absenteeism did not relate to the presiding officer. Several states lacked representation because of financial problems and unsettled directorships. Overall, those few delegates who were present settled only one matter of importance; they agreed to submit weekly progress reports to Mitchell. These were necessary because Mitchell was required to report on black political activities in the West. At the Chicago sessions with Mitchell, directors elaborated on extensive plans for reaching prospective black voters with the New Deal message. For the most part, these state officers were proud of the organizational achievements in their respective

34. Thompkins to M, September 4, 1936; M to Thompkins, August 18, 1936; Julian D. Rainey to M, July 22, 1936; M to Rainey, July 24, 1936; M to JAF, August 18 and September 22, 1936; JEM to Ambrose O'Connell, September 26, 1936; Thomas C. Hennings Jr. to JAF, September 16, 1936, MP.

35. CD, DNC, Eastern and Western Budgets, Weekly Expenditures; M to Ada L. Johnson, January 28, 1937; Rainey to M, July 31 and August 3, 1936, MP. After years of confinement due to illness, Ammar Patterson Mitchell died September 29, 1936.

states. This was reflected in their initial field reports to Mitchell. Henry U. Mease's boastful claims about the Iowa Negro Democratic League's successes typified the reports that flowed in to Mitchell. At the outset, Mease dismissed Republicans. Undaunted by their optimism, he was certain "the fight in Iowa can be won with proper financial and other aid such as speakers that are effective and good publicity." He boasted that everywhere in Iowa, black Democrats were "organized and clicking." In the beginning, Mitchell was hopeful, too. Excepting states with leadership woes and the irritation of Thompkins, his greatest grief came from Chicago's Stevens Hotel, which refused to rent rooms to the Colored Division. Otherwise, reports to Farley conveyed encouraging news: "I wish to assure you again that the outlook is exceptionally bright and the Negro, notwithstanding the Republican propaganda, is approachable and lends a listening ear to the Democratic appeal." As was true in general of campaigners, Mitchell's greatest obstacles were limits of time and money.[36]

As the election entered its final weeks, monetary problems grew into a major concern. When spread over eleven states, the western division budget soon proved inadequate. Frustrated and irritated at the end by the effects of underfunding on campaign work, many black state directors filled their weekly reports with excuses related to meager finances. Mitchell offered little hope or empathy to overwhelmed workers. Instead of cheering them on with words of support and agreements about a need for cash infusions, he accused directors of fraud and mismanagement. There was a hollow ring to this, however. Weeks before state directors were noting monetary problems in their field reports, Mitchell grumbled to New York about "entirely inadequate" funding. Regarding finances and various state officers, the greatest problem related not so much to quantities of money but more often to its rather slow disbursement. Since payments from the western office invariably arrived later than expected or not at all, confusion and fears reigned. In most cases when staffers submitted expenses to Mitchell, they expected quick reimbursements for personal outlays. Since turnabouts were seldom fast, Mitchell faced frequent inquiries about overdue money. Usually, his answers to legitimate questions were rude and unhelpful. The fault for much of the confusion and misunderstanding, however, originated in Mitchell's haphazard setup. After the Democratic party had entrusted him with authority to distribute funds, he did not set up adequate guidelines. Failing to have

36. M to CFD, August 6, 1936; O. B. Jefferson to M, August 14, 1936; FBR to M, September 9, 14, and 18, 1936; M to FBR, September 12 and 21, 1936; PDJ to M, September 21, 1936; M to Mease, September 24, 1936; Mease to M, September 18, 1936; M to JAF, August 7 and 31, and September 7, 14, and 25, 1936; M to Powell, September 18, 1936, MP.

good procedures in place subsequently led to inconsistent and abusive practices. Soon thereafter, ugly charges were made by "colored" campaigners who had accumulated travel expenses while championing a candidate. Of course before incurring debts, nobody had expected problems recouping their legitimate expenses from Mitchell's office in Chicago. Yet, many trusting staffers discovered stiff resistance. For not paying workers, Mitchell used two excuses. He either claimed their trips had not been authorized, or he determined their travels had not related exclusively to Roosevelt's reelection. To staffers' consternation, regardless of reasons for a nonpayment of vouchers, he was unfair. Overall frustrations from such whimsical nonsense eventually culminated in Ohio staffers suspecting a fraudulent misuse of funds. Resentful of their "dirty and false insinuations," Mitchell struck back with his own assertions. He claimed the accusers were "chisselers [sic]" who deserved punishment. Reneging on obligations and creating Democratic enemies were not the results hoped for by the Democratic leaders who had set up the two colored divisions. Farley and the National Committee had hoped an experiment of two black directors would lead to eventual coordination between the many state colored organizations and to improvements in FDR's popularity among African Americans. Mitchell also had wanted something more rewarding than confrontations with dissatisfied, "disgruntled persons" and fights over "false reports." Furthermore, the lack of a freer hand to create a more personal corps was another disappointment. Still, there was reluctance on his part to have all individuals who were "not helping the cause any . . . [to be] speedily called home."[37]

The last weekly campaign reports contained almost no organizational news. Instead, they covered Democratic rallies. To substantiate claims of successful events, directors often included news clippings. From all indications, Mitchell was not at all skeptical about incoming feedback. Like state staffers, he saw a landslide of black votes for FDR. At any rate, that was his prognosis for Farley on October 14. According to Mitchell, "I have every reason in the world to believe that President Roosevelt will carry all of these states, and that the Negro will vote from sixty-five to

37. M to Charles Michaelson, August 25, 1936; M to Meese, September 30, 1936; DsL to M, November 1, 1936; E. E. Pruitt to M, October 6, 1936; CFD to M, September 22, 1936; M to CFD, September 18, 1936; FBR to M, October 24, 1936; Alberta Draper to M, n.d.; M to Pruitt, October 8, 1936; John C. Walker to M, October 20, 1936; PDJ to M, September 21, 1936; M to PDJ, September 22, 1936; James C. Thomas to M, January 23, 1936; M to Thomas, January 24, 1936; C. Oliver and James E. Prowd to M, January 26, 1936; M to A. E. Patterson, March 27, 1936; undated statistical data compiled before M's appointment; unidentified clip, July 24, 1936; JAF to M, June 8, 1936; M to JAF, October 22, 1936; Alexander to M, October 19, 1936, MP; *Defender,* August 8, 1936.

eighty-five percent Democratic. I think it is most remarkable the manner in which they are responding to us and to our cause."[38]

Although Democrats were negligent of African Americans on some fronts, care was taken to tailor campaign literature for their consumption. For the task, National Director of Publicity Charles Michaelson employed Harlem physician C. B. Powell. Among his duties, Powell had charge of assembling and mass-circulating materials for the Colored Division. By all accounts an accommodating individual, Dr. Powell complied as well as possible to Mitchell's demands on his understaffed seven-member African American publicity team. In addition to the nonsalaried director, the staff consisted of a cartoonist, two secretaries, and two staff writers. As manager in charge, Powell had a thankless job. Without funds to cover all printing costs, just satisfying the western division's requests for literature demanded skill. On top of that, Powell patiently endured Mitchell's unpleasant demeanor and criticisms. Despite scant contributions, the doctor's office accomplished much. Overcoming poor funding with strong determination and dedication, the office managed somehow to circulate scores of diverse news releases to friendly newspapers, magazines, and a news bureau. For spreading among prospective black voters, Powell's staff distributed 125,000 copies of "Take Your Choice" to Roosevelt campaigners. Nonetheless, the accomplishment represented only a fraction of the field requirements. As a result, requests for campaign literature often went unfulfilled. Shortages left gaping holes in many previously targeted areas. In key states such as Illinois, Michigan, and Indiana, a literature crisis severely hampered work under Mitchell's leadership. To plug gaps, Mitchell asked for and received help from Chicago's *Metropolitan News*. However, resorting to such rescues did not increase Mitchell's respect for Powell's unit. Despite all, Mitchell figured rather prominently in the doctor's work. Mitchell's partisan speeches about Roosevelt and the New Deal made perfect copy for handbills. During 1936, Powell's office arranged with the federal printing office for reprints of Mitchell's flamboyant attacks. Since these came directly from the pages of *Congressional Record*, they made ideal handouts for Colored Division workers because Congress's official seal legitimized their contents. During the 1936 campaign, several thousand citizens received Mitchell's polemic explanation of the differences between how Democrats and Republicans approached blacks. Moreover, the African American partisan contributed

38. Pruitt to M, October 6, 13, and 16, 1936; Jefferson to M, September 26, 1936; PDJ to M, October 16, 1936; CFD to M, October 11, 13, and 17, 1936; DsL to M, October 28, 1936; Horne to M, September 28, 1936; FBR to M, October 10, 1936; M to JAF, October 6 and 14, 1936, MP.

several sections to the Colored Division's most widely used and distributed pamphlet, "Take Your Choice."[39]

Although essential to the campaign, literature did not provide the main spark in 1936. The most vital campaign tools were lecturer teams from state political organizations, the National Speakers Bureau of the Colored Division, and pools under Mitchell's and Rainey's control. Since these lecturers were paid weekly salaries and per diems, finding orators willing to travel and speak on behalf of the president did not pose problems for the two directors. Moreover, with separately earmarked funds for hiring speakers, Mitchell was in a position to reward offers to personal acquaintances and "worthy" servants with Chicago Machine endorsements. Since he relied so much on these sources for candidates, there were times when state leaders resented intrusions from outside their jurisdictions. Hence, favoritism occasionally backfired on Mitchell. Like him, state directors of "colored" organizations also wanted the privilege of being able to reward allies with the honors and salaries associated with speaking for Roosevelt's reelection. There was more to a speaker's job than oratory; describing appearances was important, too. Consequently, reports flowed into Mitchell's Chicago office from all eleven states under his direction. As sources of information, they were not especially useful because of their tendencies to exaggerate events so much that they created false images of the campaign's progress. Accordingly, large auditoriums always overflowed with excited FDR supporters, and correspondingly, every speech ended with thunderous applause. More importantly, audiences left with lasting enthusiasm for the president. The returns from black-populated western precincts eventually contradicted what speakers had offered Mitchell. Despite sanguine forecasts of a Democratic landslide among African Americans, only a minority abandoned the GOP in 1936. Landon and the Republicans held onto traditional black support in the West.[40]

39. M-Powell exchanges, August–November; Publicity Department, CD, DNCC, Report and releases, "Boston Leader Flays Landon," "Mrs. Fauset Sees Value of Mrs. Roosevelt in White House," et al.; Draft and final edition of "Take Your Choice"; M to JAF, September 24, 1936; M to Powell, September 25, 1936; Mease to M, September 28, 1936; M to Mease, September 24, 1936; Pruitt to M, October 6, 1936, MP.
40. CD, DNCC, Roster, National Speakers Bureau; M to CFD, September 29, 1936; Pruitt to M, October 6, 1936; A. L. Garvin to M, August 12, 1936; Alonzo Bowling to M, September 26, 1936; M to Robinson, September 19, 1936; Emory Smith to Morgan, October 26, 1936; Alexander to M, September 30, 1936; FBR to M, October 6 and 8, 1936; Robert H. Beverly to M, August 25, 1936; Mease to M, October 12, 1936; Charles W. Tinsley to M, August 6, 1936; Jefferson to M, October 19, 1936; Lilly to M, October 20, 1936; Western Division, Illinois Report, MP; Indianapolis Hoosier Sentinel, September 18, 1936.

Mitchell's role in "colored" activities was significant. For one thing, he was the most sought-after orator. Because of great demands for his presence, he could have spoken nonstop from September to November 4. Staffers sought him when their fortunes were sagging, and they desired him when all was going well. Moreover, in attempts at improving their favor among black constituents, Democratic officials, such as Missouri's Thomas Hennings and Ohio's Byron B. Harlan, used Mitchell's draw as a black congressman. Wisely perceiving his value as an attraction, they wanted him in their districts, influencing black voters. Notwithstanding great unpopularity in some circles, Mitchell was still a special headliner. Wherever and whenever plans called for him to stump for FDR, crowds and attention would follow. Clearly, Mitchell had not diminished as an attraction. Bad press and all the negative connotations aside, blacks were as anxious as ever to see and hear "their" congressman, and he obliged them and Democrats as often as time and other considerations permitted. On the campaign trail for Roosevelt in 1936, Mitchell used what for him was standard partisan fare. Succinctly described as a succession of useful laws, the New Deal received citation as the greatest effort of all at involving commoners in government, and he credited Roosevelt with being the friendliest president ever to blacks. Finally, in order to relax audiences, Mitchell injected political humor into his oratory. An explanation for why the GOP had quickly dropped the sunflower as its symbol was his favorite story. Shifting voices, Mitchell credited a woman from "Hicksville" with discovering the secret behind a floral emblem's sudden abandonment. "In this part of the country we have always had a purpose for sunflowers. Ever since I was a little girl, sunflowers have been planted around the privy down at the end of the lot. They sorta hide the place and protect those who use it; and the more the privy is used the bigger the sunflowers grow;—and now I wonder what stink the Republicans are trying to cover up by the use of sunflowers in 1936."[41]

Among western division blacks, in addition to dual roles as spokesperson for and coordinator of "colored" efforts to reelect an incumbent president, Mitchell used an Illinois state capital appearance to protest racial discrimination. Billed as Mitchell Day by sponsors, his arrival in Springfield was conceived as a draw to enlist downstate blacks in Roosevelt's bid for a second term. However, a stir over a hotel's policies toward blacks soon blurred the real reason behind Mitchell's appearance in central Illinois. What transpired during a fifteen-hour stop proved a memorable

41. Byron B. Harlan to M, August 15, 1936; Hennings to JAF, September 8, 1936; Mease to M, October 6, 12, and 13, 1936; handout, Grant County (Indiana) Colored Democratic Club, October 12, 1936; Alexander to M, September 30, 1936, MP; *Carbondale Free Press*, October n.d., 1936; campaign story, "Sunflower," MP.

lesson in defiance of local customs. After an uneventful escort from the
railroad depot to a state legislator's office, Mitchell learned that the office
would be his Sangamon county headquarters. There were no complaints
from Mitchell until a waiter appeared from the St. Nicholas Hotel to
take the guest's breakfast order. Thereupon, Mitchell inquired why he
could not obtain service across the street in the hotel dining room. The
polite reply was that the establishment did not accommodate blacks.
Provoked, Mitchell grabbed his belongings and marched off to the hotel's
front entrance. There, he met a stunned bellboy who tried desperately
to pacify him while anxiously attempting to direct him to a rear door.
Becoming angrier than ever, Mitchell shoved his luggage into the astonished employee's hands and led him into the lobby. Observing what
had been in progress, the hotel's manager quickly intervened, trying at
this point to divert a most unwelcome customer to a private room and
proposing that breakfast could be taken there. The solution, however,
did not satisfy Mitchell. Against management's wishes, he boisterously
refused to accept food under such demeaning arrangements. After bitter
exchanges between Mitchell and the hotel official, a local arrangements
committee member conversed privately with the hotel manager. Upon
finishing, they informed Mitchell "that they could not serve Colored
people in the regular dining room, as Springfield is a small town and
purely Southern in sentiment, as far as mixing of the races is concerned."
Unmoved and undeterred, the offended officeholder stormed into the
general eating area, demanding immediate service, which he quickly
received to the stunned amazement of everyone around him. Then hours
later at noon, just to confirm a point, he led a mixed-race delegation back
to the hotel's main salon for dinner. Afterward for weeks, Mitchell's bold
crusade for civil rights was still the talk of central Illinois. But for his part,
he did not attempt to use it in his own reelection campaign against Oscar
DePriest.[42]

As manager of the western division, Mitchell got mixed reviews.
Among supporters, none seemed more appreciative than Emory B. Smith
and O. B. Jefferson. Immediately after the election, both took time to
praise Mitchell's campaign organizing efforts. Jefferson's postelection
compliments were a reflection of earlier sentiments he had shared with
Farley. Three weeks before the election, there had been mention of "fine
cooperation" and "helpful advice." After the election, Jefferson spoke to
Farley and credited Mitchell with "handling this most difficult assignment." For having had an opportunity to work with Mitchell, there was

42. *Chicago Metropolitan News*, September 26, 1936; James S. LeVine to M, September 15, 1936; M to LeVine, September 16, 1936, MP.

a note of personal satisfaction. But in addition to fights over reimbursements, other complaints surfaced about Mitchell's management of the western division. After visiting Kansas in the middle of the campaign, Lawrence Oxley, adviser on black affairs to the Department of Labor, concluded Mitchell was "doing absolutely nothing" there. How much of Oxley's opinion was a misreading of Mitchell's role in Kansas's leadership vacuum and what part came from personal differences with the lawmaker cannot be determined. For similar reasons, it is difficult to evaluate Perry Thompson's negative assessments of Mitchell. Just about anything other than a positive verdict from a longtime Chicago critic of the official would have astounded anyone deeply involved in Bronzeville politics. Based on firsthand knowledge, Thompson's prediction was that "it will be a bit difficult to work with Mitchell." Compounding matters, Thompson disagreed with Mitchell about "sticking to the theory that if Roosevelt hasn't done enough for the Negro to merit his vote—then the hell with their votes."[43]

For the Democratic party, Mitchell's problems with Rainey were potentially more embarrassing than a jaded attitude. Early in their campaign jobs, Mitchell and Rainey worked productively together. In October, though, Rainey let loose some ill-timed words about Mitchell after excessive drinking in a Harlem saloon. Suddenly, everything positive in the relationship deteriorated. Through a friend who heard Rainey's bellowing wish for Mitchell's defeat, Mitchell learned of Rainey's true feelings. Confidentially then to Farley, Mitchell expressed outrage with Rainey's indiscretion. Claiming not to be "thin-skinned," he still did not enjoy being a besmirched victim of a jealous drunkard with an incapacity to check defamatory outbursts.[44]

While the majority of African American votes did not go to FDR in 1936, the fault was hardly Mitchell's. Two aspects of the 1936 presidential election and the black populace were more or less beyond Mitchell's control: how blacks related to Roosevelt, and how they related to the Republican party. FDR and the New Deal were precipitating powerful shifts of old allegiances, but the shift was more gradual than Mitchell's estimates. His predicting a landslide was an honest mistake. To Mitchell, the fact that so many more African Americans were coming to Democratic rallies in 1936 than ever before was a definite indication of a swing from the GOP. Unforeseen by him, strong binding traditions among black voters had prevailed in November, as blacks chose Alf Landon over Roosevelt.

43. EBS to M, November 5, 1936; Jefferson to JAF, October 14, 1936; Jefferson to M, November 5, 1936; DsL to M, October 21, 1936, MP; Thompson to EGB, September 21, 1936, RP.
    44. Earl Brown to M, October 6, 1936; M to JAF, October 7, 1936, MP.

Just as the director had little to do with FDR's momentum, there was no way for him to overcome habitual Republican voting by blacks. Even if their votes did not reflect it in 1936, African Americans were moving closer to becoming participants in a gigantic political upheaval. Unknowingly, they were adopting the spirit and sentiments of two humble citizens who expressed support to their "Mistah Roosevelt." A Miami woman told how Roosevelt had "been a life saver to us." Notwithstanding obstacles to her own voting, she wanted on behalf of the race to "send up our prayers for you." Aware of his popularity, the Floridian understood something was happening among blacks. As she viewed it, "There isn't a Civilize[d] Colored person that would [not] vote for you." A black from the Midwest had even more emphatic feelings for FDR. "Honestly," he wrote Mitchell, "I think that Roosevelt is a second Jesus Christ and it would be a calamity if he did not get a vote of confidence from the people that he has so loyally defended the past three years."[45]

While circumstances within the Democratic party's Colored Division in 1936 seemed dismal at times, matters were worse for Republicans. For them, the year's presidential contest looked like their first one without solid African American support. Loyalists such as Perry Howard and Claude Barnett stayed in the GOP, but many other blacks did not. In an otherwise bleak election, Jesse Owens's willingness to campaign was a bright spot. Although Mitchell shrugged off the track star's possible impact, Owens's presence brought much anxiety to the western division. Even with Democrats in command with many advantages in 1936, worries about losing voters to Republicans persisted because the GOP was concentrating more money on the Negro electorate than was the Democratic party. In addition to complaints about Landon flushing money into black communities, Mitchell's team perceived the Democrats to be ineffective at countering hostile propaganda. Many of the campaign workers were relative newcomers to the harsh realities of political races. As a result, they tended to overreact to GOP assaults on the president. For example, Republicans charged that many dimes collected in FDR's fight against poliomyelitis were ending up in a Georgia clinic that did not admit and treat affected black children. After learning of the accusation, Indiana state head Freeman B. Ransom was gripped with fright. For dealing with the challenge "of keeping propaganda from poisoning the minds of our people," he sought Mitchell's advice.[46]

45. Aileen Byron to FDR, October 9, 1936; C. C. Galloway to M, August 17, 1936, MP.
46. Powell to M, September 4, 1936; PDJ to M, October 1 and 7, 1936; CFD to M, October 15 and 21, 1936; FBR to M, October 13 and 19, 1936, MP; *Omaha Guide*, October 10, 1936; *Kansas City Call* clip, n.d., BP.

Some legacies of the Colored Division lived on after 1936. One such legacy was the crisis of reimbursements. Unlike other times when Mitchell ignored or belittled accusations, there was no scaring off those who sought repayments. The determination to recover expenses was greatest in Ohio because its state staffers had a distinct advantage; they could set their cases before Roosevelt. Unresolved recoveries reached him through a White House staff employee, who was a friend of the Ohioan entrusted with collecting unsettled claims. Alerted that black Ohioans had become "a good deal down on Congressman Mitchell," FDR asked Farley to "get someone to look into it and get it straightened out without bringing . . . me into it." Insofar as any financial records supported the claims, Roosevelt ordered Farley to "destroy them." Even with this high-level involvement, Mitchell did not retreat from earlier allegations that the claimants were "chiselers" guilty of "a silly effort to shake the National Committee down for money." He could take such a hard stand because one factor was favoring it; W. Forbes Morgan was dead. He was the only committeeman with any knowledge of the Ohio disputes and the mess of conflicting testimonies. With nobody in a position to refute the bases for nonpayments, Mitchell was secure. For collecting on unpaid claims, Ohioans were at a disadvantage. Without fear of refutation, Mitchell could stick to a story that Morgan had directed a strict accounting to ensure that campaign compensations went only for authorized election work. Without financial records to check, scholars must assume from similar experiences in neighboring Michigan (where workers never recovered all their expenses) that neither Mitchell nor the party ever reimbursed three thousand dollars in claims to the Ohioans.[47]

What began as a drift to Roosevelt in 1936 was becoming a surge before the 1940 election. By the last quarter of 1940, increases in FDR's popularity among African Americans had reached such high levels that a landslide for him seemed inevitable. It was not the only major change in 1940. Just as in Philadelphia four years earlier, Mitchell was before a podium as a speaker when the Windy City hosted the Democratic National Convention. Now, however, his participation did not cause an incident. "Cotton Ed" Smith was absent altogether from the party's quadrennial event, and no other demagogic disputant emerged to mar Mitchell's appearance. Hence, arrangements by the National Broadcasting Company were the most momentous thing about the event. NBC provided coast-to-coast transmission of Mitchell's address. Such radio coverage was special

47. FDR to JAF, August 28, 1937, RP; JAF to M, September 14, 1937; M to JAF, September 29, 1937; for Michigan, see: M to Edmund C. Shields, January 25, 1937; Shields to Morgan, January 14 and February 2, 1937; M to Morgan, January 25, 1937, MP. Mitchell had begun spelling "chiseler" correctly.

because no other black had ever delivered a political address over national airwaves. Here in effect was a unique feat, a radio broadcast bringing a black Democrat into the homes of millions of white Americans.[48]

Mitchell's part in overall 1940 Democratic strategies changed, too. For all practical purposes, the strife-torn Colored Division, with its many splintered organizations scattered among several potentially decisive states, was gone. For all that, dismantling the division was not easy. Many Democrats, black and white, wanted its life extended. Curiously in this battle for its survival, African American activists who were interested in greater power in party affairs unwittingly joined forces with the most uncompromising segregationists. Both of these groups had opted for continuing the Colored Division. The African American position resulted at a closed-door meeting of black Democrats. Within the party, blacks advocated a representative body to champion the race's interests. Dubbed the "jim-crow convention" by its critics, it met days before the official convening of party delegates. With blacks gathered in rump session, it occurred to Mitchell that their preconvention assembly was a cause for a GOP celebration. From a critic's vantage point, Democrats now appeared to have closed party deliberations to African Americans and were ignoring the race's party leaders. Besides giving some potential ammunition to the GOP in its campaigns for minority votes later in 1940, the rump session was a source of irritation for another reason; Bill Thompkins and Edgar G. Brown were behind it as cosponsors. Since Mitchell had been loathing them for several years, there was no chance of enlisting his participation. The disrespectfulness of Thompkins and Brown toward many white Democratic leaders and their militancy on racial matters had never sat well with Mitchell. Several prominent black Democrats boycotted all sessions of the preconvention that constituted itself as the National Colored Democratic Association, but only Mitchell received harsh treatment. Interestingly, though, there were no personal denunciations of him in the NCDA report forwarded to James Farley because by its resolution, the assembly had stamped Mitchell so "obnoxious to the association" that his leadership would be rejected if the party should ever decide to name him to another top post. Even if the NCDA had not shared its assessments of Mitchell, Farley was aware of animosity brewing among African American Democrats toward the congressman. Consequently, there was no choice but to abandon plans to resurrect anything resembling in scope the Colored Division of 1936. Except for two shadow organizations established with Mitchell and Rainey in more

48. Reprint, CR, 76th Cong., 3d sess., July 22, 1940, MP; Chicago Sunday Bee, July 28, 1940; Oklahoma City Black Dispatch, July 27, 1940; Afro-American, July 20, 1940.

or less honorary leadership roles, the Colored Division was nonexistent because not much materialized from the 1940 edition. Lacking unity and support, directors Rainey and Mitchell were left virtually powerless and penniless. Nothing in 1940 matched the scale of 1936. The example of Michigan illustrated just why Mitchell could achieve little. Bitter memories still lingered there after he had blocked recoveries of campaign travel expenses.[49]

With no Colored Division to manage in 1940, Mitchell experienced his first relatively easy presidential election in sixteen years. He enjoyed himself, doing what always had gone well. He spoke on behalf of fellow Democrats. Considered a pleasurable pursuit, campaigning for House candidates brought him into eventual contact with the Democratic Congressional Campaign Committee and chairman Lyndon Baines Johnson. As its head, Johnson soon appreciated Mitchell's kind willingness to help. For a reward, LBJ collected four hundred dollars from fellow Texans in the House of Representatives as their donation to Mitchell's reelection. While working for Democrats in 1940, Mitchell embarrassed at least one incumbent candidate. In an act of public bravery and moral principle, he did not deliver a scheduled speech in Wichita for Congressman Jack Houston. As in Springfield four years earlier, the black headliner did not allow himself to be a victim of a hotel's policies. In some respects, though, the black officeholder was more peeved at the local arrangement committee's decision to side with a lodging facility than with the hotel's refusal to honor his reservation. Still, by announcing an irreversible cancelation, Mitchell left rally sponsors scrambling after a new speaker. Although days later he forwarded regrets to Houston for "a gross misunderstanding," there was steadfastness to his conviction that unfortunate circumstances had forced his withdrawal from his speaking commitment. With a carefully worded explanation to the Kansas incumbent, Mitchell included a full refund of an advanced per diem. Overall, his defiant spirit and pluck earned Mitchell more respect and praise from blacks than criticisms from white Kansans.[50]

The end of Roosevelt's third campaign marked a terminal point of sorts in FDR's relationship with Mitchell. Mitchell had offered his help in Roosevelt's presidential victories of 1932, 1936, and 1940, and most conceivably, he had given some legitimacy to Democratic appeals to

49. M to JEM, August 8, 1940; M to JAF, July 23, 1940; FBR to M, September 1, 1940; M to Joseph C. Coles, September 13 and 20, 1940; Coles to M, September 16, 1940, MP; *Buffalo Star*, August 30, 1940; *Afro-American*, July 20 and September 7, 1940; *Louisville Leader*, August 31, 1940.

50. *Mt. Vernon Register* (Ill.) and *Centralia Sentinel* (Ill.), n.d.; Lyndon Baines Johnson to M, October 23, 24, and 29, November 1, 4, and 15, and December 4, 1940; M to Johnson, October 29 and December 3, 1940; Edward J. Flynn to M, October 10 and 15, 1940; M to Jack Houston, November 3, 1940; Carrie Robinson to M, November 3, 1940, MP; *Wichita Kansas Journal* and *Wichita Negro Star*, November 1, 1940.

African Americans. On almost every roll call before Congress, Mitchell had sided with the president. In addition, he had been a rather consistent New Deal spokesman both on Capitol Hill and nationally. Yet in 1940, after Roosevelt's first-time capture of a majority of black votes, there seemed less need for a lackey such as Mitchell in the Democratic party. From all appearances, the novelty of a black Democrat in Congress had lost both its importance and vitality. As the new majority of a minority, African American Democrats had already begun aligning themselves behind better political leaders than Mitchell. As evidenced by preconvention rumblings in 1940 and later by angry responses from Michigan, Mitchell had perhaps become an embarrassment and a liability for the Democrats. Earlier when leaders of the executive branch had ignored his advice and judgments, there had at least been tolerance toward a tool of the Chicago Machine. Cast by bosses to be the Democrats' first black in Congress, Mitchell had pleased the party just because he had not upset the Roosevelt administration. Personal peculiarities and eccentric behavior had not seemed to matter so long as he had not aroused Southern white sensibilities and had not upset the Democrats' fragile coalition. Administration officials, party members from Capitol Hill, and Democratic national committeemen had sighed with relief after that first win over Oscar DePriest in 1934, and they generally had liked Mitchell's performance in Congress and his conspicuous contributions to the Democratic party. Nonetheless, his true value as a pioneer had been largely symbolic. Despite lapses into docility, Mitchell was a good transitional figure for the Democrats. Initially after an election to the House as an avid Rooseveltian, he excited both black urban masses and country folk. Remarkably, he could accomplish this feat and still soothe Southern Democrats' worst fears about empowering blacks. Prior to Mitchell's rise, whenever a leading person in the party had broached proposals that African Americans be added to party ranks in Dixie, there had been overwhelming suppression; forces driven by reaction and fear had united. Now, however, with dies cast by Mitchell and a subsequent abandonment of Lincoln by a black majority, there could be no retreat. African Americans were coalition partners in a revised Democratic federation. From the NCDA in 1940, Democrats were placed on notice to heed the race's demands. Farley's decision in 1940 not to reconstitute an active Colored Division illustrated the first effects of a political revolution on the party. Ultimately, then, a pragmatic decision to slate Mitchell, a black man and a Democrat, by a white ward boss under pressure from Bronzeville contributed to shifts in party loyalties among blacks and to greater party incongruity. No discussion of Mitchell and Roosevelt would be complete without noting the fact that the president's black ally on Capitol Hill did not publicly criticize nor attempt to amend administration-backed legislation.

Reluctant Black
Representative

6

I n January 1935, when Arthur W. Mitchell anxiously stepped forward for the mandatory congressional oath of office, citizens observed a black Democrat slip inadvertently into a capacity that did not square exactly with his previously announced aspirations. From his slating in September to the January ceremony, Mitchell had adamantly denied that his future would include the role of representative at large for black America. He had insisted his primary interests would be to citizens of the First District, to the president, and to all Americans. Yet he could not avoid completely an obvious conflict of interests for him and an unwanted burden—African American welfare. No matter what he might have said or done to dodge or minimize responsibilities to what many regarded as his most natural constituency, some realities about America were going to upset Mitchell's plans. Most importantly, as the first black Democrat in Congress, he would not escape recognition. He also could not avert the resultant consequences of citizens associating him with black predecessors, for reluctance had nothing to do with results. Mitchell could deny—from whatever platform or before whichever group—that blackness would not affect or distinguish him, and he could loudly shout that he would not crusade with a special agenda of assistance to African Americans struggling against racist injustice and discrimination, but none of these wishes would really matter. The real situation did not resemble Mitchell's perceptions. According to his rhetoric aimed at the white South, Mitchell had planned to blend as inconspicuously as possible into the general House membership. But the distinction of race, etched deeply into the national character, would dictate a special view and judgment of Mitchell, a man of African heritage conspicuously placed among whites. There would be completely unique standards applied to him. Interestingly, neither his black nor his white followers—be they friends or enemies—would have wanted it differently. Always, they compared Mitchell's record and reputation only to the DePriest legislative model and to nobody else's; there were never comparisons to other lawmakers because citizens would never confuse a black Democrat with them.

By favoring him with a letter soon after the opening of Congress in 1935, a young black schoolgirl from North Carolina inadvertently challenged Mitchell's pretenses about color's insignificance. She had written to beg an autographed picture of "her Congressman." Her act of designating him for the honor left an unmistakable imprint. According to her innocent assessment and confession after his win, she had developed strong kinship bonds for the Chicagoan. They had resulted, volunteered the girl, because of racial pride and assurance. Knowledge that he—a man of her racial background—would soon occupy a House seat had led her to request his photograph. Encountering a teenager's naïveté and dreamy sentiments might have done no more than flatter if Mitchell had not faced similar attentions from kindly black adults. Like her, they had not accepted his reservations about not wanting consideration as "their Congressman." Their outpouring of emotional expressions would indicate that Mitchell's statements about not desiring such entrapments had not taken hold. Inasmuch as there was no escape for him, one question would remain: How devoted would Mitchell be to African Americans?[1]

Mitchell made a mockery out of strangers who tried to steer or influence him. A good example was the experience of Chicago's Afro-American Protective League. It had wanted to school Mitchell in racial consciousness because there were mounting fears that he neither comprehended nor appreciated the significance of his references to blacks or to himself. Noting for the newcomer to Congress why "the name 'Negro' means nothing," the League's officers endeavored as a matter of pride to demand his use of "Afro-American" or "Ethiopian." Dismissing all this as foolishness, Mitchell insisted that there would be no changes in his appellation for the race. Thus, "Negro" would continue to suit him except during moments of anger when he sought to insult or denigrate persons of African heritage. Then, "darkie" became his favored term of derision. Significantly, in spite of his own use of such contemptuous terms, Mitchell, to his credit, showed neither tolerance nor patience toward whites who insisted on inflammatory references to African Americans. For example, in 1936, he directed harsh criticism at a major Washington newspaper for its use of "dusky" in a front-page headline introducing opera's Marian Anderson.

1. Pauline Jenkins to M, January 31, 1935; for reminders and replies, see: L. Joseph Bickham to M, January 1935; William T. B. Hill to M, May 4, 1939; M to Hill, May 5, 1939; "Chickens Come Home," n.d.; Dabney to M, January 22, 1935; M to Alcorn, March 6, 1935, MP; Dickerson interview; *Journal and Guide*, June 22, 1935; *Afro-American*, June 8 and 15, 1935; *Pittsburgh Courier*, March 9, 1935.

With profuse apologies for his "ineptitude," a chastened editor quickly accepted Mitchell's reprimand.[2]

Overall during his first term, Mitchell tended toward ambivalence about himself and his race. Ambiguities existed because he did not know how to wrestle with racial attitudes and identity. At a loss before 1937 about how to note strong feelings, he simply attempted as much as possible to disassociate himself from many minority matters. During this self-denial era in Mitchell's life, these connections were embarrassments that he perhaps could overcome through cultivating impressions of his dissimilarity to most other African Americans. According to biographer Joyce Ross, Mary Bethune was also inclined toward these same negative expressions. Ross attributed race depreciations before whites to desires to couch real demands. Although Mitchell could employ double-talk in similar fashion, he also held some genuine contempt for blacks.[3]

Interestingly, though, Mitchell did not necessarily advise racial submission. In a candid exchange with Bronzeville native William F. Thornton, he counseled the black engineer to stay the course by continuing his supervision of a white crew in Alabama even if it might prove difficult at times. After technical studies at the University of Illinois, Thornton experienced much personal discomfort while trying to manage fellow technicians at a Tuskegee Resettlement Administration project. His complaints to Mitchell about being unable to cope with the unusual circumstance triggered a surprising response. Citing the situation as "a rare opportunity" for an African American, Mitchell asked why Thornton could not change his attitude for the benefit of other blacks. Rather than capitulate to white pressures, Thornton was requested to value his management position as a milestone for the race. As Mitchell counseled, "Our [African Americans'] conditions in this country, as to improvement, depends very largely upon our ability to successfully handle white people. It is not only a rare art, but a necessary art, and nothing pleases me more than to see a Colored man with training placed in a position such as you are now in and use the proper tact in order to make himself beloved rather than despised. I repeat, I regret exceedingly the fact that you seem not to be able to make it with the white people under your charge."[4] Illustrative of Mitchell's first-term complexities and inconsistencies, his advice characterized all the mixed signals coming from him. On civil rights, he was offering such

2. R. H. Johnson and Ray Barkley to M, June 5, 1935; M to Johnson and Barkley, June 8, 1935; M to Dungee, March 26, 1936; Cephas interview; M to WRC Broadcasting Station, March 15, 1937; M to Lowell Mellett, February 19, 1936; Mellett to M, February 20, 1936, MP; *Defender*, January 19, 1935; *Washington Daily News*, n.d.

3. Survey of Mitchell correspondence and speeches to whites; Ross, "Mary McLeod Bethune and the NYA," 4–6.

4. Thornton to M, February 24, 1936; M to Thornton, February 26, 1936, MP.

diverse opinions that varying positions from him could easily have been interpreted as support for almost any political perspective. At one time or another, Mitchell teetered from conservative to radical, passive to militant, with each description appropriate to a particular issue or event before him. Hence, from one moment to the next from 1935 to 1937, in response to the enigmatic politician's easy movements within a rather broad ideological spectrum, contemporary judgments of Mitchell swung from condemnation to praise. As with sudden changes in Chicago's weather, Mitchell's attitude toward civil rights was tempestuous.

Abrupt moves were representative of his strong instincts and desires for political survival. To survive, he found adjustment necessary and more beneficial than consistency. Whenever reactions from the Democratic party or the Chicago Machine indicated disfavor, retreat or retraction followed without hesitation. In his research on African American leaders, scholarly Ralph Bunche found so many leaders exhibiting mixed-behavior tendencies that he classified them distinctly. According to Bunche, these prominent blacks could cross "the entire gamut from sane, sober restraint to downright and deliberate 'kowtowing,' 'pussy footing' and 'Uncle-Tomming.' " Moreover, he observed "many honestly conservative Negro leaders who are convinced that within the existing racial situation the Negro can make best progress by slow, patient but determined plodding along, by a restrained approach to the problems of the group, so designed as to avoid stirring up any more racial feeling than already exists." Individuals with these beliefs tended to "be suave Uncle Toms with white[s] and harsh tyrants among Negroes. They are often given to berating Negro[e]s and are apt apologists for the white attitudes toward Negroes." If based only on superficial observations of Mitchell, Bunche's generalizations and simplifications applied to him. However, Mitchell displayed too many complexities for him to fit entirely into one of Ralph Bunche's neat categories.[5]

One thing was certain about Mitchell: he detested "trouble makers." By his definition, these included activists and protesters.[6] Clearly an adherent of Booker T. Washington's formulas for racial progress, Mitchell mostly preferred legal remedies and education to peaceful or violent confrontation. Essentially just a flexible blueprint "hammered out for the Negro [as] a philosophy of the dominant white population" according to Bunche,

---

5. Ralph J. Bunche, "A Brief and Tentative Analysis of Negro Leadership," September 1940; compare to David McBride and Monroe H. Little's "The Afro-American Elite, 1930–1940: A Historical and Statistical Profile," 105–19; Karen L. Kalmar, "Southern Black Elites and the New Deal: A Case Study of Savannah, Georgia"; Douglas C. Abrams, "Irony of Reform: North Carolina Blacks and the New Deal," 149–78.

6. For an example, see Mitchell's opinion of a rebellious Howard University student in his letter to Morgan, March 19, 1936, MP.

the Tuskegee approach "was a pragmatic doctrine of 'getting along' and of making the best of things as they are." Like Washington, Mitchell imagined improvement as a cause-and-effect, step-by-step process, with accelerations resulting only from practical training that had been geared to useful vocational preparation. As Mitchell summed up education, "It is a pity that so many [black] students leave our schools with A.B. degrees. Why can't more of them study for the bachelor of science degree? This is a scientific age, and the world is calling for scientists. I want to see some of our colored boys invent something." Mitchell also agreed with Washington on another point: he concurred that basking in self-pity would not benefit the race. He believed that dwelling on slavery's injustices would not advance African Americans. As he was fond of telling black listeners, there were only two things that could solve their problems: education and hard work. With his often-repeated platitude about labor's own rewards, Mitchell would liken himself to Joe Louis and Jesse Owens. "Most of us hold ourselves back thinking that we are being mistreated." Nevertheless, "color does not hold a man back." Eventually, Mitchell disparaged relief's effects upon his "group." Since he believed government-sponsored relief programs were causing blacks to depend on public largesse, he thought the programs contradicted his beliefs in individual responsibilities. "Only as the Negro is given the opportunity to work out his own economic salvation can any progress be made in the solution of the problem" of black poverty, he advised.[7]

Not astonishingly, Mitchell tried to honor Booker T. Washington. At his behest, Congress designated Washington's birthday as a special day for eulogies. Then on April 5, 1937, Mitchell proceeded fellow legislators to a Capitol rostrum for delivery of a passionate, thirty-minute address, "Booker T. Washington's Life: A Legacy for the Nation." As the moving spirit behind a day of tribute, Mitchell received much praise and gratitude from admirers of Tuskegee's founder. As a follow-up, he initiated and led efforts to restore Washington's Virginia birthplace. The plans called for building a museum and a log-cabin replica of Washington's boyhood home on vacant land near Hale's Ford. When completed, the museum would house Washington mementos. Mitchell believed in the project so much that he committed himself personally to purchasing the site. There were two conditions to meet, however. A title transfer to him would be

    7. Bunche, "A Brief and Tentative Analysis," 14; Unidentified Atlanta newspaper, February 14, 1938; JMc to M, December 31, 1942; M to Woodson, May 5, 1939; Thomas R. Harrison to M, April 10, 1935; reprint, CR, 75th Cong., 2d sess., April 5, 1937, MP; Oakwood Junior College Acorn (Huntsville), n.d.; Charlotte Observer, April 24, 1939; Wilmington Morning Star, April 22, 1939; CR, 74th Cong., 2d sess., 5887–88; Defender, October 29, 1938; Oklahoma City Black Dispatch, October 16, 1937.

contingent upon a guarantee from the Commonwealth of Virginia to pave a road to the remote spot and upon sold subscriptions to fund the project. In the end, even a pledge from Representative Willis Robertson of Virginia to lobby for the access artery failed to secure the necessary appropriations for road construction. Consequently, without tax levies, Mitchell never took out his option on the land. Thereupon, in quick succession, the project lost its sponsorship and its momentum.[8]

Mitchell also showed interest in honoring other African American role models. Despite suggestions of inconsistencies between Mitchell's attitude toward the race and time spent on its heroes, he was devoted to and interested in African American history. Many of his addresses to congressional and other audiences traced the roots and development of Africans in the United States. Furthermore, Mitchell was a regular donor to the Association for the Study of Negro Life and History. He also participated in National Negro History Week, and he counted historian and fellow accommodationist Carter G. Woodson of Howard University among his closest friends. Reflecting passion for the race's past achievements, Mitchell's most memorable campaign centered on the brave accomplishments of black polar explorer Matthew A. Henson. Convinced recognition of the pioneer's important contributions to Admiral Robert E. Peary's successful Arctic Circle conquest of April 6, 1909, was long overdue, Mitchell assumed the task of helping the cause in 1936. By then, Henson, almost seventy years old and living in poverty, was no longer remembered as the man who had planted an American flag on the North Pole. Obtaining assistance for Henson meant so much to Mitchell that he even enlisted personal enemies as his allies in the cause. Mitchell seemingly willed himself to overlook political considerations and past grudges, and all selfish aversions to working with foes such as Eugene Kinckle Jones of the Urban League and Fred R. Moore of the *New York Age* suddenly vanished. Left speechless by the turnabout, many of Mitchell's most persistent detractors had neither the cause nor its champion to fight this time. After having established a broad base of support, Mitchell dropped a relief-and-recognition bill for Henson in the House hopper on April 20, 1936. Eventually designated H.R. 12388, it was unlike earlier ill-fated attempts at pensioning Henson because the new effort would provide more than monetary aid. To symbolize a black explorer's "loyalty, bravery, and valor," it would authorize minting of special commemorative

8. L. M. McCoy to M, Ligon A. Wilson to M, March 20, 1937; M to Work, March 22, 1937; Jacob L. Reid to M, September 24, 1937; M to Reid, December 6, 1937, MP; *CR*, 75th Cong., 1st sess., 2110, 3149; *Journal and Guide*, April 10, 1937; *New York Sun*, September 7, 1937; *Newport News Star*, September 18, 1937; *Franklin News-Post* (Va.), September 17, 1937; *Chicago Herald and Examiner*, September 8, 1937; *Roanoke Times*, October 21, 1937.

gold coins. In "recognition for the service rendered to Admiral Peary," Henson would benefit from an annual pension of twenty-five hundred dollars allocated from funds earmarked to the Bureau of Veterans' Affairs.[9]

After its assignment to the Committee on Coinage, Weights, and Measures, H.R. 12388 began gathering African American support. Even perpetual Mitchell nemeses such as Walter White of the NAACP and *Afro-American* editor Carl Murphy were behind the lawmaker on the Henson commemorative coin. When congressional hearings commenced on May 22, 1936, all the incongruous pieces had fit together so well that Mitchell was positioned to introduce an impressive lineup of supporters to committeemen. Matthew Henson was also present. Although the House panel recognized and then generally quizzed their honored guest about conquering the North Pole, he likely did not favorably impress many committee members. Self-conscious and modest, Henson was a rather dull witness. By all accounts, the day belonged to Mitchell; he gave a strong performance before his fellow congressmen, orchestrating and controlling everything on Henson's behalf. Mitchell opened with a long rambling introductory address that detailed the bill's features, Henson's life story, and the justifications for granting Henson a pension. Mitchell closed the proceedings by calling ten diverse witnesses who all agreed that Henson deserved recognition and compensation. Wedged between their short speeches were testimonies from absent supporters of the bill. Overall, the session was not so much an inquiry as an opportunity to recount a black hero's contributions. Consequently, presenters at the hearing introduced nothing new about the polar adventurer. To spectators following a day of deliberations, it seemed as if the committeemen's politeness had come more out of courtesy for a colleague than from genuine interest in Mitchell's bill. As a result, there was not much surprise when the committee did not recommend H.R. 12388.[10]

9. EKJ to M, February 4, 1935; Woodson to M, April 8 and May 15, 1935; M to Woodson, April 24, 1935; EKJ to M, April 10, 1936; M to Fred R. Moore, April 24, 1936; MNR, "Congressman Arthur W. Mitchell Strikes Another Blow in behalf of the Negro," April 1936, MP; speech, "The Negro a Factor in the History of the World," February 7, 1940; *Atlantic City Eagle*, February 11, 1939, MP; *Defender*, May 2, 1936; *CR*, 74th Cong., 2d sess., 5750, H.R. 12388. For accounts of Henson, see Robert H. Fowler's "The Negro Who Went to the Pole with Peary"; also see Floyd Miller's *Ahdoolo: The Biography of Matthew A. Henson*.

10. U.S. House of Representatives, Committee on Coinage, Weights, and Measures, Hearing, "For the Recognition of Matthew A. Hensen [*sic*]," 74th Cong., 2d sess., May 22, 1936, 1–19; MNR, May 23, 1936; WW to M, May 21, 1936; Moton to M, May 21, 1936; M to EKJ, Moton, and Garnet C. Wilkerson, May 19, 1936; EKJ to M, May 20, 1936; Moore to M, May 18, 21, and 28, 1936; M to Moore, April 24, May 19, and June 1, 1936; M to Murphy, May 19, 1936; Murphy to M, May 21, 1936, MP; *Afro-American*, April 15, 1936; *New York Journal and American*, January 26, 1936.

Mitchell obviously expected no political ramifications from his support of Washington and Henson. His personal decisions to promote and assist these individuals had come without reservations. They had not resembled African Americans whom Mitchell eschewed. Washington and Henson had been openly appreciative of their opportunities, and they had not protested publicly to gain recognition or achieve change. Led by his misguided sense of patriotism, Mitchell disdained those blacks who were not appreciative of their "opportunities" and who voiced their discontent. His intolerance extended to those who complained too loudly about American injustice and to activists who demonstrated to address problems. In his scheme, these were "cry-baby Negroes" or "born trouble makers." As Mitchell explained to the *Dayton Forum,* opera's Paul Robeson personified what should be disdained: "All of us know what it is to suffer from the injustice and prejudices heaped upon us by the majority people, but I pity the fellow who gives most of his time to thinking of these and overlooks the opportunities that this country gave him." Mitchell disliked radicals and opposed communism. According to him, Karl Marx's philosophy offered nothing to African Americans. Mitchell's opinion of leftists was so dogmatic and irrational at times that he told some representatives of suspicious-sounding organizations to refrain from visiting him at the Capitol if their intentions were to represent the Communist party. After approaching Arthur Mitchell for an appointment, one Jewish leader interested in discussing fascism and anti-Semitism learned of this paranoia. In Mitchell's judgment, Reds had been "so very inconsiderate in their conferences that it is very unpleasant and unsatisfactory to receive them."[11]

The situation at Howard University provided a good example of Mitchell's suspicions of communists. During his first term, he made dubious speculations about communist infiltrations into the institution under President Mordecai Johnson. Concerns about possible communist influence at Howard, however, had not originated with Mitchell. In 1933 after Johnson's baccalaureate sermon, protests about his disloyalty had arisen from Oscar DePriest. During one year of Red baiting, DePriest had become Johnson's scourge. For both Howard University and Johnson, the attacks had been disastrous. From some quarters at the university, the defeat of DePriest brought loud cheers, for nobody could damage the school's reputation more than the black Republican had done. On February 3, 1935, a formal tea reception held in honor of DePriest's Democratic successor demonstrated the university's expectation of goodwill from Mitchell; the

11. *Dayton Forum,* February 23, 1940; M to *Forum,* February 26, 1940; M to Morgan, March 19, 1936; M to Abe Feinglass, October 23, 1937, MP; *Philadelphia Independent,* August 10, 1941.

reception was a clear signal of awaited positive advances with someone new. Well attended by both faculty and staff, the special social function at Sojourner Truth Hall was a welcoming event to introduce and reintroduce Mitchell to new people and old acquaintances and to encourage his support; Johnson hosted the event. From this beginning, relations between Johnson and Mitchell quietly deteriorated. All signs of compatibility were gone by June. Their acrimonious estrangement occurred in part because Mitchell had been partial in a Howard power struggle between Dean Kelly Miller and President Johnson. To discredit the head of Howard and involve outsiders in an internal fight between rival factions and administrators, Miller used a smoke screen of radicals' access to many campus facilities. Johnson's tolerance and laxity no doubt had contributed to a leftist presence at the school, but this issue only partially explained Mitchell's unfolding role in a strident internal affair. Ultraconservatives on almost every subject involving race and radicals, Mitchell and Miller were longtime personal friends. Above all, his relationship with Miller accounted for much of Mitchell's curiosity. Regarding many procedural questions, Miller and many other old-guard members of the Howard community were antagonistic toward Johnson. According to reliable sources, resentment had begun with Johnson's selection. After the board had bypassed Miller for Johnson, there was no generous acquiescence to a secondary role. Still resentful and vengeful about the whole matter in May 1935, Miller finally received his long-awaited chance to entangle and perhaps even topple his rival. On May 18, with Julius Rosenwald funds and under the combined auspices of Howard's Social Science Department and an autonomous Joint Committee on National Recovery, economists, sociologists, and mixed laymen assembled at Howard to convene the Conference on the Economic Condition of the Negro. The conference, held despite the protests of Miller, attracted radicals with far-out leftist ideas, and brought accusations to the effect that Howard's president had sanctioned communistic deliberations. Sanctimoniously, in an open letter addressed to Johnson and circulated among university trustees and House members including Mitchell, Miller both instructed and warned. From the president, Miller wanted explanations for why there had not been an attempt at countering and censuring radicalism at the conference. In addition, there were challenges to Johnson's tenure at Howard. In pleas to trustees and Congress, Miller embodied a case for dismissal that cited a series of specific charges against the president.[12]

While Miller was composing a challenge to Johnson, Mitchell was on a House subcommittee tour of Howard. At the besieged Johnson's request,

12. KM to MWJ, May 24, MP; *Washington Post*, May 20, 1935; *Philadelphia Tribune*, June 6, 1935.

a six-member contingent was on campus to observe teaching. Johnson was present at this superficial inspection, escorting guests and personally strolling with them to answer their questions. Nothing surfaced then to indicate special concerns or displeasures with Howard University or its officers. Mitchell, in the general spirit of the day's conversation, expressed a hope that the Negro institution would never inculcate such radical teachings in its class offerings as many newspapers had implied. In reply, Johnson referred eloquently to a liberal tradition of rights, adding glibly that Howard would sooner forfeit congressional funding than suppress oratory. With no signs of lawmakers' disapproval arising out of the visit, Johnson sighed, considering his critics sufficiently answered. After he had apparently skirted the controversy about radicals, a rapid succession of reversals jolted him. In an instant, the House subcommittee's friendliness had given way to accusations. Jed Johnson of Oklahoma reacted first. Unhappy with what he had seen and heard as a visitor, he placed President Johnson on notice with a warning about severe and dire consequences that would follow from abetting radicals and communists at a tax-supported facility. A legislative investigation would transpire if Howard did not implement immediate corrective measures to rid itself of revolutionary leftists. Not long after Johnson's ultimatum, Mitchell announced similar plans for cleansing the university. Citing negative reactions to the Conference on the Economic Condition of the Negro while showing his own lack of comprehension of the official's preference for "academic freedom to federal government support," Mitchell supported a House probe and *Congressional Record* publication of Miller's open letter.[13]

Reactions to the threats came from many directions and reflected diverse viewpoints. Mitchell's brother John and GOP National Committeeman Perry W. Howard were among those favoring congressional investigation. Seldom one to question a sibling about politics, John Mitchell was proud that his older brother was planning to "tame" Johnson's "high handedness." Perry Howard was convinced of "Communistic" plots to win over students. Relieved that a politician was interested in doing something about the problem, Howard set aside his habitual partisanship long enough to praise Mitchell for "waging a righteous fight." Other onlookers were viewing matters differently. "Under the Microscope," a weekly editorial feature from the staff of the *Philadelphia Tribune*, attributed the whole controversy to Miller's "jealousy," reasoning the "old man hates to see Howard [University] make progress without him." Regarding Mitchell's participation, several opinions were not necessarily kinder. "His statements," noted one columnist, "prove clearly that his major

13. KM to MWJ, May 24, 1935; Jed Johnson to MWJ, May 24, 1935, MP; *Defender*, June 1, 1935.

concern is to carry [sic] favor with white Southerners. He wants to prove
to them that though a colored person is a Congressman from Illinois, he
still has the ability to carry his hat in his and lick the hands of his masters
like a cur dog." No less abrasively, another critic agreed that Mitchell's
token subservience had been compounding the situation. However, this
critic did not find a Southern hand on Mitchell's shoulder but a demand
on him to court Chicago bankers and gangsters, "his predatory bosses" for
whom he had been missing few chances to repay for his election victory.
Congress's strongest voice against the Howard University investigations
belonged to Marion A. Zioncheck, a Democrat from Washington state
interested in defending Johnson. Considering evidence against the president as "hearsay," Zioncheck promised Mitchell a fight if he persisted
about publishing Miller's letter in the *Journal*. There was also advice from
Zioncheck. If Mitchell needed a worthy cause, Zioncheck submitted that
it should be fascism. As he put it, "the way to avoid fascism is to allow
freedom of speech," not digressing "off on a tangent" as Mitchell had
done with Howard University.[14]

Meanwhile, there were indications that Mitchell was having second
thoughts about a vigorous challenge to academic freedom. In what looked
like a plea for a friend's affirmation that alleged communists at a Negro
university must be pursued, he unburdened everything on T. V. Smith
of the University of Chicago. Clearly perplexed by the matter at hand,
Mitchell was hoping Smith—a philosophy professor who once had offered
him a noncredit course at Columbia University—might agree that Johnson was a "misfit." However, the professor did not embrace such brash
conclusions; rather, he favored discretion and abandonment of reckless
applications of patriotism. According to Smith, "More scoundrels find
shelter under its fine folds than under any other guise. This is my only
fear about your stirring the communistic pot against Howard." After
defending free speech, the educator pleaded with Mitchell to "pray twice
before using in your own intelligent and learned way that instrument
of the passionate and unruly against our beloved Howard University."
Mitchell waited days before answering Smith. There were no hints of
agreement. Spurning the advice to cancel his attack, he noted plans to proceed with a congressional address critical of Johnson. Such oratory would
be crucial because Johnson had "gone entirely too far in . . . the right of the
University to academic freedom." After summarizing Johnson's alleged
aid to communism, Mitchell, convinced that legal intervention had been

14. John to M, June 2, 1935; Howard to M, May 28, 1935, MP; *Philadelphia Tribune*,
June 6, 1935; *Louisville Leader*, June 22, 1935; *Afro-American*, June 1 and 22, 1935; *New
York Age*, June 8, 1935; *Washington Times*, June 4, 1935.

justified, tried again to persuade Smith. Under oath of office to uphold the Constitution, Mitchell considered himself bound "to protect Howard University from what might be the most damnable influence that could be marshalled against any institution designed for character and citizenship building." In his opinion, the university's salvation would surely depend upon drastic measures. Yet, as poised as Mitchell appeared to be on June 17, 1935, to deliver knockout blows to a man judged treasonous to country and Howard University alike, all actions were suspended until Congress's fall term. By October, when Mitchell resolved again to push a full congressional investigation of Johnson, interest in Howard University had waned. This meant the question of whether or not its president had allowed Howard to become a seedbed of Marxism in 1935 would be unanswered. As for Mitchell's role in the meaningless Red scare, all must have faded completely from memory because he was on campus five years later, addressing graduates of Howard's class of 1941. Never once in his commencement talk did Mitchell attempt to link communism to Howard's past or to President Johnson seated nearby on a flag-and-flower-bunted dais.[15]

Worries over Reds allegedly infiltrating Howard represented only one example of Mitchell's ongoing concern over their targeting blacks for recruitment. Although he imagined them in several places, his obsession became their influence and operation of the National Negro Congress. Mitchell had an unshakable belief that after its establishment by Howard faculty in 1935, the NNC had either been the brainchild or the handmaiden of Communist party agents bent on capturing African American loyalties. He spent much of his congressional career seeking to influence House colleagues to notice and not be duped by "this child of the depression." Conceived and launched just months after Mitchell's legislative debut and the notorious Howard conference, the NNC was an apolitical umbrella federation that had been formed to coalesce diverse African American thoughts and opinion into a combined drive for improvements. On St. Valentine's Day, 1936, Chicago's Eighth Regiment Armory opened to the first annual NNC meeting; 817 delegates arrived after braving subzero temperatures to travel to the Bronzeville fortress. Mitchell was among the missing; beforehand, he had announced he would boycott all the proceedings. Consequently, his absence was conspicuous and duly noted by Congress organizers. However, nobody could fault them for having not tried to entice his attendance. First by formal invitation and later by personal

15. M to Smith, June 8 and 17, 1935; Smith to M, June 9, 1935; Executive Committee Resolutions, Chicago Chapter, Howard Alumni Association, October 28, 1935, MP; *Afro-American*, July 27, 1935; CR, 77th Cong., 1st sess., appendix, 3009–11.

visits, they had worked at coaxing his presence, but he "did not have time to talk about this." Several factors had been behind his reluctance to be involved. No doubt because of NNC origins and founders, it never gathered support from Howard's conservatives. A so-called radical clique at the university—the very group that only months earlier had dragged Kelly Miller into conflict with Mordecai Johnson over campus academic freedom and activism by Reds—had chartered the NNC. Meanwhile in Chicago, police menaced delegates and threatened to close the Armory.[16]

Because he had boycotted the NNC convention, Mitchell had no first-hand experience with the organization or its sessions. Had he attended, he would have found nothing harmful emerging from the proceedings. Delegates representing many divergent groups sought common ground in Chicago. Stressing unity, President Asa Philip Randolph called upon African Americans to solve their own problems. Although few in the Armory doubted the wisdom of this premise, Mitchell's conclusions about forging racial progress seldom reflected Randolph's opinion. Mitchell stressed interracial partnerships as the source of betterment. As late as 1939, Mitchell imagined a coalition of well-meaning whites and black gradualists in the South cooperating to achieve common goals. At least, this was his recurring message: "Our problems will be solved by our ability to encourage the white man to believe in us and to work with us. We should foster a better estimation of ourselves in the opinions of the white man, who in turn will show greater respect, admiration, and the friendliest of spirit. We negroes ourselves should go forward on our own initiative and do the job of solving our own problems." For Mitchell and the NNC, the question of white involvement was a minor point of divergence. The NNC's openness fostered a broad-based coalition that conferred memberships on all African Americans; this openness made Mitchell's dissidence easier. In the beginning when radicals represented a minority in the NNC, their insignificant presence gave Mitchell an excuse to criticize its general organization. With the likes of James W. Ford of the Communist party on its rolls and in its councils, the NNC had not only outfitted Mitchell with absolute proof and reason to complain about its revolutionary infiltrations and influences but also had excused

16. *Afro-American*, January 25, 1936; Bernard Eisenberg, "Kelly Miller: The Negro Leader as a Marginal Man," 187. For a balanced account of the NNC, see Lawrence S. Wittner's "The National Negro Congress: A Reassessment," 883–901. Pro-HUAC accounts are less useful; see for instance Wilson Record's *The Negro and the Communist Party* and *Race and Radicalism: The NAACP and the Communist Party in Conflict*, Harold Cruse's *The Crisis of the Negro Intellectual*, 171–80, or Lewis Coser and Irving Howe's *The American Communist Party: A Critical History, 1919–1957*, 356. Balanced but difficult to follow is Harvard Sitkoff's *A New Deal for Blacks—The Emergence of Civil Rights as a National Issue: The Depression Decade*, 258–60.

his nonparticipation. Laxity of another sort would exacerbate the NNC's problem of radicals. The organization's guidelines and purposes were so general that control of local chapters became impossible. Since the NNC lacked rules, activists seized power to foment as much trouble as possible. With a combination of leftist demands and use of pickets, boycotts, rent strikes, and other collective actions, the radicals succeeded in humbling municipalities, landlords, shopkeepers, and businesses. While activism was winning concessions, it further aroused Mitchell's suspicions and indignation with the NNC. To demonstrate his disapproval and garner white favor, Mitchell enjoyed distancing himself as much as possible from demonstrators by doing things such as breaking through their picket lines to enter boycotted stores.[17]

After an initial period of trying to federate African American energies into an amalgam with common general purposes, the NNC began in 1940 to reflect John Llewellyn Lewis's United Mine Workers. Now more than ever to outsiders like Mitchell, it appeared to generate closer Communist party affiliations. In point of fact, it had relinquished so much control to John Davis and other radicals that Randolph no longer felt there was any confidence left in his presidency. Hence, he implied his only option would be resignation. Discovering no rush on anyone's part to alter his negative impressions, Randolph delivered a farewell address to delegates. Feeling that Randolph's resignation had vindicated his long-standing hostilities toward NNC actions, Mitchell was overwhelmed with so much joy that he read the departed president's resignation speech into the *Congressional Record*. Mitchell also added his praise for the crestfallen Randolph's unwillingness to continue in a radical-infested body. Mitchell took the occasion to laud every black who had not yielded to the temptations laid out by wild leaders who wanted defiance of civil law and alliances to hostile objectives. There was one carefully couched admonition in Mitchell's commentary: "If there should ever come a day when the Negro yields to these [radical] influences it will be because of the activities of such white organizations . . . as the Ku Klux Klan. . . . white America should take due notice and immediately modify its attitude in Government and in economic opportunity toward the Negro; give him the same chance and . . . consideration that is given all other racial groups. If this is done there need never be any fear of the Negro going astray."[18]

17. *Wilmington Morning Star*, April 22, 1939; *Charlotte Observer*, April 24, 1939; *Defender*, October 29, 1938, and January 7, 1939; Tittinger and Dickerson interviews.

18. *CR*, 76th Cong., 3d sess., 5336–37, appendix, 2944–45; *Cleveland Gazette*, June 1, 1940. For details of Randolph and Reds in the NNC, see Jervis Anderson's *A. Philip Randolph: A Biographical Portrait*, 229–40 or Paula F. Pfeffer's *A. Philip Randolph, Pioneer of the Civil Rights Movement*, 32–43.

Mitchell's distrust of the NNC illustrated something important about his life. He did not affiliate with organizations whose main purpose was uniting blacks. For a brief period after Randolph's NNC resignation, Mitchell held respect for the union organizer. But nothing lasting could be forged between these two very different men. Among other things, Mitchell and Randolph did not agree about collective actions or unions. Except for a few involvements in labor litigation while practicing law in Chicago, Mitchell did not participate in organizational drives aimed at black workers. Several times, for example, in responses to pleas from Red Caps and sleeping-car porters for assistance in struggles for collective bargaining, he demonstrated no interest in helping the two black-dominated unions. In 1935 when the Wagner Labor Bill came under consideration, he adamantly ignored pressure for an amendment to declare all hiring discrimination illegal. As a result of negative reactions toward unions and workers, Mitchell became a target of organized labor's criticisms.[19]

According to contemporaries, few blacks acquainted with Mitchell trusted or liked him. His obvious selfishness usually accounted for poor relationships. He was only in office two months when a complete stranger from Texas attacked him for being "a black-faced mouthpiece for the white race" and a "numbskull." Several weeks later on his first return to Bronzeville as a congressman, Mitchell was greeted with a similar indication of hostile feelings. This time, it was unfriendly fight fans at the Savoy Ballroom, who catcalled him. Instead of permitting him to enjoy an evening of boxing, they "roundly booed" after a ring announcer asked everyone to stand and acknowledge Mitchell. With more decorous reservations, even less hostile people inveighed against him for hostile actions. From observations during Mitchell's long tenure as president, brother Sigmas acknowledged concerns about his priorities. He had raised doubts among fraternity members about whether he intended to "devote special attention to Negroes" and keep the race "FIRST." Mitchell's beliefs contributed to his poor standing. Acting out of his belief in Booker Washington's agrarian romanticism, Mitchell made odd and unpopular commitments to the rural South as the ideal setting for blacks to live. According to Mitchell, blacks who lived next to understanding whites were fortunate. These African Americans received invaluable benefits from whites. Mitchell, in interpreting the ongoing migration of blacks to cities for Kelly Miller, expressed his belief that there was almost no possibility the urban immigrants could ever outstrip other more fortunate individuals who

19. Douglass E. Johnson to M, January 25, 1935; Howard D. Gould to M, May 28, 1935; M to Gould, May 31, 1935, MP; MacNeal to WW, May 27, 1935, NAACP; "Labor Leaders Attack Mitchell for Miner Statement," December 1941; "Mitchell Slaps Back At Labor Critics," "Mitchell's Labor Policy Ill-Advised," December 1942, BP.

had remained on Southern plantations and farms; in Mitchell's mind, "the south with its temperate seasons and agricultural possibilities, offers the Negro his greatest opportunity." On migration—and on so many other black issues—there was unanimity between Mitchell and Miller. In Miller's opinion, "A Negro family rooted and grounded in the agricultural life of Alabama has a much more promising prospect than if [it were] transferred to the sidewalks of New York. One shudders to predict the future of a Negro child brought up in a seven story flat of a Harlem tenement house."[20]

Referring to the Southern countryside as the preferred choice of African Americans illustrated how well Mitchell knew and understood the region's psyche. Frequently, he mentioned "a growing tendency [among whites] . . . to be more considerate of the Negro's rights in that section of the country." For example, in 1937 after an automobile tour of Southeastern states, Mitchell returned to Capitol Hill speaking enthusiastically about a "growing liberality" in Dixie. Openly excited about its implications for blacks, he incorporated some auspiciously positive conclusions into his replies to Southern black petitioners after help with problems. For this genre of appeals, he used a stock answer: "I do not hold myself out as being the representative of all the Negroes in the United States, and shall not permit anyone to persuade me that this is right or sensible. It would be a sad day, indeed, if we must depend upon one man to represent us in a body of four hundred and thirty-five. I am therefore urging Negroes all over the United States to use the Congressmen from their particular districts in every possible way. This is one of the best ways to make friends and strengthen our case in the House of Representatives."[21]

Mitchell extracted other conclusions from his favorable assessments of the South as well. Early on, he determined from personal experiences and twisted logic that blacks possessed natural affinities for the rural South. It seemed that additional travel and observations only reaffirmed his old beliefs and supplied him with new ideas such as an unworkable resettlement scheme. According to Mitchell, even FDR "appeared interested" in a proposal to involve the federal government in resettling "homesick" black migrants on vacant Southern farmland. As Mitchell imagined the plan in operation, several thousandfold unskilled African Americans

20. CR, 76th Cong., 3d sess., appendix, 3011; Louisville Leader, June 1, 1935; Pittsburgh Courier, March 9, 1935; Argus, January 17, 1936; Thomas L. Dabney to M, January 22, 1935; KM to M, January 25, 1939; M to KM, February 7, 1939; in letters to M, November 7, 10, 12, 17, and 21, 1937, R. D. Bowen of the Farmers Union confirmed Southern sentiment for Mitchell's "farm-is-best" philosophy, MP.
21. New York Times, November 22, 1937; H. H. Dudley to M, March 26, 1935; M to Dudley, March 28, 1935; M to L. L. Dolphin, June 3, 1936, MP.

who had fled the rural South for metropolitan areas only to encounter joblessness and hostility would gladly participate in a resettlement plan if there were opportunities anew to live on farms because it would restore their personal pride and make them productive again. By Mitchell's calculations, resettling would not drain taxpayers. Self-supporting because of its conversions of "idle, unhappy city-dwellers into happy, productive farm dwellers," it would generate another benefit; resettlement would showcase every "change which has come about in the Southern attitude towards Negroes," and thereby "speed progress" on other fronts. The politician phrased his doubtful opinion as follows: "The South is much more tolerant toward the Negro than it used to be. By and large the Southerner of today is in favor of giving the Negro a 'break,' and would be glad to see him better himself." Of course, Mitchell's reverse migration plan was an unworkable, naive concept. An attempt predicated on relieving ghetto residents' suffering at the expense of depressed farmers would only exacerbate already low commodity prices and halt progress toward allegedly better race relations.[22]

Mitchell also believed, based on his view of the South, that several places would reinstate black voting privileges after the race's act of petitioning. According to his reading of the situation, sustained drives to restore suffrage would not confront resistance in Virginia, North Carolina, Texas, Tennessee, Oklahoma, and many urban areas. These places were ready to reenfranchise African Americans en masse, whereas the reestablishment of voting would come selectively elsewhere. African American lethargy, Mitchell blamed, explained why so few blacks had been bothering with registering, voting, and participating actively in politics: "Racial tolerance has increased tremendously in the south in the last 10 years. A new generation of white persons has grown up. . . . But the Negro still is not availing himself of his rights. He is not voting. If the Negro got into politics and had a voice in the election of the sheriff and other county officers, we'd need no lynching law. He could protect himself against lynching." It must be added that Mitchell's counsel had not come within earshot of Southern whites; he gave it privately in a black newspaper owner's office. Except for a streak of last-hour boldness during his last term, all his suggestions about blacks voting in the South occurred before Northern audiences or in correspondence to sufferers of Dixie oppression and injustice.[23]

---

22. M to Ad Wimbs, July 2, 1935; MNR, April 12, 1939, MP. Although the FSA did resettle some blacks, its purpose was not to return all who longed for the South back to Southern countrysides, as Mitchell was advising.

23. *Oklahoma City Daily Oklahoman,* October 9, 1937; *Lafayette Sun* (Ala.), n.d., MP; *Gastonia Daily Gazette,* September 17, 1937; *Ashville Citizen,* September 16, 1937;

Mitchell's Southern initiatives drew mixed reactions. References to Dixie tolerance certainly did not impress Claude Holman. Directed to drive his boss's "big car down South" in September 1937, Mitchell's secretary begged to "be excused from making this trip." Claiming "a deep rooted fear," Holman was "very nervous just thinking about it. . . . I welcome the assignment of any other duty." Although Mitchell scoffed at Holman's fear, he had been overtaken by fear himself some twenty months earlier. Having learned that racists had circulated flyers with distorted information about his views on interracial marriage, Mitchell had noted concerns about personal safety to the mayor of Columbus, Georgia. Before venturing into the Peach State, he wanted reassurances. No wonder every statement from Mitchell about a new day in Dixie was so astounding to a writer calling himself "Chicago Citizen" that he asked, "Mr. Mitchell do you think by any means we the colored people of Chicago sent you to congress to propose or contemplate on such a plan [as resettlement], do you think . . . the people of your district elected you to a $10,000 a year job to socialize or represent them [white Southerners?] . . . [If yes,] get your family and your Resettlement plan and run along to the south." Southern whites also gave Mitchell's observations mixed reviews. "Liberals"—here, advocates of Booker Washington's path to racial progress—appreciated his positive utterances about blacks and the South. One brave Alabama editor even dared to suggest that Southern state legislatures all needed "one or two Negroes of the Mitchell type . . . to speak for their race." In what amounted to a rare public acknowledgment of Dixie's shortcomings in race relations, there followed frank admissions that "the Negro race in America is given so little opportunity for self-expression" and that blacks "have rights [that] should be recognized." In sharp contrast, "conservatives" had different perspectives on Mitchell. They had no quarrels with his general assumptions about Dixie superiority, but there were objections to his constant referrals to inevitable change. Claims of a regional transformation with black beneficiaries angered diehard segregationists because there were no desires on their parts to improve anything for the minority. To express resentments, racists often addressed hate-filled letters to the lawmaker or otherwise threatened him. According to advice from one unhappy bigot who was resenting references to progress, Mitchell should "see what happens [to] niggers [who] want to mix with white people." Ultrareactionaries such as Mississippi Senator Theodore Bilbo

Augusta Chronicle, September 20, 1937. Answers to the following Southern black correspondents in 1935, M to: Portsmouth Political and Civic Club, January 11; William L. Purifoy and McCloud Rayford, April 30; Calvin Drummond, July 27; William Kelso, July 9, 1936; W. L. Horne, May 23; Leroy Perkins, December 18; Luther P. Jackson, March 16, 1937, MP.

were even more extreme. Bilbo and other back-to-Africa proponents provoked Mitchell. Suppositions from them that African Americans would accept persuasion and would leave were "exceedingly foolish and absolutely impossible." With "all of its faults, this country has given me an unusual opportunity; greater, I think, than any other country would have given me." The South's racial minority also had mixed reactions to Mitchell. Support came from Norfolk publisher-editor P. B. Young because of the overtones of Booker Washington in Mitchell's ideas. According to Young, a highly respected conservative, Mitchell fostered "better racial relationships and political understanding [with] such recognition as you have received at their [white] hands." To others, Mitchell's images of "happy" blacks frolicking in Southland bliss under the watchful guidance of benevolent whites did not sit well. Critics imagined no advantages accruing from an insensitive official who did nothing but tell "the Negro his faults," and there were queries about what kind of leader preferred attacking African American victims to assaulting their oppressors. Meanwhile, what was perceived as Mitchell's "pussyfooting" prompted others to question if he possessed any wisdom or courage.[24]

Circumspection characterized Mitchell's handling of New Deal shortcomings. Under advisement to be still, he refrained from ever questioning Roosevelt, and he resisted criticizing FDR's policies and programs. For example, when Norman Thomas and members of the Southern Tenant Farmers' Union protested the Agricultural Adjustment Act's awful effects upon sharecroppers in Arkansas and Missouri, Mitchell ignored the largely black movement. He did not decry National Recovery Administration failures nor claim, as many sharp-witted critics did, that NRA stood for "Negro Removal Act," "Negroes Ruined Again," or "Negro Rarely Allowed." Moreover, he did not follow his friend Robert R. Moton's lead in investigating Southern employers to ascertain if they might be guilty of using dual codes to discriminate against black workers.[25] Although Moton and Mitchell had generally agreed, their public views on

24. Holman to M, September 15, 1937; M to L. C. Wilson, January 30, 1936; see M to W. A. Fountain Jr., March 21, 1935, for Mitchell's explanation of "a vicious and wicked slap at" him by the *Atlanta World;* "Chicago Citizen" to M, April 24, 1939; "A Word to the Wise" to M, n.d.; Frank Burnett to "You Dirty Nigger," n.d.; no name to M, April 12, 1937; D. L. Goins to M, April 11, 1938; M to Goins, April 20, 1938; M to H. T. Allen, May 4, 1939; M to KM, February 7, 1939; unidentified clip, "Chickens Come Home," MP; *Afro-American,* May 2, 1936; *Anniston Star,* November 18, 1934; *St. Paul Recorder,* October 7, 1938; Bunche, "A Tentative Analysis," 74–75.

25. For July-December 1933, Moton's letters reveal commitment to finding wrongs within the NRA, MotP; *CR,* 76th Cong., 2d sess., 1543; W. Ellis Stewart et al. to M, April 15–20, 1935; M to Stewart et al., late April 1935; M to Henry A. Wallace, April 25, 1935; Wallace to M, May 6, 1935; E. L. Powell to M, February 27, 1935, M to Powell,

blacks and the operations of the Civilian Conservation Corps and Works Progress Administration differed. With silence, Mitchell excused himself from responsibilities in these areas. If there were reasons, he often cited nonjurisdiction as his basic objection to tackling agencies' overt racism and discriminatory practices. Every occurrence outside his First District almost automatically was beyond his legitimate sphere of influence and therefore was another representative's duty. When it came to avoiding awkward and difficult responsibilities, Mitchell could dumbfound his critics with absurd excuses for not intervening in controversies. A favorite excuse was humbuggery about members of Congress being under sworn commitments to represent all constituents equally and fairly. At times almost sardonic with many hapless petitioners after his help, Mitchell could be so dispassionate that he advised Deep South solicitors to turn first to their own lawmakers for help. No fool, he did not use the same approach with persons capable of publicizing his lame excuses for ignoring racist policies. Much slyer at dodging their issues or controversies, he evaded criticisms by offering to investigate if first someone could present some evidence to warrant a probe.[26]

Mitchell even spurned opportunities to influence changes. In 1936, on a rare visit to his constituency, Bronzeville resident and National Bar Association president George Lawrence entreated Mitchell to serve on an NBA committee on legislation. Obliging in part, Mitchell accepted an honorary role. Doubtless his reluctance to take on a more substantial role related for the most part to committee chairman Thurgood Marshall. Mitchell simply did not want the risks associated with working with a young attorney from the District of Columbia with an established record of activist interests in civil rights. Although Mitchell was good at protecting his vital personal interests, nothing in his record indicates cowardice. It was not wise, for example, to insult or corner him because his strongest tendencies were for self-defense. After allegedly distorting his stand on racial segregation with a claim that "he was crusading not for the elimination of Jim Crowism but merely for the 'equal accommodations' stipulated in most of the State laws," Time-Life editors learned a lesson about him. Mitchell angrily countered, "I am unqualifiedly opposed to all forms of racial segregation." Stacked against his pro-South leanings, Mitchell's statement might seem at odds with other conclusions. Yet there was no conflict, because his tenure in office split in two periods. Especially

March 1, 1935; Moton to McIntyre, July 29, 1935, M to McIntyre, August 2, 1935, FDR to M, August 21, 1935; Bowen to James Roosevelt, November 25, 1935, MP.

26. Murphy to M, March 6 and 9, 1935; M to Murphy, March 7, 1935; Kelso to M, June 28, 1935; Thornton to M, September 19, 1935; E. S. Handy to M, November 2, 1937; M to Handy, November 5, 1937, MP.

in his first term and certainly less in his last three, Mitchell's Chicago bosses were checking his conduct. To some extent, therefore, he could be excused for not always being bold and courageous. Rather than attempt to follow an independent course from his first day in Congress as many African Americans had wanted, he proceeded cautiously, abstaining from actions that might wrench the party. At the outset, he showed nimble-wittedness toward civil rights and the South. For this he should not be chastised too severely. As a recipient of Democratic favors, Mitchell had two options: sacrifice a House career, or move slowly. The officeholder's peculiar advice in communications came from his dilemma of being in an awkward situation between blacks and the Chicago Machine. More than any other factor, it resulted because he could seldom afford to reveal what he was really thinking. Although Mitchell doubtlessly believed in the suitability of the rural South for illiterate African Americans, he did not always support the way they were treated in the region. Reluctant to give opinions publicly about Southern injustice, he revealed them in correspondence to a select group of trusted friends. To Kelly Miller, there were empathetic expressions for the blacks who had fled Southern oppression. Mitchell might not have foreseen positive gains from their departure, but at least he had some understanding of their motivations:

> Many of these people have left the south with great reluctance, but there were conditions in the south over which they had no control, which made their abode in that section not only uncomfortable, but unsafe. Many of them, under the leadership of educators and ministers, sought to follow the instructions of Dr. Booker T. Washington ("Let down your buckets where you are") . . . , but to them the risk of life became so hazardous and so great they, like the oppressed of other Nations of the world, sought safety and comfort, and the best possible opportunity to live and support themselves and their families, by leaving their homes and going to other sections where they thought these things could be had.

Elaborating, Mitchell blamed the exodus on lynching, jury exclusions, denials of justice, and unequal educational opportunities.[27]

Ever cautious and careful with his inner thoughts, Mitchell entrusted most opinions only to confidants, but occasionally he divulged his true feelings to strangers. Important as his letters to friends are as sources of insights into the real person, none revealed as much as the correspondence

27. TM to M, January 6, 14, and 25, 1936; M to Murphy, May 27, 1937; M to I. Van Meier, May 24 and 27, 1937; Van Meier to M, May 25, 1937; M to Willie Miller, January 23, 1935; M to KM, February 7, 1939, MP; Lawrence interview; *Durham Morning Herald*, November 12, 1941.

he wrote while enraged. His passionate reply in 1935 to a local church federation officer illustrates the point. In a form letter sent to every member of Congress, a California church official insulted black women with blanket insinuations about their alleged widespread sexual promiscuity. Reading the minister's affront to the general moral character of black women so angered Mitchell that he answered the aspersion with wrathful indignity. The racist insults prompted him to retort if there ever had been some consideration given "white Christian gentlemen" as the harbingers of immorality. "You have only to look at the color of the Negro in this Country to see that the white man, in preaching his sermon on racial purity, is perhaps the biggest hypocrite God has ever permitted to live."[28]

Mitchell's most conspicuous service as a representative of blacks came through his speaking engagements. Hundreds of invitations to give public addresses reached him. Few blacks rivaled Mitchell's appeal as a public spokesman. Joe Louis and Jesse Owens were better-known black personalities, but nobody could refute Mitchell's celebrity status. During eight years on Capitol Hill, he attracted thousands of printlines in black newspapers. When black college students were asked to identify the period's most prominent African Americans for a survey taken in the late 1930s, a staggering 69.3 percent of those surveyed recognized the lawmaker; in comparison, 59.7 percent could place Walter White of the NAACP. On odd years in his congressional tenure, Mitchell went on extended Southern tours. The first, two months after his arrival in the House, included participating in Founders' Day activities on the campus of Morris Brown College in Atlanta, praising FDR and the New Deal in Nashville, lecturing educators in Birmingham, and addressing farmers in Murfreesboro and Jackson, Tennessee. As a freshman lawmaker, Mitchell penetrated Dixie four times. No stop was more provocative than his visit to Wilson, North Carolina, on February 17, 1935. As government professor C. H. Hamlin's invited guest, Mitchell became Atlantic Christian College's first black assembly speaker.[29]

In Mitchell's drive to showcase the South and prove its critics wrong, he scheduled events to initiate integration. They did not always proceed

28. Mitchell interview; M. F. Harbaugh to M, May 17, 1935; M to Harbaugh, May 21, 1935, MP; *East Tennessee News* (Knoxville), May 11, 1939.

29. Bunche, "A Tentative Analysis of Negro Leadership," 190–92; samples from 1935: Hamlin to M, January 20 and February 12 and 18; M to Hamlin, January 22; programs, Founders' Day, Morris Brown College, March 12, and Nashville New Deal Progressive League, March 31; Fountain to M, January 18 and March 14; M to Annie Howard, March 23; Oscar W. Adams to M, March 9; M to J. W. Jones, March 21; M to Hale, March 14; Alcorn to M, March 3; M to J. F. Lane, February 12, MP; *Raleigh News and Observer*, February 18; *Nashville Banner*, March 7; *Murfreesboro Daily News-Journal*, March 12; *Journal and Guide* and *Washington Tribune*, March 23.

according to plans, however. Occasionally instead of Southern hospitality, Mitchell was met with unreceptive, hostile greetings. In Birmingham, this was Howard College's reaction. Due to "unforeseen circumstances," President Harwell G. Davis hastily withdrew a student club's invitation to Mitchell. Although mitigating Southern racists was Davis's real motive for canceling the appearance, Davis, when pressed for explanations, cited Mitchell's "partisan" record, and said that there had been all too many examples of Mitchell stirring up "political strife" for Howard College to welcome him. A closer look at Davis's decision reveals that it probably related more to reaction to a black man addressing whites at an Alabama Baptist college than to polemics. Racially inflammatory handbills circulating around the college proclaimed Mitchell's visit an "affront" to "Southern ideals and traditions" and a move "to destroy white supremacy." Just the idea of the invitation touched off spirited debate among Alabama journalists. One liberal editor, observing that every previous appearance by Mitchell in Alabama had indicated that "he would have said nothing to affront or offend anyone," called the cancelation "an unfortunate episode" and Davis's decision "sadly misguided." Seeing matters from another perspective, a Tuscaloosa reporter did not fault Davis; rather, he said, there was no comprehending the motivations for inviting Mitchell. To the Tuscaloosan, an appearance by Mitchell would have represented deceptiveness and hypocrisy at their worst because Southern Baptists in charge of Howard College had not intended to accept anything but Southern majority attitudes. Why, probed the journalist, would Howard, a college with entrenched discriminatory covenants and conservative traditions, suddenly open itself to a black speaker?[30]

Overall, certain trends emerged from Mitchell's speaking appearances. For one thing, there were few First District speeches; most exceptions occurred during elections when he addressed Bronzeville churches and civic bodies. Secondly, Mitchell felt rather uncomfortable speaking before nonpartisan Northern audiences. Weeks after taking office, there was one nightmarish episode in New York that affected his future engagements. While at the Bethel Young Peoples' Lyceum, a rude audience hissed and booed Mitchell's comments about the Roosevelt administration's friendly intentions toward blacks. The uncivil behavior left him so unnerved that just the prospect for disrespect at a forthcoming engagement caused Mitchell to cancel. Threatened and repeated discourtesies indicated wide disapproval of Mitchell's race-flagellating criticisms and apologies. Within no time, he had acquired so many enemies that he was

30. *Montgomery Advertiser, Birmingham News,* April 24, 1936, *Montgomery Alabama Journal,* May 6, 1936.

on a constant lookout so that he could shun any potentially dissentious audiences. Since his remarks had been drawing jeers, catcalls, and boos before general audiences in the North, he did not book many more appearances outside the South without Democratic sponsorships. Thus, he avoided hostile blacks as often as possible. However, disagreeable black newspapermen were not skirted this easily. Encounters with them were often confrontational because of Mitchell's refusal to accept or respect the inquisitive nature of reporting. Furthermore, journalists with prying questions about his policies and attitudes caused him insecurity and discomfort, and he also resented their critical articles that claimed he neglected African Americans. At times, Mitchell was so disrespectful of differing viewpoints that his inclination to retaliate led to humiliation. Of the many heated bouts with a hostile black press corps, none proved more ridiculous than the one that occurred during his second month in Congress, when he and Annie Mitchell were on their way to a White House reception and he spotted an *Afro* news team on the sidewalk fronting the Mitchell apartment. Irritated by this perceived invasion of his privacy and frustrated by the *Afro*'s apparent hostility, Mitchell felled the pair of newsmen, smashing a photographer's camera in the process. Later when asked to explain why the assault had occurred, Mitchell noted his displeasure at having men camped at his doorstep for pictures and a story of an event that deserved no publicity. "What if I was going to the reception?" he asked inquisitors trailing him for his version. Obviously not at all regretful for what had happened, Mitchell implied it should serve as a reminder to anybody bent on disturbing him. "I'm no coward. I'll fight if I'm mistreated. They may call me a 'hat-in-hand-Negro' but I'm afraid of no man, white or black. I'll not move one inch from minding my own affairs to disturb anyone but if any one of these detractors dares to face me, I'll demonstrate what I mean."[31]

After battles with unfriendly black journalists, Mitchell always found numerous allies. His supporters often expressed grave concerns about hostile reporting, but in Mitchell's judgment, their fussing was not necessary. Feigning general imperviousness to published critiques, Mitchell boasted of not being "bothered in the least by calamity howlers and the

31. *Defender*, January 23, 1937; M to George Haynes, January 17, 1935; program, Bethel Young Peoples' Lyceum, January 27, 1935; Samuel Westerfield to *Afro-American*, February 1, 1935; N. B. Ellis to M, February 25 and April 4, 1935; M to Ellis, April 2, 18, and 19, 1935; L. F. Coles to M, November 29, 1937; M to Murphy, July 25, 1935; Murphy to M, February 8, 1935, MP. Eardlie John to M, April 24, 1936, MP, is a typical rebuttal; editorials in the anti-Mitchell press (*Defender*, *Afro-American*, etc.) indicate why so many people had been alerted to Mitchell's record before his appearances. *Philadelphia Tribune*, April 18, 1935; *Defender*, February 9 and March 2, 1935; ANPNR, February 8, 1935, BP; *East Tennessee News*, February 14, 1935; *Journal and Guide*, February 9, 1935.

adverse criticism which they are making. . . . I expect to go on the even tenor of my way . . . without fear or favor of any man or any group of men. This applies to newspapers as well as to men." As he noted another time, there was no reason to give "any worry or uneasiness about adverse criticism appearing in the Negro press. . . . As long as there is real progress, why give a moment thinking about criticism?" Instead of expressing concern, Mitchell preferred striking back at enemies. As he put it, "I think there has been entirely too much camouflage and ballyhoo in the speeches of those who have purported to lead us from darkness into light, and instead of leading us into the light that they have talked about many times, have proceeded to lead us farther into the dark. This I do not propose to do."[32]

Mitchell was reluctant in the beginning to name his nemeses, but after six months as a congressman, he was readily exposing his detractors. Leaders of what he and several black reactionaries were dubbing "the national Association for the Advancement of certain people" headed his list. He described them as "self-centered individuals looking for an opportunity to serve themselves and conducting what I regard as a shameful racket at the expense of Race and in the name of a fair deal for the Race." Although Mitchell was supposedly "paying absolutely no attention to the foolish critics who have never done anything themselves and who will always object to those who wish to do something substantial for the Race and for the Country," his attacks on his critics indicate how much they had annoyed him. Otherwise, he certainly would have done a much better job of concealing his personal dislike of "such men as William Pickens and others of his ilk who have been foremost in criticising everything I have endeavored to do." Unknown to Mitchell, Pickens was an NAACP orator without influence. *Afro-American* publisher Carl Murphy, A. N. Fields of the *Defender,* NAACP rightists Walter White and Roy Wilkins, and Washingtonians William Hastie and Edgar G. Brown ranked among Mitchell's severest critics in open forums while P. B. Young of the *Norfolk Journal and Guide* and J. E. Mitchell of the *St. Louis Argus* were his most avid supporters.[33]

Although some of Mitchell's ill feeling toward civil rights activists seemed to have had deep-seated roots, there was a honeymoon period

32. To M from: C. Francis Stradford, February 5, 1935, John W. Bussey, March 1, 1935, Philip A. Parham, March 20, 1935, George T. Kersey, August 3, 1935, Cleveland L. Longmire to M, June 10, 1936; M to Sydney Thompson, January 24, 1935, Monroe L. Plant, January 29, 1935, Stradford, February 7, 1935, PBY, March 2, 1935, Thomas W. Brown, March 21, 1935, Turner, July 24, 1935, Coles, November 30 (1937); Locke to *Defender,* October 27, 1938, MP.

33. M to Wimbs, July 2, 1935, and Watkins, July 29, 1935, MP; impressions drawn from author's extensive black press survey.

after his 1934 win. Nervously, a truce, with restraint shown by both the NAACP and the politician, existed for months. Neither side harmed the other nor exhibited anything but cordial respect. Before its final collapse, surface harmony between the two irreconcilable forces survived for almost four months. Missing documentation precludes against offering any definitive assessments about who to blame for breaks in peaceful relations, but evidence at hand suggests responsibility for the rupture rested with NAACP officials. Enough goodwill had existed as late as February 22, 1935, for the Cleveland chapter to honor Mitchell at its annual dinner dance. Soon thereafter, however, Mitchell learned of an unflattering *Crisis* editorial that attacked him for lacking interest in the District of Columbia committee, affronts to black journalists, and general disregard of the race: "THE CRISIS is loathe to believe anything that comes out of the Jackson, Miss., Daily News, but Mr. Mitchell is starting out as though he means to justify that paper's assertion that the new congressman is a 'white folks' Negro and will do anything they tell him to do.' THE CRISIS is concerned about the reputation of the race even if Mr. Mitchell is not, and so we set down the fervent hope that if he cannot be discreet, he at least will remain silent." After reading this, Mitchell unleashed his anger at the NAACP. A man disinclined to forgive and forget, he considered the editorial a call to arms. As a believer in chivalry and the Southern code of honor, he could not let such harsh disparagement pass without countering with an appropriate response in kind. Therefore in response to J. E. Mitchell's well-meaning suggestion that he venture to St. Louis in June for the NAACP annual convention, Mitchell gave proof of his angry brooding. As he put it to a friend in Missouri, "nasty, cheap editorials" and the NAACP leadership's total lack of appreciation for thankless, dedicated congressional work surely explained why there would be "no invitation from the N.A.A.C.P."[34]

Except for private expressions of dissatisfaction, Mitchell did not immediately answer his critics from the NAACP. While he withheld public comment, adversaries were assailing his proposal for an industrial commission to handle Negro affairs. Introduced in late January 1935 and touted by Mitchell as the single most important idea ever introduced in Congress to improve the general status of African Americans, the proposal duly went to the House Clerk and became H.R. 5733. Mitchell soon began a campaign on its behalf. According to his first press release, the legislation would do for blacks what the Bureau of Indian Affairs had done for Native Americans. Through appointment of a five-member council with

34. Alexander Martin Jr. to M, February 19, 1935; JEM to M and M to JEM, April 6 and 8, 1935, MP; *Crisis*, February 1935; see Moore, *A Search for Equality*, 82–83, 98–110, for evidence of other blacks' dissatisfaction with civil rights leaders.

alternating five-year terms, control of African American welfare would pass to the executive branch. Blacks would have majority rights because at least three of the five memberships on the governing board would be reserved for African Americans. Short on specific details, the proposal placed in Section 4 its only definitions of council power, and these were broad. It provided flexible mechanisms and authority to study general interracial labor problems, stimulate and encourage tolerance, and develop harmonious resolutions of black-white social adjustment. According to H.R. 5733, commissioners could not take up issues without first obtaining clearances from governors, state attorneys general, or federal officials. Once so engaged, the special task force for minority welfare could proceed with investigating problems, formulating new policies, recommending regulations, and advising on legislation. For the latter, however, action would depend upon receipt of presidential authorization. For all practical purposes, the board would not have power to initiate or lobby. Still, the goals were ambitious even if Mitchell's plan only called for a first-year operating budget of two hundred thousand dollars.[35]

Assigned to the Judiciary Committee, H.R. 5733 became Mitchell's first obsession after arriving on Capitol Hill. Over a four-month period, it seemed that whenever he was not speaking on its behalf, he was trying to gather support for it by other means. Among others, governors appeared on a solicitation list. Responding to Mitchell's many efforts, both whites and blacks agreed to back a Negro Commission. AME bishops, educators from Tuskegee, Wilberforce, Lane, and Howard, conservative newspapermen, businessmen, attorneys, longtime associates, and scores of ordinary citizens were listed as solid endorsers and unqualified supporters. Elks of the World praised the concept of H.R. 5733, boosting the plan editorially in their publication, *The Eagle*. Politicians led by black New Dealer Mary Bethune and several members of Congress assisted. New York Representative Emanuel Celler and Illinois Senator James Hamilton Lewis introduced companion bills. An industrial commission bill for blacks was not a new cause for Celler, though. Previously without success, he had offered bills similar to H.R. 5733. Of course, there were negative responses too. Overall, foes did not receive very kind treatment from ·Mitchell. The NAACP was one exception, though. Since in the beginning only a scattering of local NAACP chapters criticized H.R. 5733, Mitchell chose to ignore the organization. As he said and did nothing in retaliation, unanswered criticisms of his lawmaking and of H.R. 5733 accumulated. The first indications to him of how the bill's opponents might respond came just weeks after its introduction. For opponents of the bill, the idea

35. *CR*, 74th Cong., 1st sess., 1991; copy of H.R. 5733, MP.

of concentrating so much accountability for African American welfare in a five-man commission was a frightening prospect. As one critic phrased his concerns, "My fear would be a tendency to shift all the responsibility for decent treatment to the Negro to this commission and blame the commission for everything that went wrong." The worry expressed here was increasingly shared; in some cases, early enthusiasts echoed skeptics after studying the proposal more thoroughly. However, grassroots reactions against the plan's adoption never matched the greater volume of favorable mail. Immediately after H.R. 5733's introduction, there was not enough black opposition to worry its sponsor. Excepting perhaps Tuskegee's Monroe Work and Governor Horner, opponents appeared outmanned, fragmented, and unknown. Overall, opponents of the bill looked so powerless and anonymous that Mitchell could easily ignore them without dire consequences. As he had been after his 1934 election victory, Mitchell was under tight press vigilance. But he had already labeled his most adamant vilifiers as partisan Republicans undeserving of his attention. With his huge appetite for confronting sniping journalists, there appeared at this point to be more irritation than concern for general critiques. For example, his reactions to the *Defender* were mild. Even if the newspaper's criticisms brought almost no response in the beginning, its staff refused to give him ground. Relentlessly as well as passionately, the Chicago weekly bombarded its readership with articles critical of H.R. 5733. Whether based upon genuine concern about the bill or vindictiveness toward its sponsor, *Defender* stories reflected a prevailing attitude among Mitchellphobes in journalism; blacks, enemies warned, must "approach the discussion of this bill with studious apprehension occasioned by the very delicate sensibility of the sponsor of the bill."[36]

Slow to mount a campaign against Mitchell's proposal, the NAACP eventually became the fulcrum of opposition. The unmistakable actions taken by the Illinois branch on May 5, 1935, at Evanston, Illinois, reflected

36. PBY, February 9, 1935, SJ, Harris, EJS, February 11, 1935, Westbrooks, Wilson, February 12, 1935, Wright, Lane, Stradford, February 13, 1935; W. J. Walls, February 14, 1935, Work, February 19, 1935, Woodson, February 21, 1935, Fountain, February 26, 1935, Maude E. Brown, March 7, 1935, Locke, March 11, 1935; PBY, Spaulding to M, June 3, 1935; M to governors, March 15–20, 1935, M to PBY, February 11, 1935, M to Work, March 1, 1935, M to Brown, March 11, 1935; Maudelle B. Bousfield to M, February 14, 1935; Horner to M, March 18, 1935; David Jenkins to M, February 26, 1935; Dingle to M, March 5, 1935, MP; *Atlantic City Eagle,* March n.d. and *Richmond Times-Dispatch,* July 13, 1935; *Argus,* February 22 and May 17, 1935; *Journal and Guide,* March 2, 1935; *Chicago Tribune,* April 29, 1935; *Afro-American,* May 11, 1935; *Defender,* February 23, March 9, May 4 and 18, June 8, and August 3, 1935; "What *Leader* Readers Think," *Louisville Leader,* March 23, 1935; *Philadelphia Tribune,* July 25, 1935; *Detroit Guardian,* March 9, 1935.

a general groundswell against H.R. 5733 in NAACP circles. Assembled in annual state convention, delegates petitioned Illinois members of Congress. Their resolution noted how "American citizens . . . of Negro ancestry are more interested in legislation designed to make truly effective the Constitution . . . than they are in any such paternal interest." By the time of the Illinois statement, Walter White and others on the NAACP executive board had already lost respect for Mitchell. Yet, the top leadership had not laid plans to engage him publicly. Even at this point, from all appearances, NAACP leaders were hoping to find some peaceful way to work out differences with Mitchell. Besides, squabbling with Mitchell over his bill might weaken their chances of shaping and influencing him in the future. Simply put, there still were neither plans nor a consensus to mobilize nationally against H.R. 5733. Everyone at the New York headquarters of the NAACP stuck to White's position. Like the anxious Illinois petitioners, he did not want the race to become " 'wards' of the government," but unlike them, he did not worry about its prospects; Capitol Hill contacts had all but assured him of the bill's slim chances.[37]

Relative tranquility prevailed between the NAACP and Mitchell until a staffer shattered the peace in mid-July. Apparently without prior consultation, William Pickens submitted a letter for publication in the *Afro-American*. It mirrored mounting dismay and disgust with Mitchell. According to Pickens, Mitchell's proposal for a Negro commission reflected no "gray matter" and was "the dumbest thing ever offered as a threat to our race" because it could potentially "reduce us to the status of the American Indian." Although the NAACP staff officer was careful not to link his personal opinions of H.R. 5733 to the NAACP, his attempted disassociation did not matter in the end. Just the fact that Pickens was questioning the intelligence of Mitchell and his supporters was enough to erode whatever opportunities still existed to bridge the gaps between the two headstrong forces. Fueling the fire, Charles H. Houston of the NAACP legal staff compounded Pickens's deed by going to a congressional committee looking into H.R. 5733 with rather damaging testimony on June 21, 1935. To any onlooker familiar with the NAACP, these two efforts suggested a piecemeal attack by the organization's leadership. Mitchell's friends were at least certain of this. Consequently, they struck back venomously at Pickens and Houston in particular and the whole leader corps in general. J. E. Mitchell was a strong advocate of H.R. 5733. The inferences to his and Mitchell's brain impairments so personally infuriated the St. Louis newspaperman that an editorial counterattack

37. Resolution, Illinois State Conference of NAACP, May 5, 1935; a sampling of White's indifference is in his letter to Louis Lautier, March 12, 1935, NAACP.

followed immediately. In articles, J. E. Mitchell characterized Pickens as a "complete failure" whose only interest was "cash." Furthermore, he made allegations about the NAACP member wanting to settle a personal vendetta with Congressman Mitchell. According to reports in the *Argus*, the vendetta stemmed from the congressman's not helping Pickens to win a Haitian ministerial post. On its editorial pages, the *Argus* charged that Pickens had reached the gloomy conclusion that "easy money" from inclusion on the Negro Industrial Commission would again elude him: "Poor Pickens. His situation really amuses us. His associates in the N.A.A.C.P. are so much wiser than he. They probably are sitting back giving him the horse laugh while he makes a jackass of himself." During the *Argus*-Pickens spat, something less personal and more important in the NAACP's relationship to the bill unfolded. Attacks on Congressman Mitchell became increasingly more open. Houston's memorandum on H.R. 5733 to the House Judiciary Committee in late June was a portent of a new public policy. In his short rebuttal to the bill, Houston did not mention the NAACP. Even so, anyone attending the hearing who was the least bit familiar with Houston's legal practice would have equated his opinions of law with the New York–based civil rightists. In the midst of several NAACP local branches demanding a united campaign against H.R. 5733 and anti-Mitchell editors pounding relentlessly at it, policy shifted at NAACP headquarters. The organization's leaders developed a stronger inclination to publicly oppose Mitchell's bill. However, no official policy percolated down to rank-and-file NAACP members. As a consequence, they were left to draw personal conclusions from Houston's and Pickens's individual drives against the bill. Indeed, two more things must be underscored about their remarks: their speaking out apparently did not have NAACP clearance, and there would be no official attempt to galvanize opinion against the Negro Industrial Commission. In order to leave no doubts about it, Houston reaffirmed the point at the annual National Bar Association Convention. Satisfied that he had disassociated his personal stance from his official position in the NAACP, Houston asserted that fellow lawyers must approve a strong resolution against adopting a bill that would thwart the race's best interests: "It seems to me that such a commission will merely offer another resort for the buck-passing propensities of administrations which seek to duck issues on problems concerning the Race." On August 3, 1935, black delegates took Houston's challenge, voting unanimously against H.R. 5733.[38]

38. *Afro-American*, June 29 and July 20, 1935; *Argus*, July 5 and 26, and August 2, 1935; JEM to M, July 25 and August 25, 1935; JEM to Prattis, August 20, 1935; latter to JEM, August 21, 1935; M to JEM, July 31 and August 28, 1935, MP; House Judiciary

Meanwhile in Bronzeville, Chicago NAACP branch president A. C. MacNeal was busy with local forces, working to form an effective national body against the bill. Coming as no great shock to Mitchell, MacNeal's efforts were thought the involvements of a longtime nemesis and his many lunatic followers. From his onetime membership in the Chicago chapter, Mitchell recalled "foolish bickerings . . . [and] petty jealousies existing inside our own Race." Claiming now to be unaffected, Mitchell pledged not to allow himself "to be pulled aside from this task [of pushing H.R. 5733] by your organization nor by any similar group."[39] MacNeal was equally headstrong in his determination to stop H.R. 5733. Under his relentless prodding, Chicago branch members kept their views before the national leadership. Refusing to relent, they expected more clamoring from New York. After pushing the Illinois convention to commit itself decisively against the plan, MacNeal vented his frustrations at Roy Wilkins for being too timid and passive. To educate the legislators in Washington about NAACP opposition to Mitchell, MacNeal was after guidelines and permission to begin a correspondence drive. Although NAACP headquarters in New York seemed unaffected by the Chicago branch's demands, a series of unnoticed and unpublicized actions commenced to bring the NAACP position quietly forward to key government officials. White, for instance, was in contact with James Lewis, confirming that the "Association does not favor the passage of this bill." Although Senator Lewis had heard rumors about negative reactions toward the bill, White's acknowledgment startled him. Befuddled by its meaning, the Illinois Democrat solicited Mitchell's comments. Thereupon, the battle lines changed; Lewis's revelations enraged Mitchell. Within days, Mitchell accused the NAACP of selfishness and deceit, while maintaining its leadership consisted of "self-centered individuals looking for an opportunity to serve themselves and conducting . . . a shameful racket at the expense of the Race." More than all others, White was at the heart of these angry reactions because he had raised "his puny voice against this bill."[40]

This was the first installment of Mitchell's enduring public contempt for the NAACP. The sores worsened in late August after a disclosure of

Committee, *Hearing on H.R. 5733*, June 18, 1935, 39–40; 1–38, 41, for supportive testimony; Gay to Houston, July 25, 1935; Gay to RW, August 19, 1935; Murphy to Pickens, July 30, 1935; Thomas A. Curtis to Pickens, August 23, 1935; NAACP Press Service to Editors, September 3, 1935, NAACP; *Defender,* August 3 and 10, 1935; *Amsterdam News,* August 10, 1935.

39. *Defender,* August 3, 1935; MacNeal to M, June 24, 1935; M to MacNeal, June 27, 1935, MP.

40. MacNeal to RW, August 5 and 29, 1935; MacNeal to "Walter and Roy," August 7, 1935; WW to James H. Lewis, July 26, 1935; M to WW, August 6, 1935, NAACP; M to Watkins, July 29, 1935; M to S. L. Greene, August 6, 1935, MP.

White's correspondence with Roosevelt about H.R. 5733. The debating over the bill placed the Roosevelt administration in an awkward position. Without an apparent place to turn, it found itself caught between a reliable House Democrat and civil rights forces. Under these circumstances, nobody at the White House knew how to respond. Meanwhile, there was no dilemma for Mitchell. To a *Norfolk Ledger-Dispatch* reporter on August 31, 1935, he claimed "nearly everything the association does is vicious." Coming from the highest-ranking black official, these were sensational words. As a consequence, newspapers around the nation printed the hot story, quoting Mitchell either to defend or criticize the NAACP. Black reporters and editors overwhelmingly rebuked Mitchell's statement, but there were editorial plaudits from Dixie. To the delight of many Southern white journalists, Mitchell had caused a dilemma at the NAACP; after his hard challenge, there was a feeling that its assertions about legitimacy and support among African Americans had been shaken.[41]

As a result of Mitchell's continuing outbursts, all chances for H.R. 5733's passage vanished altogether. At one point, he even labeled NAACP leaders "a bunch of Communists." In every respect, Mitchell's loss of temper did more to augment and publicize opposition by Houston, Wilkins, White, and Pickens than they had ever contemplated themselves. Their correspondence and actions had indicated resignation, passivity, and mild disapproval. If they had caused Mitchell problems, common sense would have dictated arrangements to produce a negotiated settlement. Instead, Mitchell gave in to his emotions, foolishly launching a vicious dead-end counteroffensive that left both sides so alienated and hardened that neither could refer to the other without using invectives. Since ugliness did not moderate, final chances for rapprochement disappeared. Without a resolve to conclude a peaceful settlement, Mitchell was doomed to ineffectiveness under the NAACP's constant watch and scrutiny. Wilkins worried so much that his secretary had orders to "blue-pencil . . . articles . . . concerning Congressman Mitchell" in the black "only" press.[42]

Overall, mixed signals resulted from Mitchell's actions between 1935 and 1936. It is hard to imagine that he had given much forethought to how peculiar and inconsistent his responses must have looked to observers. Examples of his different reactions abounded. Often when he directed statements at blacks, there were no encounters with discrimination to

41. WW to FDR, August 16, 1935; McIntyre to E. M. Forster, September 6, 1935, RP; PBY to WW, October 3, 1935, MP; *Afro-American*, July 27, 1935; *Crisis*, October 1935; *Defender*, September 28 and December 7, 1935; *Pittsburgh Courier*, October 26, 1935; *Chicago South Side News*, October 17, 1935.
42. M to Hatton W. Summers, July 15, 1935; M to W. V. Gregory et al., July 31, 1935, MP; *New York Age*, October 19, 1935; RW to Miss Jackson, November 3, 1935, NAACP.

report. Moreover, seemingly everyone in official Washington extended him fair treatment. Privately, however, he was complaining. During 1935, the Washington affiliate of the American Automobile Association became a subject of his grumbling. He sought congressional assistance to overcome prejudicial policy-writing practices in the District of Columbia. One year later, Mitchell chastised San Diego officials because they had tolerated employment discrimination at the city's exposition. Yet after Italy's brazenly brutal attack against hapless Ethiopia, there were no forthright indications of his true feelings about Italian aggression. Given the reality that much of Chicago's "Little Italy" was in the First District, he did not dare to offend its inhabitants. His January 11, 1935, letters to the nation's governors were another example of Mitchell's penchant for duplicity. Only hours after insisting his responsibilities did not extend beyond Chicago's near South Side, he was volunteering to "render you [state executives] any service in the fight against crime in your state." Needless to say, there were no explanations from Mitchell about how the offer could fit into his self-imposed parameters of congressional representation. In a way, it did not matter because he determined to use his first term as a hiatus to pacify the jittery nerves of apprehensive whites in his party. Then again, if Mitchell's "Tom-like" behavior disappeared after he had established himself as being unlikely to "run around over the country agitating and stirring up a lot of trouble," African Americans could always forgive "their" Congressman for earlier negative actions and excesses.[43]

43. Hubert Utterback to E. A. Nash; George Burnham to M, January 19 and 24, 1935; M to Burnham, January 22 and 25, 1935; M to J. W. Brown, January 25 and February 12, 1935; Brown to M, February 8, 1935; M to Ella R. Hutson, January 25, 1935; M to Damon W. Lyons, February 13, 1935; M to Arthur G. Falls, July 22, 1935; Falls to M, February 6, 1936; M to Eugene Talmadge et al., January 11, 1935; Talmadge et al. to M, January 14–16, 1935, MP; *Philadelphia Tribune*, June 13, 1935; *Afro-American*, July 13, 1935; *Defender*, October 19, 1935; *Amsterdam News*, February 15, 1936; *Journal and Guide*, February 22, 1936; *Washington Tribune*, February 25, 1936.

Temperate Black
Representation

F or African Americans, Arthur Mitchell's second term was decisive because it showed which directions he would follow later in his legislative career. During Mitchell's first year in Congress, debates and controversies over whether blacks would benefit from the Negro Industrial Commission outlined in H.R. 5733 should have clarified what actions and activities might be expected from him in his subsequent years in office. The dialogues and discussions over H.R. 5733's merits and deficiencies illustrated the difficulties involved in trying to be the special representative at large for black Americans. However, in the closing months of Mitchell's tenure, he began to contradict oversimplified measures of him. Although Mitchell had in many ways seemed in conflict with NAACP-given descriptions of what fitted an ideal black lawmaker, he would begin moving closer to the NAACP's ideal after 1936. Mitchell had never intended to enter Congress with a civil rights agenda that conformed to NAACP standards, but eventually he would promote civil rights with temperate zeal. Insofar as helping his reputation, a turnabout would do little. Unfortunately, his dependence on the Kelly-Nash Machine prevented a spectacular break from his early congressional record. Therein was the rub between Mitchell and many civil rights activists. There could not be clear enough signals of change for all to see after his first term of carefully plotted and performed Uncle Tomming.[1]

As a good Democrat and Machine loyalist, Mitchell worked to establish a consistent record of placing party and politics above race. He knew from the beginning where his first loyalties must be placed. To maintain requisite peace and harmony between Congress and Pennsylvania Avenue—essentials to the progress and survival of Democratic programs—political

---

1. WW to J. C. Austin and to MacNeal, April 3, 1937; confidential memorandum, WW to Edward Costigan, April 2, 1936, NAACP.

bosses from both Chicago and the capital warned Mitchell that they would not tolerate intraparty turmoil or troublesome actions and demands on behalf of African Americans. The first signs of this came as early as September 1934. One warning sufficed because it was unambiguously clear. To ensure that the basic lessons for Windy City political survival were comprehended by Machine lackeys, Nash and Kelly periodically reviewed their essential rules. From these reminders, Mitchell learned that there would be no toleration of attempts on his part to repeat Oscar De-Priest's troublesome meddling into Southern affairs or New Deal policies. For the sake of Democratic tranquility and job security, bosses commanded Mitchell's adroitness at toeing a tight line and following instructions.[2]

Consequently, the progressive escalation of NAACP antagonism toward H.R. 5733 aided Mitchell. As his relationships with civil rightists soured irreversibly, his popularity with House colleagues from Dixie rose significantly. Ironically, the first real indication of how he might gratify whites who were defensive about Southern rights occurred in conjunction with antilynching. For the better part of thirty years, antilynching measures had been a favorite cause of the civil rights establishment. From appeals in 1911 for sane and just treatment of people awaiting trials, the drive advanced so much by 1933 that the NAACP had enlisted Congressman Edward Costigan and Senator Robert Wagner as cosponsors of antilynching legislation. Thus by the time Mitchell entered Congress, the NAACP already had secured adept leadership in its fight to stop and punish vigilantes.[3] With roles so firmly established, supporters of anti-lynching legislation presumed rival proposals would only weaken their efforts to enact a meaningful bill into law. Newcomers with alternative antilynching proposals would only bring confusion to a settled issue. Nevertheless, on January 22, 1935, Mitchell hopped into the fray. Not remarkably, few civil rightists found anything in Mitchell's participation to celebrate. Troubled reactions followed primarily because of a common opinion about his introduction of a conflicting proposal: it would dilute the cause and thereby inflict significant damage to whatever chances there might be to enact a meaningful measure. Immediately, therefore, many Costigan-Wagner advocates complained about his unsolicited intrusion. The superfluousness of it, they said, might lead to needless destruction of existing unity and cohesion that had been gathering behind an NAACP-sponsored bill. Repeatedly, they pondered the same question: If Mitchell's interests in the issue were genuine and his objectives constructive, why

2. Tittinger and Mitchell interviews.
3. Robert L. Zangrando, *The NAACP Crusade against Lynching, 1909–1950*, 3–121; Stephan Early to Malvina Schneider, August 5, 1935; Eleanor Roosevelt to Early, August 8, 1935, RP.

did he not simply join an already allied force against the heinous act of lynching? Then there would be neither confusion nor divisive effects deriving from his commitment. Now with rival bills before legislators, several officers of the civil rights establishment suspected that there might be good reason for opponents of antilynching measures and their accomplices to begin rejoicing; there was obvious friction between the highest-ranking black officeholder and the NAACP. After all, seeing such disagreement over how to proceed against murderous mobs and permissive law enforcement officers, opponents could also claim confusion and uncertainty as their rationale for inactivity.[4]

At first, the NAACP attributed Mitchell's introduction of an alternative bill to inexperience, but later his independent actions became a source of conflict. For Mitchell's part, he cited three reasons for offering a new bill, H.R. 4457. First of all, the NAACP draft did not set "forth in clear and unmistakable terms just what acts constitute the crime of lynching under its provisions." According to his next assertion, H.R. 4457 incorporated a superior feature. By its terms, injuring or killing a prisoner under state custody would constitute a federal crime; the NAACP bill in the congressional hopper excluded this consideration. Finally, Mitchell discussed constitutionality. Supported by alleged assurances obtained from "some of the greatest constitutional lawyers in the country," he promised H.R. 4457, unlike the Costigan-Wagner bill, could not be watered down or overruled in the nation's courts. Countering, the NAACP did not allow Mitchell's claims to pass without challenge. Curiosity about the identities of Mitchell's "greatest" attorneys led to inquiries that brought a confidential answer on February 3, 1935. According to Louis Lautier, one of Walter White's confidants in Washington, the attorney behind H.R. 4457 was Benjamin L. Gaskins, "the ablest colored lawyer at the bar of the District of Columbia." For consideration, a copy of H.R. 4457 and unsolicited advice accompanied Lautier's disclosure. In order to grasp opposing viewpoints on antilynching, NAACP adviser Charles Houston should

4. Loren Miller, article, n.d., BP; *Washington Tribune,* January 26, 1935; *Afro-American,* April 27, 1935; *Defender,* January 27, 1940; *Oklahoma City Black Dispatch,* May 25, 1935; Early to Schneider, August 5, 1935, RP; RW to JEM, April 16, 1935; WW to MacNeal, May 13, 1935; MacNeal to M and Illinois congressional bloc, February 25, 1935; Katherine Gardner to WW, February 14, 1935; WW to M, January 30, 1935; Dingell to WW, January 22, 1935; Thomas F. Ford to WW, January 11, 1935; Frank W. Fries to MacNeal, April 7, 1937; RW to MacNeal, March 11, 1937; TM to Robert S. Hartgrove, April 7, 1937, NAACP; *CR,* 74th Cong., 1st sess., 784; Clarence T. Nelson to M, January 26 and February 4, 1935; M to Nelson, January 28, 1935; EJS to M, January 30, 1935; M to Sabath, March 5, 1935; Resolution, Colored Citizens of New Orleans to Robinson, January 30, 1935; M to WAW, April 24, 1935; Ludlow to M, July 21, 1937, MP; White, *A Man Called White,* 167, 172.

consult Gaskins. At least, this was Lautier's suggestion to White. If there ever had been Gaskins-Houston exchanges on legalities, the influence was minimal because Houston remained fully committed to an original draft.[5]

Like other NAACP leaders, Houston insisted the organization's bill would offer better protection. To demonstrate its advantages, the NAACP commissioned Houston to compare S. 24, the Costigan-Wagner bill, with H.R. 4457. Applying professional detachment to provide fair and equal coverage to corresponding provisions, legal counsel to the association stacked the two legislative proposals' respective sections beside each other in opposite columns. There was a good reason for the exercise; the attorney wanted to pinpoint differences in order to show how the proposals would handle both lynchers and law enforcement allies. Through the employment of self-explanatory comparisons, Houston obviously thought persuasive arguments supporting one bill over the other would prove unnecessary; looking at two proposals in this way was effective. Any objective analyst interested in picking the superior bill could easily discern differences. At swaying opinion from the weaker bill, the NAACP counselor succeeded. Compared to Mitchell's feeble legislative attempt at dealing effectively with lynch mobs, S. 24 was more effective due to its stiffer penalties and better descriptions of offenses. It started with a clear, concise definition of what, in fact, constituted a mob action, whereas H.R. 4457 offered no clarifications. Furthermore, Mitchell missed entirely the point of vigilantes depriving victims of their entitlement to equal protection and due process. In all respects regarding constitutional guarantees of individuals' inalienable rights, there were substantial differences in the proposals. In Mitchell's bill, if government officials were also perpetuators of or participants in mob actions or conspired to permit usurpations of justice, their actions constituted felonies. The Costigan-Wagner section covering such tacit approvals and involvements categorized the same offenses as criminal actions. These were not just crimes against individuals; they represented wanton violations of victims' constitutional rights to trials. Although both bills allowed litigation, there were important legal differences. Unlike H.R. 4457, which permitted victims or their heirs to begin civil suits in federal courts, S. 24 stipulated empowerment of U.S. district attorneys to initiate legal procedures against the governmental jurisdictions. Potential jail sentences were also stiffer under the NAACP bill. Instead of H.R. 4457's maximum sentence of ten years, the stiffest

5. RW to Jayne, February 23, 1935; Lautier to WW, February 2, 1935, NAACP; House of Representatives, 74th Cong., 1st sess., H.R. 4457; MNR, January 25, 1935, MP; ANPNR, January 28, 1935, BP.

penalty for officials convicted either of assisting, abetting, or participating in a lynch mob was imprisonment for twenty-five years.[6]

During the first session of the Seventy-Fourth Congress, not much occurred on the issue except for some periodic swipes at antilynching by grandstanding Southern congressmen. House and Senate chairmen deadlocked both bills in committees, refusing to hear or schedule testimony. Frustrated with the logjam, NAACP sponsors tried to force their bill to the Senate floor, but a disciplined Southern filibuster killed their effort. Meanwhile, public sparring by Mitchell and the civil rights establishment over rival bills was limited to a few short exchanges. Neither side demonstrated much inclination to aggravate the other over antilynching. Championing or defeating a Negro Industrial Commission bill seemed more urgent in 1935. But already by the midway point of the session, interest had waned for consolidation of a superior group representing blacks. Dialogue now concerned which bill—H.R. 4457 or S. 24—would be a more effective deterrent to lynching. As often was the case with matters involving Mitchell and his detractors, contests in 1936 and afterward between him and top NAACP officials disintegrated into unpleasant exchanges that were punctuated by false accusations and character defamation. Clearly over antilynching bills, the fault for escalating ugliness rested with Mitchell. Attorney Arthur B. Spingarn had directed Walter White to leave the congressman alone. Through large donations and control of NAACP legal proceedings, the white lawyer wielded much power in the organization's decisions. In early 1936, Spingarn instructed White to inform staffers that he would be "very much opposed to any campaign against Congressman Mitchell." It became the final directive on the subject. About this commanding authority, Professor Joyce Ross is correct; Spingarn's orders were obeyed, and the NAACP executive council seldom overruled advice and leads from brothers Arthur and Joel Spingarn. Their generous contributions had strings that allowed them to dictate policies and procedures.[7]

If anybody in the NAACP deserved rebukes from Mitchell in early 1936, it was A. C. MacNeal of the Chicago chapter. MacNeal unsuccessfully tried to provoke a national onslaught on H.R. 5733. Subsequently when these efforts were underway, he attempted to enliven the congressional antilynching debate. Acting on personal initiative, MacNeal polled several

6. Houston, Comparative Analysis of S. 24 and H.R. 4457, NAACP.

7. *Washington Daily News*, April 26, 1935; *Chicago Tribune*, April 17, 1935; Fred Greenbaum, "The Anti-Lynching Bill of 1935: The Irony of Equal Justice—Under Law," 78–83; Memorandum, WW to Pickens, January 4, 1936; Pickens to Arthur B. Spingarn, January 6, 1936; WW to Crews and Elisha Scott, February 8, 1936, NAACP; B. Joyce Ross, *J. E. Spingarn and the Rise of the NAACP*, 163, 197, 218.

House members to ascertain their positions on the Mitchell and Costigan-Wagner bills. Afterward, there was a vendetta. To all who had supported H.R. 4711 went individual reprimands. In exceedingly poor taste for a branch head of a respected organization, MacNeal's unkind replies to lawmakers eventually forced an unwanted dilemma on Walter White. Curious members of Congress wanted clarification for MacNeal's unauthorized acts on behalf of the NAACP. Left on his own to defend or attack the foolish insults of a "loose cannon," White ultimately chose to ignore MacNeal's remarks. Since White was striving hard to pacify everyone as much as possible, a statement of any kind would only provoke someone. On several occasions, White offered Mitchell olive branches. During a two-month frame between March and May, White, in his efforts to settle misunderstandings and foster cooperation, patiently made no fewer than six overtures to Mitchell. In the final analysis, these determined efforts at prevailing upon Mitchell to join the NAACP's antilynching campaign netted nothing but frustration. For his attempts at enlisting the headstrong Mitchell in a joint struggle, neither the reasoned prodding embodied in a series of lengthy letters nor personal sessions in Mitchell's Washington office persuaded the stubborn politician. From every indication, there were no intentions on Mitchell's part to associate with the NAACP. Instead, he concentrated on excuses for not siding with White. Skirting White's efforts required clever maneuvering, for Mitchell did not want to appear as an abettor of lynch mobs. Aware as well of his reelection bid later in the year against DePriest, he did not want to risk being remembered for opposing something as emotional as antilynching legislation. Thus, the trick was to disguise his obstructionism in order to keep DePriest from capitalizing too much from his conflicts with prominent blacks over mob justice and murder. Mitchell's conniving was in marked contrast to White's sincere attempts to explain to him that his congressional colleagues' kind words had probably been nothing more than worthless flattery and that his help was crucial to the success of an NAACP-sponsored discharge petition aimed at bringing an antilynching bill to the House floor.[8]

After putting his devious mind to work, Mitchell found a reasonable excuse with which to resist the NAACP. Heeding suggestions that his superior bill should be abandoned in favor of the inadequate offerings of others would constitute an unconscionable dereliction of duty to black

8. MacNeal to Leonard W. Schuetz et al., January 29, 1936; Schuetz et al. to MacNeal, January 20, 1936; Mollison to Illinois branch offices, January 23, 1936; Raymond S. McKeough to WW, March 28, 1936; WW to Sabath, April 4, 1936; Dingell to WW, April 13, 1936; WW to M, March 14 and 21, April 13, and May 14, 1936; M to WW, March 16, 1936; Chicago Branch to M, April 24, 1936, NAACP; M to JEM, March 25, 1936; M to Andrew C. Brown, April 18, 1936; M to Harriet S. Butcher and to Harry T. Carter, April 23, 1936, MP.

citizens, he slyly insisted. Coming back with this comeback foiled and outflanked White. Hence, all White's persistence relating to a petition drive under NAACP sponsorship and with aid from Frederick Van Nuys of Indiana ended in disappointment. Ever resourceful as an effective counterstrategist, Mitchell replied that his participation now with the NAACP would surely be interpreted as implied support for a weaker legislative solution. Using a ploy of dissatisfaction for long-awaited revenge, he achieved the sinister objective of wreaking havoc on House petitioners because these legislators had ignored H.R. 4711 in favor of S. 24. Months before White's final appeals to Mitchell, there were blacks who suspected his mind could not be changed. At first, while trying to make sense out of the impasse, the exasperated White did not blame Mitchell's intransigence on a conspiracy. After experiencing a series of failures with Mitchell, however, White reached a somewhat different conclusion. Now, he suspected that Mitchell's nonreceptivity was the result of secrecy-bound outsiders. In early April, Senator Costigan learned that White's suspicions of "Congressman Arthur Mitchell of Illinois . . . [were] apparently being used by certain forces to try to block any action" on Van Nuys's move to discharge. Given the weird set of circumstances before White, charges of conspiracy seemed feasible enough. However, benefits of hindsight and research negate it altogether; there simply is no hard evidence to link Mitchell's obstinacy to a prolynching cabal.[9]

Apparently buoyed by successfully upsetting the NAACP, Mitchell went to the press. His goals were to expose White as a liar and an advocate of inferior legislation and to provoke defensive posturing. In a resourceful move on May 5, 1936, Mitchell passionately appealed to a carefully selected group of Negro newspapermen rather than wait for much-anticipated criticisms for not having signed Van Nuys's petition. Earlier by letter, he had divulged his views on antilynching legislation while lashing out at White. In this correspondence, which was certainly intended for public consumption, Mitchell had described White as a "vicious" and "selfish" man "bordering on insanity." Even worse for the race, according to Mitchell's indictment, White had turned a good organization into "a racket . . . for the purpose of getting what money and notoriety he can for himself." Within days of this totally wild assessment, *World* editor Jacob R. Tipper leaked a copy of Mitchell's vicious letter to A. C. MacNeal. Soon thereafter, White was privy to how MacNeal planned to deal with Mitchell's attempt at character assassination. Besides branding Mitchell "public enemy number one among Negroes," MacNeal

9. MNR, "Congressman Mitchell of Illinois Takes the N.A.A.C.P. Severely to Task," n.d., MP; WW to M, March 21, 1936; confidential memorandum, WW to Costigan, April 2, 1936, NAACP.

proposed treatment in kind. As he put it, "To be delicate in the matter would be fatal. You may as well throw a gang of bricks and you may as well discard powder puffs and use musket gas, tanks, and ten-ton trucks." Although White did eventually criticize Mitchell in Chicago for his role in keeping antilynching legislation bottled up in committee, it was Bill Pickens's assignment to fell Mitchell and his supporters. Not bashful in a partisan role, Pickens chided people in Bronzeville to redeem themselves. They could amend for a "folly" by refilling the seat left "vacant" in Congress by DePriest's departure. Shortly thereafter, Roy Wilkins joined Pickens in Mitchell-bashing.[10]

Meanwhile, Mitchell let up on the NAACP. Without explanations for his differences with the organization's leaders, he reverted to a states-manlike demeanor. With his goals satisfactorily achieved, perhaps he contemplated no benefits accruing from continuing hostilities. After his contribution to delaying antilynching legislation, it seemed as if Mitchell sought magnanimity until another round of NAACP-backed legislation popped up to threaten and disrupt the Democratic coalition partners. In the process of abandoning dialogue, Mitchell left debating to surrogates. With Mitchell as the culprit in the proceedings, it became pointless to belabor his part because his defenders could easily cry partisanship in an election year that featured a most elusive congressman as Franklin Roosevelt's best-known black supporter. In strictest confidence, *Courier* owner and Democrat Robert Vann noted as much for White. After reading the Pittsburgh publisher's compelling advice to tread softly, the NAACP leader recognized that problems could result from besmirching Mitchell. Therefore, White conceded to political reality. If he and other civil rightists desired to gain leverage with the Democratic party, their nonpartisan-ship was needed. In effect, White was forced to suppress Pickens "until you hear from me further." Then in early August, the NAACP leader-ship council settled the irritating dilemma of how to handle Mitchell during an election year. In the best interests of civil rights, the council agreed to lay off him. White had wanted to proceed cautiously against Mitchell, but Wilkins reminded the council that they were "in a pocket so far as Mitchell is concerned"; negative actions could easily be "in-terpreted as fighting Mitchell's place as a Democrat in the Democratic setup."[11]

10. M to Tipper, Vann, et al., May 5, 1936, MP; MacNeal to WW, May 8, 1936; Vann to WW, with an ANP article by Pickens, July 1, 1936, NAACP; *Afro-American, Defender, Louisville Leader,* May 9, 1936.

11. M to MacNeal, May 25, 1936; M to W. F. Reden, June 17, 1936; MP; Vann to WW, July 1, 1936; WW to Vann, July 8, 1936; WW to Pickens, July 18, 1936; WW to RW, August 4, 1936; RW to WW, August 5, 1936, NAACP.

The reluctant hands-off policy benefited Mitchell. As its primary result, no reputable truth squad circulated in Bronzeville to correct and challenge his false campaign releases on antilynching. White and Wilkins surely had not sought to render Mitchell indisputable as mob terror's greatest enemy, but their decisions partially had this effect. Still, in their defense, it could be rightfully argued that not much preceding their secret communications and the subsequent confidential compacts to disengage the NAACP from Mitchell's campaign had produced anything resembling a backlash against Mitchell. Excepting critical remarks by individual NAACP members and political partisans, there was almost no rebuttal to his claims of holding a principal role in antilynching efforts. As usual with Mitchell-phobes, they did not create serious problems for him; he dismissed their claims as the false actions of partisans, unworthy of his time. He could blunt attempts at rallying black masses against his reelection because despite what foes had written or spoken about his noncontributory role, Mitchell could take comfort in knowing public ignorance and a desire for a black national hero compensated to favor his candidacy. Sincerely told as the correct version of events, Mitchell's distortions and half-truths were more believable than his foes' exposés.[12]

Prior to White's and Wilkins's resignation to his superior political position, Mitchell had already seized antilynching as his cause. Using manipulation and skillful twists of truth to emerge as a great champion of the most popular civil rights issue of its time, he demonstrated mastery at transforming his national political status into positive positioning. Now more important than ever with a tough election in progress, his speeches on lynching to Congress and Northern audiences assumed new meaning as vital instruments of his self-aggrandizement. For circulation among African Americans, Democrats reprinted "The Suppression of Mob Violence" and "Lynching the Blackest Crime in America Today." By early August, Democratic efforts were already in place to bill Mitchell as the most effective fighter against justice's enemies. In forging a generally useful image of himself among blacks, white extremists aided Mitchell. Celebrated and media-hyped confrontations with hardcore segregationists added a degree of credibility and luster to his reputation. Foolish antics by Georgia's Governor Eugene Talmadge and Senator "Cotton Ed" Smith created good impressions of Mitchell's efforts. When Talmadge ignored a solicitation to share his opinions of murdering mobs roving freely in his state, Mitchell wisely issued a press release to belabor the governor's silence, and he followed by further pressing the matter in his speeches. Thereafter, Smith's foolish but widely publicized walkout at

12. Mitchell interviews; *CR*, 74th Cong., 2d sess., 8540–53.

the 1936 Democratic National Convention brought new focus on Mitchell as the major source of racists' irritation. Spectacles such as Smith's exit generated large bold-faced headlines in the black press, but how many readers failed to contemplate all the unnecessary confusion Mitchell's noncooperation had created earlier during a NAACP-supported petition drive? As a result of their decision not to hammer at Mitchell's record in 1936, NAACP leaders were in a vulnerable position. They were forced to watch their nemesis triumph easily for a second time over Oscar DePriest. Unfortunately for them, Mitchell's unwanted reelection created the potential for a second round of conflicts over whose solution better deterred crazy mobs from lynching jailed suspects. This time around, however, a six months' respite from each other's criticisms appeared to have had a mellowing effect upon Mitchell and the NAACP leadership, because after the first weeks of the Seventy-Fourth Congress and reintroductions of the antilynching proposals, relations between Mitchell and the NAACP seemed to have turned friendlier. All outward signs suggested that productive, more gentlemanly decorum was somehow going to replace all acrimony left from earlier debates between seemingly irreconcilable foes over just how best to proceed legislatively against ghastly usurpations of citizens' judicial rights.[13]

Relations had improved enough, in fact, that two congressional principals on lynching legislation—Joe Gavagan and Arthur Mitchell—could agree to a verbal commitment. In exchange for assurances of support for Gavagan's legislation, Mitchell expressed willingness to defer on antilynching. At one point as a meaningful gesture of goodwill, he even went so far as promising to sign his name after Gavagan's on an eventual discharge petition. Harmonious unity endured until March 8, 1937, and Chairman Hatton Sumner's announcement that his House Judiciary Committee would begin hearings soon on Mitchell's bill, H.R. 2251. Suddenly fortified with hope of its passage, Mitchell forgot his pledges to Gavagan. Thereafter, he was back to his old tricks. First, he reneged on his promise to sign a discharge petition, and then in a pitch for House support, he encouraged its members to follow his example, forsaking the NAACP-backed bill. While Mitchell was lining up witnesses for committee appearances on behalf of H.R. 2251, Walter White and the NAACP leadership were also busy, warning friends about the consequences of working with Mitchell. Believing the worst, officers expected a cat's-paw role from Mitchell. Accordingly, they were suspicious of Sumner and the members of the House antilynching bloc. Civil rightists feared these same Southerners

13. Reprint, *CR*, 74th Cong., 2d sess., 7557; *Louisville Leader* and *Afro-American*, April 11, 1936; *Defender*, June 6, 1936; Mollison to WW, November 7, 1936, NAACP.

might sucker Mitchell into false conclusions. As events later proved, there were justifications for their suspicions. Enemies of federal antilynching legislation were able to convince Mitchell that their amending and weakening of H.R. 2251 had been done only to ensure its passage. Despite "a complete emasculation" at the insistence of Southern committeemen, the overhauled bill did not lose its blinded sponsor's support. Throughout H.R. 2251's ordeal, Mitchell insisted nothing had happened to its content. His defense was outrageous; it was if he were pleading that a smiling man had teeth, when everyone else knew they were missing. As legal experts rebutted Mitchell's contention that H.R. 2251 had retained its effectiveness at preventing mob seizures, he compounded his own ridiculousness with crude posturing at critics, discountenancing them as fools. Although Sumner had been successful at duping Mitchell, Mitchell's wrong reactions again spoke volumes for how there could be mayhem with every issue involving him and the NAACP in an important Capitol debate. For the moment, both sides were more obsessed with gaining credit and glory than with peaceful settlement. For neutral lawmakers, rivalries between Mitchell and the NAACP inner circle about how to eradicate lynching more than likely diminished their sense of urgency and drained their desire to legislate. With two sides bombarding Capitol Hill with letters belittling the other's efforts, everything seemed trivial. From the outset, NAACP executives had feared negative reactions from harsh campaigns against Mitchell, but they did not yield even if there were private concerns about their bill's constitutionality.[14]

As a final step to legitimizing his credentials as an antilynching spokesman, Mitchell took his campaign to the American public on April 5, 1937. During a statesmanlike radio address carried across the nation by Columbia Broadcasting System affiliates, he spoke humbly and eloquently of the need for federal action. As he told listeners without elaboration, H.R. 2251 was "the best bill," but "authorship . . . means little to me

14. Unsigned memo, "Mitchell's Pledge to Gavagan," April 3, 1937; WW to Austin, April 3, 1937; RW to MacNeal and RW's memo, "Help Pass Anti-Lynching Bill," March 11, 1937; MacNeal to WW, March 17, 1936; WW to MacNeal, March 15 and 23, 1937; Thomas J. O'Brien to MacNeal, April 6, 1937, NAACP; *Afro-American,* January 26, 1937; FDR to M, March 30, 1937; M to FDR, April 1, 1937; M to RW, March 11, 1937; EKJ to M, March 30, 1937; Howard to M, April 16, 1937; hearing transcript, House Judiciary Committee, March 31, 1937, MP; *Portland Northwest Enterprise,* March 26, 1937; WW to Austin, April 3, 1937, WW to JEM, April 9, 1937, NAACP, 28th Annual Report; WW to William F. Illig, February 16, 1937; RW to MacNeal, March 11 and April 6, 1937; WW to MacNeal, March 15 and April 5, 1937; MacNeal to WW, March 17 and April 3 and 8, 1937; O'Brien to MacNeal, April 6, 1937; Mann to Illinois Congressmen, April 7, 1937; WW to Mann, April 10, 1937; JEM to WW, April 5, 1937; WW to George K. Hunton, April 12, 1937; J. A. Gregg to WW, April 9, 1937, NAACP; WW to FDR, April 1, 1937, RP; *Washington Post,* April 6, 1937; *Detroit Tribune,* April 17, 1937.

as compared with the importance of the legislation itself." If Sumner's strategy had been to complicate matters by rushing Mitchell's amended bill to the House for a vote, it backfired. A House roll call on April 7, 1937, resulted in decisive defeat for H.R. 2251, 257 to 123; by better than a two-to-one tally, a majority decided not to discuss the bill. Afterward, Mitchell's breakdown of the tabulation revealed an odd coalition of Republicans, Gavagan supporters, and Southern Democrats joining to vote against the bill. Anguished, the bitter sponsor of H.R. 2251 lashed out, blaming GOP partisans and "misguided Democrats" for what he perceived as a tragic loss. At first, no kinder to one group than another for his bill's defeat, Mitchell went so far as to tell a Pennsylvania Democrat, "You can go to hell!" Later in the process of apologizing for his remark, Mitchell emphasized how Republicans had been the real culprits. Negative voting, he charged, had been their revenge for him turning so many blacks into Democrats before the last election. Confidence among supporters of the Gavagan bill probably caused part of the lopsidedness of the vote against taking up H.R. 2251 on the House floor. NAACP bill supporters seemed certain of another chance to express themselves on antilynching this session; petitioning on behalf of Gavagan's bill had succeeded. If the attainment of enough signatures to release their proposal to a House vote accounted for the Judiciary Committee's move to bring H.R. 2251 forward to Congress, some wonder should be expressed at Southerners' clumsy disposal of Mitchell. With much at stake in uniting to support Mitchell's weaker bill over the stronger NAACP bill, the much-acclaimed Solid South mustered little unanimity. Its failure to coalesce behind an accommodationist's meager offering pushed a valuable ally into the opposition's fold.[15]

Unlike a year earlier, Mitchell kept his word to Gavagan in 1937. In Mitchell's legislative career, this was a pivotal point. Although too proud to acknowledge the effects of his bill's defeat on his decision, it had forced him into the NAACP's embrace. First to Congress April 12 and three days later to the nation, Mitchell spoke favorably of the NAACP-backed bill. To the House, he urged "every Member who believes that this disgraceful crime that has blotted our history so many years should be wiped out vote for this bill." Then while addressing issues of the Gavagan bill such

---

15. Radio address reprint, CR, 75th Cong., 1st sess., April 6, 1937; Kersey to M, April 8, 1937; M to J. Burrwood Daly and to Democratic supporters, April 9, 1937; reprint, CR, 75th Cong., 1st sess., April 7, 1937, MP; Washington Post, Washington Evening Star, Washington Times, April 7, 1937, Christian Science Monitor, April 8, 1937, Chicago Daily Times, April 9, 1937, Journal and Guide, Argus, April 10, 1937, Columbus Advocate, April 17, 1937; CR, 75th Cong., 1st sess., 3385, appendix, 747–48; NAACP, 28th Annual Report, NAACP; Zangrando, The NAACP Crusade against Lynching, 143.

as its constitutionality, he turned logician, asking how in one instance Congress could apply inherent powers to provide migratory birds federal protection and then in the next claim similar authority could not be used to defend prisoners in jails. If there were no legal worries with helping fowl, then there should be no judicial problems with saving human lives. Mitchell's raised voice had less of an impact on the bill's outcome than did a gruesome event at Duck Hill, Mississippi. As Gavagan's bill moved toward consideration, word reached the House floor of an especially brutal double lynching near the Deep South hamlet. Graphic details of the savage murders repulsed even Southern Democrats such as Maury Maverick of Texas; the impact was enough to create a large majority for antilynching forces, 277 to 120.[16]

For Mitchell, something of a personal milestone was buried in the sweeping vote. The bill had represented his break from the ranks of Southern apologists; on antilynching, he had joined the NAACP in a legislative struggle. Ironically, betrayals by Dixie "friends" over antilynching legislation had seemingly lifted a monkey off Mitchell's back. Mitchell began to assume a much more active role on behalf of blacks, but he could not discard altogether his old ways of projecting the image of an "Uncle Tom." By occasionally humiliating himself with subservience, he retained a reputation for being a "safe niggraw." His acts of servility to whites remained, but Mitchell's deeds indicated more dutiful attention to African Americans. But inasmuch as a change had transpired, few of his critics noticed much difference. Remembering Mitchell's first term in Congress, they heard little thereafter to indicate he was moving to meet their expectations of a black representative. Friction continued therefore between Mitchell and the civil rights establishment. However, no discord would again equal the confusion and hostility arising from the competing antilynching bills. For the remainder of Mitchell's congressional tenure, opponents of antilynching bills succeeded at stalling all antilynching legislation before Congress. Almost ritually, Gavagan's bills advanced before the House for debate and resolution, and just as routinely, Mitchell spoke and voted in favor of them. A lone highlight occurred during the 1940 campaign when accusations were made against Republican congressmen for "trying to buy back the Negro vote" with support of bills against lynching. The charge touched off a heated exchange between Mitchell and New Yorker Hamilton Fish about whether or not "the colored vote is for sale." Mitchell questioned Fish about the GOP's true motives for being so suddenly interested in African Americans: "They did not send

16. *CR*, 75th Cong., 1st sess., 3385, 3541–42; Zangrando, *The NAACP Crusade against Lynching*, 143–44.

Negroes to West Point, not even the distinguished gentleman from New York. . . . What has kept him from doing that if he is so friendly toward us? Why all this interest in the Negroes at this particular time?"[17]

In contrast to his antilynching proposals, Mitchell's strong initiatives to reform the Civil Service Commission were supported by the NAACP. Although Mitchell had stated in 1935 that eliminating CSC barriers to facilitate greater and fairer employment of blacks in the federal government would be one of his major legislative goals, he took no action until 1937, the year of his temperate turn toward representing black interests. Previously, he had not done much more than introduce a bill prohibiting required submissions of photographs as a Civil Service prerequisite to further processing and considering a candidacy, and he had won over President Jerry O. Gilliam of the National Alliance of Postal Employees. Nevertheless, correspondence from victims of discrimination accumulated in Mitchell's files. Their letters reflected a common contention: good test scores seldom merited jobs with the federal government. Mitchell actively relaunched a three-pronged assault on unfair hiring on January 26, 1937. In what would become H.R.s 2249, 3691, and 3692, he offered solutions to three perceived faults with CSC operating policies and procedures. His first bill substituted fingerprints for the oftentimes required photographs. H.R. 3691 was more complex. Written in rather ambiguous language, it tried to set up procedures to mandate that all job selections must be on the basis of highest scores achieved on competitive examinations. In cases of ties, Mitchell wanted names alphabetically arranged, with first entries having priority. The third bill provided general specifications for employment officers to follow. With a job's posting, if gender were going to affect qualifications, there must follow then and there in a full public disclosure the sexual preference of applicants. The bill had a simple purpose; it intended to curb the practice of CSC officers bypassing minority applicants. To disqualify black job seekers from the tops of hiring lists, administrators charged with screening candidates often claimed that only one gender could qualify. Although none of the three reform bills ever received committee action, they signified Mitchell's new attitude toward tackling discrimination. Compared with his previously lukewarm record on civil rights, Mitchell's stand was now stronger and should have caused civil rights leaders to reevaluate him. To committed individuals in the race's struggles for freedom, there were signs of cooperation coming

17. DeFrantz to M, July 15, 1937, NAACP; *Argus*, April 30 and July 30, 1937; M to Flowers, August 3, 1937; Dutton to M, October 31, 1937; reprint, *CR*, January 9, 1940, and M to L. F. Coles, January 13, 1940, MP; *CR*, 76th Cong., 3d sess., 173–77, 188–89; *East Tennessee News, Journal and Guide, Argus, Louisville Leader,* January 13, 1940; *New York Age,* January 2, 1940.

from Mitchell. Perhaps an old foe at last had become a new ally, discretely offering in his way evidence that civil rights supporters could have sanguine expectations from him in overcoming everyday challenges and problems encountered by African Americans in pursuit of public-sector employment. Although the *Crisis* editorial board and Charles Houston admitted "Mr. Mitchell's bill deserves whole-hearted support from all groups interested in employment opportunities for the race," a corresponding willingness to follow Mitchell did not materialize.[18]

Nevertheless, on questions involving racial identification on federal forms and applications, Mitchell had moved from being an apologetic accommodationist to an activist. Near the end of January 1937, after having received a complaint from Bronzeville about processing procedures at the Social Security Administration, Mitchell suddenly became curious about the rationale behind asking beneficiaries and taxpayers to identify themselves by race on form SS-5. Shortly thereafter, his search for explanations involved Roosevelt. In a most reassuring reply to Mitchell's doubts about good intentions, the president explained that the question about the applicant's race existed "solely for purposes of more accurate identification in dealing with the vast numbers of persons who will be carried on the Social Security rolls." Believing FDR's twist that nothing else was involved, Mitchell did not pursue the matter again.[19]

Yet, he was determined to fight vigorously in Congress against racist hiring practices. Although the battle for an end to job discrimination had high stakes and involved sacrifices, Mitchell willed to challenge it through legislation. He pledged himself to securing congressional approval of three reform bills. His zeal and strong will eventually aggravated Commissioner Harry B. Mitchell of the Civil Service Commission. When requested to chair hearings "to eliminate injustices against the Negroes of this country," the commissioner refused, snapping disdainfully that he could "see no basis for Mr. [Arthur] Mitchell's charges." The bureau

18. S. D. McRae to M, January 11, 1935; Jerry O. Gilliam to M and WW, April 22, 1936; M to Gilliam, April 23, 1936; AME resolution, Virginia Annual Conference, April 17, 1936; Bessie McLurkin to M, February 6, 1937; Rudolph Almento to M, February 7, 1937; Zerobia Gray to concerned, February 7, 1937; Jennie Means to *Washington Tribune*, February 6, 1937; Locke to M, January 28, 1936; William E. Taylor to M, February 6, 1937; LeFlore to M, February 26, 1937; Houston to M, March 10, 1937, MP; *Postal Alliance*, February; H.R. 10587, 74th Cong., 2d sess., January 24, 1936; H.R. 2249, 3691, 3692, 75th Cong., 1st sess., January 1937; *Washington Tribune*, January 26, 1935, and February 6, 1937; *Springfield Daily Republican*, January 15, 1937; *New York Age*, February 6, 1937; *Defender*, February 13, 1937; *Crisis*, March 1937; *Afro-American*, December 18, 1937.

19. M to FDR, January 25, 1937, MP; FDR and Hans Morgenthau Jr. to M, February 24, 1937, RP.

head's cavalier response enraged Mitchell so much that he sought and gained House permission to address the issue of how job prejudice was occurring under the Pendleton Act. In a December 15, 1937, speech, he labeled Civil Service "the rottenest and the most unfair department of the Government toward Negroes of any that is now in existence." Although the Committee on Civil Service buried Mitchell's bills, they made an impact. Charges of prejudice within the CSC aroused its commissioner, and Mitchell's determination silenced his critics in the NAACP. Above all, by raising his voice, Mitchell demonstrated his willingness to assume minority interests. In many ways, however, the transition from NAACP foe to active participant in efforts to reform federal hiring practices was a logical shift. Throughout his life, Mitchell generally favored fairness for talented blacks as much as he opposed clamoring agitators. Unlike those who demanded the same constitutional rights for everyone, Mitchell believed in selectivity; only blacks with nothing to concede to whites should have obstacle-free paths to success and full privileges.[20]

In practice, this philosophy helps to explain Mitchell's role in opening up service academies to gifted blacks. Convinced that his congressional and moral duty required him to select only the best young men, he did not adopt a policy of appointing only African Americans; that would set a poor example. Since the First District was a racial polyglot, good representation dictated fairness to everybody. Besides, if he, a black, named candidates exclusively on the basis of qualifications and not race, perhaps other lawmakers from equally heterogeneous districts would adopt a similar policy. Unsaid but practiced were two additional factors behind Mitchell's color blindness. Equal treatment provided a nice cover to masquerade paybacks to Machine politicians. On several occasions, Mayor Kelly sought Mitchell's help in securing academy placements for the sons of friends. Without fail, Mitchell delivered. In early 1936, it was Joe Tittinger's son, George, soliciting a West Point appointment and obtaining one in return the following June from Mitchell. However, the young man's low entrance scores would subsequently disqualify him.[21] There were interesting stories behind other white selectees, too. While

20. Misc. undated AP clipping, MP; *Postal Alliance* 23 (March 1938); Mitchell interviews.

21. List, DePriest's U.S. Military Academy appointees, n.d.; Tipper to M, July 13, 1935; M to Inez G. Vickery, July 15, 1935; George J. Tittinger to M, February 7, 1936; M to Tittinger, February 11, 1936; George G. Sadowski to Charles Roxborough, June 4, 1936; M to Sadowski, June 5, 1936; E. T. Conley to M, June 5 and July 27, 1936; L. R. Walker to M, June 26, 1936; M to James Watlock, March 23, 1937; EJK to M, May 3, 1938, and May 9, 1939; M to EJK, January 14, 1936, May 5, 1938, and May 11 and 17, 1939; M (transferring a 1940 appointment) to Claude V. Parsons, May 15, 1939, MP; *Philadelphia Tribune,* March 28, 1935.

Gilbert and Wilson Reed were boarding at a private military school, their wealthy Southern-born parents lived comfortably in Chicago's Loop. The brothers' respective selections to Annapolis and West Point illustrated how Mitchell enjoyed favoring white descendants from Dixie. Years later, Mrs. Inez Gilbert Reed grew nostalgic in discussing her family's black benefactor. Unembarrassed about the relationship, she mentioned a cordiality between the Reeds and Mitchell. As the boys' mother explained it, a friendship between members of her family and the "Negrow" had begun after an inquiry was made for Gilbert about Naval Academy entrance procedures. Mrs. Reed cherished fond memories of her family hosting Mitchell one weekend away from Chicago at the Reeds' Crystal Lake summer estate, and of Mitchell's reciprocation years later in Virginia. Mrs. Reed also recalled a small memento Gilbert had received during his first visit to Washington. For a keepsake, "Mistah" Mitchell autographed a small American desk flag. According to Professor Jimmie Lee Franklin's studies, such interracial acts of friendship and social intercourse across Southern lines were commonplace. As Franklin interpreted these, "Shared experiences and a sense of place among blacks did not necessarily imply acceptance of . . . discrimination." For Mitchell, relationships of this type were a means to promote "Good-Will Between the Races." To give it meaning in 1938, for example, he saved one appointment for a white teenager from Columbus, Georgia. For maximum effect, Mitchell expected the prospect to keep the deal to himself until he could announce it during an upcoming speech from the steps of a county courthouse. This was asking too much of the young man, however. After his appointee prematurely leaked details of the plan, Mitchell regretfully withdrew his offer, irritated that the intended recipient could not keep their secret.[22]

In naming his first candidate for West Point, Mitchell apologized that it could not have been a white boy. He explained his disappointment this way: "But owing to the fact that this is my first appointment the members of the organization in Chicago who have much to do with matters of this kind in the district, thought it imperative that the first appointment go to a member of my own Race to meet an argument that has been made against me to the effect that I am neglecting the interest of the Negroes wholly in my official appointments." Herein lies a key to understanding Mitchell's predicament. On occasions, he had obligations to fulfill. Hence, he deferred the tasks of finding and naming a black principal and two alternates to the Second Ward's Joe Tittinger. After having relieved himself

22. Vickery interview; Jimmie L. Franklin, "Black Southerners, Shared Experience, and Place: A Reflection," 14; M to Joseph Gatewood Jr., August 5, 1938, and May 1, 1939; Gatewood to M, August 9, 1938, MP.

of a debt by selecting black candidate Emory J. Joseph to West Point, Mitchell announced that future appointments would reflect a "50–50 colored and white" policy. True to his word, he named a white as the second recipient. Editorially, both the *Philadelphia Tribune* and the *Afro-American* thought the distribution should not be even because equal generosity had not come from other legislators. As an editor explained, "The situation as it actually exists, not as we would like for it to be, is that unless the colored Congressman appoints colored cadets to West Point, none will be appointed." Yet, according to an informal poll taken in 1936 of Democratic lawmakers by an *Afro-American* reporter, there was a great faith in competitive examinations that preceded acceptances because they guaranteed merit appointments. As one Illinois colleague of Mitchell understood color's effect, "I didn't know whether they [candidates] were white, black, blue, or orange."[23]

Apparently, there was no knowledge of how Mitchell nominated his young men. Nevertheless, by 1936, his attempts at balancing his appointments had upset Chicago NAACP members so much that there were threats to turn his policy into a campaign issue. Months before the organization's August moratorium on Mitchell, Chicago branch secretary C. A. Hansberry requested a racial breakdown of his appointees because "delay in this matter has seriously embarrassed an effort to place the facts concerning Congressman Mitchell before the voters." Mitchell succumbed somewhat to the pressure to appoint more African Americans to service schools. He launched national searches to uncover the most gifted young blacks. At first, secretary Claude Holman was in charge of locating them, but Holman did not find many qualified candidates. As soon as his secretary's failure was obvious, Mitchell expanded his efforts to locate tough, talented African American youths willing to "submit to the rigid discipline at these institutions." To assist him in the talent search, Mitchell turned to black pastors, principals, and Charles H. Houston. Once word spread of Mitchell's earnest drive to find qualified black applicants, solicitations arrived from everywhere. From 1936 until his departure from Congress in 1943, his expanded spanning-the-nation program located blacks from Virginia, New York, Georgia, and the nation's capital. All promised to endure hardships at Annapolis and West Point. There were marked differences in Mitchell's attitudes toward minority qualifiers, too. Just after his 1937 surrender on antilynching, he demonstrated interest in their welfare and progress at the two academies. Heretofore, Mitchell had

23. M to Vickery, July 15, MP; *Journal and Guide*, July 20, 1935; *Chicago Tribune*, July 13 and 19, 1935; Tittinger and Kirkpatrick interviews; *Afro-American*, July 20, 1935, and January 18, 1936; *Philadelphia Tribune*, August 1, 1935.

shown only cold indifference for black appointees and Felix Kirkpatrick, the talented DePriest nominee who had been systematically expelled from West Point on demerits on December 7, 1935. Without so much as a whimper of protest from Mitchell or signs of interest in their pleas for aid, the personal cases of dismissed men had not garnered support for investigations or help with reinstatements. In a turnabout, candidates after 1936 were more fortunate. From behind the scenes, there were still calculated moves on the parts of students and officers to oust black enrollees, but now at least there was a government official who cared about their plight.[24]

Life was difficult for black cadets. For his toughness at West Point, fellow students nicknamed Kirkpatrick "Iron Man." Years later, he recalled how racism had defied his hopes to succeed. Mostly Southern corpsmen forced him to suffer extraordinary taunting and hazing. Their cruelty brought him many unnecessary demerits, as did the fact that he could not share a room with other students. Of officers, the former plebe best remembered Commandant Simon Bolivar Buckner because of his condonation of pranks and mischievous behavior. Since Buckner never intervened to curtail unfair treatment, there obviously was no desire on his part to see the U.S. Military Academy integrated. It took nearly twenty months in Congress before Mitchell finally acknowledged that African Americans were experiencing hardships at the academies. Encouraging letters to Midshipmen James Lee Johnson and Gilbert L. Reed were his first signs of empathy and interest. Besides the usual advice from Mitchell about success and its relationship to hard work, the correspondence was personal, containing individual messages to each man. To Reed, Mitchell gave specific instructions to aid Johnson, "the first colored boy to be admitted to Academy for nearly seventy years." On the other hand, for the black inductee's personal benefit, Mitchell offered cheering words with which to overtake "difficulties and trials." Bear in mind, he advised Johnson, "when you will feel like throwing up the sponge, you have thousands pulling for you." In the note, there was also Mitchell's pledge to "never be too busy to come to your rescue if it is necessary."[25]

The thoughtful letter arrived at an opportune time. Midshipman Johnson had been under siege. Devious upperclassmen had "told a deliberate

24. C. A. Hansberry to WW, May 27, 1936, NAACP; M to Holman, December 30, 1935; M-Houston exchange, March 14, 18, and 21, 1938; M to pastors, 1936–1938; Arthur E. Gilmer, June 13, 1939, Olive M. Diggs and Lochard, March 27, 1939, Ira F. Lewis, June 4, 1942; Foster to M, April 29, 1936; M to Foster, March 16, 1937, MP; Kirkpatrick interview; *Defender*, May 4 and July 27, 1935, January 11, 1936, and May 30, 1942; *Washington Tribune*, January 10, 1936; *Journal and Guide*, January 11 and 18, 1936; *Argus*, January 17, 1936; *Afro-American*, January 18, 1936.
25. Kirkpatrick interview; M to Gilbert L. Reed and to JLJ2, August 4, 1936, MP.

falsehood" about him, which, if believed by academy authorities, would prompt an early expulsion. Just the thought of having been remembered with Mitchell's encouragement and commitment uplifted Johnson's spirit. As the appointee admitted years later, there had been torturous moments to withstand at the Naval Academy. Johnson did not enter Annapolis directly after high school; there had been almost three years' preparation at the Case School of Applied Sciences when word from home in Washington arrived in Cleveland of his candidacy's review. An announcement of Mitchell's national search to locate qualified blacks had produced an excellent recommendation from the drill team commander at Dunbar High School of the District of Columbia. Johnson's former teacher had considered the Washington public school graduate ideally suited for an appointment. Nobody could have been more perfectly matched for placement at Annapolis than Johnson. Physically fit from fencing and track, popular with Case classmates and staff, and academically sound, especially in mathematics and applied sciences from his major in engineering, he met every requirement for naval officer training. Plus, ships of all descriptions had been his lifelong hobby and passion, as his bedroom in Washington filled with models of his design and fabrication attested. Grateful that such a perfect black candidate had been found to break the Navy's color line, Mitchell announced Johnson's appointment in April. Even if his family and friends were skeptical about how the Navy—"the most arrogant, overbearing, and deeply dyed in race prejudice of any department of government"—might treat a black whose single greatest ambition was officer training at Annapolis, James remained optimistic. Six pleasant terms among Case's mostly white student body and faculty had given him confidence, and thorough, back-to-back medical checks by his family's physician and a retired medical corps doctor had confirmed good health. Before reporting for duty in late July, James's only real concern was an address given on an application. To skirt a congressional appointments-at-large policy, his sponsor had filled in a Chicago address. Until Mitchell reassured him about intent and the law, James worried about a falsification.[26]

Johnson's arrival and settlement at Annapolis changed all his expectations. In a flash, dreams of a challenging Navy career turned into a nightmare. Sophomores and juniors were away on traditional summer cruises, while inductees were on campus with seniors. Yet every absent

26. JLJ2 to Mother and Daddy, July 22, 1936; L. W. Mills to JLJ2, December 21, 1936; Clare Barkalow to Mr. and Mrs. James L. Johnson Sr., June 23, 1936; Theodore M. Focke to JLJ2, February 15, 1937; M to JLJ2, March 9, 1936; Cleveland Gazette, April 25, 1936; misc. unidentified clippings, June 27, 1936; Francis J. Grimke to Mr. and Mrs. Johnson, February 19, 1937, JFP; C. W. Nimitz to M, April 8, 1936, MP; Johnson interview.

midshipman appeared to know about Johnson. A spectacle, his presence at school stimulated many diverse reactions, everything from surface cordiality to open hostility. Middies from Arkansas were most unmerciful, shouting every imaginable racial slur at him. Later, he learned that there had been debates and bets among the middleclassmen at sea about the duration of his stay. Yet, as devastatingly incomparable as the whole experience had become, he expected abatement after his tormentors' introductions to him. Contrary to wishes for an end, students pledged to his removal persisted. From "cracking jokes" to him while in rank to rushing into his room after nightly taps, racists never tired of finding ways to give him demerits. Still, James marched off to do extra duty, knowing their will to taunt could not match his endurance. As bad as things were, his letters rarely hinted of despair or foul play. Parents and "Auntie" learned mostly of good moments, such as doing well on the shooting range, being on a winning drill company, and enjoying Navy football games. Except for August 6, 1936, when Johnson assessed classmate relationships, there was no communication with Mitchell. In his only letter, the plebe judged other midshipmen either as "antagonistic," indifferent, "afraid," or "tolerant" and helpful. Being one or the other, middies reflected naval officers. Sparse with details about them or his ordeals, Johnson seemed much more interested in leaving favorable impressions and exhibiting gratitude than in criticizing or complaining. For instance, there was nothing about having to board alone. Also in late August, there was no reference to Lieutenant Commander Lemuel P. Padgett or to the Tennessee-reared officer's reprimands because of Johnson's attendance at Rear Admiral and Mrs. David F. Sellers' reception and his total ignorance of a black's "place"; Padgett was the midshipman's battalion leader. According to Johnson, his parents had sheltered him so much that he had not known much about protocol and racism before receiving Padgett's crude introduction. Well-meaning but naive, Johnson had not comprehended racism's totality at Annapolis until it was too late. From childhood, he recalled how loving parents had succeeded very well at shielding him from racism, and then his positive interactions at Case had deceived him about the generalities of interracial relationships. Sheltered from prejudice and inexperienced in hardships from racism, the young man did not know enough to prepare for the worst at Annapolis. Worried that letters filled with the ghastly truth would upset his parents, he failed to document personal anguish from being Annapolis's unwanted pioneer.[27]

27. Johnson interview; JLJ2 to Frank and Daddy, August 23 and September 1, 1936, JLJ2 to Mother and Daddy, September 20, 1936, JLJ2 to Auntie, October 30, 1936, JFP; JLJ2 to M, August 6, 1936, MP.

A definite need for supportive materials arose after Johnson's first term and his father's receipt of a letter from Academy Superintendent Sellers. The letter mentioned a record of 181 demerits, or fifteen more than academy conduct rules allowed. During the past decade, stressed the admiral with Texas roots, only 113 middies had ever accumulated so many bad marks. Trying to show both interest and concern, Sellers wrote how he had hoped Padgett's advice to an erring charge would "be all that is necessary." Knowing that he had "interviewed your son and attempted to impress upon him the seriousness of his situation" without apparent effects, Sellers advised James Johnson Sr. to "use . . . influence in calling to your son's attention the seriousness of his present situation and the importance of overcoming such habits of carelessness or indifference which he may have."[28]

Johnson's father put careful thought into his reply. Unlike an original draft that pled with "each person there to think of him as another midshipman instead of a Negro," his final answer reflected calculation. All critical expressions of outrage at the racism his son James had suffered were missing from the letter sent to Sellers. Instead, the father mentioned appreciation for Padgett's interview and gave his "assurance [from talking to James] that it will have the effect on my son"; paternal advice had been "impressed on him that it is necessary for him to give extra and continuous attention to details to prevent the accumulation of . . . demerits." As for his son's supposedly dismal deportment, he attributed it to "overanxious rather than careless and indifferent" behavior and to "a certain tenseness in his situation." A contrite response closed with another "tahnk [sic] you" to Sellers for "fairness and . . . a square deal."[29]

The apologetic response to Sellers was both curious and ill-advised. Days earlier before placing James at the admiral's mercy, James Johnson Sr. consulted with Mitchell. In a frantic search for truth about prejudicial treatment at Annapolis, the parent gave Mitchell a copy of Sellers' letter. Johnson wanted to know why racist attacks against his son had been allowed to continue. To accommodate him, Mitchell began checking. The congressman's first inquiries were made on January 29, 1937, or four days before the father's self-defeating letter to the superintendent. Without mincing words to Sellers or Roosevelt, Mitchell stipulated that discussions on Johnson would be imperative. Simultaneous to making himself understood about the urgency of meetings, Mitchell asserted that forces hostile to Johnson at Annapolis were plotting his departure. He was especially blunt and accusatory toward Sellers, claiming a total incapacity "to understand how officials at the Academy, whose duty it is to see that

28. David F. Sellers to JLJ1, January 27, 1937, RP.
29. JLJ1 to Sellers, draft and reply, February 2, 1937, JFP.

all students are dealt with fairly, could permit any mistreatment of one of my Race." Four days after writing to ascertain for himself what had occurred, Mitchell visited Annapolis. After listening to James Johnson Jr., he spoke to the midshipman's battalion leader. Described later as a free exchange, the chat detailed the autumn term. Every naval officer who had had contact with the cadet, Padgett confided, had been "leaning over backward to help," but nothing could save him from more demerits except closer attention to posted time changes. There had been improvements in Johnson's deportment and English, but Padgett predicted "something may come up any minute." After finishing with the officer, Mitchell checked battalion files. The details of Johnson's ordeal were recorded there on index cards. Laid before Mitchell were threats—from "Let's string him up" to "Let's treat him like we treat the 'nigger' down our way"—and proof of prejudicial treatment. There in the records, Mitchell found registered protests from Sellers, his commanding officers, and midshipmen to Johnson's presence at the admiral's August reception for freshmen. Moreover, Mitchell read notations about an "unduly severe" English professor and a student ringleader behind "a lot of checking on Johnson."[30]

During early February, Johnson's situation consumed most of Mitchell's time. Following his on-campus meeting with Padgett and his search through hundreds of pages of midshipmen records, Mitchell consented to Sellers' request for a Capitol Hill meeting. During a subsequent session, Sellers gave a positive synopsis of Johnson's steadily improving conduct and scholarship. On account of progress, Sellers assured Mitchell that there were no disciplinary actions contemplated against the black midshipman. Still, within days, on the morning of February 11, 1937, the Academic Board confronted him with a resignation form to sign. Afraid to comply, the student resisted, refusing to cooperate with the panel's request for his signature. Bewildered by the unexpected demand on him, Johnson asked for permission to wire the Capitol for advice. Turned over to Padgett for an answer, the student soon found himself in the company of a person whom he would describe almost thirty-seven years later as "one of the finest confidence men I'd ever seen." From a session with the battalion leader, Johnson recalled in 1974 how Padgett had pretended empathy and "affectation of friendliness" in order to cajole away a four-year stipend to study at Annapolis.[31]

30. M to FDR and to Sellers, January 29, 1937, RP; Reed interview; transcript, Mitchell interview of Lemuel P. Padgett Jr., February 4, 1937; M to Sellers, February 3, 1937, MP.

31. Johnson interview; JLJ2, "The Circumstances of My Resignation," February 11, 1937, MP; *Washington Post*, February 13, 1937.

No one at Annapolis would tell Mitchell if his attempted intercessions had precipitated the U.S. Naval Academy's rush to remove Johnson
from its rolls. From all indications, Sellers did not appreciate Mitchell's
interference or his implications of bigotry at Annapolis. Whether these
had contributed in any way or not to the Academy's actions, Johnson
understood from a "slip of the tongue" that top-level officials had plotted
Johnson's withdrawal. About the Academy's haste to get a withdrawal
signature, "The Department had planned . . ." was the embarrassing start
to a then-muted explanation begun by an Academy lieutenant. Catching
a mistake in progress, the red-faced officer never completed what might
have been a most revealing sentence. Reactions to Johnson's resignation
came quickly. For such "grave injustice," Mitchell felt both shock and
betrayal. Although several accomplices had participated in plots against
Johnson, none "disappointed" him more than Sellers. He had received
Sellers' verbal assurance just one week earlier not to act against Johnson without prior consultations. Sellers' promises had therefore become
fallacious and meaningless. After "the treatment of Johnson," Mitchell
readdressed the superintendent, notifying him that "there should be a
Congressional investigation of the conduct of the officers of the Academy
and all others." Mitchell then followed up on his threats, drafting two
resolutions for Congress's consideration. One required the Speaker's appointment of a seven-man committee to investigate conspiracy charges
against officers and students, and the other demanded transmissions by
Secretary of the Navy Claude Swanson of every appropriate record to a
House select committee looking into the aforesaid allegations. Coupled
with these efforts, Mitchell tried again to involve Roosevelt in the matter.
Since the president had ignored his earlier appeal to talk about Johnson,
Mitchell wired Roosevelt on February 13 to recommunicate his request
to confer. Suddenly, everything concerning a black midshipman changed
from private worries to public indignation; now, the matter demanded an
executive response. Mitchell was given an appointment with Roosevelt on
February 16, 1937. Even if rather accustomed from such sessions to "expect
to ring no backing bells," Mitchell was more poised than usual to obtain
something from the meeting. Afterward, he apparently felt the session
had gone his way. At least, he indicated success to several news reporters
gathered outside the White House. As if to say "evidence of skullduggery"
laid before FDR was in a briefcase at his side, Mitchell pointed toward
a leather satchel. Then he summarized matters: "There is no doubt in
my mind that the boy had been railroaded out," but "we will get fair
play" from an executive inquiry. Regardless of the result, the official
vowed, other black appointees would soon enter Annapolis. Separately
for the benefit of white newspapermen, FDR meanwhile confirmed that
an investigation would get "to the bottom of matter." Pending the probe,

noted an official White House communique, the standings of Johnson and all other students coerced into resigning would be on hold.[32]

With activities seemingly abounding on their behalves both on Capitol Hill and in the White House, Johnson along with 144 other midshipmen had presidential permission to remain at Annapolis in "civvies," awaiting final resolutions of their cases. Meanwhile, James Johnson Sr. received the Navy's official explanation. It came from Captain Forde A. Todd, the Commandant of Midshipmen. He attributed Midshipman Johnson's dismissal to academic problems in English and history, deficient eyesight, and conduct unacceptable for a future naval officer. Ironically, just as the report arrived at the Johnson household, the Navy informed Mitchell of a vacancy at Annapolis. Shortly thereafter, the Johnsons contacted Mitchell to ascertain his opinion of their son's desired immediate return to Case. Feeling it best for him, Gertrude and James Johnson explained how enrolling at once would permit their son's entry in the second term. Besides, if his presence were needed at a Washington or Annapolis hearing, there could always be travel on short notice from Cleveland. Perceiving no problems from granting a release, Mitchell agreed that James Johnson should resume his studies in Ohio. With a prepared statement, Johnson was ready for reporters awaiting his arrival at Case. His statement completely contradicted the U.S. Naval Academy's official interpretation. He attributed his low marks to racism. Johnson described a bad grade and his former situation this way: "There is no course in the marking of which personal opinions, prejudices, or interpretations plays such a dominant part as in English as taught at the Navy Academy." Furthermore, extra duty assignments had raised barriers to academic improvement. For every ten hours of assessed demerits, there had been daily routines to work off time. Without penalties to consider, there would have been supplementary tutoring, Johnson concluded, and it would have raised him at least one letter grade in mathematics. According to his complaint, his daily ordeals had robbed him of valuable composition time. Since some upperclassmen had "required [me] to keep my room in better condition than others," there had not been enough time to organize and compose better English themes. As Johnson admitted in 1974, writing had never come easily for him; he either painstakingly "carved out letters" or he suffered the

32. Johnson interview; JLJ2, "The Circumstances of My Resignation"; *Washington Post*, February 13, 14, and 17, 1937; Sellers to M, January 30, 1937; M to Sellers, February 13, 1937; drafts of different resolutions; M to *Pittsburgh Courier*, February 15, 1937, MP; Wires to FDR: M, February 13, 1937; The American Society for Race Relations, February 18, 1937, RP; misc. undated clippings, JFP; *Indianapolis Recorder*, February 27, 1937; *Amsterdam News*, February 20 and 27, 1937; *Washington Capitol Daily*, February 20, 1937; *Afro-American*, February 20, 1937; *Defender*, March 6, 1937.

consequences. By his assessment, all blame for his prejudicial treatment had ultimately belonged to the Naval Academy officers because they had not condoned his attendance at Annapolis. All their affected friendship and kindness had only covered their deep-seated resentments toward blacks. Years after Johnson's "resignation," Gilbert Reed corroborated the dismissed student's contentions about official duplicity. According to Reed, Johnson had been as capable as anyone at Annapolis, but racist Naval Academy administrators had abetted acts against him.[33]

Gertrude Johnson broke her silence, too. In an open letter for curious *Washington Tribune* and *Afro-American* readers, she revealed her son's Annapolis nightmare. A doubter in the beginning, like others, about a black's chances at the Academy, she had cautioned her son about "stumbling blocks and difficulties," but he had countered that it would have been "doing my people an injustice not to enter." At the Naval Academy, he had endured so many "humiliations, insults, prejudices, and discriminations" that he had been "representing not just James L. Johnson, Jr., but the Negro race." As a result of his suffering, all African Americans owed her son the highest respect. By releasing statements to two area newspapers, the Johnsons angered Mitchell. Until a completion of investigations into the dismissal, he had expected the family's full cooperation and silence. Even before the newspaper articles, there had been strains between the Johnsons and Mitchell. The first indications arose during a February 24 telephone conversation. Curious to ascertain how several probes were progressing, James Johnson Sr. asked Mitchell if there had not been any positive results to report. The timing of his inquiry could not have been worse. Moments earlier, a most disappointing report had come to Mitchell's attention. It had confirmed rumors from Capitol Hill that Secretary of the Navy Claude A. Swanson had indeed closed the Johnson case. Unsure about his next move, Mitchell inquired about James's whereabouts. Informed he had moved back to Ohio to finish studies at Case, Mitchell exclaimed angrily that all his investigating was "through as far as I am concerned." Shocked to hear this, Johnson Sr. considered the response rather ludicrous because earlier in the week Mitchell had endorsed his son's return to Cleveland. The unwarranted outburst would confirm the Johnsons' suspicions of Mitchell. For several days, they had been wondering if "Mr. Mitchell is of an impetuous disposition" inclined to rendering "snap judgement"

33. Forde A. Todd to JLJ1, February 15, 1937; Navy Department Bureau of Navigation to M, February 18, 1937, MP; *Washington Tribune*, February 20 and 27, 1937; penciled notes about a Mitchell conversation, n.d.; JLJ1 to the Office of the Dean, February 14, 1937; Todd to JLJ1, February 15, 1937; JLJ2 to Mother and Daddy, February 25, 1937; "Significant Facts," JLJ2 explains a discharge, JFP; Johnson and Reed interviews; *Afro-American*, February 27, 1937.

and "spur of the moment" remarks, and they had been questioning whether their son's case might not be "bigger than Mitchell." Now with a confirmation of their suspicions, they were ready to call in the NAACP to investigate their son's miseries at Annapolis. Later after regaining composure, Mitchell indicated his personal probe into the circumstances leading to James's involuntary departure from the Naval Academy would not end just because of Roosevelt's acceptance of Swanson's verdict.[34]

Resolving to continue his inquiry after Roosevelt had pronounced the matter dead characterized Mitchell's sudden about-face on civil rights issues. Although he would utter nothing critical about Roosevelt, he made no attempts to withhold his personal impressions of Swanson's investigation or of the Department of the Navy. To an interracial audience, Mitchell reaffirmed his earlier opinions about the "railroading out of Johnson." According to Mitchell, the alleged probe conducted by Swanson was no more than a "Star Chamber" effort at "white washing the culprits."[35] Of course because these comments had come from a normally uncritical black apologist for the administration, they attracted much attention. No previous issue involving Mitchell had generated as much emotional interest and concern as the case of the fallen black midshipman. For speaking out, Mitchell received commendations from longtime detractors such as the NNC's John P. Davis. Spontaneous congratulations arrived from all sections of the country, and numerous people offered assistance. After his son's elaborations of the Naval Academy's mistreatment of and unfair disposition toward Johnson, an anonymous midshipman's father conveyed his family's wishes for sympathy to the victim and success to investigators. Other correspondents disagreed with Mitchell's stand; for aiding a "Nigger Naval Officer," "yellow Nigger" and " . . . hole," Mitchell received hate mail.[36]

Over the next months, unabated resolution and cooperative personal contacts sustained Mitchell as he continued to investigate everything behind Johnson's ouster. Congress accepted the Navy's self-serving

34. Draft and final statement, Gertrude Johnson, n.d.; JLJ1 to M, February 13, 1937; draft notes about M, n.d., JFP; *Washington Tribune* and *Afro-American*, February 27, 1937; Johnsons to M, February 28 and resolution draft, n.d., MP; *Washington Star*, February 24, 1937.

35. M to Stephen M. Young, Daniel E. Wiseman, Baptist Ministers' Conference of Washington and Vicinity, American Society for Race Tolerance, February 25, 1937, MP; *Atlantic City Eagle*, March 5, 1937.

36. Sample mail to M: JPD, February 17, 1937; Charles A. Brown, March 4, 1937; North Harlem Community Council, March 1, 1937; EJS, February 19, 1937; R. A. Gillem, February 16, 1937; Kirkpatrick, March 7, 1937; James Wechsler, February 17, 1937; J. Arnow, February 20, 1937; Young, February 22, 1937; Wiseman, February 16, 1937; anonymous, February 17, 27, and June 18, 1937, MP.

explanations, but he refused to surrender his race's right to attend the Naval Academy. All along, he had surmised the Navy's probe would be nothing more than a useless "white wash." Inasmuch as his investigation was hampered by his lack of authority and powerlessness to subpoena key defense witnesses or impound Academy records, his personal probe pursued only three main leads. The first came from an *Afro-American* headline story about two midshipmen who had allegedly plotted to "get" Johnson. Since a Kansas jury had convicted a black man of murdering the father of one of the Academy masterminds, the young man in question, a senior, had bragged about hating and resenting all blacks. With no more of a lead to follow, Mitchell struggled to ascertain if there had been some relationship between Johnson's unwarranted demerits and the newspaper article's allegations about prejudicial motives. Working first with a tip that there might have been peculiar inducements for Johnson's mistreatment, Mitchell and Claude Holman turned to Kansas City for answers. Despite his modest resources, Mitchell was able to gather enough information to conclude by mid-March that just as the *Afro-American* had reported, the Annapolis cabal's ringleader was a surviving son of a slain trolley conductor, and the convicted murderer was a black. However, this was circumstantial evidence, and further speculating without sworn admissions would be meaningless. Even without authority to interrogate witnesses or the suspect, Mitchell still had found more than Swanson; he had confirmed a viable cause-and-effect connection to Johnson's demerits. Academy special regulations were the second concern of Mitchell's private investigation. Because he had requested a copy, Admiral Sellers provided a manual detailing all the Navy's rules applying to midshipmen. The Annapolis handbook showed how much subjectivity was involved in judging specific rule violations. Again if he had been empowered, Mitchell now had in his possession the wherewithal to press Academy officials about Johnson's allegations. It would not have been difficult for a lawyer to illustrate how a black midshipman's conduct might have been judged under one set of rules, and white classmates under another less rigid code. Unfortunately for Johnson, Mitchell lacked prosecutorial powers to accuse anyone, congressional authority to hear evidence, or a popular mandate to demand Johnson's reinstatement.[37]

Mitchell did not begin the last installment of his investigation until the July resignation of George J. Trivers Jr., Johnson's black replacement. If the two young men had anything in common, it was their Washington

37. Houston to M, March 1 and 27, 1937; M to Houston, March 8, 1937; Holman to Roy Garvin, March 5, 1937; Garvin to Holman, March 8, 1937; Lucile Bluford to Holman, March 9, 1937; Holman to Bluford, March 13, 1937; M to Sellers, March 13, 1937; Sellers to M, March 15, 1937, MP; *Afro-American*, February 27, 1937.

public high school backgrounds; there, however, similarities ended. Complaining of racism, Trivers quit after only three weeks as a midshipman. Revelations that another black appointee might have endured torment so enraged Mitchell that he demanded an immediate appointment with Forde Todd, the Academy's acting superintendent. On the following day, July 7, 1937, Mitchell and Attorney Emory B. Smith arrived from Washington to launch a thorough investigation into every circumstance surrounding Trivers's resignation. After separate interviews with Trivers and Todd, Mitchell was convinced that his candidate was not "the fighting type." Nevertheless, there had been something rather suspicious about Todd. Consequently, upon returning to Washington with Smith, Mitchell solicited naval records to check on Todd's background. After finishing with him, Mitchell subjected the dossiers of Sellers and Padgett to similar scrutinies. There can only be speculation about these searches because Mitchell neither mentioned nor recorded what his intention had been for the examinations; he also never indicated if the exercises had served a purpose or had led to any specific conclusions. If there were aftereffects from his independent investigation, they were not publicized. Mitchell's preliminary charges about Swanson "white washing" facts and about the Naval Academy "railroading" black appointees were correct, and certainly Mitchell's unauthorized probe was more thorough than the Roosevelt-sanctioned one that had promised to go "to the bottom" of Johnson's dismissal.[38]

Prior to the uproar over James L. Johnson's treatment at Annapolis, none of Mitchell's black appointees to West Point had been admitted. Several had been named, but all had failed the Academy's admission test. Attrition caused by Felix Kirkpatrick's forced departure in 1935 and by the graduation the next year of DePriest appointee Benjamin O. Davis Jr. had left the school all-white until James D. Fowler's registration in July 1937. Since Fowler was Mitchell's first black nominee to gain admission to West Point, Mitchell made several precautions to ensure his success. First of all, Mitchell carefully watched over the young man from Washington, goading and encouraging him to "measure up to the same standard and, if possible, a little higher standard than that acquired [sic] by white

38. M to Bureau of Navigation, Navy Department, March 10, 1937; Nimitz to M, March 13, 17, June 22, and July 19, 1937; M. D. Day to M, April 30, 1937; Conley to M, July 19, 1937; M to PBY, July 9, 1937; M to Adolphus Andrews, July 7 and 19, 1937; Andrews to M, July 24, 1937; M memo, July 6, 1937, MP; *St. Louis Post-Dispatch*, June 16, 1937, *Columbus Advocate*, July 24, 1937, *Washington Post*, July 9, 1937; *East Tennessee News*, July 15 and August 5, 1937; *Argus*, July 23, 1937; *Washington Tribune*, July 10, 1937; U.S. Naval Academy, "Letter of the Superintendent to Parents and Guardians of Midshipmen," 1936, JFP; McIntyre and Claude Swanson to FDR, February n.d.; Sellers to Swanson, February 24, 1937, RP.

classmates." In addition to the letters to Fowler, Mitchell conversed with his mother and advised West Point Superintendent Jay L. Benedict to guard the black student from racists "out to get" him. Moreover, Mitchell designated one of his white nominees as Fowler's guardian angel, to be a special "acquaintance" and render "what he can to make it comfortable for this young man." In June 1941, after four years working "my utmost to prove that a Negro is fully capable of more than holding his own in competition with representatives of the white race," Fowler survived a "list [of] obstacles" and was graduated into the army as a commissioned officer. Noting for Mitchell on June 4, 1942, that the congressman's two other African American appointees were "held in high esteem" at Army, Major General F. B. Wilby remembered from the 1941 commencement how the audience had reacted to hearing an announcement of Lieutenant Fowler's name. As the officer recalled it, "a greater ovation was bestowed upon the colored graduate . . . than was received by the honor man or the man who graduated last."[39]

Increasingly, the army's policy of racial segregation grated on Mitchell. However, during his first congressional term, it had not excited him particularly. Hence, the NAACP had not succeeded at interesting him in its campaigns to halt further deterioration of the all-black Ninth and Tenth Cavalries, open specialized branches to blacks, and qualify them for more than mess and commissary duties in the Navy. Rather than cooperate and fight to alter restrictive War Department policies, Mitchell rationalized away the discriminatory military practices. As Mitchell claimed during his weak first term, "There are many elements that enter into this matter that the ordinary person is not aware of." There was also circumspection on his part about adding "colored" Army Air Corps training at Tuskegee Institute.[40] James Johnson's departure from Annapolis in 1937 placed new demands on Mitchell. Assuming now that he had more than a general interest in the Navy's prejudicial attitudes toward blacks, mess attendants began placing their woes before him. Even if these men's plights received more sympathetic hearings than they would have earlier, Mitchell could do little about their situations. According to his conclusions for the NAACP and Charles H. Houston in 1938, Mitchell felt blacks would have to show greater will to avail themselves "when the opportunities are

39. Conley to M, May 15, 1937; M to Vickery, June 29, 1937; James D. Fowler to M, November 26, 1937; M to Fowler, December 1, 1937, and July 20, 1938; M to Jay L. Benedict, June 18, 1938; Benedict to M, July 15, 1938; M to F. W. Wilby, May 27, 1942; Wilby to M, June 4, 1942, MP; *Defender,* July 30, 1938, and June 14, 1941.

40. M to E. C. Johnson, June 27, 1935; William D. Leahy to MacNeal, June 3, 1935; MacNeal to Swanson, May 26, 1935, and MacNeal to M, June 24, 1935, MP; M to Pickens, Houston, and WW, September 3, 1935; M to WW, October 21, 1935, NAACP; *Chicago World,* June 29, 1935; WW to FDR, January 2, 1936, RP.

offered." Without stronger determination, there would not be progress. As he put it, "I do not understand how we can ever break this prejudice down" without a foursquare push. As proof, Mitchell cited his personal frustrations with trying to find black replacements for Johnson and Trivers. Since there had not been success at finding "the right type of colored boy," he could "not see any need of making a lot of noise about opportunities which we already have and which we are not using."[41]

In his second term, Mitchell displayed another sign of his increased willingness to assert his political independence. For two years after refusing to seek a place on the District Affairs Committee, his involvements in District of Columbia affairs had been destructive. By stirring up Howard University over Reds and contesting a progressive black's appointment to the municipal bench, he fully estranged himself from Washington's civil rights leaders. The first positive sign that he might seek atonement for his misguided actions and arcanal silence for institutional racism in the District of Columbia occurred during April 1937 with his hard push to persuade Attorney General Homer S. Cummings to consider Emory B. Smith, a young African American attorney, for one of two vacancies on the police court bench. Although the bid failed, it was a forerunner of Mitchell's meaningful initiatives in capital affairs. In 1938, for example, he issued sharp rebuttals in Congress to Capitol Hill budget cutters who wanted to transfer fifty black women from the National Training School for Girls to Industrial Home; due to overcrowded conditions at Industrial Home, removing them, he correctly maintained, would become "a national scandal" and "one of the most disgraceful things that this Congress could do." After this, if there were still any doubts about Mitchell's resolve to mind black interests in Washington, a controversy over a Marian Anderson performance in 1939 should have settled them. Prejudice toward the young black contralto provoked Mitchell. After Anderson's successful tour of major European cities and a brilliant performance at Carnegie Hall, an agent booked her into Washington's Constitution Hall for an early 1939 recital. Thereupon, the Daughters of the American Revolution drew the color line, refusing to open their auditorium to a black artist's performance. Their racist decision so infuriated Mitchell that he paralleled her problems with the DAR to the Nazis' treatment of Jews. "I wouldn't be surprised if Hitler knew of this, the D.A.R.'s would get a medal from him," the official snapped to an Associated Press reporter moments after the ban. Although uttered in haste, his comment was not recanted. Unlike his quickly forgotten first-term flare-ups over racism, Mitchell's fury over

41. M to Swanson, March 8, 1937, Frank B. Wilson Sr., March 18, 1937, C. Lavender, October 18, 1937, Houston, March 14, 1938; James Witlock and Ralph Waters to M, March 18, 1937; Andrews to M, March 15, 1937; Lavender to M, October 19, 1937, MP.

Anderson stayed on his agenda. Some three months later, in a letter to remind the DAR president-general of Crispus Attucks, there was no relenting; he was still demanding "an explanation for all this hubbub."[42]

Mitchell had gradually built up to expressing such bold reactions. During his second term, reactions to a provocatively worded inquiry about mixed marriages foreshadowed future responses; one letter had an uproarious effect upon him. The letter's author learned definitively from Mitchell that all such weddings were private affairs between consenting adults and were nobody else's business. If there were negative reactions, they resulted from whites who were frustrated by their inability to foster an "idea of superiority in the minds of . . . children." As an effect, the irate congressman postulated, "it [had become] necessary . . . [for them] to pass many discriminating laws, trying to put over . . . bluff as to . . . inherent superiority," when in fact, all the decisions should belong to participants and "not . . . fool agitators."[43]

By 1940, with much of Europe and eastern Asia engulfed in turmoil and bloody conflicts, the role of blacks in America's preparation for a global war became a more significant interest for Mitchell. At a August 16, 1940, meeting with Roosevelt, he discussed the subject with the president. In the meeting's aftermath, Mitchell showed greater militancy and activism on wartime matters and blacks. On August 28, Congress heard a positive report from Mitchell on his meeting with Roosevelt. Among other things, Mitchell claimed to have secured a written assurance from the War Department that it would not raise "a combat division composed exclusively of Negro personnel either in the regular army or in the national guard." Important as the announcement might have seemed as some kind of testimonial to Mitchell's efforts on behalf of African Americans, it still paled in comparison to something else he slipped into his address. As glibly as possible, he bid a rather discrete farewell to years of gradualism. Few contemporaries caught his "contention that racial prejudice in the Army and in the Navy—in fact, in all branches of our national defense—should be wiped out, and should be wiped out immediately." Still a politician and not a professional civil rights advocate, Mitchell did not want to act so overtly that his action would flaunt militancy at Roosevelt and the Democratic Party. Hence, he reverted to more familiar sycophancy after receiving a warm invitation to participate actively in a proposed protest march on Washington. Slippery as ever to organizer A. Philip Randolph, Mitchell feigned pressing out-of-town business as a reason for declining.

42. M to Cummings, April 12, 1937; Elwood Street to M, March 17, 1938; M to Mrs. Henry M. Robert Jr., April 11, 1939, MP; *CR*, 75th Cong., 3d sess., 3659, 8537; *Washington Evening Star*, March 18 and April 2, 1938; *Defender*, January 28, 1939.
43. M to Arthur M. Weber, February 26, 1938, MP.

Later, Mitchell ridiculed everyone who credited Randolph's threat of a mass demonstration with having forced Roosevelt to issue an executive order that created the Fair Employment Practices Commission.[44]

Mitchell might not have been party to public protests, but there was other evidence confirming his break with his past. Most notably, his final-term speeches to Congress contained far less patience and more anger than ones given earlier in his political career. By hammering home unabashed attacks on racial injustice, he seemed to be seeking reversals of all perceptions that he was a "Tom." Whether these confrontations resulted from Mitchell's disillusionment or the Machine's loss of clout over him, he did not say. Whatever had caused his transformation, the results showed up in his orations. Advancing from monotonous scripts of diatribe and partisanship, he shifted over to lamentation and instruction on the nation's inconsistency toward blacks. Although Mitchell left few clues to indicate his secret ambitions, everything in his final congressional addresses suggest strong wishes to be remembered as the minority's representative who probed and pricked at the national conscience insofar as his words could showcase the differences between lofty war goals and the realities encountered by African Americans. By exposing unfair treatment by whites, he obviously expected amelioration of wrongs and gratitude from blacks. In particular, his July 24, 1941, address—"The Negro Discriminated Against in Our National Defense Program"—became a model for future lectures: "At this very moment," he reminded House members, "when this country is straining every nerve and fiber to prepare itself for defense against subversive doctrines and activities, calling loud and long for workers in every field, the Negro is not included except in the most limited way." Mitchell targeted the sources of problems, charging specific corporations and unions with racism before imploring his listeners to inquire if these unfair practices could "exist in a real democracy." No less mindful of problems and hypocrisy after the United States entered the war, he coupled his pledge of support to an expectation on behalf of blacks who were prepared to "give all . . . , including . . . life, for the success of our effort to withstand Hitlerism." On December 8, 1941, with completion of Congress's acceptance of military intervention, his hope was that "those in power and authority . . . will cause this country to recognize the Negro as a full-fledged citizen." According to Mitchell's view, if a black soldier offered his life in the defense of liberty, he "should be given the largest and fullest opportunity to live for his country without

44. Memo to Watson, August 8, 1940, RP; *CR*, 76th Cong., 3d sess., appendix, 5306; *Afro-American*, September 7, 1940; Randolph to M, June 11, 1941; M to Randolph, June 18, 1941; M to Turpin, July 15, 1942, MP; *Philadelphia Independent*, August 10, 1941.

any type of racial discrimination." Mitchell repeated the theme several times before his congressional farewell in late 1942. At directing attention to hostilities inflicted on uniformed blacks, no effort surpassed his speech "Negro Soldiers Discriminated Against." Under arcanal circumstances, a secret memo meant for the Adjutant General reached Mitchell. Used as background to his sensational speech of February 18, 1942, it also became the basis of a protest to Major General Robert Donovan about a disturbing racial incident in Houston. In Houston, white municipal and military police were accused of calling uniformed blacks "nigger soldiers." Everyone concerned, warned Mitchell, should not forget that Singapore's conquest by Japan had come from Great Britain's "refusal and failure to recognize and use the native soldiers." Similarly, he predicted, the United States could be defeated if it insisted on wasting African American talent and resources. His protest to Donovan and a request ended Mitchell's moralizing. What he wanted next was inclusion of his complaints to the general in the *Congressional Record*. By his reckoning, the anticipated publicity from publishing the address might shame government and military officials into a mobilized attack against every type of insensitivity toward blacks. By reacting positively, Secretary of War Henry L. Stimson indicated to Mitchell that his strategy of exposing racism had produced desirable effects; the Cabinet officer promised "suitable remedial action."[45]

Disturbing as prejudicial attitudes and behavior were, Mitchell found even more vicious forms of discrimination. In his opinion, all types of institutional restrictions and limitations did not belong in a democratic society. It was also his judgment that neither race, color, nor religious convictions should advance or hinder Americans. Given his conviction, the Navy became a good target because of its closed opportunities and admitted bigotry. Secretary of the Navy Adolphus Andrews had confessed as much on October 15, 1937: "Experience of many years has demonstrated that men of the negro race, if enlisted in any other branch than that of messman . . . , cannot maintain discipline among men of the white race over whom they may be placed by virtue of their rating." Since evidence had not suggested changes in attitude, Mitchell appealed to Roosevelt to ameliorate the Navy's dismal record. Rather than attempt to tackle every Navy discriminatory policy toward blacks, Mitchell concentrated on a specific frustration. On July 22, 1942, in an attempt to ascertain why the Navy had not been allowing blacks to be physical training instructors,

45. *CR*, 77th Cong., 1st sess., appendix, 3574–75, 9525–26; *CR*, 77th Cong., 2d sess., appendix, 210, 290–91, 607–8, 2790–91, 4298–99; confidential memo from an unnamed civilian aide to Henry L. Stimson and to the Adjutant General, February 9, 1942; M to Stimson, February 14, 1942; Stimson to M, February 23, 1942, MP; *Kansas City Call*, February 27, 1942.

Mitchell directed inquiries to Navy Secretary Frank Knox and FDR. According to the quest, "rank discriminations" had sunk African American morale. As for "protecting the welfare . . . [and] wiping out this terrible discrimination which is retarding the nation in its effort to win this war," Mitchell still had faith in the administration. However, neither Knox nor Roosevelt conceded to anything being wrong with the Navy. Just as with other groups in society, blacks were giving full support to the war effort; for their patriotism, they were obtaining "the same basic training." In effect, then, Knox denied contentions that certain vocational opportunities went exclusively to whites. Contrary to false rumors in circulation, he countered, all placements in the Navy were "entirely open for Negroes." Although the facts contradicted Knox on this point, there were no direct challenges from Mitchell to his overoptimistic conclusions. Nevertheless, many times in the last months of Mitchell's congressional career, there were references to the two-front war being waged by black fighting men. Not only did African American servicemen face Axis enemies at sea and on battlefields, Mitchell contended, but they also were fighting "against those Americans who are trying to keep . . . [the minority] race down." Careful not to disclose who "those Americans" were, Mitchell claimed blacks had been suffering prejudice in "every branch of government, and usually in industry, business and social life." There was much pointing to a "lack of knowledge about Negro history and culture," white self-aggrandizement, and negative "propaganda" from many popular radio programs—such as Amos and Andy—with demeaning caricatures and Hollywood motion pictures that cast stereotyped images. In the twilight of his political career, Mitchell answered the title of his speech "Does White America Know the Negro?" with an emphatic no.[46]

Perhaps at this point, he could have asked Black America if it really knew him. After his first-term accommodation had evolved into clearly temperate militancy and impatience during the remainder of his tenure, everything seemed to reflect a revised attitude. In the spring of 1937 after his silent movement from hesitancy to involvement, Mitchell favored changes to the Harrison-Black Education Bill that would have removed financial discrimination wherever segregated schools were operating. He also supported the NAACP on the Wage and Hour Bill, opposing proposals for regional variations. In neither instance did he assert himself,

46. Andrews to Houston, October 15, 1937, NAACP; M to FDR, July 22, 1942; M to FDR and Frank Knox, July 22, 1942; Randall Jacobs to Harry C. Graves, July 13, 1942; FDR Memo to Knox, July 27, 1942; Knox to FDR, August 1, 1942; FDR to M, August 4, 1942, RP; Knox to M, July 29, 1942; CR reprint, 77th Cong., 2d sess., July 21, MP; San Diego Union, September 12, 1942; UCLA Daily Bruin, September 18, 1942; Waterbury Republican, October 6, 1942; Pittsburgh Courier, December 19, 1942.

but at least he had begun to clarify his stance on racial discrimination. A first hint of where he might stand in the future on bigotry came in a letter to Philip Murray dated January 25, 1937. Asked by the union leader to assist the CIO in Pittsburgh with organizing black steelworkers at a membership meeting, Mitchell declined, citing personal and adamant opposition to their recruitment into "separate organizations from the great body of workers." As Mitchell explained to Murray, such "separation of races inevitably leads to race discrimination." In this instance, there was a complete misunderstanding of Murray's point. Here, the goal was not the segregation of African Americans into separate locals but into the main CIO organization; to reach the goal, Murray thought a special appeal to Mitchell would help.[47]

After developing a policy of disassociating himself as much as possible from movements that promoted or practiced racial segregation, Mitchell ironically gave impetus to the American Negro Exposition of 1940. At first, there were problems securing congressional appropriations for an exhibition, but finally his bill, H.R. 8826, passed, giving Mitchell his first legislative triumph. Even if the sixty-day event staged in 1940 lost money and failed by many hundred thousand to draw the anticipated two million visitors, it still had importance. A first in congressional history, it had developed entirely from the efforts of an African American member. At Mitchell's request, Congress granted seventy-five thousand dollars "to demonstrate to the citizens of America the accomplishments of the Negro." More important, Congress did not strip away the bill's provisions that ensured blacks would prevail over the fair's governing boards. Thus, blacks were responsible for plans and operations. Mitchell and Tuskegee President F. D. Patterson were on the American Negro Exposition Auxiliary, while black Chicagoan Truman K. Gibson managed everything as executive director.[48]

In 1942, Mitchell used the powers at his command to intervene in a Detroit public housing dispute. A large influx of white workers to a key arsenal of democracy were causing major residential shortages near defense plants. Inasmuch as Detroit's situation was not unique, federal

47. Furman L. Templeton to M, March 10, 1937; M to Katye H. Steele, March 24, 1937; WW to M, October 20 and November 24, 1937, and May 18, 1938; Philip Murray to M, January 25, 1937; M to Murray, January 26, 1937; M to Donnelly, December 1, 1937; Samuel E. Spalding to M, May 25, 1937; M to Spalding, May 27, 1937, MP.

48. House and Senate, 76th Cong., 3d sess., H.R. 8826 and S. 3821, March 7 and April 22, 1940, respectively; House and Senate, 76th Cong., 3d sess., Report No. 1979; CR, 76th Cong., 3d sess., appendix, 4275; Chicago Sunday Bee, May 19, 1940; pamphlet, "American Negro Exposition"; FDR to M, June 5, 1940; Barnett to M, March 11 and 19 and August 7, 1940; M to Barnett, March 13, 1940; Gibson to M, August 14, 1940, MP; Gibson and Dickerson interviews.

officials set up the Division of Defense Housing Coordination to locate housing accommodations. Early in its life, a "raw decision" would strike "a great blow to Negro morale" in the Motor City. The Division took two hundred units of newly constructed housing originally designated as the Sojourner Truth Homes by the city and redistributed them to white workers. The decision caused immediate problems because from the beginning, with the city housing authority's first publicity releases about the project, the entire large subdivision had been promised to African Americans. The callous and racist breach, which prioritized whites over Detroit's most poorly housed and overcrowded population group, galvanized the black community into mass mobilization under the Reverend Horace A. White, the only African American on the municipal housing commission. Resultant protests by activists from Michigan chapters of the NNC, locals of the United Automobile Workers, and branches of other activist organizations took form in picketing at the city housing office and appeals to Washington. White appealed to Mitchell to gain Roosevelt's intercession and to offer thoughts on how to proceed to reverse the unfair federal housing decision. Mitchell, angered by the events in Detroit, agreed to attempt to influence key people in Washington. After discussing strategies with White, Mitchell implored Roosevelt to "give the matter serious thought." Meanwhile, following Mitchell's counsel, White laid everything out for presidential secretary and confidant Marvin H. McIntyre. Alerted to the facts of the case, the administration seemingly reacted with panic because just as America had begun unifying behind a full commitment to wage war, a disturbing racial brawl over two hundred apartments in Detroit was threatening to cut into that unity. Endeavoring "to avoid an open fight at this time," McIntyre asked Defense Housing Coordinator Charles F. Palmer to see "if your Advisor on Negro Affairs can do anything to call White off." To fulfill McIntyre's hope of persuading Mitchell "to phone out" to Detroit, frantic attempts were made to reach the black congressman. After several telephone calls without making any contact with Mitchell, McIntyre at last located him in Virginia. With no need to coax, Mitchell gave conditional support to finding a solution to the administration's embarrassment. Since Palmer had initiated demands for a hearing, there was agreement between him and Mitchell that a settlement should originate in Palmer's office. To facilitate the concerned parties, Mitchell arranged a conference for January 29, 1942, attended by a small delegation of black leaders from Michigan and Palmer. By the following day, the Housing Coordinator could boast to McIntyre how one good session had "straightened out" a mess "to the satisfaction of everybody concerned." Palmer was only half correct, though. Due to his backtracking to the original demands of restoring Sojourner Truth to the minority, the settlement only pleased blacks. A month of turbulence and protest by whites attested to their displeasure with Palmer and the return of Sojourner Truth to only African American tenants. In bringing about a complex settlement, Mitchell's contributions as both mediator and counselor should not be undervalued. To Roosevelt, he provided very detailed criticism of an insensibly dumb act, and, vital to cooling off tense residents, he went to White with moderating advice at a moment in the crisis when reasoning with the president could still lead to directives to investigate. Then his behind-the-scenes work with McIntyre and Palmer eventually assembled all parties for a problem-clearing session.[49]

Perhaps the best evidence of Mitchell's maturation and transformation occurred during House debates over a bill to outlaw poll taxes. On October 13, 1942, during one of Mitchell's finest moments on Capitol Hill, he purged leftover remnants of his old self to denounce "many of our Representatives [who] are not in favor of democratic government in our own country." In a hard-hitting speech, there were no partisan references to the GOP or pusillanimous defenses of how well whites in the South were treating blacks. Rather, he spoke of the "demogogic [sic] office seekers" who had been using African Americans' presence to create "a prejudicial condition which has not only meant oppression to the Negro, but has meant bodily harm, fear, and in many cases mob violence and death." Finally unmindful at last of the presidential coalition, Mitchell identified the true culprits as Southern Democrats. "We are here listening to men seriously and almost violently opposing the rights of the Negroes to participate in government . . . when the Negro is wearing the uniform of this government, bleeding and dying, and making every sacrifice . . . that this government might live." A series of West Coast talks delivered in his final month in office climaxed Mitchell's temperate move toward supporting civil rights. One address was particularly noteworthy. Given in December to a racially mixed audience in San Francisco, it completely rebuffed all promises he had made some eight years earlier when he first took office. Now, Mitchell said "scores of men in the United States congress . . . would rather see the axis powers win this war than to grant the Negro his rights as an American citizen." Also noteworthy about the speech, there was no glossing over Southern faults. Mitchell's previous

49. Horace A. White to McIntyre, January 19, 1942; H. A. Wallace to McIntyre, January 16, 1942; M to FDR, January 10, 1942; Baird Snyder III to McIntyre, January 15 and February 20, 1942; McIntyre to M, January 16, 1942; Gloster B. Current to FDR, January 23, 1942; Watson to FDR, January 24, 1942; McIntyre note to FDR, n.d. and Charles F. Palmer, January 19, 1942; Prentiss M. Brown to Watson, January 24, 1942; Watson to Brown, January 26, 1942; Palmer to McIntyre, January 20 and 30, 1942; OEM, Division of Defense Housing Coordination, Policies Regarding Sites for Defense Housing for Negro Occupany, January 28, 1942, RP; M to FDR, February 6, 1942, MP; best for background are Harvard Sitkoff's "The Detroit Race Riot of 1943," 183–206 and August Meier and Elliott Rudwick, *Black Detroit and the Rise of the UAW*, 176–87.

praise for Dixie's understanding whites had turned harshly to criticism. Referring to a mob's recent lynching of two teenage boys in Mississippi, Mitchell considered its brutality "as reprehensible as any crime which has been committed by Nazis or the Japanese."[50]

The fact that Mitchell's farewell tour had taken him west and not south was symbolic in itself. After defeating DePriest in 1934, he had stirred controversy by rushing southward. In many respects, the tour had represented a first-term orientation. Both as a means of calculated survival and as an honest reflection of his deep-seated beliefs about Southern superiority, Mitchell had done and said all in his power to please and appease Dixie politicians. Now, after eight years and a more-or-less unnoticed transition to temperate African American representation, Mitchell fittingly chose the West and not the South to reveal his transformation into a spokesman and champion of racial issues. Unfortunately for his reputation, there had been almost no devotion or attention to promoting his personal metamorphosis. As a consequence, it never occurred to friends or foes alike to reevaluate their earlier opinions and images of him. On the eve of his departure from Congress, of course, there were no pressures on him to satisfy Kelly and Nash in Chicago. Thus, it can be concluded that Mitchell's actions were not especially courageous. Had they come years earlier, late in his first term, for example, there is good reason to think that African Americans would have noticed his challenges to racism.[51]

The circumstances surrounding Mitchell's retirement are ambiguous. Since he was only fifty-nine years old and in good health, neither age nor a physical disability contributed to his departure. With investments and a generous pension guaranteed by congressional service, he had enough financial security to expect a comfortable retirement, and for years he had been longing to live on a country estate. All who knew his goals and aspirations understood this much about him, and they realized money would not affect him one way or the other. In addition, though, murky Chicago decisions had precipitated his departure. Everything had gone wrong after William Dawson—"Chicago's Ballyhoo Man Number One" to Mitchell just days before the ouster of Joe Tittinger—had assumed powers over the Second Ward. Since the new Democratic boss and Mitchell had been exchanging hyperbole like the aforementioned insult only days before Dawson's ascent, there remained such bad blood between them that seemingly neither backtracking nor flattery could ever relieve all their ill feelings for each other. Besides, Dawson and Mitchell possessed similar makeups and were equally ambitious; this meant that neither

50. *CR*, 77th Cong., 2d sess., 8151–52; notes from Mitchell speeches, December 1942, BP.
51. M to William Nunn, November 3, 1942, MP.

could tolerate the other's rivalry. An anonymous tipster had surmised what might happen with these two men in the same political party. Weeks before the November 1940 elections, she had warned Mitchell to "be on your guard with Dawson." In less than one year, her prophesy was fulfilled.[52] Machine bosses, in a decision based on political realism, had decided to dump Mitchell. To Mayor Kelly's embarrassment and in complete defiance of secret orders, Mitchell had not stopped litigation against three Chicago-based railroad corporations. With the next chapter devoted to Mitchell's lawsuit, there is no need to examine it here. But excepting most unusual circumstances, strokes of independence such as Mitchell's lawsuit were not tolerated by the Machine. Dawson had had a hand in the decision to dump Mitchell, too. Playing on speculation about a possible Mitchell-Dickerson showdown in 1942, he had frightened insiders into looking for a successor to Mitchell to avoid such a confrontation. To make matters worse for the inner circle, Dawson was claiming his organization could not deliver a win if popular but refractory Dickerson were a challenger. In essence, then, Dawson, by proclaiming his own personal chances against the undesirable pair of Mitchell and Dickerson as excellent, had quietly pushed himself as the best alternative for the Machine's hold on the First District congressional seat. Yet in doing so, he withheld his role in arousing Dickerson to challenge Mitchell. On May 22, 1941, ready for leaving public life and facing new horizons, Mitchell went peacefully, accepting his inevitable fall and involuntary retirement from Kelly-Nash servitude. He remained silent about the details because of the mayor's promises of new assistance. Thereafter, speculations about Mitchell's future went adrift. There was some talk about him eventually seeking another House seat, whereas his closest associates imagined him being nominated to the federal bench. Forever hopeful, he watched Dawson's defeats of Dickerson in the primary for the party nomination and of William King in the general election for his House seat. Patient and quiet throughout the two elections, Mitchell was apparently waiting for Kelly's "promise." Although never Dawson's friend, Mitchell supported his nemesis, confident of future rewards. Moreover, he found glee in Dickerson's defeat; afterward to the loser, "the most conceited man in the United States," he sent a sarcastic congratulatory telegram.[53]

52. Clayton, *Negro Politician*, 56; a friend to M, October 15, 1940; Frances S. Smith to M, December 18, 1938; M to Smith, December 21, 1938, MP; Tittinger interview; *CR*, 77th Cong., 2d sess., 9649–50.
53. *Defender*, May 24, 1941, and February 7 and April 18, 1942; ANPNR, February 1942; Gibson to Barnett, February 5, 1942; Barnett to Gibson, February 10, 1942, BP; FDR to McIntyre, January 30, 1942; William Henry Huff to FDR, October 15, 1942, RP; Huff to M, October 13, 1942; M to Huff, October 23, 1942; M to EBD, April 15, 1942, MP.

Supreme Court Triumph against Railroad Discrimination

With its necessary uncouplings and couplings completed, train number 45 of the Rock Island Line began moving out of the station at Memphis the morning of April 21, 1937, for its routine Southwest run. A stop at Bluff City for Arthur Mitchell had required luggage transfer from a Pullman carriage bound for New Orleans on the Illinois Central to a first-class coach going to Arkansas and beyond. Soon the locomotive and trailing carriages inched out of Tennessee across the Mississippi River, and in minutes, the train carrying Congressman Mitchell sped through the delta of eastern Arkansas. After the clickety-clack sound of wheels pounding rails had turned rhythmic, a conductor appeared in the Pullman car to punch tickets. Scanning the rows in the first-class coach, he spotted a most unfamiliar sight, a black passenger seated among white riders. Stunned, the conductor moved swiftly forward to confront the offender of Jim Crow's code.[1] Tired from a night's rail travel and exhausted from the demands of a congressional routine that had included both disappointment and compromise over antilynching legislation, Mitchell was on his way to Hot Springs' relaxing waters and was in no mood for trouble. He had paid the extra one-cent-per-mile surcharge to enjoy comfortable first-class travel. Besides, he believed his rank as a member of Congress should entitle him to certain privileges such as relief from the many state statutes that required racial separation on public carriers. Unfortunately for him, though, railroad conductor Albert W. Jones was not interpreting matters this way. Since Arkansas law demanded segregation and provided no exceptions on account of status, Mitchell must retire to another coach—the old smelly one at the

1. *Mitchell v. Frank O. Lowden, James E. Gorman, and Joseph B. Fleming, Chicago, Rock Island and Pacific Railway, Illinois Central Railway Company, Pullman Company,* Docket No. 27844 before the Interstate Commerce Commission [hereafter cited at all lower judicial levels as *M v. Rock Island*]; *Journal and Guide,* May 15, 1937.

train's front reserved for blacks. Mitchell loudly protested, indignantly identifying himself as a congressman and trying to argue his first-class ticket had entitled him to the best section. Thereupon, Jones informed the startled lawmaker that skin pigmentation, not professional status, was what counted. As Jones phrased his ultimatum to Mitchell to move to the Jim Crow car or face arrest, "It don't make a damn bit of difference who you are as long as you are a nigger you can't ride in this car!" Humiliated by the crass order, Mitchell did not utter another word as he moved to the "colored" coach. Indeed, even the coach must have been better than jail under an Arkansas sheriff's watch.[2]

To understand why Mitchell had purchased a first-class ticket when he had obviously known about Southern railroad practices, one must retrace some of his previous demands on transportation companies. After all, he had once come to Washington in 1919 as a Southern black educator with bold advice to Congress to forbid segregation on carriers. Although he had made the recommendation, it would not be until 1935 when he was a congressman himself that he looked seriously at discrimination's effects on his personal travel. Thus, the Rock Island incident followed a two-year struggle to obtain first-class travel privileges. His battle began with an Atlantic Coast Line clerk in Goldsboro, North Carolina. In preparation for a return trip to the capital, Mitchell had tried to purchase a Pullman birth, but the local agent refused to sell him first-class accommodations. Irritated that his congressional status had not exempted him from the Southern caste system on April 27, 1935, Mitchell decided to set the matter of privilege before the railroad. In order to distinguish himself from less famous African Americans, he wanted special identification. General Passenger Agent George P. James complied, presenting Mitchell with an official letter to show and ordering all station masters to "extend to him every consideration and courtesy . . . in the perfection of his trans-portation arrangements when a patron of this railroad." Obviously, it was a breakthrough for Mitchell. Only days earlier, a similar request to the Southern Railroad System had netted different results. According to the Southern department head, Mitchell could not be granted an exemption from segregated travel arrangements because black riders had not com-plained about hardships. Besides, the Southern "could not very well afford to establish a precedent of this kind." At the same time he was attempting to reverse disliked railroad policies, Mitchell sought influence over taxi operators in Washington. On April 24, 1935, he decried the Diamond Cab Company's discriminatory practices. According to his complaint, its

2. *Journal and Guide*, May 15, 1937; ICC, *Initial Brief of Arthur W. Mitchell*, April 18, 1938, 23.

drivers had not been stopping for blacks. Diamond president Harry C. Davis pled for empathy, noting how the fleet had been operating under the Independent Taxi Owners Association's management. According to Davis, only tougher congressional regulations of taxis in the capital could guarantee "perfect service at all times." Given Davis's good explanations and promise to discuss the complaint with the offending driver, Mitchell retreated, satisfied that "things of this kind ought to be handled as peacefully and quietly as possible . . . I have personally seen to it that this matter was given no publicity."[3]

Mitchell's belief in his rights as an interstate traveler aboard the Rock Island in 1937 was backed by a few weak legal precedents to support his stance. The doctrine affirming segregation's full compatibility to equality had been firmly established by the *Plessy* decision in 1896. In the next four decades, the Supreme Court had done almost nothing to guarantee equal facilities. Of the six alleged discrimination-in-transportation cases taken before the Supreme Court, only one, *McCabe v. Atchison, Topeka, & Santa Fe*, had any bearing whatsoever on Mitchell's presence in a first-class coach. With the *McCabe* decision in 1914, the court did bring some clarity to earlier separate-but-equal judgments. Insofar as comforts and facilities, one race could not be denied what another had received. One group's lack of demand for equivalent services was no justification for denying it those services. Theoretically, then, blacks had won the right to travel on sleepers, dining cars, and first-class coaches; railway companies had no legal right to determine for themselves when demanded passenger comforts constituted unjustifiable financial burdens.[4]

If a court were to evaluate the Rock Island Line's practices in strict accordance to the instructions of *McCabe*, it would be forced to find that the railway company had patently abridged Mitchell's rights as an interstate passenger. Unresolved, however, was whether the Supreme Court in 1914 had actually meant for carriers to supply coaches whenever blacks demanded first-class service, or whether it had simply wished to show the impractical nature of segregation from a constitutional perspective.

3. *Wilmington Star*, November 11, 1898; *Afro-American*, June 12, 1937; *Journal and Guide*, May 21, 1938; M to General Passenger Agent, Atlantic Coast Line Railroad, July 9, 1935; George P. James to M, July 15 and August 3, 1935; M to General Passenger Agent, Southern Railway Company, July 2, 1935; Frank L. Jenkins to M, July 3 and 17, 1935; M to Jenkins, July 9 and 15, 1935; M to Diamond Cab Company, April 24, 1935; Harry C. Davis to M, April 27, 1935; M to Davis, April 30, 1935, MP.

4. Sarah M. Lemmon, "Transportation Segregation in the Federal Courts since 1865," 179–80; Raymond Pace Alexander, "The Upgrading of the Negro's Status by Supreme Court Decisions," 139–40; ICC, *Annual Reports*, 1887–1943; *Tariff World*, May 22, 1926; Robert G. Dixon Jr., "Civil Rights in Transportation and the ICC," 199–206.

Regardless, *McCabe* had clearly had little effect on the Department of Justice or the Interstate Commerce Commission; neither had ever shown any inclination to enforce separate-but-equal accommodations on railroads. Hence, Southern carriers maintained a color line, and they consistently reserved their most inferior equipment for blacks. In general, "colored" on coaches had become associated with cars where passengers sweltered in summer and froze in winter, and where dirt, wear, and putrid smells overwhelmed; seldom did blacks receive first-class facilities upon demand. On those infrequent occasions when blacks had obtained births and drawing rooms, only supply-and-demand and the whims and fancies of local station masters had been factors. Consequently, Mitchell had much to prove.[5]

When Mitchell was forced by Conductor Jones to leave his first-class accommodations for a seat on the colored car, it should become clear why he considered it an insult. As Mitchell sat amidst filth, there was scowling and brooding over intolerable conditions. That he, a congressman, could be forced from the comfort and luxuries of a Pullman parlor car by some surly conductor irked him so much that he would not allow the matter to pass without a challenge. Mitchell's legal practice and experience might have been limited, but he knew when somebody had denied him his legal rights. On the way to Hot Springs, he promised himself that he would go over the constitutional implications later with Attorney Richard E. Westbrooks of Chicago. Perhaps, just one productive meeting with Westbrooks would yield the basis for a proper cash settlement. After all, Mitchell supposedly pondered, Jones had affronted his personal honor as well as the dignity associated with an esteemed public office.[6]

Two invigorating weeks at Hot Springs' Pythian Hotel and Baths restored Mitchell's vitality. In body and spirit, he was ready for battle. After a fortnight's fishing, boating, hiking, and mineral bathing at a lodge catering especially to members and friends of an African American fraternal order, he returned to Illinois, knowing consultations must occur soon if legal actions were to begin against the Rock Island Railroad. Although Mitchell never gave any reasons for choosing Westbrooks, it seems obvious that Westbrooks was a trusted ally who would advise expertly without extracting too much in return. Westbrooks's modestly successful criminal and civil practice coupled with service as the Liberian consul general had gained him a modicum of respect from black members of the bar. However, it would have taken more than courtroom skill to draw

5. *New York Times,* May 16, 1937; Anne O. Bennof to author, May 7, 1979; Raymond Pace Alexander, "Recent Trends in the Law of Racial Segregation on Public Carriers," 401–7; Dixon, "Civil Rights in Transportation," 198–204.

6. Mitchell interview.

Mitchell to Westbrooks. Westbrooks must have understood Mitchell's ego rather well, for he seemingly was always prepared to allow his special client to dominate their relationship. Those who knew both Mitchell and Westbrooks commonly believed that the key to peaceful relations with Mitchell was for other African Americans to humble themselves before him, and that this is how Westbrooks appealed to Mitchell. Altogether too many acquaintances had been able to observe Mitchell in action to dismiss their common assessment as speculation. In all probability, the same factors explain why Mitchell could not go to the NAACP with a legal problem that involved civil rights. He simply had no desire to risk what was considered his great chance for glory and reputation. Far more secure in Westbrooks's company, Mitchell had in all likelihood conferred freely about his humiliating morning on the Rock Island, knowing his descriptions of the train trip's unpleasantries would remain his to exploit. After listening to Mitchell, Westbrooks advised that there were grounds to sue because the carrier had breached a contract to provide a specific service.[7]

Preparations for a major lawsuit began immediately. Westbrooks diligently searched Arkansas statutes for legal references, and he consulted both state and federal court proceedings to discover judicial interpretations and precedents. Arkansas law had required Jones to order Mitchell from the train's only first-class Pullman coach car. There were specifications stating racial separation on public carriers must be maintained. However, the clause represented only half of the statute; Westbrooks also found that it guaranteed equality. For the purposes at hand, Arkansas court records yielded nothing of value; state justices had ruled on separation, but they had never defined the meaning of the separate-but-equal provisions in state statutes. Conversely, a search through federal cases brought Westbrooks to *McCabe* and opinions about wrongfully abridging personal entitlement to all accommodations. A fifty-thousand-dollar personal damage lawsuit based solely upon the principles stated in *McCabe* was filed against the Rock Island, Illinois Central, and Pullman companies on May 10, 1937, at the Federal Circuit Court in Chicago. Westbrooks took the suit there because Mitchell had bought his tickets and had begun his journey in the Windy City. As an accompanying action of a civil proceeding on his client's behalf, Westbrooks appealed to the Interstate Commerce Commission for a hearing. Since neither he nor Mitchell had ever been before the regulatory body as practicing attorneys, both needed

7. Ibid.; *East Tennessee News*, May 20, 1937; interviews with all black Chicagoans listed in the bibliography, but especially those with Gibson, Dickerson, Motts, Brown, Cyrus, and Lawrence because they knew both men.

certification. With their completion of this preliminary in early June, they were prepared for the greatest legal battle of their lives.[8]

The black press gave front-page coverage to Mitchell's lawsuit, and he quickly went from coward to hero. Many newspapers detailed his forcible ejection from the first-class car, and to illustrate his experience, they repeated Conductor Jones's vile language to "their" congressman. Moreover, several articles explained how the episode had embarrassed Mitchell and affected his health. More important for Mitchell than what newspapers were reporting was the lawsuit's overall effect on his sagging image; the news coverage elevated him to new pinnacles of personal popularity. A number of hostile weeklies even reversed their positions on him. Suddenly in their editorials, Mitchell emerged as a paladin of honor and pride. Now among black journalists, there was a consensus of favorable opinion directed at Mitchell; he had acted bravely, beginning favorably the long process of personal redemption. Most black followers of early proceedings in the case seemed to agree, and they praised Mitchell for his lawsuit on behalf of African Americans. After a flood of supportive mail reached him following the announcement of his lawsuit, Mitchell began responding with form letters that included both gratitude and confident predictions of success. If necessary, he would engage the culpable railroads on appeal all the way to the Supreme Court, he wrote. To assist him in the struggle, there were calls on his many well-wishers "to speak out in unmistakable terms on this Jim Crow business" and for conventions to boycott those states that could not guarantee all blacks equal travel accommodations. As he described this attitude for one minister, "It strikes me that the leading Negroes have pussy-footed on this question long enough."[9]

To establish cause based upon precedent and to lay some bases for damages, Mitchell's complaint filed at the Cook County Circuit Court contained several specific allegations. According to the brief, Jones's tone and language, coupled with his threats, had weakened Mitchell's health. A substantial increase in his already high blood pressure required expensive medical treatment and additional rest. Besides subsequent health problems, there was the matter of legality. According to the plaintiff, Jones's ouster order had not followed the law as expressed in *McCabe*. The justices had been very clear about this; since there was a first-class ticket,

---

8. Westbrooks to M, May 23, 1937; ICC Applications, June 2, 1937; typed copy, Arkansas Separate Car Law; reviews, Arkansas court cases involved with same, MP.

9. *New York Times*, May 11, 1937; *Atlantic City Eagle*, May 14, 1937; *Defender, Atlanta World, Pittsburgh Courier, Afro-American, Denver Colorado Statesman*, May 15, 1937; *Chicago Sunday Bee*, May 16, 1937; *Louisville Leader*, May 22, 1937; James D. Pouncey to M, April 30, 1937; Ulysses S. Keys to M, May 11, 1937; Patrick B. Prescott Jr. to M, May 17, 1937; Z. Dallas Hicks to M, May 27, 1937; M to Prescott, May 21, 1937; M to R. L. Gray et al., May 12, 1937; M to the Reverend C. E. Chapman, May 22, 1937, MP.

the conductor was under judicial obligation to place Mitchell on another Pullman car. In a legal sense, the ticket in the passenger's possession was similar to a contract. By its terms, the holder was fully entitled to every specified service. Beyond Jones's denials and intervention, the ticket had given the rider rightful possession to placement in Pullman-standard accommodations. The litigation strategy was very simple. Since the Constitution demanded equality, Mitchell and Westbrooks sought to establish beyond all doubt the distinct differences between first-class and colored-car travel. Once there was agreement to this, proving how the carrier had trampled on Mitchell's rights would follow. Despite Mitchell's possession of a first-class ticket, the conductor had forced him to retire to an inferior second-class coach. Thus Mitchell's suit did not attack segregation per se, but rather it tested to determine if all carriers were under any obligation to supply equal services to riders upon demand. Insofar as blacks and civil rights, its objective was limited to gaining judicial reassertion of the unconstitutionality of offering unequal accommodations based upon race. Besides seeking a proof of principles, Mitchell sought some monetary redress for the humiliation and stress he had suffered from Jones's ouster.[10]

For the court's evaluation, Westbrooks used Mitchell's vivid description of his train ride through Arkansas. Mitchell's testimony drew a poignant contrast between the well-appointed Pullman coach's fine accommodations and the colored car's sparsity. For passenger comfort, the first-class carriage featured sinkbasins complete with running water, soap, and towels, as well as writing desks filled with stationery. There were magazines to read, and riders had porters at their command. Furthermore, the luxurious coach was divided so as to offer many compartments, berths, and drawing, smoking, and lounging rooms, as well as an observatory deck; meals were served privately in coupés and publicly in the dining car. For an extra penny per mile, whites choosing the Rock Island's best service received comfortable seating aboard spacious, clean, bright vehicles with good ventilation and air conditioning. Nothing similar existed for blacks. According to Mitchell's written testimony, none of the amenities of the first-class coach had been found in the colored-only section. The colored coach consisted of separate areas to accommodate baggage, black passengers, and the train's crew. Compounding its congestion, the small area was unpleasant. Mitchell remembered vividly how the space assigned blacks had seemed "poorly ventilated, filthy, filled with stench and odors eminating from the toilet and other filth, which is indescribable." Such disparity surely constituted "wilful, wanton, malicious, arbitrary, and intentional" wrongdoing.[11]

10. *Mitchell v. Rock Island*, Circuit Court No. 37-C-5529, May 10, 1937.
11. Ibid.

The defendants filed separately in answer to Mitchell's charges and lawsuit. The Chicago, Rock Island and Pacific Railway Company was in court receivership, but two corporate attorneys represented its trustees. In their initial response of June 5, 1937, or twenty-six days after Mitchell's complaint, they registered a feeble defense. Although their argument rested on the constitutionality of the Arkansas Jim Crow law, the railroad lawyers in essence challenged everything about the lawsuit's main contentions. Claiming Mitchell's assertions were inconsistent with the facts, the defense counselors filled their defense with rebuttals and denials. There was also a categoric rejection of Mitchell's argument that possession of a ticket was tantamount to entitlement to Pullman accommodations. The attorneys also asked Mitchell to produce hard medical evidence linking his Rock Island experience to subsequent health problems. Furthermore, they called on him to prove Jones's mistreatment, and they scoffed at his charges of putrid smells and filth. In sum, there had been no denigration or humiliation; Mitchell had experienced "the equal comforts, pleasures, privileges and safety afforded or enjoyed by other first-class passengers who had paid the same fare and price as the plaintiff." In other words, the Rock Island had allowed no discriminatory practices against its passengers, and therefore, just as every rider before him, Mitchell simply had not suffered "any undue or unreasonable prejudice or disadvantage as the result of any conduct of these defendants." As for the issue of segregated intrastate passenger travel, the defense attorneys reminded the court that the State of Arkansas, not the railroad company, was responsible for enacting the laws and setting the rules. According to the state's Separate Coach Law, certain prohibitions governed passenger seating, and the railroads had a legal responsibility to separate whites and anyone with "a visible and distinct admixture of African blood" during a train's operation in Arkansas. In addition, countered the defense, if railroad employees failed to segregate riders by race, the state could fine them for noncompliance. Therefore, the Pullman car had definitely been off limits for Mitchell. Since its other occupants had been scattered in private drawing rooms and compartments, Jones's only legal recourse had been to order Mitchell to leave. The Rock Island did concede to Mitchell on one point, however. Since he could not occupy a Pullman seat, he should not have been charged for a first-class fare. Consequently, the railroad offered to refund him $3.74, or the difference between what the plaintiff had paid for transportation from Memphis to Hot Springs and the proper amount for a day-coach passenger's second-class journey.[12]

12. Ibid., Boe and Taylor of June 5, 1937.

During the following week, the Illinois Central Railroad Company rebutted Mitchell's charges. Illinois Central's attorneys claimed the company was not accountable for what transpired between Memphis and Hot Springs on another carrier. The IC had only sold Mitchell first-class service as far as Memphis; thereby, it had fulfilled its obligation. After Mitchell's Pullman car was uncoupled in Tennessee, another railroad had taken over the responsibility for his travels, the attorneys argued. From that moment on, the Illinois Central had neither owned nor operated the train and had not employed its crew. Hence, argued the defense counsel, Illinois Central sought exclusion from the litigation. Just for the record, though, there were disputations of the suit's many allegations. Particularly, IC attorneys wanted to examine Mitchell's medical proof. They also expressed doubts about his possession of a round-trip first-class ticket from Chicago to Hot Springs when Jones had allegedly confronted him. For this second leg of the journey, Memphis to Hot Springs, the defense doubted Mitchell's claims of having paid an extra fare to reserve a Pullman compartment.[13]

After Westbrooks had filed a civil lawsuit with the Circuit Court, he and Mitchell prepared a parallel suit of high value. In the first action, Mitchell and Westbrooks were after monetary damages for injuries suffered. But before an Interstate Commerce Commission hearing, Mitchell sought to determine the legality of forcing blacks to day coaches when they possessed Pullman tickets. In addition, there was a simultaneous demand on railroads to provide standard services to all passengers, race notwithstanding. Filing on September 2, 1937, Westbrooks submitted Mitchell's complaints and demands to an ICC examiner. In scope and definition, the requests placed before the ICC commissioners set new precedents. Never in the ICC's fifty-four-year existence had anybody asked its regulators to resolve this many social and minority issues at once.[14]

Meanwhile the lawsuit seemingly had placed some pressure on the Rock Island. A first indication of the litigation's importance had occurred with the railroad's assignment of two lawyers to the case. Later, in August on its now infamous Hot Springs–Memphis run, it replaced all old and battered Jim Crow cars with modern streamlined coaches equipped with running water, air conditioning, flush toilets, and comfortable seats. Nobody at the Rock Island would say whether the company had planned the installations before or after the legal suit. Nevertheless, just the sight of these cars for black travelers seemed a tacit admission that the company

13. Ibid., John W. Freels and Herbert J. Deany, IC Answer, June 14, 1937.
14. *Railway Age*, September 4, 1937; Answer of Defendant, the Pullman Company, *Mitchell v. Frank O. Lowden et al.*, September 22, 1937; ICC, *Annual Reports*, 1914–1937.

had not offered Mitchell separate-but-equal treatment during his contested trip.[15]

On November 3, 1937, the ICC notified all parties that a hearing before Examiner William A. Disque was scheduled for December 10, 1937, in Chicago. Since the hearing would require much preparation by Mitchell and Westbrooks, the two decided that the five weeks provided to assemble facts, contact individuals for eventual testimonies, and organize a case were inadequate. After asking, they won a necessary postponement; Disque reset the ICC hearing for March 7, 1938.[16] Throughout the preparation period, Mitchell found that unwanted advice was easier to obtain than sworn testimonies from individuals familiar with the Rock Island's operations in Dixie. Scipio Jones was one lawyer who agreed to help with some prehearing preparations. Since he lived in Little Rock, it became Jones's assignment to gather testimony on the nature of Jim Crow coaches in service before April 22, 1937, on the Memphis-Hot Springs run and to support the testimony with photographs. Anticipating a groundswell of enthusiasm from African Americans distressed over decades of discriminatory rail practices, Jones encountered much resistance instead. To his astonishment and Mitchell's irritation, African Americans were more than "a little timid" about cooperating. Photographers refused to venture into railroad yards with their cameras, and sworn affidavits were equally difficult to obtain. Fears of reprisal were so great that Jones finally advised that testimonies would have to be gathered outside the state from former Arkansas residents and others familiar with travel there.[17]

In the midst of Disque's extension, Congress reopened after a holiday recess. While waiting for the ICC hearing in March, Mitchell was entrusting most of the work of preparing for it to Westbrooks. Meanwhile, he was on Capitol Hill, introducing a largely symbolic bill for legislative consideration. Though the bill had no chance of passage, it encouraged many civil rights advocates because in it Mitchell had proposed to terminate de jure racial segregation in interstate transportation. Even if banning segregation "ought to become a law promptly," as a *Cleveland Gazette* editorial writer recommended, the same writer was correct to note that the bill "doubtless would [become law] if it were not for the southern Democratic 'Cracker' majority in both Houses of The Congress." W. Robert Ming Jr., an attorney

---

15. Westbrooks to SJ, September 18, 1937, MP; *Defender,* September 18, 1937.

16. W. P. Bartel to M, November 3 and December 6, 1937, and January 14, 1938; M to ICC, November 3, 1937, MP; *Railway Age,* November 6 and December 11, 1937.

17. Westbrooks to SJ, September 18, 1937; SJ to Westbrooks, September 23, 1937; M to SJ, October 17, 1937; SJ to M, November 6, 1937, MP. Difficulties enlisting help hindered the NAACP during its legal campaigns to erase Southern discrimination, too; see Mark V. Tushnet's *The NAACP's Legal Strategy against Segregated Education, 1925–1950.*

from Chicago who specialized in civil rights law, hailed the bill's general objectives and praised its constitutionality, but he judged it to be too vague. In Ming's opinion, it needed amendments to eradicate ambiguities and provide for civil and criminal liability.[18]

Finally, on March 7, 1938, Mitchell and Westbrooks met the railroad defense attorneys for the first time. More than just a black-white contest before ICC Examiner William A. Disque, the hearing was a spectacle pitting Bronzeville against LaSalle Street, "jitney" practitioners against establishment lawyers. On hand to champion the railroads were corporate barristers sharpened by years of specialty work and multiple appearances before ICC hearings; there to offer complaint were two advocates relegated by prejudice's yoke to criminal, civil, and domestic cases involving a downtrodden minority's unnoticed legal squabbles. The hearing was unique in one more respect; for first-time use in preparing stenographic minutes, phonograph discs recorded everything. There are, therefore, accurate transcripts of the transpirings. After calling the hearing to order, Disque asked Westbrooks to proceed. Thereupon, Mitchell's attorney complained of just having received a copy of Pullman's answer; having the complaint admitted into the record got Westbrooks off to a good start. Then with most unexpected verve, he charged into the Rock Island trustees, accusing them of violating revised ICC rules and motioning to have their disposition deleted from the record. What the defense had not done was "admit or deny specifically and in detail each material allegation of the pleading answered." Before concluding a stunning introduction and calling in the first witness, Westbrooks appeared to astonish Disque by noting another ignored ICC provision: "An answer denying that an alleged discrimination is unjust . . . should state fully the grounds relied upon in making such denial." With his splendid beginning, Westbrooks not only surprised everyone present with his opening salvos and his command of law and legal procedure but also accomplished several other feats. First, he placed both Disque and the corporate lawyers on notice that the case was serious and that he understood how to proceed. Second, by citing the defense's slovenliness and procedural errors, he had established some bases for appeals to the judiciary. Clearly, by his obvious conversance in ICC rules governing complaints and answers, Westbrooks had carried round one, placing the railroads on guard.[19]

18. 75th Cong., 3d sess., House of Representatives, H.R. 8821, January 5, 1938; *Daily Worker*, January 6, 1938; *Argus*, January 14, 1938; *Washington Capitol Daily*, January 6, 1938; *Philadelphia Tribune*, January 13, 1938; *Louisville Leader*, January 15, 1938; *Cleveland Gazette*, January 15, 1938; W. Robert Ming Jr. memo, March 1941, NAACP.

19. ICC, Stenographers' Minutes of Docket No. 27844, March 7, 1938; *Railway Age*, July 9, 1938; *Defender*, March 5 and 12, 1938.

Mitchell was the first of several witnesses called by Richard Westbrooks. Mitchell tediously retraced the entire ordeal of his journey to Hot Springs. During his well-coached testimony contrasting first-class luxury to day-coach squalor and sparsity, Mitchell did not miss any details. Following him to the witness stand were five prominent Bronzevillians. Each claimed to have had a familiarity with Rock Island passenger service in the South. Before residing in Chicago, they all had lived in either Arkansas or Oklahoma. As a result, they had ridden the carrier's Jim Crow coaches, and their testimonies corroborated the lead witness about the presence of filth, odors, and smoke on Rock Island's colored-only cars. By introducing these men and bringing forth their testimony, Westbrooks fortified Mitchell's contentions about the stark inequalities of colored coach travel. The testimony included an eyewitness account of chained prisoners in transit having been placed alongside black passengers, and another account of how "drunken men of the white race [were] being brought out of the car used by white passengers into the Jim Crow car where colored ladies were riding, and the drunken men would heave all over the seats." One witness remembered a colored car that was "dirty with peanuts and tobacco juice all over it" and "covered with railroad dust from the engine."

The defense relied little upon cross-examination; its strategy clearly rested upon Conductor Jones's testimony and on the constitutionality of the Arkansas Jim Crow law. Railroad lawyers spared Mitchell and three of his witnesses from interrogation. The two witnesses who were questioned did not endure probing cross-examinations. At the hearing, Albert W. Jones was the only person who experienced intensive grilling. He was on the witness stand for two-fifths of the entire deliberation, suffering through Westbrooks's thorough round of cross-examination. Arrogant and unflappable throughout his ordeal, Jones used many condescending phrases like "very gentlemanly" to describe Mitchell's reaction to instructions to vacate the first-class parlor car. There was pride in the conductor's testimony, especially when he noted that no black had ever received first-class seating during his thirty-two years of service to the railroad. Yet, his unabashed racism and braggadocio made Jones a weak defense witness. Seizing upon these attributes, Westbrooks was able to wring many valuable admissions from the uncoached railroad employee. During one exchange, Jones inadvertently blurted out his agreement with all of Mitchell's major contentions about unfair treatment. Among the admissions, Jones confessed to a double standard of selling first-class spaces to whites but not to blacks. Jones also freely distinguished between the day coach service available for African Americans and the first-class accommodations. Candidly, he branded the two "not equal." By not pausing to consider the consequences before answering honestly, the blunt railroader worked against the defense and supported Mitchell's claims. In addition, there were no refutations from two other company witnesses. Both were veterans on the Rock Island; one employee was a brakeman, and the other was a mechanical foreman. Under Westbrooks's cross-examination, they also freely admitted to travel inequities. According to their statements, colored-only coaches did not match Pullman accommodations.

Had Disque followed *McCabe,* both the testimony and the evidence presented dictated a pro-Mitchell settlement. Simply stated, the railroad had not given or maintained separate-but-equal facilities. Since every witness had substantiated this, any fair verdict would surely have entitled Mitchell to redress. After a final witness had concluded his testimony and Disque had adjourned the session, it would have been reasonable enough to expect favorable recommendations from Disque to the ICC. Westbrooks had advanced the case perfectly; he had found several flaws in the proceeding, and he had wrested confessions of inequities from every defense witness. Still, on May 4, 1938, Disque proposed a dismissal of Mitchell's complaint. Neither wrongdoing nor unfairness had affected Disque's decision. Rather, he had drawn from practicality and financial accountability. As the examiner phrased it, "comparatively little colored traffic" could not "warrant the running of any extra cars. Only differences in treatment that are unjust or undue are unlawful and within the power of this commission to condemn, remove and prevent." Disque did not dispute Mitchell's possession of a first-class ticket, but he found nothing wrong with ousting its holder from a Pullman coach to an inferior accommodation. In a strange ruling, profits had supplanted judicial process and precedent. Since the railroads had complained that separate-but-equal service would drain corporate treasuries, there was full consent to separate-but-unequal service. Apparently, Disque had never considered a better cost-cutting solution; his findings altogether ignored integration as a possible solution.[20]

Mitchell and Westbrooks categorically rejected Disque's conclusions and challenged the examiner's ruling. According to ICC rules, all parties in disagreement with an examiner's findings had twenty days to file their formal protests. By submitting a thirty-two-page rebuttal on May 27, 1938, Westbrooks and Mitchell just beat the filing deadline. Altogether, the two lawyers had found eight glaring faults with Disque's evaluations. Relying upon a 1907 conclusion from *Edwards v. Nashville, Chattanooga & St. Louis Railway Company,* the separate-but-equal ruling in *McCabe,* and Albert W. Jones's testimony, Mitchell and Westbrooks challenged

20. ICC, Stenographers' Minutes of Docket No. 27844, March 7, 1938; *Railway Age,* May 7 and 14 and July 9, 1938; *Defender,* March 5 and 12, 1938; *Washington Post,* May 5, 1938.

the main assertions in Disque's ruling. Restating how the Rock Island had "flagrantly violated" ICC rules with improper answers to their contentions, they forcefully denied that they would accept segregation—even for a lawsuit—as the examiner had maintained. Presumably, Disque had missed the assertions about Arkansas' "abominable, unjust, and un-American" statute. Mitchell and Westbrooks had been ignoring its validity altogether because interstate circumstances had been the basis of their suit. According to a major premise from Judge Charles Evans Hughes in *McCabe*, states could never claim any jurisdiction in cases where passengers had crossed state lines. Since there had been an unbroken trip from Chicago to Hot Springs, it was not necessary to contest a "diabolical" law's constitutionality. From Mitchell's and Westbrooks's perspective, Disque's advice to reject an important right was incorrect: "Every American citizen financially able to travel first-class" should be able "to pay for first-class transportation and receive first-class accommodations and facilities throughout his journey." The suit did not attempt to specify how the railroads might supply separate-but-equal first-class accommodations for black passengers—whether railroads should satisfy the demands by desegregating, partitioning, or adding coaches. The suit's only stipulation was for *McCabe*'s reaffirmation because it would erase volume as an excuse to discriminate in interstate passenger travel.[21]

Mitchell's exceptions extended the case. All oral arguments had to be repeated before an ICC quorum. Adhering to standard procedures, the federal regulatory body set July 6, 1938, as the date to rehear summations. On hand to listen to pleas from both sides were eight commissioners. Wallace T. Hughes represented the Rock Island, and Mitchell retained Westbrooks. Protocol demanded defense and plaintiff presentations and allowed impromptu interruptions for commissioners' comments and questions. Mitchell led off the proceedings with another succinct recounting of his misfortunes aboard the Rock Island train bound for Hot Springs. On a couple of points, commissioners stopped him for clarifications. There were no deviations during a second round of testimony, however; Mitchell kept to his original story and strategy. By plan, everything moved to a pithy summation question for the ICC: "A colored man who buys a first-class ticket . . . traveling interstate, because he happens to enter a state where there is segregation, can the conductor and can that state, or the laws of that state rob this man of the right which he has acquired under the constitution?"[22]

21. Exception on behalf of plaintiff to report proposed by William S. Disque, Examiner, May 24, 1938, ICC Docket No. 27844.
22. ICC, Stenographers' Minutes, Docket No. 27844, July 6, 1938, MP; *Railway Age*, June 18 and July 19, 1938; *Defender*, June 4 and July 16, 1938.

Wallace Hughes followed Mitchell. Now well briefed and better prepared than he had been before William Disque, the LaSalle Street lawyer
no longer appeared nonchalant and overconfident. Earlier, his judicial
arguments had been devoid of forethought and logic, and Westbrooks had
completely overshadowed his listless performance. Markedly different
this time, he was primed for legal confrontation. His opening was an
impassioned critique of the claim to first-class accommodations. A three-
cent-per-mile ticket, Hughes lectured, was "not a contract whereby a
railroad undertakes to guarantee . . . a pullman accommodation. You may
buy here in Washington a first-class ticket and unless there is a pullman
accommodation available that ticket does not guarantee any more than it
could guarantee Congressman Mitchell." Mitchell's negligence had com-
plicated everything; before journeying to Arkansas, he had not bothered
to book a Pullman seat. Therefore, Hughes explained, the Rock Island
could not be liable or responsible for the consequences of his carelessness.
After blaming Mitchell for not obtaining first-class reservations, Hughes
turned to Arkansas law, characterizing its Jim Crow statute as a "police
regulation" and "not a regulation of commerce." To support the legal
definition, Hughes cited two cases involving interstate travel and arrests
under state segregation laws. In both, state supreme courts had used the
Tenth Amendment reserved-power clause to uphold convictions.[23]

Westbrooks testified last; he concentrated on the suit's primary premise.
Mitchell's possession of a first-class ticket had entitled him to Pullman-
coach service; intrastate commerce, passenger volume, state police powers, and segregation had no bearing whatsoever. To illustrate what was
involved, Westbrooks drew an analogy between his client's situation and
that of a produce shipper who had not been given refrigeration after
paying for it. Why would not the same principle apply in both circumstances, he asked. In both cases, victims had paid for services, and carriers
had not provided them. Next, Westbrooks broke down systematically
the contention of Hughes that inadequate black demands for first-class
seating could not justify costly special services. Westbrooks questioned if
laws had ever required plaintiffs to "prove how many . . . were denied"
as a prelude to their validity. According to high court opinion, Westbrooks
added, "it is the individual who is entitled to the equal protection of
the law."[24]

Westbrooks's plea completed the formal hearing. Now the work of
sifting through conflicting testimonies to reach an equitable verdict rested
with the ICC. Both the Fourteenth Amendment and *McCabe* favored

23. ICC, Stenographers' Minutes, Docket No. 27844, July 6, 1938, MP.
24. Ibid.

Mitchell, but a legacy of noninterference in Southern states' rights was favoring the Rock Island. Heretofore, legal questions with sociological implications had never interested the ICC; in fact, more than thirty years had elapsed since its last action on a civil rights appeal. Yet in the Mitchell case, it had a charge to determine if a black passenger's rights to first-class seating on an interstate carrier should outweigh regional Jim Crow traditions and a railroad's pursuit of profits. More than five months passed before the ICC announced its decision. On November 25, 1938, following William Disque's example, a majority of the commission favored an outright dismissal of Mitchell's complaint. A conservative group, the ICC members found insufficient grounds to enforce better services for blacks on carriers, and they continued viewing passenger segregation as a policing matter "for State authorities." In their report, matching demand to accommodations took precedence over other concerns. Apparently, they had dismissed as irrelevant all associations between injustice and allocation of first-class facilities by race. Blacks' lower demand for dining, parlor, and observation coaches had been reason enough not to warrant partitions or extra cars. Following Disque's example, they had not even given consideration to recommending desegregation. Dissenters on the commission were divided. Two commissioners supported the plaintiff: "when the railroad refused complainant Pullman accommodations and required him to ride in the coach provided for colored passengers, it violated the act in failing to furnish him substantially similar accommodations to those furnished white people willing, as he was, to pay therefor." There were also two compromise opinions between the majority and the pro-Mitchell faction. One foresaw practical difficulties from enforcing equal accommodations for blacks, but held that nevertheless, the railroads should provide Pullman spaces and meal service to everyone. The other commissioner conceded "unjust discrimination" and "undue prejudice" had occurred, but he was so satisfied with the recent inaugurations of modern coaches for black passengers' comfort between Memphis and Hot Springs that, in his opinion, every reason to punish the Rock Island had disappeared.[25]

Black reactions to the ICC's dismissal were predictable. Stunned by it, Mitchell asked for a rehearing to restate his case because a majority on the ICC had "obviously" overlooked important court decisions as well as the wording of several statutes. Later on Capitol Hill, he reintroduced his bill outlawing the segregation of interstate passengers. Overall, his double onslaught—protests to reporters and legislation in Congress— was winning him African American acceptance. The *Cleveland Gazette*'s

---

25. *Railway Age*, December 3, 1938; *Washington Evening Star*, November 25, 1938.

reaction was typical. With poignancy, the black weekly's editor accused commissioners of malfeasance for not recognizing Mitchell as an American citizen "entitled to such protection and treatment, under the laws of the country, which the ICC was created to enforce." Responses from most blacks were similar. Heeding the advice from President Harry H. Pace of Supreme Liberty Life Insurance Company and its other influential officers, the National Negro Insurance Association announced a membership boycott on January 14, 1939. Delegates planning travel in six months to Los Angeles for the annual convention were urged to shun the Rock Island because of its support of discrimination. There was another form of black response. Claude A. Barnett was uncertain of Mitchell's abilities to handle an important case. For an expert's assessment of the situation, the news bureau chief turned to Charles H. Houston of the NAACP. Specifically, Barnett sought the professor's candid impressions of Westbrooks's credentials, explanations of the National Bar Association's position, and thoughts on the prospects of Mitchell succeeding against the railroads. Although Houston expressed "complete faith in Mr. Westbrooks' ability, energy, and courage," still, he was worried about Westbrooks going alone without NBA participation. As for a final outcome from Mitchell's suit, Houston excused himself, pleading that he had not studied case records and briefs. Despite Houston's professed unfamiliarity with the issues, the NAACP was among many organizations offering assistance to the plaintiff. After the ICC dismissal, Secretary Walter White promised "whatever help the NAACP can give in ending this nefarious practice" of segregating Americans.[26]

The dismissal of Mitchell's lawsuit produced notable side effects. Before the suit, the composition of the ICC had not worried leaders of the civil rights establishment. Now after the stand against Mitchell, it mattered; scrutinizing candidate credentials suddenly became important. With Roosevelt's appointment of J. Haden Allredge to the Commission in early 1939, fellow Alabaman and NAACP activist J. L. LeFlore of the Mobile branch investigated, asking Allredge: What are your "attitude[s] toward the matter of equal travel accommodations for white and colored alike, and . . . Section 3, subsection 1, of the Interstate Commerce Act, . . .

---

26. ICC, Petition of Arthur W. Mitchell, Complainant, for Rehearing and Reargument, January 21, 1939; ICC, Reply of same to Answers given by Frank O. Lowden et al., February 9, 1939; Miller Press Statement of December 8, 1938, "Congressman Mitchell Turned Down by the Interstate Commerce Commission"; Townes to All Members of the National Negro Insurance Association, January 14, 1939; WW to M, January 13, 1939; LeFlore to M, February 11, 1939, MP; *Cleveland Gazette,* December 10, 1938; *Railway Age,* February 4, 1939; *Defender,* January 14, 1939; *Daily Worker,* March 16, 1939; *Chicago Sunday Bee,* December 15, 1940; Barnett-Houston exchange, December 6 and 9, 1938, BP.

dealing with . . . discrimination?" Begging Roosevelt to "consider only persons of unquestionable fairness, devoid of race prejudice," LeFlore set these as minimum qualifications.[27]

Unsuccessful at obtaining ICC reconsideration, Mitchell went to federal district court on April 19, 1939, with an appeal for a hearing. On the grounds of arbitrary and erroneous constructions of law and the misapprehensions of ICC regulatory powers, his petition asked the tribunal to declare the ICC's order null and void. Furthermore, Mitchell argued, the ICC finding conflicted with federal law. Three judges given the assignment to rule on the case decided Mitchell's plea had raised so many questions that they scheduled a continuation hearing for May 27, 1940.[28] On May 27, Mitchell and Westbrooks strode into court, fully prepared to argue their case against the ICC dismissal. There to counter their efforts were eight railroad attorneys and J. Stanley Payne, the ICC's Senior Assistant Chief Counsel. Judge William M. Sparks presided, and two judges of the district court sat en banc. The proceedings opened with Mitchell, and then Westbrooks testified. They limited their remarks to a detailed review of the incident and accusations that the ICC had not protected Mitchell's rights. Payne followed, but his obvious misrepresentations and evasions irritated the judges. For insisting Mitchell's only legitimate claim had been for a one-cent-per-mile refund, the ICC attorney suffered a scoffing rebuke from the bench. Of the three judges, Sparks seemed most exasperated with Payne's oversimplifications of complex legal questions. At one point, the presiding judge informed Payne that the matter before them "is not a question of overcharge. It is a question of getting the accommodations." Before any of the eight corporate lawyers could appear, Sparks ordered them to be brief and add substance, or they would be silenced and dismissed. His point made, the judge ordered Wallace Hughes to proceed. Following instructions, the Rock Island attorney referred to Jim Crow as "a very serious national question," one that even Congress would not debate. For evidence of desegregation's volatility and complexity, Hughes pointed to Mitchell's bill; it had failed two times to reach the House floor for a vote. The defense counselor insisted that this fact dramatized the issue at hand. How could a railroad—regulated by myriad state and national laws—be expected to decide on infringements of the Constitution, Hughes pondered, if Congress—with its legislative authority to enforce

27. LeFlore to J. Haden Allredge, February 10, 1939; M to LeFlore, February 15, 1939; LeFlore to FDR, April 4, 1940, MP.

28. *Railway Age*, February 11 and March 25, 1939; U.S. District Court, Northern District of Illinois, Eastern Division, Mitchell Petition, April 19, 1939; District Court, Separate Answer of Frank O. Lowden et al., June 16, 1939; District Court, Intervention of ICC, June 15, 1939.

the Fourteenth Amendment—could not improve on its long record of procrastination and noncommittal. Using a brilliant courtroom maneuver, Hughes charged the court to consider the Rock Island's predicament in light of national lawmakers' inaction on the Mitchell bill. Then there could be some government soul-searching of a disturbing problem.[29]

The court ruled against Mitchell. In a brief order of less than 150 words, released on June 27, 1940, the three judges decided the ICC had not acted outside the law to contravene the Constitution, but due to the case's several complexities, they dismissed themselves from all jurisdiction in the dispute, thus discharging the complaint. Except to note general accord with the ICC's judgment, the federal panel did not justify or explain its ruling. Correspondingly, references to what Sparks had detected as inconsistencies in Payne's testimony and what he had been belaboring to establish as the central issue—the plaintiff's right to equality—gained no mention whatsoever in a decision to resolve nothing.[30] News of the district court's verdict did not shock Mitchell, and it caused no wavering in his resolve to proceed against the railroads. Almost from the beginning, he had considered a right to first-class service so important that, if necessary, he would appeal all the way to the Supreme Court. Conceivably more was at stake for him than civil rights. For a man without formal legal training, arguing a case before the nation's highest tribunal involved probably more than just winning the lawsuit; it would be an acclamation of his courtroom skills and certification of his professional credentials. It is not speculation to assume that he believed a favorable decision might enshrine him as a great legal champion of African Americans. As Mitchell mused over the consequences and prospects caused by judicial cowardice, he had thoughts of advancing his case to the Supreme Court. Then perhaps, he pondered, he might be vindicated before his unsympathetic critics.[31]

On August 23, 1940, Mitchell surprised nobody following the case when he filed an appeal notice with the district court. His petition, a routine preliminary step to possible Supreme Court action, alleged the three district court judges had committed forty-three errors; it asked for correction and appropriate relief. Specifically, Mitchell's appeal claimed the jurists had overlooked sustaining evidence, the Constitution, and federal laws such as the ICC Act in the course of having failed to discharge a jurisdictional ruling of the case. Moreover, their nonrecognition of rights to first-class

29. District Court, Proceedings, May 27, 1940; *Des Moines Iowa Bystander,* May 30, 1940; *Kansas City Plaindealer, Argus,* May 31, 1940; *Washington Tribune, Afro-American, Defender,* June 1, 1940.

30. District Court, Findings of Fact and Conclusions of Law, June 27, 1940; ICC, *Annual Report,* 1940, 143.

31. Mitchell interview; MNR, January 9, 1939, MP.

service, equal accommodations, and travel sans discrimination, plus their general misunderstanding of the distinctions between *inter* and *intra*state commerce, had contributed to an incorrect decision. On the day of the petition's filing, Judge Sparks granted appeal to the Supreme Court, while fixing the corresponding bond at three hundred dollars.[32]

The appeal process was a judicial adventure for Mitchell and Westbrooks. Sensitive about their Supreme Court inexperience, the pair nevertheless handled all assistance offers with consistency. They steadfastly asserted their control of the case, and they denied any need for outside intervention. While maintaining progress toward a favorable outcome, they remained confident of success, but in point of fact for their appeal, the two men were having some problems assembling the necessary components and preparing a satisfactory brief within the allotted time. With little more than two months to master what other lawyers had learned during long apprenticeships at major law firms, Mitchell and Westbrooks were not coping well with the time constraint. Thus once again, they requested and received a thirty-day postponement. The Supreme Court set Thursday, November 21, 1940, as their last filing day. Mitchell and Westbrooks appreciated the delay; it would offer them ample time to prepare several hundred pages of testimony and documentation, research previous court cases more thoroughly for relevant precedents, draft the necessary briefs, and provide the required jurisdictional statement. On Monday, November 18, 1940, their deadline beaten by three days, the two men submitted their petition. It was a significant feat with symbolic value; no African American had ever argued a personal case before the Supreme Court. From a legal perspective, Mitchell was correct about the case's importance; it would be a litmus test of judicial will to enforce bilateral aspects of *McCabe*'s separate-but-equal doctrine.[33]

Mitchell's Supreme Court appeal consisted of a series of well-documented legal arguments involving jurisdictional and constitutional rights. For the most part, however, the brief was no more than a fortified restatement of previous presentations. Again, traffic volume was dismissed as a legitimate defense for denying accommodations to all riders. In language more convincing than that used in their pleas before the ICC and the district court, Mitchell and Westbrooks reasserted their complaints about the railway company's denial of Mitchell's personal rights. The offer of a penny-per-mile refund would never suffice. Its insultingly meager

32. District Court, Notice and Petition for Appeal, Order Granting Petitioner an Appeal to the United States Supreme Court and Fixing the Amount of the Bond, August 23, 1940; *Kansas City Star*, August 30, 1940.

33. Mitchell interview.

compensation of a few dollars could not undo all the physical strain and anguish Albert W. Jones had caused aboard the Rock Island train in 1937. As a finale, there was a forceful conclusion about why custom had not justified discrimination.

Articulate and dynamic as the Westbrooks-Mitchell case was, it still was dismaying some segregation foes. They thought that in its overall scope, the lawsuit had not pursued enough relief. To Mitchell's many remaining critics, his Supreme Court appeal was just another reminder of how he had compromised black interests. Contrary to activists who had been wanting to achieve integration by court fiat, Mitchell was demanding only first-class service. Critics such as those in the NAACP were still faulting the criteria for the suit. Mitchell and Westbrooks had structured their strategy around attaining the judicial goals promised by earlier decisions such as *McCabe* that had distinguished intrastate from interstate commerce and had mandated providing without exception separate-but-equal facilities. It had not occurred to Mitchell and Westbrooks to study the theories and concepts of liberal attorneys and progressive law journals; the two men were judicial conservatives. Without many recent precedents to build a more ambitious case against de jure segregation in transportation, they had not imagined much beyond suing for access to first-class travel. To obtain a favorable judicial review in 1940, they were in pursuit of less than an overturn of Jim Crow. They claimed that a number of diverse legal precedents had helped to disassociate their appeal from Arkansas authority and statutes. Arkansas jurisdiction did not apply to matters at hand. Instead, logic, law, and precedent dictated that Mitchell, a Pullman-ticketed passenger, had been engaged in peaceful interstate travel when a serious legal error occurred. In interfering with Mitchell's first-class seating arrangement, Albert W. Jones had threatened arrest, using nonexistent constitutional authority; therefore, his actions had constituted an illegal transgression of rights. The perspectives of law embodied in the brief were concise and sound; the black lawyers had based everything upon established constitutional powers. Simply stated, their challenges boiled down to a question of whether or not states could impose their traditions and laws on through passengers. Westbrooks maintained that as long as Mitchell had held a valid first-class ticket, his right to a vacant Pullman seat had prevailed over all conjured-up supersedings of state laws that had been segregating races physically by color. No such authority could exist in cases that spanned state borders because the Constitution had obliged courts to protect against encroachments of federal regulatory powers in all interstate transits. Selective Supreme Court recitations on limits of state jurisdictions over commerce had supported Westbrooks's conclusions. On

December 16, 1941, the Supreme Court agreed to review the case against the Rock Island.[34]

The appeal and the Court's willingness to hear the case caught the Roosevelt administration in a dilemma. Despite the case's significant potential for political consequences, it demanded a Department of Justice response because the United States was a codefendant. Since the district court and ICC decisions had sided with railroad defendants and not the plaintiff, Attorney General Robert H. Jackson was involved as the nation's chief counsel. Although nothing required him to defend previous judgments, he was obliged to review the facts and issue a government memorandum to the court. Politically speaking, there could be several repercussions from taking sides. Regardless of the government's response, it was certain to trigger attacks because of the main issue's delicacy. Segregationists would interpret a pro-Mitchell stance as a personal affront and interference in Southern states rights, whereas every friend of civil rights would view an attempt to uphold earlier judgments as evidence of the administration's hostility toward blacks. Afraid or not of political fallout, Jackson courageously sided with Mitchell. Early in March 1941, he instructed Solicitor General Francis Biddle to file a twenty-page memorandum with the Supreme Court. Succinct but definitive, it contained Department of Justice arguments for reversing the appellant court's decision. Among several reasons cited, the nonapplicability of Arkansas law in the proceeding received strongest emphasis. Jackson asserted, "so long as white passengers can secure first-class reservations on the day of travel and the colored passengers cannot, the latter are subjected to inequality and discrimination because of their race." Furthermore, Jackson dismissed cost as a legitimate reason to discriminate: "however great these [practical problems of removing injustice] may be, the common carrier which undertakes to segregate its colored passengers must pay the cost." Moreover, the ICC got a scolding because of its application of state law to an interstate case and its ruling that demand and volume somehow worked hand in hand to circumvent individual rights.[35]

Segregationists reacted with alarm and fear to the Department of Justice's commitment to support Mitchell. They were especially apprehensive about all the implications of Mitchell's suit and the risks of a chain reaction. Although Mitchell had not been seeking integrated railroads, there were still concerns among Jim Crow's many upholders because the

34. RW to JEM, April 23, 1941, NAACP; *Dayton Forum*, December 27, 1940; *Railway Age*, December 21, 1941; U.S. Supreme Court, No. 577, *Arthur W. Mitchell v. The United States of America, ICC, Frank O. Lowden, et al.*, Appendices to Brief for Appellant, Brief for the ICC, Statement as to Jurisdiction, 1940.

35. *Mitchell v. U.S.*, Memorandum for the United States, March 1941.

suit represented an attack on state powers to enforce racial separation. At stake, they feared, was a right to "police" African American passengers during their movements across state lines. Since sustaining authority seemed essential to maintaining segregation, Dixie leaders had reason to fret. Alabama Attorney General Thomas S. Lawson was the first to react to the perceived perils. Perhaps more than officials in other states, he worried openly that a decision favorable to Mitchell would affect the South's ability to hold onto its rigid color line in transportation. On March 13, 1941, Governor Frank M. Dixon joined Lawson in urging a joint response from brethren states. As a follow-up, Lawson invited Southern counterparts to Montgomery on March 20 for a conference on the Mitchell case.[36] As a direct result of Lawson's initiative, ten Dixie states joined in an amicus curiae brief. For the record, it stated what the Southern states regarded as proper subject matter in the Mitchell case decision. In response to the Department of Justice memorandum, their counterappeal attempted to exclude a consideration of segregation from the verdict. Without mention of Robert H. Jackson or debate of the case's merits, the Southerners argued for an unobstructed ruling on the plaintiff's claim to first-class accommodations. To leave an impression that racial segregation was not central to their position, the state attorneys general used Mitchell's own statements and testimony freely. Their claims of support for Mitchell's bid to acquire first-class accommodations were absurd, but more than anything, issuing a brief so late into the Court session only proved the degree of desperation and fear that had swept into the South after Jackson threw his support to Mitchell's case. Clearly the Southerners' brief was a bid for time; without documents or legal preparation to fight for Jim Crow in court, the ten attorneys general preferred postponements of constitutional tests into the validity of the Arkansas Separate Coach Law and of the legality of intrusions into interstate commerce under state police powers. Tacit concessions to African Americans—claiming they deserved to have access to equal coaches—were Dixie's way of asking the Supreme Court to delay its judgment of Jim Crow. Given the context of Mitchell's established pro-Dixie record, the knowledge that the Southerners' brief had been made with his full cooperation did not astonish his foes. Still, Mitchell's willingness to assist the South proved especially irksome and frustrating to the NAACP's top leaders because he had not allowed them to file a subsequent friend-of-the-court brief as their rebuttal to the segregationists.[37]

36. Frank M. Dixon to Southern governors, March 13, 1941; R. M. Harper to J. M. Bonner, March 14, 1941; Paul B. Johnson to Dixon, March 17, 1941, FMDP; *Montgomery Advertiser*, March 13, 14, and 16, 1941; *Montgomery Alabama Journal*, March 13, 1941.
37. *Montgomery Advertiser*, March 21, 1941; *Montgomery Alabama Journal*, March 20 and 21, 1941; *Railway Age*, April 28, 1941; Hastie to Marshall, January 24, 1941,

Meanwhile, the Supreme Court began hearing arguments on March 13, 1941. On this, the same day as the Lawson-Dixon invitations, in a courtroom jammed with news reporters and interested spectators, Mitchell testified on his own behalf. Dramatic as the setting was, his testimony did not change; his complaints on this occasion were the same as those presented earlier at ICC and district court hearings. He spoke of blacks suffering gross unfairness every time they sought special railroad privileges, and he stood by his original contentions. He was not making a fight against segregation; his case dealt with entitlement to first-class accommodations. When defense attorneys countered that the limited demand for black seating did not justify either subdividing or adding cars for African American riders, Chief Justice Charles Evans Hughes advised integration as a solution to the problem of low numbers. As the defense pondered "a sentiment for segregation . . . , The question then would be whether the railroads would have any other customers in the dining car."[38]

Mitchell's Supreme Court appearance touched off another angry exchange between Roy Wilkins and J. E. Mitchell. After Wilkins's abrasive initial reactions to the Supreme Court testimony, trouble flared again between the two bitter rivals. It began on March 29, 1941, when Wilkins used a weekly column in the *Amsterdam Star-News* to attack Mitchell's suit. Since the lawsuit promised no relief from segregation, there could only be marginal benefit to the race. At least, this was Wilkins's prediction. Harshly and vindictively, he likened Mitchell to a selfish ogre whose only interest was personal accomplishment and whose disengagement from all constructive social movements entitled him to the epitaph, "Greatest Mistake in Negro political history." The NAACP official's critique inflamed J. E. Mitchell. The St. Louis publisher disputed Wilkins's claims about the lawsuit's minimum effects on African Americans, and he challenged the civil rights leader to leave his comfortable New York office and become part of a suit on behalf of "ordinary Negroes who are 'kicked around' in the Jim Crow cars." According to the exasperated journalist's speculations, Wilkins would not prompt such a suit because he and so many other NAACP officers "would rather criticise the effort of the man who will really do something for his race." The controversy did not die with an *Argus* editorial; Wilkins reacted to it with a response that lacked much of the passion and venom of his newspaper attack on Mitchell.

NAACP; *Mitchell v. U.S.*, Brief for the States and Commonwealths of Arkansas et al., Amici Curiae; Lawson to M, April 19, 1941; M to Lawson, April 23, 1941; M to Hastie, April 16, 1941, MP; Hastie to M, April 16, 1941, BP.

38. *Louisville Courier-Journal, New York Times, Washington Post, Philadelphia Inquirer, Baltimore Sun, Boston Herald, Springfield Daily Republican,* and *Chicago Tribune,* March 14, 1941.

Wilkins's reply was more a rationale for his differing with the lawsuit and a defense of the NAACP transportation record than an assault on J. E. Mitchell. Wilkins swept aside the suit as a breach-of-contract action, while noting that it was not a civil rights matter; Mitchell's concern was not with Jim Crow cars per se but with the Rock Island Line's refusal to honor his Pullman ticket. Regarding the NAACP's noninvolvement in the case, Wilkins absolved it, notifying J. E. Mitchell that the congressman had spurned the organization's offers of assistance. As for the NAACP's record in transportation cases since its beginnings in 1909, Wilkins proudly pointed out how it had always been ready to assist in struggles for equality and justice, but this did not mean its officers had been "roving the country trying to make legal cases." Such acts would be counterproductive and totally senseless, for "the accusation can be brought against them in court that they are employed by an organization whose purpose is to fight cases of this sort."[39]

As the final salvos were recorded in the Wilkins-Mitchell dispute, the Supreme Court justices were preparing a decision. Although much had been said and written about the case, few observers anticipated the verdict Chief Justice Hughes delivered on April 28, 1941. Reversing the decisions of both the district court and the ICC, the U.S. Supreme Court ruled unanimously for Mitchell. The Court seemingly had not concerned itself with logistics or profits because its rendering argued for equality in service and against racial privilege. Suggestion-free, their verdict for the plaintiff did not manifest how rights might be attained, and there was no timetable. As for explanations, jurists did not tender many interpretations. The Constitution guaranteed Mitchell's rights, and passenger volume was not an adequate excuse for negating or abridging his freedom. Regarding the ICC dismissal and the district court's nonjurisdictional claims, the eight justices answered with a mandamus. All inquiries to determine unjust or unlawful acts were, in fact, the regulatory body's legal duties, and law charged district courts with reviewing ICC actions. Nonetheless, in many respects, decisions from *Mitchell v. the United States et al.* left more legal questions unanswered than resolved. Following the advice of *amicus curiae* submitted by the Southern state attorneys general, the Court had not considered segregation's legality, choosing to sidestep the issue altogether.[40]

Triumphant headlines and page-one spreads in the nation's newspapers greeted Mitchell's victory. All across America, major dailies tended

---

39. *Amsterdam News*, March 29, 1941; *Argus*, April 4, 1941; RW to JEM, April 23, 1941, NAACP.

40. *Mitchell v. U.S.*, Opinion of the Court; *Railway Age*, March 22, 1941; ICC, *Annual Report*, 85–86.

to view the Supreme Court ruling as a win for equal services, while black editors elaborated about its possible meaning for African Americans. Knowledge that eight justices had upheld the right of blacks to equal travel accommodations introduced rays of hope and jubilation into the columns of black newspapers. Among black journalists, predictions of a new era of travel for the minority were commonplace. Amidst all the excitement, the newspapers occasionally got carried away. For example, those dependent upon ANP coverage of the verdict were guilty of exaggerating the effect of the ruling. For ANP subscribers, reporter Albert Anderson called the verdict "a slap at the south," this, because of an "apparent failure of the southern attorneys-general to influence the court." Contrariwise, the Southerners' brief had succeeded in removing racial segregation as an issue in the case. *Nation* gave the best overall analysis. It gave a backhanded compliment to the Supreme Court justices for doing "the neat legerdemain of approving segregation by attacking discrimination." Cautioning its readers to avoid premature jubilation, *Nation* dampened expectations, arguing the "Supreme Court had not helped matters by evading the most important issue."[41]

Overall, news of the Supreme Court decision for Mitchell received mixed reactions. Looking at the ruling for possible effects on railroading, *Railway Age* understood it meant the addition of sleepers, diners, and observation cars. From Montgomery, Alabama, Jim Crow's survival brought sighs of relief to state officials. "It is travel as usual," one noted gladly for the ANP. Attorney Raymond Pace Alexander's hopeful assessment gave encouragement to blacks. For critics and skeptics guilty of stripping the decision of its importance, the founder of the *National Bar Journal* countered with an optimistic reply. Even if segregation survived the verdict, any barrister familiar with the effect of legal precedents upon future decisions should appreciate the Court decision as "an opening wedge and a long step toward the eventual eradication of jim-crow legislation." NAACP officials did not share Alexander's perceptions. Their displeasures from the outset with Mitchell's litigation and his "go it alone" resolve had indicated why a minimum judicial result would do little to cheer them. For Marshall, White, and Wilkins, the case ended where it had begun, inappropriately. Totally misdirected from the start, its outcome reflected Mitchell's stubborn unwillingness to take advice

41. *Des Moines Register, Chicago Tribune, Richmond Times-Dispatch, Oklahoma City Daily Oklahoman, New York Daily News, New York Times,* and *Baltimore Sun,* April 29, 1941; *East Tennessee News,* May 1, 1941; *Dayton Forum, Kansas City Call, Argus,* May 2, 1941; *Indianapolis Hoosier Sentinel,* May 3, 1941; *Des Moines Iowa Bystander,* May 1, 1941; *Cleveland Call and Post, Defender, Indianapolis Recorder, New Orleans Louisiana Weekly,* May 3, 1941; *Chicago Sunday Bee,* May 4, 1941; *Nation,* May 10, 1941.

and to challenge Jim Crow. As one organizational spokesman put it, "The time for real jubilation and for belief that democracy is being attained will come when the courts unequivocally strike down all methods and modes of segregation." For leaders of the civil rights establishment, a good chuckle was about the only good thing to emerge from *Mitchell v. The United States et al.* Following a well-meaning supporter's telephoned congratulations on the "NAACP win" at the organization's headquarters, White noted for Marshall how "parenthetically this would probably cause Mr. Mitchell to have apoplexy." Conversely, the critical reservations from NAACP officers likely resulted from bitterness and frustration at not having had a role in the judicial proceedings and from Mitchell's allegations about the suit's effect on black public opinion of them. If Mitchell needed reinforcement to support these viewpoints and to confirm how his popularity had soared, there were scores of flattering letters and cables in his office.[42]

Mitchell's case did not end with the high court's decision and the jostling between supporters and critics. Justices had entrusted a number of unresolved matters for settlement to the federal district court and the ICC. The procedure for a reversal called for district judicial remanding. The original three-judge panel entered its final orders of annulment on June 20, 1941, and then it refunded Mitchell's three-thousand-dollar deposit. Finally, it assessed court costs against the three corporate codefendants. The conclusion to *Mitchell* came on November 10, 1941, when the ICC officially withdrew its dismissal and ordered the railroads to change its discriminatory policies before December 24, 1941. Unclear and general about what would constitute noncompliance, the ICC directive did not give any specific instructions or penalties. Separately from an out-of-court settlement of his civil lawsuit, Mitchell recovered court costs and received $3,750.[43]

In the final analysis, Raymond Pace Alexander offered a correct reading of the Supreme Court verdict in 1941. Prospects for a "new psychology" had resulted from *Mitchell v. The United States et al.* Apathy, fear, and doubt among blacks lessened after the verdict. Individual citizens were writing

42. *Railway Age,* May 3, 1941; ANPNR, May 4, 1941, BP; Raymond Pace Alexander to M, May 9, 1941, MP; WW's Memos to TM, April 30 and May 1, 1941; WW's statement for the *New York Post,* April 29, 1941; RW to Prattis, May 5, 1941; RW to M, May 5, 1941; TM to George F. Miller, May 6 and 13, 1941; Miller to RW, March 28 and May 3 and 12, 1941; RW to Miller, May 9 and 14, 1941, NAACP; *Crisis,* June 1941; *Cleveland Call and Post,* May 3, 1941; see MP for April 29–May 4, 1941.

43. *Railway Age,* August 9 and November 22, 1941; ANPNR, December 1941, BP; *Defender,* June 28, 1941; *CR,* 77th Cong., 1st sess., 4296; ICC, Transcript, November 10, 1941; Mitchell interview; canceled check dated November 2, 1945, MP.

Mitchell, inquiring if they might also have grounds for legal actions.[44] In far greater numbers, blacks were looking to the courts to right racial injustice. Historically, more litigation involving transportation discrimination came during the decade after *Mitchell* than during any previous ten-year period. As a law professor observed, Mitchell's successful challenge to the railroads ushered in the "modern era of transportation desegregation." From Montgomery to Memphis, during a generation of unequaled civil rights legal activism, *Mitchell* loomed importantly as a precedent for lawsuits.[45] Notwithstanding harsh contemporary NAACP judgments of the case, the organization showed a bittersweet dependence upon *Mitchell* in several suits litigated with Association resources and counsel. Prime examples were *Jackson v. Seaboard Air Line Railway Company* and *Mays v. The Southern Railway Company.* Use of *Mitchell* took two forms. If a suit's goals were limited to securing equal facilities, the litigant's brief and the Court ruling served as bases of copycat litigation. On the other hand, when desegregation was the complainant's objective, civil rights attorneys cited it as one of their many building-block cases.[46] Retrospectively, nobody captured the vitality of the Supreme Court decision better than Langston Hughes. In "The Mitchell Case," a column circulated to ANP subscribers, the black poet laureate shared his impressions and disappointments:

> I see by the papers
> Where Mitchell's won his case.
> Down South the railroads now
> Must give us equal space.
> Even if we're rich enough
> To want a Pullman car,
> The Supreme Court says we *get* it—
> And a diner and a bar!
> Now, since the Court in Washington
> Can make a rule like that,
> If we went to court enough we might
> Get Jim Crow on the mat

44. M to Dunjee, March 13, 1942; William Y. Bell Jr. to J. B. Hill, May 25, 1942; Samuel Plato to M, May 23, 1942; James H. Levenson to M, July 9, 1942; M to Levenson, July 15, 1942, MP; *Railway Age*, February 14, May 16 and 30, and November 7, 1942; *Chicago Sunday Bee*, May 31, 1942.

45. Dixon, "Civil Rights in Transportation," 198–241; Loren Miller, *The Petitioners: The Story of the Supreme Court of the United States and the Negro*, 365–67; Alexander, "Recent Trends," 401–13.

46. Westbrooks to TM, July 30, 1941; TM to Westbrooks, August 1, 1941; *Jackson v. Seaboard Air Line Railway Co.*; *Brown et al. v. Southern Railway Co.*; *Mays v. Southern Railway Co.*, Legal Files, NAACP.

And pin his shoulders to the ground
And drive him from the land—
Since the Constitution ain't enough
To protect a colored man—
And we have to go to court to make
The crackers understand.
But for poor people
It's kinder hard to sue.
Mr. Mitchell, you did right well—
But the rest of us ain't you
Seems to me it would be simpler
If the Government would declare
They're tired of all this Jim Crow stuff
And just give it the air.
Seems to me it's time to realize
That in the U.S.A.
To have Jim Crow's too Hitler-like
In this modern age and day—
Cause fine speeches sure sound hollow
About Democracy
When all over America
They still Jim Crowing me.
To earn a dollar sometimes
Is hard enough to do—
Let alone having to take that dollar
To go and sue![47]

47. Langston Hughes, "The Mitchell Case," BP.

Retirement Amid Roses with Little Recognition

9

1943–1968

Retirement for Mitchell meant more than leaving Capitol Hill; it meant the realization of a lifelong pursuit based upon wistfulness for the South. The life of a Southern aristocrat had long been his dream. Having the splendor of a stately, pillared mansion, indulging in gentlemanly pleasures such as hunting, fishing, horseback riding, and show gardening, and augmenting everything with some mundane dabblings in law, politics, and investments had been his goals because he had not forgotten Alabama's genteel men and women; memories of them had remained, buried deeply in his soul. From trips with Robert R. Moton to Oak Knoll at Capahosic, Mitchell remembered fellowship and fishing, but mostly he recalled Virginia's majesty. As with most things, he planned his retirement carefully. His plans, based upon models of the ideal plantation estate, surfaced first in 1939 with his purchase of twenty-eight acres of lush farmland from an estate located off U.S. Highway 1 and seven miles south of Petersburg.[1] Here on the banks of Hatcher's Run and the site of a bloody Civil War battle, Arthur Mitchell constructed a "showplace." Corinthian in its architectural design, the fourteen-room estate house was built by black craftsmen working under Mitchell's watchful supervision. True to a dreamer's plans, it was a magnificent structure, reflecting Tara and featuring a spacious dining salon, four bedrooms, a family room, and a home study. Although there had been concern for outward elegance, the building's cold interior lacked cheerfulness and sociable character. Somehow, a guest entering Mitchell's colorless mansion could not help but feel something of the estate master's frigid austerity in the absolutely

---

1. M to Moton, July 25, 1935, and May 19, 1937; M to A. W. E. Bassette Jr., July 16, 1937; compilation of black teachers from Dinwiddie County, Virginia, 1939, MP; Mitchell interviews; *Pittsburgh Courier*, November 28, 1942; *Journal and Guide*, September 24, 1949.

stark, drab furnishings. Nothing in the building was ever allowed to be misplaced. Grimly decorated, a large sitting room exemplified Mitchell's fetish for neatness. It was so structured and perfectly arranged that it resembled a funeral parlor more than a living room. Pictureless, with chairs and sofas placed at long distances from each other, the room did not suggest warmth or cheerfulness to its occupants. The study, "Mitchell's room," was perhaps oddest of all the chambers. Belonging to "the Congressman," it doubled as library and office. With its orderly, stacked, glass-enclosed lawbooks, bound volumes of the *Congressional Record*, USDA yearbooks, and selected biographies of famous American heroes such as Washington and Lincoln, the cryptlike vault of a room showcased a large desk that faced a long wall and one dozen perfectly placed chairs. With everything on such an exaggerated scale, Mitchell either had sought to shape impressions of grandeur for himself or had expected regular delegations for advice and consultations.

Gorgeous magnolias, pecan trees, various spruces, and varieties of cedar were visible from a circular drive curving from the highway to the house. Not far away stood "magnificent gardens and the cultivated fields," the sources of Mitchell's greatest pride and pleasure. In order to create Dinwiddie County's loveliest horticultural display, he invested more than twenty thousand dollars and countless hours. With its two thousand different plants, one hundred hollies, one thousand rose bushes, and a sunken pool, Mitchell's estate attracted about a thousand flower fanciers of both races every May 15 for personal inspections. Just beyond the great spectacle of colors and fragrance, Mitchell kept some perfectly tilled rows of tomato vines, okra, watermelons, cantaloupes, beans, and peas. Also on the estate were several well-maintained outbuildings for poultry, livestock, farm implements, and a tractor. Named after its flowers and his second wife, Mitchell's estate became known as Rose-Anna Gardens.[2]

Living in the South along Jefferson Davis Highway amid greenery fittingly fulfilled Mitchell's farewell-address pledge to his congressional colleagues. Just as he had promised in his parting speech, they would have found him the following day outfitted "in overalls" at his mansion "built . . . by the side of the road." In accordance with most Mitchell decisions, his retirement from Congress followed careful deliberations about how he would like to leave office. During a farewell to House members on December 16, 1942, Mitchell withheld the most important detail. If his bowing out from Chicago politics had not been especially

2. Author's impressions; Mitchell and Cephas interviews; *Pittsburgh Courier*, November 28, 1942; *Journal and Guide*, September 24, 1949.

graceful, there was something statesmanlike about his Washington exit. Before leaving, he helped to reelect a supportive colleague from West Virginia, and to his idols John McDuffie and Franklin D. Roosevelt he sent his very special gratitude. For the president, he had generously kind words "for the splendid and encouraging manner in which your administration has handled the affairs of this nation, particularly those things vitally affecting the safety, welfare and progress of the Negro." Forever grateful, Mitchell could not forget McDuffie, who had "made a distinct contribution to my election possibility." McDuffie gained Mitchell's pledge "to again engage in the work of building better racial relations between the colored and white people." In return, Mitchell received praise from both sides of the House aisle. Speaking for Republicans, New Yorker Hamilton Fish ignored partisanship long enough to salute a political rival for having been a "credit to his constituents and to his race." John Sparkman of Alabama spoke for many liberal Southern Democrats, commending a native son for a "most helpful, patient, and tolerant" role in the region's black-white relations.[3]

After a life of fanfare, Mitchell adjusted well to his new surroundings. Always a Jeffersonian at heart, he was proud to be associated again with agriculture. In letters to friends, he mentioned his new life as a "Dirt Farmer," telling of hard work, weather problems, and produce sales.[4] Besides gardening and farming, he filled his life with other diverse activities. During periods of restlessness and boredom, he had sufficient money to pursue many diversions. Whenever it became especially dull around the country estate and Petersburg, he found quick relief motoring to Washington for political chatter with former congressional contemporaries. Moreover, the Mutual Housing Company still operated in the District, and it always demanded something. Although many years ago he had entrusted a professional real estate company with the everyday management of the company's apartment buildings, there remained many small tasks to perform at three rental properties. After Mitchell acquired his Washington properties in the early 1920s, they survived many changes under their owner. After many tenants, Mutual Housing's buildings were showing wear and old age. As principal stockholder, Mitchell recognized that if the once-modern flats were going to retain any value, he would have to oversee periodic maintenance and repairs.[5]

3. *CR*, 77th Cong., 2d sess., 9537, 9649–50; Jennings Randolph to M, October 21, 1942; M to FDR, November 16, 1942; M to McDuffie, December 29, 1942, MP.

4. *CR*, 76th Cong., 3d sess., 1009–10; undated MNR; M to McLendon and to Maude Scritchfield, August 20, 1943, MP.

5. M to F. M. Pratt, February 20, 1935; M to Albert G. Langhorne, September 14, 1935; M to Lerly W. Sanchez, May 26, 1937; Mutual Housing Company, statements and stockholder voting shares, 1935–1957, MP.

A job of the kind Mitchell had hoped to obtain after retirement finally reached him at the end of his first year away from the Capitol. In late 1943, he became the War Department's "colored" military camp inspector. Six weeks before leaving Congress, he had volunteered his service to Director James F. Byrnes of the War Stabilization Board, but the former justice was unable to offer him anything. Somewhat disappointed but still not overly discouraged in June 1943 by not receiving a special assignment, Mitchell returned to Byrnes. During his visit to the South Carolinian's office in Washington, Mitchell received Byrnes's promise that an appropriate job would be found, but as an alternative, Byrnes suggested that Mitchell contact White House assistant Marvin H. McIntyre. Mitchell was so convinced of his rare insight into racial issues that he pressed the aide on July 6, 1943, for "an opportunity to visit the Negro soldiers at the camps and on fields in foreign countries." Within a week, there were results. For discussions on "how some difficulties [for blacks in military service] that have arisen might be dealt with," Assistant Secretary of War John J. McCloy requested an appointment with Mitchell in Washington. At their July meeting, Mitchell indicated his interest in tackling the issue, but McCloy promised only to do what he could. By early October, Mitchell was so impatient that he returned with his worries to Jimmy Byrnes. Once again, there was intervention. Periodically, Byrnes questioned McCloy about progress toward employing Mitchell. Follow-up inquiries only abated after a November 16, 1943, memorandum to Byrnes from the War Department; an assignment in line with Mitchell's interests had finally developed. Appropriately, it was Byrnes who informed Mitchell of a special arrangement with the Joint Army and Navy Committee on Welfare and Recreation for someone with his insight and background to study the problems encountered by black troops stationed at remote outposts. Since Mitchell was interested, there was contact at once with the Joint Committee's Francis Keppel. Mitchell was given an assignment, but it did not include clearance to make visits to military installations. This was a rather serious handicap for Mitchell, since without clearance he would have to gather information elsewhere. Still anxious for the opportunity, Mitchell did not seem to mind the War Department restrictions on him; he accepted Keppel's conditions without protest. Requested to "visit as many communities as possible," he received orders by December 5, 1943, to depart for the West Coast by the week's end. After his hasty acceptance, Mitchell received further details of his assignment. By mid-January, the Army's John McCloy expected a treatise "on the adequacy of community facilities for Negro soldiers and on any hostile attitudes which you may find in communities toward Negro soldiers."[6]

6. M to Byrnes, November 26, 1942, and July 21 and October 23, 1943; M to McIntyre, July 6, 1943; John J. McCloy to M, July 15, 1943; Byrnes to M, October 7 and November

Although Mitchell claimed to have logged ten thousand miles and to have visited "colored" training camps in more than twelve states, his study "The Treatment of the Negro Trainee" missed the Army's goals. Five of his nine major observations did not relate to community attitudes, and he did not describe civilian facilities; Mitchell dealt instead with soldiers' feelings about the Army or vice versa. Except for generalities about the effects of segregation and prejudicial restrictions on African American military trainees' morale, his report was worthless. Simply put, it contained no anecdotal or factual examples to prop sweeping conclusions about racism, and his synopsis did not provide the War Department with details of intolerable base towns and conditions. From the materials presented, one can wonder if Mitchell ever really visited any unfriendly locales. His transmission of 1944 suggests that he had not interviewed anyone as he had been instructed; he had merely gleaned everything from thirteen pages of anonymously compiled recollections, "ONE YEAR with the 92d [black] DIVISION." Before submitting an abominable report to McCloy, Mitchell risked prosecution by notifying two black newspaper publishers that they could preview his findings, a promise he made in order to gauge their interest and reactions. If Mitchell did discuss his report with the newspapers, he did so in violation of his contract with the War Department. According to its nondisclosure clause, he was under oath to disclose nothing without clearance from the Joint Army and Navy Committee on Welfare and Recreation. No matter how clear the policy had been about secrecy, Mitchell was prepared to defy it. On December 15, 1943, he invited president Ira F. Lewis of the *Pittsburgh Courier* and *Journal and Guide* publisher P. B. Young to Rose-Anna Gardens to examine his report. As Mitchell noted in his bids to his two journalist friends: "I should like to talk over with men like yourself before reporting them to any white man." Continuing, he admitted to wanting "to take a few men like you into my confidence and get the advantage of your wisdom and experience in putting our case before the Department." Honored by the trust, Lewis expressed gratitude for having been given such opportunity to view insider documents, but told Mitchell that going to Virginia for this purpose was "practically impossible." No records indicate if Young ever viewed the confidential materials.[7]

16, 1943; Byrnes's letter of recommendation for M, December 8, 1943; December 1943 clippings; letter and memo, Francis Keppel to M, December 4, 1943; War Department News Release, 1943, MP.

7. M, "The Treatment of the Negro Trainee," 1944; anonymous, "ONE YEAR with the 92d DIVISION," October 15, 1942, to November 30, 1943; Memo, Keppel to M, December 4, 1943; M to IFL, December 15, 1943, and January 8, 1944; M to PBY, January 11, 1944; M to Gordon Hancock, January 10, 1944, MP.

Mitchell would experience both sorrow and joy at Rose-Anna Gardens. His wife's ongoing health problems were a source of disappointment. Sick periodically from 1935 to 1937, she suffered cardiac arrest in 1938. Placed in intensive care at a private Nashville hospital known for its heart-patient ward, Annie Harris Mitchell became well enough after several months' treatment to come home to Washington, but her recovery was not total. Although the tender, soft-featured woman remained in the background of her husband's full life, there were few complaints; the pair enjoyed too many pleasurable moments together for her to gripe. Childless, she anticipated opportunities to cruise into tropical West Indian ports, travel across the continent, and savor exotic places like Hawaii with her spouse. Yet, as the wife of a restless, dominant man, Mrs. Mitchell did not experience as much domestic stability during much of her marriage as she was craving; there were too many long separations to endure. As she once wrote to her husband, "The old house seems sort of empty and lonesome with no one here . . . while I am preparing breakfast." Making the most of her "dearest Precious" being absent so much, she tried communicating compassion, unselfish love, pride, and commitments instead of chronic complaints. As a devoted wife, and seemingly always unconcerned about herself, she worried first and foremost about her partner's health. Even if Mitchell thought of her when he named Rose-Anna Gardens, weakened stamina prevented her full appreciation and enjoyment of the estate. Losing her battle with her weak heart, Annie Mitchell died on March 7, 1947; she was fifty-seven years old.[8]

Mitchell was a widower for one year. At the Petersburg estate, official mourning ended with a March 20, 1948, marriage ceremony in the gardens. The union of Clara Smith Mann and Arthur W. Mitchell proved how two opposite people could be drawn together in nuptials. Except for their strong wills and their both having lost spouses, they did not have much in common. Their first meeting had been almost thirteen years before the marriage on April 27, 1935, after he accepted her invitation to New Bern, North Carolina, for a graduation address at the Craven County colored high school. Mitchell was instantly infatuated. He could not forget Mann, and the assistant superintendent of county schools pined after him as well: "I want to see you *badly*. Write to me. . . . I think of you often and fondly." His small gifts such as an autographed book about the Constitution "so pleasantly thrilled" the wife of a New Bern physician that his subsequent motor trips to the South seldom excluded detours to the coastal city for

8. *Afro-American,* June 12, 1937; *Richmond Times-Dispatch,* March 9, 1947; Annie to M, September 7 and 12, 1935, and April 20, 1937; M to Holman, May 14, 1935; Wilma Carmody to M, January 26, 1937; M to Carmody, January 16, 1939, MP.

reunions. Candid during interviews about her second husband, Clara Mitchell was disinclined to withhold anything. Emotionless, she did not flinch from discussing the disappearance of matrimonial bliss. From the outset of the marriage, Mitchell showed jealousy over her affection for three grown children. Fights often erupted after she suggested traveling to see son Bobby's National Football League games. As an extra burden, there was hostility from an ongoing affair with "the white lady from across the road." To protest Mitchell's blatant lechery, Clara once took a loaded rifle from a rack and fired at her husband's automobile from an open second-floor bedroom window, flattening two tires in the process.[9]

As long as people remembered Mitchell's congressional tenure, he received invitations to speak. Alcorn A & M College's class of 1943 heard him at their commencement exercise, and one year later in Dallas, he made a keynote address at the National Baptist Convention. Because of a sick wife and then another marriage, his speaking appearances became less frequent. Opportunities became scarcer, too. Following the NBC speech in 1944, he limited himself to two annual acceptances. The pattern continued for almost seven years. In early June 1951, during Mitchell's final lecture tour, he demonstrated before a Los Angeles audience just how much he still enjoyed controversy. Lecturing the Columbia Women's Council only a short time after President Harry S. Truman's discharge of World War Two hero Douglas MacArthur for insubordination, he entered the maelstrom with personal opinions. Describing MacArthur as a staunch nonbeliever in "equality of all Americans under the Constitution," the orator characterized the five-star general as a "rampant segregationist."[10]

Departing Capitol Hill did not diminish Mitchell's resolve to be at odds with popular opinions. His tendencies for antics and candor became the talk of Petersburg. Few blacks could forget his reaction after he received Virginia State College's personal invitation to be present when the institution feted Nobel Peace Prize laureate Ralph Bunche. According to a member of the college community, Mitchell had snapped, "What do

9. Clara Mann to M, January 19 and 25, April 2, and May 11, 1935, and one, n.d.; M to Mann, January 7 and 23 and April 16, 1935, and March 31 and May 5, 1938; Craven County, N.C., Colored Schools, Commencement Program, April 27, 1935; announcement, Mann-Mitchell Marriage, March 20, 1948, MP; Mitchell and Cephas interviews.

10. Alcorn A & M, May 1943, Fort Valley State College, June 3, 1946, Adkin High School, Kinston, N.C., May 30, 1950, Virginia Theological Seminary and College, May 30, 1951, graduation programs; Veterans and Civilians Service Organization of Virginia, Founders' Day, January 12, 1947, Sumter Branch of the NAACP, April 22, 1951, The Tri-County Church Union, meeting, October 29, 1950, programs; W. Lester Banks to M, March 14, 1939, MP; *Alcorn A & M Greater Alcorn Herald,* May 1943, *Dallas Morning News,* September 9, 1944, *Los Angeles Tribune,* July 7, 1951.

I want to go and see that old darky for?" Usually, though, his flippant
outspokenness was not always so ridiculous. In 1946, for example, he
justifiably rebuked President Truman for his inconsistency on racial issues.
Mitchell requested Truman's rationale for immediately condemning a
Jerusalem hotel bombing by terrorists after he had completely ignored
a brutal Monroe, Georgia, lynching. Five years later, he loudly objected
when official plans called for segregating blacks from whites at an upcoming Marian Anderson recital in Richmond. Upset by this affront, Mitchell
boisterously acclaimed his support for an NAACP-sponsored boycott.[11]

However, retirement still meant a sharp curtailment of Mitchell's political activities. After Franklin Roosevelt's death in 1945, Mitchell lost enthusiasm for the Democratic party. Thereafter, his political independence and
disillusionment with politics were increasingly evident. Very few elections
were of any interest to him. The first indications of his readjustment
followed the opening of the Republican-dominated Eightieth Congress
and the GOP selections of Joseph Martin and Robert Taft as Speaker of the
House and Senate Majority Leader, respectively. Noted for his unabashed
Democratic partisanship while on Capitol Hill, Mitchell surely surprised
the two Republican stalwarts by sending them congratulatory notes. His
letters may have reflected his impatience with Truman over civil rights
injustices or his approval for GOP unity during the unseating of Mississippi Senator Theodore Bilbo; Mitchell did not divulge his inspiration.
After the intraparty elections of January 20, 1947, one thing was rather
self-explanatory, however; Mitchell's compositions indicated a change of
attitude toward the Republican party. The animosities that had been so
much associated with his eight years in Congress had somehow vanished.
Mitchell not only bestowed upon Robert Taft "the highest regard for . . .
statesmanship" but also predicted the presidency for him because Taft
was the "greatest and most fearless leader."[12] Following the collapse of
the Democratic party's Colored Division in 1940, Mitchell had almost
completely disengaged from national presidential politics. Of the next
six presidential campaigns, only one remotely interested him. Thoughts
of General Dwight D. Eisenhower in the White House in 1953 worried
Mitchell so much he made inquiries about returning to politics as an
unpaid speaker for Adlai Stevenson. His willingness to assist brought
Mitchell again into close contact with veteran Democratic officeholders
such as Texan Sam Rayburn and Oklahoman Mike Monroney. In 1952,
as chairman of the Speakers Bureau, Monroney was happy to learn that

11. Cephas interview; M to Huff, July 29, 1946; M to J. M. Tinsley, January 12, 1951,
MP.
12. M to Robert Taft and to Martin, January 20, 1947, MP.

Mitchell's oratory skills might become available to Stevenson. During the buildup to the campaign, Mitchell had another reunion with less pleasant overtones. As vice-chairman of the Democratic National Committee, Bill Dawson was in contact with him. At Monroney's insistence, Dawson was placed under some obligation to solicit Mitchell's presence at a party planning session. There are no signs that Mitchell ever made the trip to Washington to confer on new campaign duties and strategies, but it is clear that Mitchell never again volunteered to participate in Stevenson's campaign.[13]

In Virginia, Mitchell participated actively in one race, the 1949 gubernatorial primary. It interested him because one of the Democratic candidates was a friendly neighbor, Remmie L. Arnold. Although the Petersburg resident would eventually emerge as Mitchell's choice for the nomination, Mitchell did not immediately endorse Arnold. Before announcing for Arnold, Mitchell extended equal opportunities to the four major contenders. From their respective platforms, each candidate was given a chance to elaborate on African American policies. Although none dared to advocate plans for racial integration, Arnold definitely showed the greatest willingness to work for the interests of the minority. Unlike his three rivals, Arnold promised equality in all his dealings with Virginians. Arnold's pledge did not surprise Mitchell. As a city councilman, Arnold had achieved a reputation for fairness. At his insistence, the city's budget had been increased so that Petersburg's blacks would be provided with an equitable share of public housing units and recreational facilities. In his search for allies, Arnold displayed unusual openness and candor about his desire for black support. Weeks before the primary, Arnold met with African American leaders to explain his positions and to enlist their aid. From his personal calls, Arnold garnered P. B. Young's editorial backing and Mitchell's involvement. In July at a rousing preelection rally held at Moore Street Baptist Church in Richmond, Mitchell gave the most visible demonstration of his support for Arnold. Among other things, he told the large audience that "I think I am as good as any white man in Virginia," but only Arnold's nomination could bring "first-class citizenship for Negroes." Then switching over to his now-familiar rhetorical style, Mitchell attacked Arnold's rivals, belittling their pledges not to mix race into the campaign. As he put it, "These candidates are not fooling anybody—the Negro is the big issue in Virginia." After watching Arnold lose, Mitchell never bothered himself again with Virginia politics.[14]

13. Rayburn to M, September 1, 1952; Mike Monroney to M, September 8, 1952; Dawson to M, September 9 and 29, 1952, MP.

14. M to Remmie L. Arnold, Horace H. Edwards, Nick Prillaman, and John S. Battle, April 2, 1949; same to M, April 4, 5, and 12, 1949; Arnold to PBY, May 19, 1949, and

Overall, Mitchell showed more interest in law than in politics. He exercised some care in selecting clients and cases, but routine legal counsel to neighbors and friends dominated his docket. More than once, there were important exceptions. In the era of McCarthyism, Mitchell once more became preoccupied with Communist party deeds. However, unlike his stands against Howard University in 1935 and the National Negro Congress during his years in Congress, Mitchell this time found himself on the other side of the fence, representing a defendant charged with communist involvement. The case involved a fired civilian worker. After Samuel L. Brown was suspended on November 22, 1954, from a nonclassifed job at Fort Lee, Virginia, he chose Mitchell to defend him against several charges. Brown's reasons for choosing Mitchell are unknown. With many serious accusations pending against him from a security board of the U.S. Army, Brown had a desperate legal problem that required an attorney with considerable courtroom skill and judicial experience. Mitchell thus was a curious choice for Brown. Nonetheless, on January 12, 1955, after Pentagon prosecutors had cited Brown with six different offenses, Mitchell was present in military court, representing the accused civilian. Three of the charges against Brown concerned alleged Communist party affiliations, two counts stemmed from falsification of information on an Army employment application and perjury, and the sixth charge was a blanket indictment that covered narcotics, assault, a probation violation, and illegal gambling. To obtain an acquittal, the self-trained and fully unprepared Mitchell turned to Constitutional questions, hoping to formulate a sound defense strategy. Unlike other lawyers with clients in similar witch-hunt trials, Mitchell did not advise Brown to seek Fifth Amendment protections from self-incrimination. Instead, at his counselor's insistence, Brown responded nervously to several queries about a Communist party cell in Buffalo, denying each time knowledge of and participation in its activities. As coached by Mitchell, Brown did confirm that he had been arrested for marijuana possession, child-support arrears, and illegal gambling. When the prosecutor persisted in going back to Communist involvement, Mitchell interrupted, asking if he must "keep going back." Thereupon, in order to examine affidavits, the judge granted Mitchell a ten-day extension. Following a short conference after Mitchell and Brown had returned to court for final arguments and closing summaries, the military board upheld Brown's earlier dismissal from all duties at Fort Lee. Although Mitchell's ineptitude as a defense attorney

to M, June 1, 1949; Archie D. Respess to M, July 9, 1949; M to August Deitz Jr., July 7, 1949, MP; *Journal and Guide,* July 30 and September 24, 1949; *Richmond Times-Dispatch,* July 10 and 13, 1949.

clearly was on display at the trial, Brown was more an innocent victim of the national Red Scare than of bad counsel.[15]

Representing Brown soured Mitchell on practicing law. After the Brown case, he almost completely abandoned the profession. In its place, he interested himself in property speculation, beginning in 1956 by purchasing a triangular plot of Petersburg acreage that he appropriately called Mitchellville Subdivision. A surveyor's draft showed sixty "High Class Building Lots" fronting Clara Drive, a new street named after Mitchell's wife. According to the prospectus, the property was "about to be hard-surfaced and paved by [the] city." For obvious reasons, there was no mention of the building sites' proximity to the tracks of the Atlantic Coast Line Railroad. When the development opened on July 21, visitors not only received free refreshments and tours of a model house but also learned of Mitchell's "EASY TERMS."[16]

As a very busy retiree, Mitchell had problems fulfilling several of his most important retirement goals. Before leaving office, he had promised that he would devote himself to improving race relations. Yet he did absolutely nothing to live up to the personal pledge until November 7, 1950. On that date, Executive Director George S. Mitchell persuaded him to attend a Southern Regional Council board meeting scheduled to convene on November 10. After hearing more about SRC programs and research and how the organization had been promoting equal opportunities for all Southerners, Mitchell affiliated himself with the biracial organization. Months later, he was an SRC spokesman, traveling from Birmingham to Galveston, speaking and advising listeners on how to improve human relations. Since his speaking tour followed a long absence from the lower South, Mitchell showed more interest in personal gratification and in personal reunions than in civil rights. Hearing and reading commentaries about how kindly age had treated him were especially flattering. Missing, however, were relevant insights for audiences. Mitchell's comprehension of the dynamics behind cultural and social changes had not markedly changed since his first Southern tour as the newly installed black congressman from Chicago. To his credit, though, he showed less tolerance for prejudicial Southern jurisprudence. In 1951, he admitted that an African American citizen "had two strikes against him when he comes in court. I have always marvelled that in the South Negroes get in jail so easily and white men get out so easily." Even more revealing on the tour, an Alabama State College audience heard what would amount to his most

15. M to Edward A. Marks Jr., May 31, 1949; transcript, *Hearing Board for the Military District of Washington v. Samuel Leroy Brown*, January 12 and 22, 1955, MP.
16. Mitchellville flyers, 1956, MP.

revealing confession about his past accommodation to whites. Owning up to Tom-like behavior, he confessed, "We are not as dumb as we sometimes pretend. We know when we are hurt. . . . The Negro has no right to ask special consideration, but he does have the right to ask the same things that all other Americans receive."[17]

Other than a swing through the South for the Southern Regional Council, Mitchell had almost no other involvement in civil rights. When asked in 1959 for an opinion about desegregating Dinwiddie County and Petersburg city schools, Mitchell gave the local reporter's question careful thought before cautioning against what he called "overnight" moves. According to his suggestion, lengthy biracial exchanges should occur first as preparatory preludes to integration. His response was curious because years earlier President Dwight D. Eisenhower's indecision at "carrying out the Supreme Court decision" of 1954 prompted his rebuke and condemnation. To Mitchell, Eisenhower had shown timidity by refusing to call a national governor's conference to implement the *Brown* ruling.[18] There is nothing to confirm that Mitchell ever supported Martin Luther King Jr., student sit-in demonstrators, or other protestors involved in myriad activities from Montgomery to Memphis. Still, in all likelihood, he probably was supportive if his praise of Robert F. Kennedy in 1961 indicates anything. After the U.S. Attorney General's emotional defense of equality in Albany, Georgia, Mitchell admired "Bobby" for having shown "great wisdom and rare courage" and for having given "hope and courage to thousands . . . working and praying for real DEMOCRACY in America." If Mitchell ever spoke similar thoughts to others, there is no record or memory of his oratory. Furthermore, nothing exists to imply or indicate that he ever marched, boycotted, or otherwise contributed support to further civil rights crusades.[19]

Early in his retirement, Mitchell referred to other goals. On a regular basis, he expressed his desires to establish an endowment and to write an autobiography. His dream, he said and wrote, was to establish a personal foundation to own and maintain Rose-Anna Gardens as a national trust for African Americans. Certain it would inspire new generations to greatness, he wanted the house and surroundings to survive as his gift to black people. For similar reasons, he long considered publishing his memoirs. Throughout his life, he had passionately collected clippings

17. George S. Mitchell to M, October 30 and November 7 and 10, 1950; program, Alabama Division, Southern Regional Council, February 13, 1951, MP; *Montgomery Alabama Journal*, February 13, 1951; *Montgomery Advertiser*, February 14, 1951; *Selma Times Journal*, February 15 and 16, 1951.
18. *Petersburg Progress-Index*, March 22, 1959, MP.
19. M to Robert F. Kennedy, May 11, 1961, MP.

and saved correspondence, thinking that someday he would use them to write a valuable self-portrait of how he, the first child of illiterate former slaves, had studied and worked hard in order to achieve prominence and success in education, business, law, and politics. Just as Rose-Anna Gardens would inspire imagination and hope, his personal story would encourage and inspire young African Americans to great feats.[20]

Mitchell failed to fulfill these promises to himself. Yet a tragedy of much greater proportions unfolded with the wasted life of his son Wergs. Wergs suffered troubling delusions, and was hospitalized for mental disorders for twenty-eight years. An only child of three marriages, Wergs Mitchell had seldom made his father proud of him. A dysfunctional father-son relationship had affected the son's development. Family needs rarely interfered with Arthur Mitchell's driving ambition. Subsequently, the father's inattentiveness combined with his high expectations contributed to the son's downfall. Wergs compiled an excellent record at a Washington high school, then graduated from the University of Michigan. After he earned a master's degree in social work from the University of Chicago and prior to his total mental collapse, he held two different jobs in Chicago. He was employed with the Illinois Emergency Relief Commission as a case worker until 1935, when agency cutbacks led to his dismissal. Through his father's political contacts in Chicago, Wergs gained new employment at once. "Mitch" received a job at the Illinois offices of the Internal Revenue Service. His first months there passed without problems, but suddenly everything in his life became unbearable. He was no longer coping with fellow workers, and he was experiencing marital problems. Compounding his difficulties at work and home, his hard-to-please father reintroduced high expectations after learning of his problems at the IRS. Spoiled and indulged while a youngster, Wergs suffered from overprotection on the one hand and from great fraternal pressures to fulfill father's dreams on the other. Content as the young man always appeared to people around him, he was suffering inside. Chronic inner pains had haunted him for years. Louder and harder, they pounded at him until they brought him down at his former wife Billie's South Side home. Thereupon, police transported him to a hospital for psychiatric observation. During Wergs's initial hospitalization, his father sent no sympathetic support from Capitol Hill. Instead, Wergs was reprimanded for endeavoring to hurt and embarrass his father with foolish stunts for attention. Rather than blame himself for Wergs's breakdown or the subsequent failures of various treatments, Arthur Mitchell accused his son's friends for the disorders. Eventually, Wergs slipped completely away from his father's

20. *Journal and Guide*, September 24, 1949; Mitchell interviews.

life. According to medical reports, the patient's mental state deteriorated so rapidly after a few years of isolation at a state hospital that doctors were diagnosing his case as hopeless. Preoccupied with his distant past, Wergs was altogether removed from reality. He spoke ramblingly and constantly about his long-deceased mother, Eula Mae Mitchell. Except for friends, whose visits his father suspended after a few months, Wergs was visited only by his mother's sister, Dr. Wilma Carmody of San Diego. On several occasions, to cheer him with recollections of Eula Mae, "Auntie" journeyed far to be with her nephew. For her first visit, she took along Arthur Mitchell's only photograph of her sister. Except for immediately after Annie Mitchell's death in 1947, all father-son contacts ceased. It was just as well, however, because the medical staff complained that the father's few attempts at relations had only made Wergs's condition worse. Wergs died on July 14, 1965; days later in a private ceremony, Arthur Mitchell buried his son at Rose-Anna Gardens.[21]

Within three years, Mitchell joined Annie and Wergs Mitchell under the trees at "The Land of A Thousand Roses." A peaceful end came on May 9, 1968, just minutes before 8 P.M. After almost eighty-five years, the famous but now almost forgotten son of Ammar Patterson and Taylor Mitchell was dead, leaving in his wake several surviving relatives including twice-widowed Clara, brother John W. of Los Angeles, sister Tommie L. Stitt in Detroit, granddaughter Melinda from Chicago, and three stepchildren. Ironically and paradoxically, his siblings had left the South in their old age, while Arthur had returned there. He had never begun writing his planned memoirs. No foundation had ever been created to maintain his cherished Rose-Anna Gardens as a grand memorial to hopes and opportunities enjoyed by African Americans. Since Mrs. Clara Mitchell had no desire to live there by herself, she sold the house and gardens to a retired Air Force officer. More a hunter than a farmer, he gained little pleasure from strenuous gardening. Left to become exactly like so many other private

21. *Defender*, November 20, 1937, and March 12, 1938; M to Sabath, December 12, 1935; M to Blaine G. Hoover, December 23, 1935, and January 21, 1936; memo, E. K. Eckert to Harrison, August 16, 1937; memo, Grace M. Welch, August 16, 1937; CHH to Charles T. Russell, August 6 and 16, 1937; Russell to CHH, August 11, 1937; CHH to Wergs, August 24, 1937; CHH to M, September 14, 1937; M to CHH, September 11 and 29, 1937; W. H. Brummit to M, November 21, 1937; O. B. Williams to M, December 10, 1937, and January 31, 1938; M to Williams, February 8, 1938; Charles F. Read to M, November 30, 1937, January 26 and October 28, 1939, and February 5, 1940; McLendon to M, June 26, 1938; M to Gert Heilburn, December 2, 1937, and January 25, 1938; M to Wabash Avenue YMCA, December 13, 1937; Diggs to M, November 24, 1937; Carmody to M, May 2 and October 11, 1939; M to Carmody, January 16, May 4, and June 6, 1939; Louis Steinberg to M, September 24, 1948; M to Steinberg, October 4, 1948; M to Haffron, March 9, 1951; Wergs to M, April 23 and 28, May 3, September 7, and October 4, 1947; obituary, July 14, 1965, MP.

residences on once-busy Southern highways, Rose-Anna Gardens passed quickly from its showplace status to an ordinary pillared house on the outskirts of a small town. At the drive to the mansion, there are no markers to the pioneering black Democratic legislator. Much like the vegetation at Rose-Anna Gardens and his son Wergs during his long hospitalization, Arthur Wergs Mitchell has been neglected.[22]

Summarizing Mitchell's place in the political transition of the New Deal Era, one anonymous ANP writer showed considerable analytical skill. As he described Mitchell's career in 1942:

> Congressman Arthur W. Mitchell is highly regarded by some people, while others hold highly adverse opinions about him. He is a man of considerable ability. His success in various endeavors causes many people who seek to discount his ability, to call him "lucky." He has the capacity for making friends among white people, particularly southern whites. It is a fair statement . . . most Negroes who have come in close contact with him do not like him . . . because he is an egotist of the first water; because he is crude and rather ruthless in his dealings with them; because he is arrogant. They say . . . he "kowtows" to southern whites outwardly . . . to serve his own ends, although inwardly he resents and despises them. . . . One who hears him speak is impressed that he is a fighter, a zealot for his people. His recent Jim Crow suit, while it does not affect the basic principles of that particular discrimination, has given him greater national prestige than he has ever known. . . . Strangely enough, Mr. Mitchell, despite what would appear . . . shortcomings galore, has . . . virtues. That is why the word paradoxical seems appropriate.[23]

Using "paradoxical" as a nutshell description of Arthur W. Mitchell's public career does not seem altogether suitable. "Complex" is definitely more descriptive of him because it is inclusive, absorbing his entire life from childhood to death and handling his tumultuous relationships and activities at several Alabama locations, in unofficial and official Washington, in Bronzeville, and in Petersburg. Absurdly, both Mitchell's contemporaries and scholars writing on the rise of black Democrats during the Great Depression have attributed his rise to "luck." A "vacuum of black leadership" is Professor Charles R. Branham's weak explanation. Branham leaves the mistaken impression that Mitchell was blessed by good fortune; he "entered public life at a remarkably propitious moment." There was "no substantial rival within the Democratic party." As for his survival through three subsequent elections, Mitchell benefited from "timing" and

22. *Richmond Times-Dispatch*, May 10, 1968, MP; author's inspection of Rose-Anna Gardens and conversation with its purchaser, September 27, 1974.
23. Anonymous memorandum on Mitchell, 1942, BP.

"conflicts within both his party and the opposition Republican party."
Indeed, Branham does rescue the African American lawmaker from an
otherwise dismal characterization by concluding that his tenure represented "more than an interregnum between the DePriest and Dawson
eras," but there are no follow-up statements to assign anything positive
and personal to Mitchell's contributions. Rather, Branham prefers to regard his years in Congress as nothing more than a beneficial hiatus, or in
his words, "a period of conflict and struggle which would transform black
leadership within both parties and alter the course of black politics." Like
the ANP writer in 1942, Branham finds a legislator who could not protect
himself from self-destruction, concluding that Mitchell "seemed destined
to sabotage each good deed with insensitivity and ineptitude." A more
careful check than Branham's of editorials and correspondence relating to
these alleged faux pas reveal much groundswell support among blacks for
all of Mitchell's excesses. Lacking in popularity and independent political
power, Mitchell had allowed himself to "speak without thinking" so much
that he had quite literally talked himself out of a personal following. Based
totally upon an incorrect premise about Mitchell's ambitions, Branham
assumes the presence of a desire for something resembling a loyal cadre.
However, in reality, Mitchell's career was the result of careful deliberation
and execution. A painstaking probe of his life reveals how infrequently
he permitted events and individuals to engulf or entrap him; as a rule, he
prevailed as the controlling force, overcoming all difficulties and people
with adroitly placed manipulation and perfected role play.[24]

Ascribing Mitchell's phenomenal overnight success in politics to luck
and good fortune both oversimplifies and underestimates his abilities and
insights as a skillful planner and plotter. Dismissing him as a "political
anomaly" indicates either a callous misreading of a complex person's
talents for adjustment or a shallow investigation into his life. Judging by
reoccurring errors in the biographical sketches of many historical studies,
the latter weakness undergirds many of the incorrect conclusions about
Mitchell's receipt of the Democratic nomination in 1934 and his subsequent eight-year congressional career.[25] From childhood through early
adulthood, a number of patterns emerged in Mitchell's life that resurfaced
later during his eventful public career. As his mother, Ammar Mitchell,
noticed early in her oldest son's development, his rows were straighter,
a good indication of his lifelong passions for detail and precision. Before
his admission to Tuskegee Institute, which would shape his philosophy,

24. Branham, "The Transformation of Black Political Leadership," 292, 318, 320–21,
365, 368.
25. Besides Branham, see especially studies by Gordon, Weiss, and Reid.

Mitchell audaciously predicted success for himself in correspondence that demanded exceptions to the inflexible school's regulations. One year there was seemingly enough for him to absorb Booker T. Washington's precepts, thoughts, and methods. A love-hate relationship with the Wizard followed. Mitchell admired and accepted every tenet of Washington's accommodationist philosophy, and he admitted his respect for Washington's status and reputation. Yet Mitchell did not hesitate to humble his hero with blackmail after the Wizard had circulated uncomplimentary reports of his chicanery in founding competing schools. Although nothing remains in four communities to remind local residents of the schools that Mitchell had begun and operated, their existence no doubt did offer positive images to their charges. A few lessons in reading, writing, and arithmetic in some respects were never as important as Mitchell, their symbol of black success. Few liked him or the compromises he was negotiating with powerful local landowners, but their feelings about him did not mean that his presence had not given isolated Alabamans chances to meet successful black visitors and to dream of better lives. Vicariously through "professor" Mitchell, detractors experienced material expressions of status heretofore unassociated with African Americans. Even if they knew a lack of scruples had contributed to his ostentation, there was still no doubt a sense of pride from seeing him, a fellow African American, in an expensive buggy drawn by a fine team of horses or from observing him in a luxurious Packard automobile that was certainly as impressive as vehicles owned by local whites. Also, by fleeing with "their" insurance money and strutting with "their" pride, Mitchell brought bravado and new dimensions to the otherwise pitiful lives of blacks in the remotest areas of backward Alabama. For Mitchell, there were benefits, too. Besides opportunities for cultural enrichment gained during summers spent at Harvard and Columbia, his experience of sealing mutually beneficial deals with prominent Southern whites prepared him for his future political career. Above all else, he extracted a basis for profitable self-growth from these interracial relationships. Even if his unadmiring critics considered him an "Uncle Tom," there is no denying that an absence of moral principles gave Mitchell extraordinary fame and wealth. Moreover, leaving one community for another miles away showed his keen judgment for knowing when to take farewells as well as his unusual capacity for contemplating contingencies. His well-orchestrated escapes to fresh starts were no more accidental or "propitious" than his entrance into elective politics in 1934.

As in education, Mitchell did not particularly distinguish himself in law. First in Washington and then in Chicago, there was nothing especially commendable about his practices. When cases demanded special skills or knowledge, his clients were not given expert legal counseling. Hence, he left them chanceless in courts of law. As a self-learned attorney, he simply could not compete with better briefed and educated lawyers. Mitchell's predictable failures at law were last evidenced with his feeble attempt at defending Samuel L. Brown. However, he made a more lasting achievement in business. For an African American population in need of modern housing, Mitchell was a gambling pioneer, introducing some of the first black-owned apartments to the District of Columbia. With his possession of these, he achieved entrepreneurial success in real estate. To doubters and critics such as Howard University sociology professor William H. Jones, Mitchell demonstrated how blacks could finance and manage rental properties as well as whites and that blacks could cope as well as anyone with living in multiple-dwelling residences. In addition, when Mitchell emerged as president of Phi Beta Sigma fraternity, it was another indication of his greatness. In the national lodge's history, no head has ever matched "little Napoleon"; his nine years as president has exceeded all others in this office. Eight times, the fraternity's members reelected him.

Mitchell's soliciting and achieving important responsibilities for Herbert C. Hoover in 1928 despite the presence of better-known black Republicans proved his ability to adroitly navigate the field of party politics. More amazing still was his move to politically crowded Chicago with the single ambition of unseating an African American congressman. It showed his resolution and determination to push himself to goals deemed unattainable by others. His daring abandonment of the Grand Old Party when most blacks were remaining in the Republican camp was one more example of his genius for weighing options and deciding correctly. Observing Joseph E. Tittinger's dilemma with black ambitions, Mitchell exploited it to full personal advantage. Professor Branham, after an excellent job of introducing black Democratic leaders from the South Side neighborhood, forgets altogether about their existence, contradicting himself with an absurd judgment about a "vacuum" among Chicago black Democrats as the primary reason behind Mitchell's elevation to prominence. If not for Mitchell's exceptional salesmanship at convincing a desperate ward heeler of his virtues as an ideal token Negro candidate, then surely Earl B. Dickerson, Edgar C. Brown, Edward M. Sneed, Bryant Hammond, Loring Moore, Corneal Davis, or Herman E. Moore would have emerged as Tittinger's more likely choice. Simply put, the chance went to Mitchell and not to one of the others because Mitchell demonstrated superior abilities to pacify white fears. Better than other contenders in Bronzeville at showing empathy to whites with "Negro problems," Mitchell could look at Tittinger in trouble with demands from militant blacks and present himself as a solution to "the problem." Mitchell's execution of this skill with the boss was so perfect that Tittinger eventually became his personal power broker with Machine overlords. With the support of a committeeman commanding an army of precinct captains, Mitchell never needed a black political force behind him. Through the span of his political career, four ward bosses asserted enough power to reelect him. Mitchell's ability to flatter their egos and then, even more amazingly, to overcome his previous harsh attacks against former foe and Republican-turned-Democrat Bill Dawson in 1940 were proof of his exceptional gift for political maneuvering and his rare talents for survival. There was another factor behind Mitchell's longevity in office. He remembered that whites were the majority in the First Congressional District. Unlike many Republican and Democratic rivals who pandered to Bronzeville, he comforted whites with reassuring promises to be fair to all residents. Then to both races, without partiality, he delivered jobs and U.S. military academy appointments. He demonstrated his expediency clearly after Italy's brutal attack on Ethiopia. Aware Little Italy's residents were his constituents, crafty Mitchell did not want to offend these biased voters with condemnations; rather, he gave a politically measured response that did not generate negative reactions from a partisan ethnic group in his midst.

Although Mitchell followed the Machine's instructions and voted according to its commands on Capitol Hill roll calls, there was more to his representation than patronage and dutiful obedience. He was powerless and had no significant legislation to his credit after eight years as Congress's pioneer black Democrat. Still, he deserves better from historians than a completely negative assessment. By no means a dynamic and powerful force who changed official Washington, this complex public official was more than "a failure as a national legislator."[26] Against some astronomical odds, Mitchell tried to defend African Americans and to push through meaningful legislation. That he did not succeed is more a reflection of the times than of his own failure. To honor Booker Washington's life and work, Mitchell was willing, if necessary, to invest his own money to emphasize how much the Wizard's birthplace meant to African Americans. His legislative bid failed, but at his insistence, Congress did set aside time for paying tribute to the great educator and leader. Mitchell also fought hard to assist polar explorer Matthew Henson, but through no fault of his own, his fellow legislators refused to give serious consideration to a pension bill. Attempts at reforming Civil Service Commission procedures went nowhere as well. His advocacy of fingerprints in place of compulsory photographs and demanded improvements in posting procedures to make them fair provoked the commissioner, but again, there was no movement on his three bills. Except for some

26. Branham, "The Transformation of Black Political Leadership," 292.

first-term excesses and grandstanding against the NAACP leadership, Mitchell worked quietly thereafter, more or less in accord with leading civil rightists, on most issues, including antilynching legislation. Unfortunately, vituperative public exchanges between him and NAACP officers in 1935 and 1936 overshadowed his later record. The evidence indicates that Mitchell was less responsible for the initial flare-up than was the NAACP leadership. Thereafter as a believer in honor, he defended his positions, outrageously at times. His resulting poor reputation among blacks who favored more militant challenges to injustice followed him into retirement. Yet on some fronts, he made fearless protests that were creditable and useful. Unlike all others in government, Mitchell refused to allow his African American appointee to Annapolis to be "railroaded out" without offering resistance and investigation. Although he discovered the truth behind James Johnson Jr.'s nightmare at the Naval Academy, it did not matter much in the final analysis because Mitchell had no support for a proper examination into officially sanctioned racism at the Navy's officer training facility. To his credit as well, he was most helpful in resolving a dispute in Detroit. He brought city and federal housing spokesmen together for useful discussions that ultimately yielded a reversal of an unfair decision that had nullified an original plan designating the entire housing park for black families. In part because of his active intervention, Sojourner Truth units were again reserved only for African American occupants. After Germany's 1939 invasion of Poland and the subsequent commencement of American rearmament, Mitchell increasingly became a gadfly with outspoken criticisms of racism in military services and in defense industries. There was also his partially symbolic four-year legal struggle against the railroads' discriminatory policies. In 1941, a long legal battle culminated in victory. The Supreme Court justices might not have struck down segregation, but their decision for a black plaintiff represented clarification and definition of equality, especially as it applied to the operations of railroads and fulfillments of constitutional guarantees of equal rights. On demand thereafter, black passengers were fully entitled to all accommodations that were available to white travelers. A wedge more than a knife in the judicial struggle against unequal treatment, the verdict might not have overturned laws separating the races, but it reinforced minority rights and was a confidence-builder for African Americans. The ruling for Mitchell encouraged new lawsuits, and the arguments used in the case became the basis of several related cases involving discrimination and African Americans.

As a cog in the Chicago Machine, Mitchell exchanged his freedom and independence for a place on Capitol Hill. Nevertheless, as a Democratic pioneer, he recognized the vulnerability and sensitivity of his position. Much was at stake. Open hostility to party members from the South could have conceivably fragmented Franklin D. Roosevelt's hold over the legislative branch, or it could have closed the Democratic party once again to African American influence and participation. Keeping his promise not to have a chip on his shoulder toward anyone, Arthur Wergs Mitchell dissipated Southern fears of him. In the process, he aided other black participants. Criticized severely for having what appeared to be an odd fascination for Dixie, Mitchell used this appearance to make a black's presence in otherwise segregated Washington Democratic circles seem natural and even comfortable. In speaking at party conventions in 1936 and 1940 and in attending Jackson Day dinners and White House receptions, he attracted only nominal whimpers of disapproval while effectively integrating his party. Also important for a black legislator, he voted with Democratic majorities. Thus, his record on roll calls contributed to a strong, problem-solving federal government. His responses to bills thereby negated several generations of Negro conservatism. Mitchell was also a vigorous spokesman for Roosevelt and for Democratic candidates. During the 1936 campaign, he had celebrity status, and demands on him to speak were overwhelming. In itself a dismissal of his insignificance, Mitchell's presence on political platforms was symbolic of a new Democratic party, one that included African Americans. Behind the scenes, whenever possible, he was steering activist black members to the sidelines. For unknown reasons, he never fully expressed his reactions to them, but the careful, accommodating politician always feared William Thompkins, Earl Dickerson, and Robert Vann. Apparently, their militancy, impatience, individual agendas, and general disregard for the delicacy of FDR's peculiar coalition worried Mitchell, but it was their lack of gratitude that probably upset him most of all. Viewing black independents as potential troublemakers capable of causing mischief and disrupting the party, Mitchell distanced himself from them and avoided their activities.

Echoing Booker Washington on many issues, Mitchell's expressions seemed irrelevant and too conservative at the time of their utterances. During the large-scale migration of African Americans to Northern cities, he warned of possible consequences for the race. In his judgment, leaving the South would not relieve problems for illiterate and unskilled rural blacks. In confidential correspondence to Kelly Miller, he expressed grave doubts about the long-term effects of urban resettlement on migrants. Similarly, even though he voted for welfare as an emergency measure to relieve the nation's most destitute individuals, he feared that welfare recipients might become permanent wards of the government. Frequently vilified for having faith in Southerners' capabilities of settling regional problems themselves, Mitchell kept his pledge to set an example by living below the Mason-Dixon Line after his retirement. Had he lived long enough, Mitchell would have felt redemption for the realization of so many of his early contentions about the South's potential for interracial progress. No longer would there be as many critics chafing at his statements about the region. Moreover, his appeals to blacks to practice more self-responsibility would no longer spark the same anger they once stirred. A quarter of a century after his death, many of his thoughts about self-reliance are encapsulated in popular rap lyrics and are espoused by strident messengers such as the Reverend Louis Farrakhan. Except for his symbolic significance, Mitchell's presence did not have as much impact on Congress as he would have wanted. On the other hand, during an era of lynching, segregation, and discrimination, no other black would have changed conditions any more than he had. Outspoken militants full of suggestions and criticism for him would have fared worse. If one of his harshest critics had been elected instead, he or she would have surely upset the white majority in control of Congress to such a degree that the results would have certainly been ostracism and ineffectiveness. Subsequently, as other black representatives elected by white-majority constituencies have shown, accommodationist views are an absolute prerequisite to political survival. As a rule, white majorities have not elected blacks to represent only the minority. Under these circumstances, black officials with majority-white constituencies have had to take a safe approach to everything involving race in order to ensure their political survival. As a brilliant politician who knew how to manipulate white people for maximum achievement of personal goals, Mitchell fully understood the limits and factors that would curtail and undermine his activities. He acted accordingly. Part of his true significance lies in what Kansas City boss Tom Pendergast, Louisville's police chief, and Tuskegee's female students recognized in late 1934 after his stunning victory over incumbent GOP congressman Oscar DePriest: his presence on the other side of the aisle from all his black predecessors was destined to make a major difference in African American political alignments. He associated himself with Franklin D. Roosevelt's presidency, and the connection stuck with a majority of the minority. The thought of a black Democrat in office was revolutionary in 1935 when Mitchell entered the House of Representatives. Hence, he had a significant role in revolutionizing the Democratic party and in the partisan debate for black votes and loyalties. If Mitchell's image does not shine brightly and positively today, it is no coincidence; for being too protective of himself, the Machine, and the Democratic party coalition, he often deserved contemporaries' reprimands and criticisms. In addition to everything else about Arthur Wergs Mitchell, his life illustrated how likability and kindness are not prerequisites or requirements for greatness and influence in politics. More than anyone else—as a man of political "firsts"—he truly was the integrator of the Democratic party as its first African American congressman.

BIBLIOGRAPHY

Manuscript Collections

Barnett, Claude A. (Associated Negro Press Files), Papers, CHS
Blaisdell, Fred W., Papers, CHS
Choctaw County (Alabama) Court Records, Butler
Dickerson, Earl Burrus, Papers, CHS
Dixon, Frank M., Papers, Alabama Department of History and Archives, Montgomery
Fitzpatrick, John, Papers, CHS
Hale County (Alabama) Court Records, Greensboro
Johnson, James L., Family Papers, author's possession
McDuffie, John, Papers, Alabama Collection, University of Alabama Library
Mitchell, Arthur W., Papers, CHS
Moton, Robert R., Papers, Tuskegee Institute, Alabama
NAACP Papers, 1934–1943, LC
Roosevelt, Franklin D., Papers, Roosevelt Library, Hyde Park, New York
Sorrentino, Anthony, Papers, CHS
Sumter County (Alabama) Court Records, Livingston
Tuskegee Institute Archives, Tuskegee, Alabama
Washington, Booker T., Papers, LC

Interviews

Brown, Oscar C. Sr., Chicago, July 28, 1971
Brummit, Mrs. William H., Chicago, May 19, 1971 (telephone)
Cephas, Marietta and James, Petersburg, September 27, 1974
Chaney, Golden W., Choctaw County, Alabama, May 13, 1979
Clarke, Thomas E., Chicago, July 21, 1971 (telephone)
Collins-Levy, Rachel, Choctaw County, Alabama, May 13, 1979
Cyrus, Bindley C., Chicago, July 27, 1971
Dickerson, Earl B., Chicago, November 19, 1970
Gibson, Truman K. Jr., Chicago, July 29, 1971

Gilbert, William E. and William L., Geiger, Alabama, April 12, 1971
Goldston, Tobe, Panola, Alabama, April 12, 1971
Harrison, Earl, Rock Springs, Alabama, May 25, 1979
Johnson, James L. Jr., Washington, September 29, 1974
Kirkpatrick, Felix, Chicago, March 27, 1971
Lane, Charles F., Chicago, July 28, 1971 (telephone)
Lawrence, George W., Chicago, July 30, 1971
Little, Fanoy, Panola, Alabama, April 13, 1971
Mason, Will, Geiger, Alabama, April 12, 1971
May, Zola, Choctaw County, Alabama, May 13, 1979
Mitchell, Clara, Lynchburg, April 4, 1970, and September 27, 1974
Motts, Leon, Chicago, July 21, 1971 (telephone)
Pinson, John, Geiger, Alabama, April 12, 1971
Reed, Gilbert L., Chicago, July 12, 1971 (telephone)
Sampson, Rufus, Chicago, July 26, 1971 (telephone)
Spencer, Alfred F., Chicago, May 27, 1971
Thornton, William F., Chicago, May 22, 1971
Tittinger, Joseph E., Wheaton, Illinois, October 8, 1970, and July 29, 1971
Vickery, Inez Gilbert, Chicago, March 23, 1971

Contemporary Published Materials

Abbott, Edith. *The Tenements of Chicago, 1908–1935.* Chicago: University of Chicago Press, 1936.
ABE *Negro Education,* Bulletins 38 and 39, Montgomery, Ala., 1916 and 1917.
Bethune, Mary. "My Secret Talks with FDR." *Ebony* 4 (April 1949): 42–51.
Chicago American Negro Exposition, 1940 Program, Chicago, 1940.
"Chicago's Record of Accomplishment under Mayor Edward J. Kelly: The Remarkable Regeneration of America's Second City under Its Democratic Mayor." Chicago, 1940.
Edwards, William J. *Twenty-Five Years in the Black Belt.* Boston: Cornill Company, 1918.
Federal Writers' Project, WPA. *Washington: City and Capital.* Washington, D.C., 1937.
Jones, William H. *The Housing of Negroes in Washington, D.C.: A Study in Human Ecology.* Washington, D.C.: Howard University Press, 1929.
National Colored Committee and the Good Neighbor League. "Has the Roosevelt New Deal Helped the Colored Citizen?" New York, 1938.
Newcomb, Charles S., ed. *Census Data of the City of Chicago, 1934.* Chicago: University of Chicago Press, 1934.

Ogden, Mary E. *The Chicago Negro Community, A Statistical Description.*
    Chicago: U.S. WPA, Illinois, 1939.
Phillips, Esther M. *Negro Health in the State of Illinois.* Springfield, Ill.: State
    Department of Public Health, 1936.
"Social Data for Chicago Communities." *Community Fact Book, 1938.* Chi-
    cago, 1938.
U.S. Congress. *CR.* 71st–77th Congresses.
U.S. Department of Commerce, Census Bureau. Records, 1900, 1910.
U.S. Deptartment of the Interior, Bureau of Education. *Negro Education: A
    Study of the Private and Higher Schools for Colored People in the United
    States.* Bulletin Nos. 38, 39. Washington, D.C., 1917.
U.S. House Committee on Interstate and Foreign Commerce, 66th Cong.,
    1st sess. *Return of the Railroads to Private Ownership, Hearings.* Wash-
    ington, D.C., 1919.
U.S. House Judiciary Committee. *Hearings on H.R. 5733, June 18, 1935.*
    Washington, D.C., 1935.
Williams, Elmer L. *The Fix-It Boys: The Inside Story of the New Deal and the
    Kelly-Nash Machine.* Chicago: E. L. Williams, 1940.

Secondary Materials

Abrams, Douglas C. "Irony of Reform: North Carolina Blacks and the
    New Deal." *North Carolina Historical Review* 66 (April 1989): 149–78.
Alexander, Raymond Pace. "Recent Trends in the Law of Racial Segre-
    gation on Public Carriers." *National Bar Journal* (December 1947):
    401–13.
————. "The Upgrading of the Negro's Status by Supreme Court Deci-
    sions." *Journal of Negro History* 30 (April 1945): 117–49.
Allswang, John M. *A House for All Peoples: Ethnic Politics in Chicago, 1890–
    1936.* Lexington: University of Kentucky Press, 1971.
————. "The Chicago Negro Voter and the Democratic Consensus, A Case
    Study, 1918–1936." *Illinois State Historical Society Journal* 60 (summer
    1967): 145–75.
Anderson, Jervis. *A. Philip Randolph: A Biographical Portrait.* New York:
    Harcourt Brace Jovanovich, 1973.
Bailey, Harry A. Jr., ed. *Negro Politics in America.* Columbus: Bobbs Merrill,
    1967.
Bain, George W. "How Negro Editors Viewed the New Deal." *Journalism
    Quarterly* 44 (autumn 1967): 552–54.
Barbeau, Arthur E., and Florette Henri. *The Unknown Soldiers: Black Amer-
    ican Troops in World War I.* Philadelphia: University of Pennsylvania,
    1974.

Bauman, John F. "Black Slums/Black Projects: The New Deal and Negro Housing in Philadelphia." *Pennsylvania History* 41 (July 1974): 311–38.

Bernstein, Barton J. "The New Deal: The Conservative Achievement of Liberal Reform." In Bernstein, ed., *Towards a New Past: Dissenting Essays in American History*, 263–82. New York: Random House, 1969.

Bernstein, Irving. *Turbulent Years: A History of the American Worker, 1933–1941*. Boston: Houghton Mifflin, 1971.

Biles, Roger. *Big City Boss in Depression and War: Mayor Edward J. Kelly of Chicago*. DeKalb: Northern Illinois University Press, 1984.

Black, Allida M. "Championing a Champion: Eleanor Roosevelt and the Marian Anderson 'Freedom Concert.'" *Presidential Studies Quarterly* 20 (fall 1990): 719–36.

Bond, Horace M. *Social and Economic Influences on the Public Education of Negroes in Alabama, 1865–1930*. Washington, D.C.: Associated Publishers, 1939.

Bracey, John H. Jr., and August Meier. "Allies or Adversaries?: The NAACP, A. Philip Randolph and the 1941 March on Washington." *Georgia Historical Quarterly* 75 (spring 1991): 1–17.

Branham, Charles R. "The Transformation of Black Political Leadership in Chicago, 1864–1942." Ph.D. diss., University of Chicago, 1981.

Brooks, Thomas R. "Big City Politics: Making the Black Vote Count." *Tuesday Magazine* (September 1971): 8–10, 26.

Bukowski, Douglas E. "According to Image: William Hale Thompson and the Politics of Chicago, 1915–1931." Ph.D diss., University of Illinois at Chicago, 1989.

Bullock, Henry A. *A History of Negro Education in the South: From 1619 to the Present*. Cambridge: Harvard University Press, 1967.

Bunche, Ralph J. *The Political Status of the Negro in the Age of FDR*. Chicago: University of Chicago Press, 1973.

———. "A Tentative Analysis of Negro Leadership." Unpublished draft.

Buni, Andrew. *Robert L. Vann of the* Pittsburgh Courier: *Politics and Black Journalism*. Pittsburgh: University of Pittsburgh Press, 1974.

Burbank, Lyman B. "Chicago Public Schools and the Depression Years of 1928–1937." *Illinois State Historical Society Journal* 64 (winter 1971): 365–81.

Capeci, Dominic J. Jr. "The Lynching of Cleo Wright: Federal Protection of Constitutional Rights during World War II." *Journal of American History* 72 (March 1986): 859–87.

Christopher, Maurine. *America's Black Congressmen*. New York: T. Y. Crowell, 1971.

Clayton, Edward T. *The Negro Politician, His Success and Failure*. Chicago: Johnson Publishing, 1964.

Collins, Ernest M. "Cincinnati Negroes and Presidential Politics." *Journal of Negro History* 41 (April 1956): 131–37.

Conrad, David E. *The Forgotten Farmers: The Story of Sharecroppers in the New Deal.* Urbana: University of Illinois Press, 1965.

Cooper, Arnold. *Between Struggle and Hope: Four Black Educators in the South, 1894–1915.* Ames: Iowa State University Press, 1989.

———. "Booker T. Washington and William J. Edwards of Snow Hill Institute, 1893–1915." *Alabama Review* 40 (April 1987): 111–32.

———. "The Tuskegee Machine in Action: Booker T. Washington's Influence on Utica Institute, 1903–1915." *Journal of Mississippi History* 48 (fall 1986): 283–95.

Cornwell, Elmer E. "Bosses, Machines, and Ethnic Groups." *American Academy of Political and Social Science Annals* 353 (May 1964): 27–39.

Coser, Lewis, and Irving Howe. *The American Communist Party: A Critical History, 1919–1957.* Boston: Beacon Press, 1957.

Cruse, Harold. *The Crisis of the Negro Intellectual.* New York: Quill, 1984.

Dalfiume, Richard M. *Desegregation of the U.S. Armed Forces: Fighting on Two Fronts, 1939–1953.* Columbia: University of Missouri Press, 1969.

———. "Military Segregation and the 1940 Presidential Election." *Phylon* 30 (spring 1969): 42–55.

Daoust, Norma LaSalle. "Building the Democratic Party: Black Voting in Providence in the 1930s." *Rhode Island History* 44 (spring 1985): 80–88.

Day, Beth. *The Little Professor of Piney Woods: The Story of Professor Laurence Jones.* New York: J. Messner, 1955.

Dixon, Robert G. Jr., "Civil Rights in Transportation and the ICC." *George Washington Law Review* 31 (October 1962): 198–206.

Drake, St. Clair. "The Negro Church Associations in Chicago: A Research Memorandum." Typed manuscript, 1940.

Drake, St. Clair, and Horace R. Clayton. *Black Metropolis: A Study of Negro Life in a Northern City.* 2 vols. New York: Harcourt Brace, 1970.

Dubay, Robert W. "Mississippi and the Proposed Federal Anti-Lynching Bills of 1937–1938." *Southern Quarterly* 7 (October 1968): 73–89.

Duis, Perry R. "Arthur W. Mitchell: New Deal Negro in Congress." Master's thesis, University of Chicago, 1966.

Duncan, Otis D., and Beverly Duncan. *The Negro Population of Chicago: A Study of Residential Succession.* Chicago: University of Chicago Press, 1957.

Dunn, Larry W. "Knoxville Negro Voting and the Roosevelt Revolution, 1928–1936." *East Tennessee Historical Society Publications* 43 (1971): 71–93.

Eisenberg, Bernard. "Kelly Miller: The Negro Leader as a Marginal Man." *Journal of Negro History* 65 (July 1960): 182–97.

Fishel, Leslie. "The Negro in the New Deal Era." *Wisconsin Magazine of History* 48 (winter 1966): 111–26.

Flock, Mary M., ed. "Autobiography of John McDuffie: Farmer, Lawyer, Legislator, Judge." Typed manuscript, n.d.

Fowler, Robert H. "The Negro Who Went to the Pole with Peary." *American History Illustrated* I (April and May 1966): 4–11, 52–55, 45–52.

Franklin, Jimmie L. "Black Southerners, Shared Experience, and Place: A Reflection." *Journal of Southern History* 60 (February 1994): 3–18.

Franklin, Vincent P. *The Education of Black Philadelphia: The Social and Educational History of a Minority Community, 1900–1950.* Philadelphia: University of Pennsylvania Press, 1979.

———. "Voice of the Black Community: The *Philadelphia Tribune,* 1912–41." *Pennsylvania History* 51 (summer 1984): 261–84.

Frazier, Edward F. *The Negro Family in Chicago.* Chicago: University of Chicago Press, 1932.

———. "Some Effects of the Depression on the Negro in Northern Cities." *Science and Society* 2 (fall 1938): 489–99.

Garcia, George F. "Black Disaffection from the Republican Party during the Presidency of Herbert Hoover, 1928–1932." *Annals of Iowa* 45 (winter 1980): 462–77.

Glantz, Oscar. "The Negro Vote in Northern Industrial Cities." *Western Political Quarterly* 13 (December 1960): 999–1010.

Gordon, Rita Werner. "The Change in the Political Alignment of Chicago's Negroes during the New Deal." *Journal of American History* 56 (December 1969): 584–603.

Gosnell, Harold F. *Negro Politicians: The Rise of Negro Politics in Chicago.* Chicago: University of Chicago Press, 1935.

———. "The Negro Vote in Northern Cities." *National Municipal Review* 30 (May 1941): 264–67, 278.

Green, Constance M. *The Secret City: A History of Race Relations in the Nation's Capital.* Princeton: Princeton University Press, 1967.

———. *Washington: Capital City, 1879–1950.* Princeton: Princeton University Press, 1963.

Greenbaum, Fred. "The Anti-Lynching Bill of 1935: The Irony of Equal Justice—Under Law." *Journal of Human Relations* 15 (third quarter 1967): 72–85.

Grimshaw, William J. *Bitter Fruit: Black Politics and the Chicago Machine, 1931–1991.* Chicago: University of Chicago Press, 1992.

Grossman, James R. *Land of Hope: Chicago, Black Southerners, and the Great Migration.* Chicago: University of Chicago Press, 1989.

Hale, William H. "The Negro Lawyer and His Client." *Phylon* 13 (spring 1952): 57–63.

Harlan, Louis R. *Booker T. Washington: The Wizard of Tuskegee, 1901–1915.* New York: Oxford University Press, 1983.

Harrell, James H. "Negro Leadership in the Election Year 1936." *Journal of Southern History* 34 (November 1968): 546–64.

Hayes, Laurence J. W. *The Negro Federal Government Worker: A Study of His Classification Status in the District of Columbia, 1883–1938.* Washington: Howard University Press, 1941.

Hero, Alfred O. Jr. "American Negroes and U.S. Foreign Policy, 1937–1967." *Journal of Conflict Resolution* 13, no. 2 (1969): 220–51.

Higbee, Mark D. "W. E. B. DuBois, F. B. Ransom, the Madame Walker Company, and Black Business Leadership in the 1930s." *Indiana Magazine of History* 84 (June 1993): 101–24.

Hirsch, Arnold R. "Chicago: The Cook County Democratic Organization and the Dilemma of Race, 1931–1987." In Richard M. Bernard, ed., *Snowbelt Cities: Metropolitan Politics in the Northeast and Midwest since World War II,* 63–90. Bloomington: Indiana University Press, 1990.

Hodges, Carl G. *Illinois Negro Historymakers.* Chicago: Illinois Emancipation Centennial Commission, 1964.

Hogan, Lawrence D. *A Black National News Service: The Associated Negro Press and Claude Barnett, 1919–1945.* Rutherford: Fairleigh Dickinson University Press, 1984.

Holley, Donald. "The Negro in the New Deal Resettlement Program." *Agricultural History* 45 (July 1971): 179–94.

Holmes, Michael S. "The Blue Eagle as 'Jim Crow Bird': The NRA and Georgia's Black Workers." *Journal of Negro History* 57 (July 1972): 276–83.

———. "The New Deal and Georgia's Black Youth." *Journal of Southern History* 38 (August 1972): 443–60.

Holt, Rackham. *Mary McLeod Bethune: A Biography.* New York: Doubleday, 1964.

Homel, Michael W. "Lilydale School Campaign of 1936: Direct Action in Verbal Protest Era." *Journal of Negro Education* 59 (July 1974): 228–41.

Hughes, William H., and Frederick D. Patterson, eds. *Robert Russa Moton of Hampton and Tuskegee.* Chapel Hill: University of North Carolina Press, 1956.

Jakeman, Robert J. *The Divided Skies: Establishing Segregated Flight Training at Tuskegee, Alabama, 1934–1942.* Tuscaloosa: University of Alabama Press, 1992.

Johnson, Charles. "The Army, the Negro and the Civilian Conservation Corps: 1933–1942." *Military Affairs* 36 (October 1972): 82–87.

Jones, Gene Delon. "The Origin of the Alliance between the New Deal and the Chicago Machine." *Illinois Historical Journal* 67 (June 1974): 253–74.

Kalmar, Karen L. "Southern Black Elites and the New Deal: A Case Study of Savannah, Georgia." *Georgia Historical Quarterly* 65 (fall 1981): 341–55.

Katznelson, Ira. *Black Men, White Cities: Race, Politics and Migration in the United States, 1900–1930 and Britain, 1948–1968.* New York: Oxford University Press, 1973.

Kellogg, Charles F. *NAACP, a History of the National Association for the Advancement of Colored People, 1909–1920.* 2 vols. Baltimore: Johns Hopkins University Press, 1967.

Kenneally, James J. "Black Republicans during the New Deal: The Role of Joseph W. Martin, Jr." *Review of Politics* 55 (winter 1993): 117–39.

Kilson, Martin. "Political Change in the Negro Ghetto, 1900–1940s." In Nathan I. Huggins, Martin Kilson, and Daniel M. Fox, eds., *Key Issues in the Afro-American Experience.* New York: Harcourt Brace Jovanich, 1971.

Kirby, John B. *Black Americans in the Roosevelt Era: Liberalism and Race.* Knoxville: University of Tennessee Press, 1980.

Kluger, Richard. *Simple Justice: The History of* Brown v. Board of Education *and Black America's Struggle for Equality.* New York: Alfred A. Knopf, 1976.

Kruman, Marc W. "Quotas for Blacks: The Public Works Administration and the Black Construction Worker." *Labor History* 16 (winter 1975): 37–51.

Lemmon, Sarah M. "Transportation Segregation in the Federal Courts since 1865." *Journal of Negro History* 38 (April 1953): 174–95.

Lichtman, Allen J. *Prejudice and the Old Politics: The Presidential Election of 1928.* Chapel Hill: University of North Carolina Press, 1970.

Link, Arthur S. *Wilson: The New Freedom.* Princeton: Princeton University Press, 1967.

Lisio, Donald J. *Hoover, Blacks, and Lily-Whites: A Study of Southern Strategies.* Chapel Hill: University of North Carolina Press, 1985.

Litt, Edgar. *Beyond Pluralism: Ethnic Politics in America.* Glenview: Scott Foresman, 1970.

Logan, Rayford W., ed. *The Attitude of the Southern White Press toward Negro Suffrage, 1932–1940.* Washington, D.C.: Foundation Publisher, 1940.

Marks, Carole. *Farewell—We're Good and Gone: The Great Black Migration.* Bloomington: Indiana University Press, 1989.

Martin, Charles H. "Negro Leaders, the Republican Party and the Election of 1932." *Phylon* 32 (spring 1971): 85–93.

Martin, Robert E. "The Relative Political Status of the Negro in the United States." *Journal of Negro Education* 22 (summer 1953): 363–79.

McBride, David, and Monroe H. Little. "The Afro-American Elite, 1930–1940: A Historical and Statistical Profile." *Phylon* 42 (summer 1981): 105–19.

McCoy, Donald R., and Richard T. Ruetten. "The Civil Rights Movement, 1940–1954." *Midwest Quarterly* 11 (October 1969): 11–34.

McDonnell, Timothy L. "The New Deal Makes a Public Housing Law: A Case Study of the Wagner Housing Bill of 1937." Ph.D. diss., St. Louis University, 1953.

McGuire, Phillip. "Desegregation of the Armed Forces: Black Leadership, Protest and World War II." *Journal of Negro History* 63 (summer 1983): 147–58.

———. "Judge Hastie, World War II, and The Army Air Corps." *Phylon* 42 (summer 1981): 157–67.

McMillen, Neil R. "Perry W. Howard, Boss of Black-and-Tan Republicanism in Mississippi, 1924–1960." *Journal of Southern History* 48 (May 1982): 205–24.

McMurry, Linda O. "A Black Intellectual in the New South: Monroe Nathan Work, 1866–1945." *Phylon* 41 (winter 1980): 333–44.

———. *George Washington Carver: Scientist and Symbol, 1864–1943.* New York: Oxford University Press, 1981.

———. *Recorder of the Black Experience: A Biography of Monroe Nathan Work.* Baton Rouge: Louisiana State University Press, 1985.

McNeil, Genna Rae. *Groundwork: Charles Hamilton Houston and the Struggle for Civil Rights.* Philadelphia: University of Pennsylvania Press, 1983.

Meier, August. "The Negro and the Democratic Party, 1875–1915." *Phylon* 17 (summer 1956): 173–91.

Meier, August, and Elliott Rudwick. "Attorneys Black and White: A Case Study of Relations within the NAACP." *Journal of American History* 62 (March 1976): 913–46.

———. *Black Detroit and the Rise of the UAW.* New York: Oxford University Press, 1979.

———. "Negro Protest at the Chicago World's Fair, 1933–1934." *Illinois Historical Journal* 59 (summer 1966): 161–71.

———. "The Rise of Segregation in the Federal Bureauracy, 1900–1930." *Phylon* 28 (summer 1967): 178–84.

Meyerson, Martin, and Edward C. Banfield. *Politics, Planning, and the Public Interest: The Case of Public Housing in Chicago.* Glencoe: FreePress, 1955.

Miller, Floyd. *Ahdoolo: The Biography of Matthew A. Henson.* New York: Dutton, 1963.

Miller, J. Erroll. "Philadelphia Negroes in the Roosevelt Elections." *Midwest Journal* 2 (summer 1950): 60–66.

Miller, Loren. *The Petitioners: The Story of the Supreme Court of the United States and the Negro.* New York: Random House, 1966.

Miller, Robert M. "The Protestant Churches and Lynching, 1919–1939." *Journal of Negro History* 42 (April 1957): 118–31.

Monahan, Thomas P., and Elizabeth H. Monahan. "Some Characteristics of American Negro Leaders." *American Sociological Review* 21 (October 1956): 589–96.

Moore, Jesse T. Jr. *A Search for Equality: The National Urban League, 1910–1961*. University Park: Pennsylvania State University Press, 1981.

Muraskin, William. "The Harlem Boycott of 1934: Black Nationalism and the Rise of Labor-Union Consciousness." *Labor History* 13 (summer 1972): 361–73.

Nipp, Robert E. "The Negro in the New Deal Resettlement Program: A Comment." *Agricultural History* 45 (July 1971): 195–200.

Ochillo, Yvonne. "The Race-Consciousness of Alain Locke." *Phylon* 47 (fall 1986): 173–81.

O'Dell, Samuel. "Blacks, the Democratic Party, and the Presidential Election of 1928: A Mild Rejoinder." *Phylon* 48 (spring 1987): 1–11.

Olson, James S. "Organized Black Leadership and Industrial Unionism: The Racial Response, 1936–1945." *Labor History* 10 (summer 1969): 475–86.

Ottley, Roi. *The Lonely Warrior: The Life and Times of Robert S. Abbott*. Chicago: Henry Regnery, 1955.

Palmer, Dewey H. "Moving North: Negro Migration during World War I." *Phylon* 28 (spring 1967): 52–62.

Paszek, Lawrence J. "Negroes and the Air Force, 1939–1949." *Military Affairs* 31 (spring 1967): 1–9.

Patton, Gerald W. *War and Race: The Black Officer in the American Military, 1915–1941*. Westport: Greenwood Press, 1981.

Pfeffer, Paula F. *A. Philip Randolph, Pioneer of the Civil Rights Movement*. Baton Rouge: Louisiana State University Press, 1990.

Philpott, Thomas L. *The Slum and the Ghetto: Neighborhood Deterioration and Middle-Class Reform, Chicago, 1880–1930*. New York: Oxford University Press, 1978.

Pinderhughes, Dianne M. *Race and Ethnicity in Chicago Politics: A Reexamination of Pluralist Theory*. Urbana: University of Illinois Press, 1987.

Plummer, Brenda G. "The Afro-American Response to the Occupation of Haiti, 1915–1934." *Phylon* 43 (June 1982): 125–43.

Pritchett, C. Herman. *The Roosevelt Court: A Study in Judicial Politics and Values, 1937–1947*. New York: MacMillan, 1948.

Raper, Arthur F. "The Southern Negro and the NRA." *Georgia Historical Quarterly* 64 (summer 1980): 128–45.

———. *The Tragedy of Lynching*. Chapel Hill: University of North Carolina Press, 1933.

Record, Wilson. *The Negro and the Communist Party*. Chapel Hill: University of North Carolina Press, 1951.

———. *Race and Radicalism: The NAACP and the Communist Party in Conflict*. Ithaca: Cornell University Press, 1964.

Reed, Christopher R. "A Reinterpretation of Black Strategies for Change at the Chicago World's Fair, 1933–1934." *Illinois Historical Journal* 81 (spring 1988): 2–12.

———. "A Study of Black Politics and Protest in Depression Decade Chicago, 1930–39." Ph.D. diss., Kent State University, 1982.

———. "Black Chicago Political Realignment during the Depression and New Deal." *Illinois Historical Journal* 78 (winter 1985): 242–56.

Reed, Merl E. *Seedtime for the Modern Civil Rights Movement: The President's Committee on Fair Employment Practice, 1941–1946.* Baton Rouge: Louisiana State University Press, 1991.

Risher, Howard W. Jr. *The Negro in the Railroad Industry.* Philadelphia: Wharton School, 1971.

Robinson, Edgar E. *They Voted for Roosevelt: The Presidential Vote, 1932–1944.* Stanford: Stanford University Press, 1947.

Robinson, George F. Jr. "The Negro in Politics in Chicago." *Journal of Negro History* 17 (April 1932): 180–229.

Romero, Patricia. "The Early Organization of Red Caps, 1937–1938." *Negro History Bulletin* 29 (February 1966): 101–2, 112.

Ross, B. Joyce. *J. E. Spingarn and the Rise of the NAACP.* New York: Atheneum, 1972.

———. "Mary McLeod Bethune and the National Youth Administration: A Case Study of Power Relationships in the Black Cabinet of Franklin D. Roosevelt." *Journal of Negro History* 60 (January 1975): 1–28.

Ross, Ronald. "The Role of Blacks in the Federal Theatre, 1935–1939." *Journal of Negro History* 59 (January 1974): 38–50.

Rudwick, Elliott M. "Oscar DePriest and the Jim Crow Restaurant in the U.S. House of Representatives." *Journal of Negro Education* 35 (winter 1966): 77–82.

Salmond, John A. *A Southern Rebel: The Life and Times of Aubrey Willis Williams, 1890–1965.* Chapel Hill: University of North Carolina Press, 1983.

———. " 'Aubrey Williams Remembers': A Note on Franklin D. Roosevelt's Attitude toward Negro Rights." *Alabama Review* 25 (January 1972): 62–77.

———. "The Civilian Conservation Corps and the Negro." *Journal of American History* 52 (June 1965): 75–88.

Schlesinger, Arthur M. Jr. *The Age of Roosevelt: The Politics of Upheaval, 1935–1936.* Boston: Houghton Mifflin, 1966.

Schwartz, Bonnie Fox. *The Civil Works Administration, 1933–1934: The Business of Emergency Employment in the New Deal.* Princeton: Princeton University Press, 1984.

Sherman, Richard B. "The Harding Administration and the Negro: An Opportunity Lost." *Journal of Negro History* 49 (July 1964): 151–68.

———. *The Republican Party and Black America from McKinley to Hoover, 1896–1933.* Charlottesville: University Press of Virginia, 1973.

Sisk, Glenn N. "Negro Churches in the Alabama Black Belt, 1875–1917." *Journal of Presbyterian History* 33 (June 1955): 87–92.

———. "Negro Education in the Alabama Black Belt, 1875–1900." *Journal of Negro Education* 22 (spring 1953): 126–35.

Sisk, Glenn S. "Crime and Justice in the Alabama Black Belt, 1875–1917." *Mid-America* 38 (April 1958): 106–13.

Sitkoff, Harvard. *A New Deal for Blacks—The Emergence of Civil Rights as a National Issue: The Depression Decade.* New York: Oxford University Press, 1978.

———. "The Detroit Race Riot of 1943." *Michigan History* 53 (summer 1969): 183–206.

———. "Racial Militancy and Interracial Violence in the Second World War." *Journal of American History* 58 (December 1971): 661–81.

Snorgrass, J. William. "The Black Press and Political Alliances: The Turning Point, 1928." *Western Journal of Black Studies* 10, no. 3 (1986): 103–8.

Spear, Allan H. *Black Chicago: The Making of a Negro Ghetto, 1890–1920.* Chicago: University of Chicago Press, 1967.

Stevens, John D. "Black Correspondents of World War II Cover the Supply Routes." *Journal of Negro History* 57 (October 1972): 395–406.

Stone, Donald P. *Fallen Prince: Black Education and the Quest for Afro American Nationality.* Snow Hill, Alabama: Snow Hill Press, 1990.

Strickland, Arvarh E. *History of the Chicago Urban League.* Urbana: University of Illinois Press, 1966.

Tatum, Elbert L. *The Changed Political Thought of the Negro, 1915–1940.* New York: Exposition Press, 1951.

Travis, Dempsey J. *An Autobiography of Black Chicago.* Chicago: Urban Research Press, 1981.

———. *An Autobiography of Black Politics.* Chicago: Urban Research Press, 1987.

Tushnet, Mark V. *The NAACP's Legal Strategy against Segregated Education, 1925–1950.* Chapel Hill: University of North Carolina Press, 1987.

Van Deusen, John G. "The Negro in Politics." *Journal of Negro History* 21 (July 1936): 256–74.

Venkataramani, M. S. "Norman Thomas, Arkansas Sharecroppers, and the Roosevelt Agricultural Policies, 1933–1937." *Arkansas Historical Quarterly* 24 (spring 1965): 3–28.

Ware, Gilbert. *William Hastie: Grace under Pressure.* New York: Oxford University Press, 1984.

Washburn, Patrick S. "The *Pittsburgh Courier*'s Double V Campaign of 1942." *American Journalism* 3, no. 2 (1986): 73–86.

Weisbord, Robert G. "Black America and the Italian-Ethiopian Crisis: An Episode in Pan-Negroism." *Historian* 34 (February 1972): 230–42.

Weiss, Nancy J. *Farewell to the Party of Lincoln: Black Politics in the Age of FDR.* Princeton: Princeton University Press, 1983.

———. "The Negro and the New Freedom: Fighting Wilsonian Segregation." *Political Science Quarterly* 84 (March 1968): 61–79.

Wendt, Lloyd, and Herman Kogan. *Bosses in Lusty Chicago: The Story of Bathhouse John and Hinky Dink.* Bloomington: Indiana University Press, 1971.

Wheaton, William. "The Evolution of Federal Housing Programs." Ph.D. diss., University of Chicago, 1954.

White, Walter F. *A Man Called White, the Autobiography of Walter White.* New York: Viking Press, 1948.

Wilson, James Q. *Negro Politics: The Search for Leadership.* New York: Free Press, 1960.

———. "Two Negro Politicians: An Interpretation." *Midwest Journal of Politics* 4 (November 1960): 346–69.

Wilson, Joan H. *Herbert Hoover—Forgotten Progressive.* Boston: Little Brown, 1975.

Wittner, Lawrence S. "The National Negro Congress: A Reassessment." *American Quarterly* 22 (winter 1970): 883–901.

Wolters, Raymond R. *Negroes and the Great Depression: The Problem of Economic Recovery.* Westport: Greenwood Press, 1970.

———. "Section 7a and the Black Worker." *Labor History* 10 (summer 1969): 459–74.

Woodson, Carter G. *The Negro Professional Man and the Community, with Special Emphasis on the Physician and the Lawyer.* Washington, D.C.: Association for the Study of Negro Life and History, 1934.

Wye, Christopher G. "The New Deal and the Negro Community: Toward a Broader Conceptualization." *Journal of American History* 59 (December 1972): 621–39.

Zangrando, Robert L. "The NAACP and a Federal Antilynching Bill, 1934–1940." *Journal of Negro History* 50 (April 1965): 106–17.

———. *The NAACP Crusade against Lynching, 1909–1950.* Philadelphia: Temple University Press, 1980.

INDEX

Abbott, Robert S., 85, 110–11
African Americans: negative impact of Mitchell's efforts upon, 12, 21–22, 45, 87–92, 144, 176–79, 190, 201–7, 210–21, 281–82; Mitchell's contributions to, 12–13, 24–25, 32, 34–35, 84, 156, 158, 180–82, 192, 196–97, 208, 222–47, 286, 289–92; evaluations of Mitchell, 15, 20–21, 53, 190–91, 197, 199–201, 243, 254, 258, 264–65, 273–74; Mitchell's integration efforts and, 30, 87, 156–58, 168–69, 172–74, 178, 208, 225, 227–28, 236–38, 249–51; in Chicago and Washington, 31–32, 47–48, 50–51; in legal profession, 34; GOP loses ground among, 36–38, 79, 145–47, 176; in fraternities, 37; Democrats appeal to, 40–44, 68, 157–75, 198–99; Mitchell's political influence on, 77, 81, 198–99; effect of New Deal policies and FDR on, 98–100, 139–40, 152–53, 194–95
African Methodist Ministerial Association of Chicago, 63
Afro-American Protective League, 177
Agricultural Adjustment Act, 194
Alexander, Raymond Pace, 274
Allredge, J. Haden, 265–66
American Negro Exposition of 1940, 244
American Youth Congress, 151
Anderson, Albert, 274
Anderson, Louis, 58, 60
Anderson, Marian, 177–78, 239–40, 285
Andrews, Adolphus, 242
Antilynching. *See* Mitchell, National Association for the Advancement of Colored People
Armstrong Agricultural Institute, 23–24, 27–28, 62
Arnold, Remmie, 286
Associated Negro Press, 71, 292

Association for the Study of Negro Life and History, 181
Atlantic Christian College, 197

Bailey, Walter T., 102
Bainbridge, Douglas, 67
Baker, Harry, 53–54
Barnett, Claude A., 71, 75, 85–86, 112, 171, 265
Benedict, Jay L., 238
Benvenuti, Julius, 105
Bethel Young People's Lyceum, 198
Bethune, Mary, 142, 178, 202
Better Government Association, 95–98
Biddle, Francis, 270
Bilbo, Theodore, 193–94, 285
Black, Hugo, 152–53
Blackstone School of Law, 33, 61
Braddan, William S., 75
Bronzeville (Chicago), 36–41, 38–39, 40, 47–50, 50–51, 53, 57–58, 68–69, 94–95, 98–99, 100–104, 104–6, 109, 110, 115–17, 118, 190, 195, 206
Brown, Edgar (of Chicago), 53, 60, 109
Brown, Edgar G. (of Washington, D.C.), 33, 74–75, 147, 200, 173
Brown, Samuel L., 287–88
Brown, William H. C., 33
Buckner, Simon B., 227
Bunche, Ralph, 179, 284–85
Burke-Wadsworth Conscription Bill of 1940, 151
Butler, Neville, 155
Byrnes, James F., 141, 154, 281
Byrns, Joseph W., 87, 152

Carmody, Wilma, 291
Carver, George Washington, 6, 80
Cayton, Horace R., 139–40
Celler, Emanuel, 202
Cermak, Anton, 45, 50